PRAISE FOR *MAYOR* ⚀ P9-DMY-038

"This book provides deep insight into the political career of Rahm Emanuel. Painstakingly researched, *Mayor 1%* provides the reader with the ability to understand the hard-line neoliberal mindset that blinds the man to the harsh realities of entrenched poverty and disenfranchisement. The relentless attacks on Chicago's working class, from the janitors at O'Hare to the librarians, mental health workers, and members of the Chicago Teachers Union have shown the true nature of a man who will have plenty of money from the billionaires to run his re-election campaign, but none of the love of the people who will not pull the lever for him. Kari Lydersen ends on a hopeful note: that Mayor 1%'s brutal reign can actually lead to a better Chicago as people get up, stand up and fight the 'power.'"
—KAREN LEWIS, PRESIDENT, CHICAGO TEACHERS UNION

"While banks and corporations continue to enjoy record-breaking profits, working families across Chicago continue to face school closings, foreclosures, and devastating privatization. Lydersen's book lifts up the extraordinary power of everyday people to stand up, fight back, dream big, and join together to make transformative change. Rarely does a journalist do such justice to the in the trenches organizing work that is vital to undermining oppressive city policies and abusive corporate influences."
—AMISHA PATEL, EXECUTIVE DIRECTOR, GRASSROOTS COLLABORATIVE

"In *Mayor 1%* Kari Lydersen surveys the expansive and deeply contested first-term record of Chicago mayor Rahm Emanuel. Her work touches every flashpoint of Emanuel's kinetic drive to govern the city as he sees fit. Along the way, Lydersen admirably and poignantly gives voice to the activist community that has become the mayor's fiercest critic, while calling out his staunchest business allies."
—ROBERT BRUNO, UNIVERSITY OF ILLINOIS AT CHICAGO

"Lydersen's book demonstrates the type of thorough investigative journalism we need in Chicago to keep all politicians and public servants accountable. It exposes the public policy that the city of Chicago and its constituents didn't expect from a Democratic mayor of the "City that Works." Lydersen's book shows the real Rahm Emanuel, leading the race to the bottom by killing off good middle-class jobs instead of upholding job standards that help build a strong workforce and the robust economy our city desperately needs."
—TOM BALANOFF, PRESIDENT, SEIU LOCAL 1

"If you want to understand how a Democrat became so reviled among the middle and working class citizens in modern day Chicago, please read this book. This is the story of organized money vs. organized people in the Second City, and the impact of what happens here ripples across the nation in our public schools, in our healthcare centers, and in our streets. It might be that Obama brought the Windy City to the Potomac, but Emanuel attempts the reverse in Chicago, and as Lydersen notes in great detail, "Rahm" might be a master at fundraising and manipulating the image of his public office, but confrontations are unavoidable when a city manager doesn't respect his electorate."
—ADAM P. HEENAN, CHICAGO PUBLIC SCHOOLS CIVICS TEACHER

MAYOR
1%

RAHM EMANUEL
AND THE RISE
OF CHICAGO'S 99%

BY KARI LYDERSEN

Haymarket Books
Chicago, Illinois

To the Chicago Mental Health Movement

Published in 2013 by
Haymarket Books
P.O. Box 180165, Chicago, IL 60618
773-583-7884
info@haymarketbooks.org
www.haymarketbooks.org

ISBN: 978-1-60846-222-3

Trade distribution:
In the US, through Consortium Book Sales and Distribution, www.cbsd.com
In the UK, Turnaround Publisher Services, www.turnaround-uk.com
In Canada, Publishers Group Canada, www.pgcbooks.ca
In Australia, Palgrave Macmillan, www.palgravemacmillan.com.au
All other countries, Publishers Group Worldwide, www.pgw.com

Special discounts are available for bulk purchases by organizations
and institutions. Please contact Haymarket Books for more information
at 773-583-7884 or info@haymarketbooks.org.

Cover design by Eric Ruder. Cover photo of Rahm Emanuel at a press conference
in Washington, DC. Photo by Olivier Douliery, Abaca Press.

This book was published with the generous support of the Wallace Global
Fund and Lannan Foundation.

Printed in Canada by union labor.

Library of Congress CIP data is available.

10 9 8 7 6 5 4 3 2

RECYCLED
Paper made from
recycled material
FSC
www.fsc.org   FSC® C103567

CONTENTS

ACKNOWLEDGMENTS

I'm very grateful to Haymarket Books for proposing and working with me on this project; to Mark Sorkin for his meticulous editing and encouragement; to Lance Selfa, Julie Fain, Jim Plank, Rory Fanning, Rachel Cohen, and the rest of the Haymarket team; to the many Chicagoans who took time to speak with me and allow me a window into their lives; to Curtis Black for invaluable editing and research assistance; to Pat Lydersen for reviewing drafts; to Chuy Campuzano, Joe Iosbaker, Matt Ginsberg-Jaeckle, Jo Patton, Izabel Miltko, Don Wiener, Amisha Patel, Andy Thayer, Jesse Sharkey, and other community and union leaders who very generously shared their ideas and insight; to *In These Times* magazine's *Working* blog and editor Jessica Stites for providing a real-time outlet for many of these stories; and to the dogged reporters at the *Chicago Reader*, WBEZ, *Chicago Reporter*, *Chicago Tribune*, *Chicago Sun-Times*, Chicago News Cooperative, Better Government Association, and other outlets that continually prove that despite the crisis in journalism, our city's proud tradition is still alive. Thank you.

NOTES ON SOURCING

From the mayoral race to the conclusion, this book is based primarily on firsthand reporting and interviews. One can assume scenes and quotes without footnotes are taken from the author's direct observation and on-the-spot interviews. Lengthier formal interviews by the author are footnoted. Analysis by pundits and columnists, investigations or reports by media outlets and watchdog groups, press releases from the mayor's office, and other documents are also referenced and footnoted throughout the book. In many cases facts and statistics are documented by multiple sources, but generally one or two sources are listed for the sake of brevity. In some cases scenes that the author observed include footnotes from other sources, so the reader can view videos or seek more information. The sections of the book dealing with Rahm Emanuel's childhood through his time in the Obama White House are drawn primarily from books and media coverage, as noted in the text and footnotes. A spokesman for Mayor Emanuel declined to speak for this book or to respond to a list of questions and main points.

RAHM EMANUEL AT BARACK OBAMA'S 2008 INAUGURATION.
PHOTO BY TIMOTHY A. CLARY/AFP/GETTY IMAGES.

INTRODUCTION

March 4, 2012, was Chicago's 175th birthday, and the city celebrated with a public party at the Chicago History Museum. The event promised actors portraying famous Chicagoans including Jane Addams, founder of Hull House and advocate for immigrants, children, and factory workers. Little did the organizers know that the show would be stolen by a woman some viewed as a modern-day Jane Addams—more eccentric and irascible, less renowned and accomplished, but just as willing to raise her voice and speak up for the weak and vulnerable.

Mayor Rahm Emanuel grinned broadly as the Chicago Children's Choir, dressed in red, sang a lively version of "Happy Birthday."

He had reason to smile.

Ten months earlier he'd been inaugurated as leader of the nation's third most-populous city, taking the reins from legendary Mayor Richard M. Daley. And while his term hadn't been a cakewalk, so far things seemed to be going well. He had inherited a nearly $700 million budget deficit and attacked it with an aggressive round of cost-cutting and layoffs. The labor unions had resisted, but ultimately Emanuel was able to strike some deals and come out on top. Meanwhile, he was moving forward with his plans to institute a longer school day, a promise that had gained him positive attention nationwide. He was already assuming Daley's mantle as the "Green Mayor": in February he had announced that the city's two coal-fired power plants would close, and miles of new bike lanes were in the works.

Emanuel had even snagged two important international gatherings for Chicago: the NATO and G8 summits, to be held concurrently in May 2012—the first time both would be hosted in the same US city.

There had been sit-ins and protests by community groups and unions related to the summits, school closings, and other issues. But Emanuel had shown a knack for avoiding and ignoring them, and so far he didn't seem to have suffered too much political fallout.

As Emanuel watched the swaying, clapping singers at the birthday party, he didn't seem to notice a crinkled orange paper banner bobbing in the crowd of revelers. It said, "History Will Judge Mayor 1 Percent Emanuel for Closing Mental Health Clinics." He'd gotten the moniker early on in his tenure. As Occupy Wall Street–inspired protests swept the nation, it was a natural fit for a mayor known for his high-finance connections and brief but highly lucrative career as an investment banker.

A staffer for the mayor or the museum did notice the banner, and told the man holding it to put it away. Matt Ginsberg-Jaeckle, a lanky longtime activist, complied, partially folding the banner and lowering it into the crowd. The song ended, and Emanuel began shaking hands with the singers and other well-wishers near a colorful multitiered birthday cake.

Then a shrill, rough voice cut through the chatter, causing heads to turn as the orange banner was unfurled and raised again.

"Mayor Emanuel, please don't close our clinics! We're going to die. . . . There's nowhere else to go. . . . Mayor Emanuel, please!" cried a woman with a soft, pale face, red hair peeking out from a floral head scarf, and dark circles around her wide eyes that gave her an almost girlish, vulnerable expression.

It was Helen Morley, a Chicago woman who had struggled all her life with mental illness but still managed to become a vocal advocate for herself and others in the public housing project where she lived, and for other Chicagoans suffering from disabilities and mental illness. For the past fifteen years she'd been a regular at the city's mental health clinic in Beverly Morgan Park, a heavily Irish and African American, working- and middle-class area on the city's Southwest Side. It was one of six mental health clinics that Emanuel planned to close as part of sweeping cuts in his inaugural budget. He said it made perfect economic sense—it would save $3 million, and the patients could move to the remaining six public clinics. But Morley and others pleaded that he didn't understand the role these specific clinics played in their lives and the difficulty they would have traveling to other locations.

Morley's eyes were fixed unblinkingly on the mayor as she walked quickly toward him, calling out in that ragged, pleading voice, her gaze and gait intense and focused. Almost all eyes were on her—except for those of the mayor, who shook a few more hands and then pivoted quickly and disappeared through a door, studiously ignoring Morley the entire time.

"Mayor Emanuel!" she cried again as he dashed out. "Please stay here, Mayor Emanuel!"

The abruptness of the exit, the cake sitting there untouched, the lack of closing niceties, and the crowd milling around awkwardly gave the impression that the event had been cut much shorter than planned.

With the mayor gone, Ginsberg-Jaeckle and fellow activist J. R. Fleming stepped up on the stage and lifted the banner behind the cake. Morley centered herself in front of them and turned to face the remaining crowd, earnestly entreating, "People are dying. They aren't going to have nowhere to go!"

Emanuel's critics and admirers have both described him as a quintessential creature of Washington and Wall Street, a brilliant strategist and fundraiser who knows just the right way to leverage his famously abrasive personality to get wealthy donors to open their wallets and to help him win races. He became a prominent fundraiser for powerful politicians in his twenties, he made some $18 million in investment banking in just two years, he played central roles in two White Houses, and he orchestrated a dramatic Democratic takeover of the House of Representatives during his six years in Congress. He clearly knows how politicking works. But being mayor is different, or at least it should be. In Washington people are often tagged as political allies or adversaries, fair game for manipulation or intimidation. In Congress Emanuel represented his constituents, but the daily grind had a lot more to do with Beltway machinations and maneuvers. Running a city, where you are elected to directly serve people and listen to them, is supposed to be a different story. Emanuel was treating Chicago as if it were Washington. Perhaps that's why, even in his brief tenure as mayor, he has seemed to find it so easy to ignore the parents, teachers, pastors, students, patients, and others who have carried out multiple sit-ins and protests outside his fifth-floor office in City Hall.

These citizens frequently note that Daley had not been particularly accessible, sympathetic, or democratic in his approach, but at least he would meet with people, acknowledge them, make perhaps token efforts to listen to their proposals and act on their concerns. Emanuel can't seem to find the time for many members of the public, they complain, even as he says he wants their input on issues like school closings. Parents, grandparents, and students with the Kenwood Oakland Community Organization (KOCO) camped out in City Hall for nearly four days trying to deliver a formal plan that community members had drafted in conjunction with university experts to protect their local school from closing and create a network of educational resources in the surrounding low-income neighborhoods.[1]

"His response was to ignore us," said Jitu Brown, education organizer for KOCO, one of the city's oldest and most respected civil rights organizations. "We had our problems with Mayor Daley, but Mayor Daley surrounded himself with neighborhood people and he himself was a neighborhood person. This man, Rahm Emanuel, has surrounded himself with corporate people. This administration is doing the bidding of corporations and robbing us of the things our parents fought for."

RAHM EMANUEL TOOK THE REINS FROM HIS ONETIME MENTOR MAYOR RICHARD
M. DALEY AND BROUGHT A NEW STYLE OF CORPORATE GOVERNANCE TO
CHICAGO. PHOTO BY C. SVEN.

If Emanuel thought primarily in terms of political and financial strategy, and the costs and benefits of how he interacted with certain people, it's understandable that he would dart away from Helen Morley. But she was clearly a woman in deep distress, both at the birthday party and at previous protests at City Hall.

Did Emanuel ever direct a staffer to contact her and see how she was doing? To take her name and follow up? Even to put a reassuring arm on her shoulder? Morley was used to people edging away from her in public; they could tell she was a little off. But she didn't appear dangerous or threatening. At the birthday party she didn't even sound angry, just desperate and afraid, literally begging the mayor to speak with her, to hear her cries.

"They knew who she was, she was at every sit-in," said Ginsberg-Jaeckle. "But she was never contacted by them, they never met with her, not once."

Three months later, Helen Morley would be dead. Her friends blamed the closing of the mental health center. Of course, there was no direct link between the clinic closing and the heart attack that felled Morley at age fifty-six. But her friends are sure that the trauma of losing her anchor—the clinic and the tight-knit community there—is what pushed her ailing body to the limit. They said as much during a protest outside the city health department offices a week and a half after Morley's death, with a coffin and large photos of her in tow.

"We don't have an autopsy or a medical examiner's report. You can't show her death was related to the clinic closure," said Ginsberg-Jaeckle. "But it would be hard for anyone to say that given her heart conditions and other conditions she suffered from, that the stress and cumulative impact of everything she was going through didn't play a major role."

If Emanuel did indeed think largely in terms of adversaries, Morley was not a worthy one for him. She was impoverished, unemployed; many saw her as "crazy," as she herself sometimes said she was. Her unhappiness with the mayor and her death would cost him no political capital.

But Emanuel's attitude toward Morley and the other members of the Mental Health Movement was perhaps emblematic of a deeper issue that would haunt him in the not-too-distant future. Although he seemed adroit at manipulating the levers of power, Emanuel did not seem to understand the power of regular Chicagoans, especially Chicagoans organized into the city's rich mosaic of community groups, labor unions, progressive organizations, and interfaith coalitions.

This failing would become fodder for national pundits in the fall, as the Chicago Teachers Union made headlines around the world by going on strike and filling the city streets with waves of shouting, chanting Chicagoans clad in red T-shirts. Emanuel appeared shocked and disgusted with the union's audacity, attacking them in a public relations campaign more reminiscent of a brutal electoral race than contract negotiations between two teams of public servants.

Few would dispute that Emanuel is a highly intelligent, energetic, efficient, organized, and hard-working individual; these are clearly qualities anyone would hope for in their elected leaders. Emanuel let hardly a week go by without announcing a major new initiative or project, many of which were applauded and praised across the board. It would be hard to question his commitment to conservation and clean energy, safe bike lanes, beautiful parks, and other aspects of a livable city. He pledged to make Chicago one of the nation's most immigrant-friendly cities, and he pushed state legislators to grant driver's licenses to undocumented immigrants and to legalize gay marriage. He courted employers, bringing thousands of new jobs to

Chicago and positioning the city as a high-tech industry hub. He made common-sense improvements in efficiency, including reforming the city's bizarre garbage collection system. After Mayor Daley left a yawning budget gap and leased the city's parking meters in a notorious deal that would leave taxpayers paying the price for decades to come, many understandably welcomed Emanuel's business acumen, fundraising ability, and determination to whip the city into fiscal shape.

But Chicagoans should have been able to expect that a leader with such skills, experience, and connections would listen to their ideas, address their concerns, and solve some of their problems—rather than ignoring them or treating them as the enemy when they questioned his actions, priorities, or motivations.

Many pundits describe Emanuel as the epitome of the modern centrist neoliberal Democrat. The North American Free Trade Agreement (NAFTA) is often viewed as a symbol of neoliberalism, a global socioeconomic doctrine with intellectual roots in Chicago. Emanuel was a key architect of the trade agreement, which ultimately cost tens of thousands of US jobs and brought social and economic devastation to Mexico.

To the extent that Emanuel genuinely wants to make the world a better place for working people, he thinks market forces and business models are the way to do it, and he clearly (and perhaps rightly) thinks that he understands these institutions far better than any teacher or crossing guard or nurse. From that viewpoint, the messy attributes of democracy—sit-ins, protests, rallies, people demanding meetings and information and input—simply slow down and encumber the streamlined, bottom-line-driven process Emanuel knows is best. But many regular Chicagoans see injustice, callousness, and even cruelty in this trickle-down, authoritarian approach to city governance. They see the mayor bringing thousands of new corporate jobs subsidized with taxpayer dollars while laying off middle-class public sector workers like librarians, call center staffers, crossing guards, and mental health clinic therapists. They see him closing neighborhood schools, throwing parents' and students' lives into turmoil. They see him (like Daley) passing ordinances at will through a rubber-stamp City Council, leaving citizens with few meaningful avenues to express their opposition to policies changing the face of their city.

This book explores Chicago's embrace of privatization and public-private partnerships: an increasingly popular urban development strategy that community and labor leaders say can be beneficial and productive if carried out right. But like residents in other parts of the country, many Chicagoans fear that the encroachment of the private sector on the public realm is increasing economic and racial inequality and sidelining unions and democratic processes. Continuing a trend championed by Mayor Daley, Emanuel has pushed for privatization of various city properties and services—including education and health care—and garnered national attention with his public-private Infrastructure Trust.

This book also details how privatization and cost-cutting, along with larger ideological debates, were central to Emanuel's battles with organized labor—long a storied and powerful constituency in Chicago. And it depicts the popular movement that arose around the NATO and G8 summits, describing how that movement became a defining struggle over civil liberties, economic priorities, and transparency at the city level.

The description of Emanuel's early life and his time in Congress, the private sector, and the Obama and Clinton White Houses was compiled through interviews and largely through reliance on books and media documenting these eras. Starting with Emanuel's campaign for mayor of Chicago and extending through his first two years in office, the content is based primarily on firsthand reporting supplemented with other media and analysis; it is also informed by my fifteen years of reporting on organized labor, immigration, community struggles, and grassroots movements in Chicago.

Although this is a book about Rahm Emanuel, it is also a story about organizations—like the Mental Health Movement and the Chicago Teachers Union—made up of regular people who are finding it harder and harder to secure basic rights including housing, health care, and a voice in their governing institutions.

I aim to explore what these actors stand for and how they pursue their goals at a time when many Americans have embraced a view of the country that pits the "99 percent" against the "1 percent," "Main Street versus Wall Street," and feel neither political party is really representing their interests.

By his second year in office, Emanuel—a famous Democrat running a city famous for Democratic hegemony—was frequently being compared to prominent right-wing Republicans including Wisconsin governor Scott Walker and even presidential candidate Mitt Romney. Such allusions were great oversimplifications, but they showed that many Chicagoans did not feel that their Democratic mayor was actually interested in democracy, transparency, or a system that genuinely seeks equity for the have-nots.

Emanuel cut his teeth in opposition research, a then-emerging field in which political operatives secure victories in part by acting as private eyes, digging up dirt or spinnable information on opponents and leveraging it for political gain. Given this expertise, and his mother's activist background, it is perhaps surprising that Emanuel did not seem to understand the history or culture of popular resistance in Chicago—or anticipate that activists and organizers would become a thorn in his side.

If there's one thing Chicagoans have demonstrated ever since the city rose out of a swamp of stinking onions, it is that they will not quietly acquiesce when they sense injustice. This rich tradition stretches from the Haymarket Affair of 1886 to the garment workers strikes of the early 1900s; from the 1968 Democratic National

Convention protests to the first massive immigration march of 2006. Like the proud Chicagoans who came before them, the Chicago Teachers Union, the Mental Health Movement, and other contemporary groups are committed to questioning and shaping the meanings of democracy, leadership, power, and justice.

Rahm Emanuel's tenure as mayor of Chicago has provided a stage for these populist and progressive institutions to grapple with other powerful forces in a drama about the continual evolution of a great American city.

THE EMANUEL BOYS GREW UP PLAYING CHESS; THEIR FATHER TAUGHT THEM TO "REMEMBER WHAT NAPOLEON SAID: 'OFFENSE IS THE BEST DEFENSE'"—AS RECOUNTED BY EZEKIEL EMANUEL IN HIS 2013 MEMOIR. PHOTO BY TOBY FRUGE.

1
A GOLDEN BOY

Rahm Emanuel was born in Chicago on November 29, 1959. His family story was one of the many quintessential American Dream tales for which Chicago is famous— first- and second-generation immigrants making good through hard work, pluck, and family and community connections.

Rahm's father, Benjamin Emanuel, was born in Jerusalem to Russian émigrés. During the struggle for independence that culminated with the founding of the state of Israel in 1948, he was active in the Irgun Zvai Leumi, a far-right-wing Zionist paramilitary organization widely described as "terrorist" for carrying out assassinations and attacks on Palestinians and the British, whom they viewed as illegally occupying Israel. The group bombed the King David Hotel in Jerusalem in 1946, killing ninety-one people. Members killed at least two hundred Arabs during the 1930s and 1940s in multiple attacks, including bombings and shootings. And in 1948 Irgun commandos carried out the Deir Yassin massacre, in which more than a hundred Palestinians in the small village were killed, including a group of men who were executed in a stone quarry.[1]

Benjamin's family adopted the surname Emanuel in the 1930s to honor Benjamin's brother Emanuel Auerbach, who had been killed in the 1930s in an Arab uprising.[2] Young Benjamin went to Czechoslovakia—he had been studying in Switzerland—in a failed attempt to smuggle guns to the Zionist underground. And he was reportedly bashed on the head by a British soldier's baton so forcefully that it left a permanent dent in his skull.[3] Author Jonathan Alter described Benjamin as a "Sabra": the term, derived from the Hebrew word for prickly pear cactus, is used to describe native-born Israelis, and also denotes "abrupt and aggressive" personalities that could "mask sensitive souls."[4]

Benjamin came to Chicago in 1953 for medical training at Mount Sinai Hospital on the West Side, where he met an X-ray technician named Marsha Smulevitz. She was the daughter of a Romanian from Moldova who had fled pogroms and arrived in

THE EMANUELS LIVED IN UPTOWN, A DIVERSE, SOMEWHAT HARDSCRABBLE NORTH
SIDE NEIGHBORHOOD, BEFORE MOVING TO TONY WILMETTE. PHOTO BY KARI LYDERSEN.

the United States alone in 1917, at the age of thirteen. Marsha's father, Herman, made a living as a steelworker, truck driver, and meat cutter, and was known as a labor organizer and self-taught intellectual.[5] Smulevitz grew up to be a civil rights activist as well; she later served as a chapter chair of the Congress of Racial Equality. At one point she also owned a North Side club that featured live rock music. She later became a psychotherapist, and was still practicing when her son became mayor of Chicago.[6]

Benjamin and Marsha married in 1955 and lived for a time in Israel before returning to Chicago, where Benjamin built his pediatrics practice into one of the city's largest.[7] Their three sons—Ezekiel (Zeke), Rahm, and Ariel (Ari)—were an energetic, competitive, and gifted bunch from early on, and the three boys would all reach pinnacles in their professions. Zeke, two years older than Rahm, became a nationally prominent oncologist and medical ethicist; he served as a department chair of bioethics at the National Institutes of Health and played a role in President Barack Obama's health-care reform legislation, carried out while Rahm was White House chief of staff. Ari, a year younger than Rahm, became a famous talent agent widely known as the inspiration for foul-mouthed, hard-charging Ari Gold on the HBO show *Entourage*. And Rahm, of course, became a prominent political operative, elected official, and fundraiser who, like Ari, was also graced with a prime-time TV alter ego: the impatient, arrogant, and profane White House chief of staff Josh Lyman on the political drama *The West Wing*.[8]

In a 1997 *New York Times* profile, Elisabeth Bumiller wrote, "Of the three brothers, Rahm is the most famous, Ari is the richest and Zeke, over time, will probably be the most important. Zeke is also, according to his brothers, the smartest. Rahm, naturally, gets the most press attention. . . . All are rising stars in three of America's most high-profile and combative professions. All understand and enjoy power, and know how using it behind the scenes can change the way people think, live and die."[9]

The boys spent summers in Israel, where they learned to speak Hebrew. They also attended civil rights protests with their mother. Until Rahm was seven or eight, the Emanuel family lived in an apartment in Uptown, a diverse, somewhat hardscrabble neighborhood near the lake on Chicago's North Side. The boys attended a Jewish day school and spent long hours together riding bikes and hanging out at the nearby Foster Avenue beach.[10] They often had to defend themselves against kids who picked on them because they were Jewish or even because they mistook Rahm—with his curly dark hair and deep tan—for an African American.[11] The Emanuels were plenty able to defend themselves; roughhousing and wrestling were a way of life for the rowdy and competitive boys, as Zeke later described in a memoir.[12] Rahm was literally born into this atmosphere: Zeke described how he and a cousin played a game called "bounce the baby," in which they jumped on a sofa bed "like a couple of jackhammers" and tried to knock infant Rahm—"Rahmy," as Marsha called him—onto the floor.[13]

The boys all took ballet lessons, and young Rahm was known to pirouette around the house. He studied at the Joel Hall Dance Center in Chicago and became a talented dancer; he was even offered a scholarship to the acclaimed Joffrey Ballet at age seventeen. Decades later the nickname "Tiny Dancer" still stuck with Emanuel, whose five-foot-seven stature surprises many in light of his outsize personality.[14]

GROWING UP

In 1967 the Emanuels moved to Wilmette, a lavishly wealthy lakefront suburb north of Chicago, where the median household income in 2010 was more than $100,000 a year and only about 1 percent of the population was African American.[15] The Emanuels lived in one of the more modest homes, not a sprawling mansion. But the boys attended New Trier Township High School, iconic as one of the nation's most elite public high schools, with academic, athletic, and extracurricular programs and facilities worthy of a university.[16] In his 1991 book *Savage Inequalities,* Jonathan Kozol contrasted the lush, privileged atmosphere of New Trier with impoverished public schools in East St. Louis, Illinois—driving home the message of two racially and economically separate Americas. NBC Chicago blogger Edward McClelland noted that "there's something about New Trier Township that ignites class resentment. It's a symbol of elite education, a finishing school for the sort of young people most of us only met by watching *Risky Business* or *Mean Girls.*"[17]

The Emanuel family was close-knit and kept its history of migration and flight from persecution very much alive. The walls were lined with photos of relatives, including some who had perished in the Holocaust. Grandparents, an uncle, and a cousin lived with them for periods of time, and stories of family travails and triumphs were told and retold.[18]

When the boys were teenagers, the family adopted an eight-day-old girl named Shoshana. Benjamin had given the infant a checkup and found she'd suffered a brain hemorrhage at birth. According to Bumiller's profile, the girl's Polish Catholic mother pleaded with him to help find a home for the baby, and after a week of debate the Emanuels decided to take the ailing child in themselves. Shoshana needed extensive surgery and physical therapy, and her childhood was reportedly full of emotional and physical struggles. After graduating from New Trier, she had what has been described as a difficult life, including unemployment and single motherhood, with Marsha later raising her two children.[19]

Writer and editor Alan Goldsher, who grew up near the family in Wilmette, later published a revealing reminiscence about the Emanuel household. In a 2012 story for the *Jewish Daily Forward,* he described Benjamin Emanuel, "aka Dr. Benny," as "a faux-crotchety alpha male, the proverbial grump with a heart of gold, the kind of person who would offer to administer allergy shots at his home rather than at his office, just because it was difficult for the patient's working mother to get her son to said office before closing time."[20]

Goldsher had to stay long enough to make sure he didn't have a bad reaction to the medication, and this usually meant hanging out in the Emanuels' backyard. "Generally, my sojourns behind the house were solitary and unexciting," he wrote.

> But every once in a while, Dr. Benny's two high school aged sons paid me a visit. It was common knowledge around Wilmette that Rahm and Ari Emanuel were bullies—hyper-intelligent bullies, but bullies nonetheless. (This was unlike their father, who only pretended to be a bully.) Rahm and Ari were, respectively, six and five years older than I was, so other than my weekly appearances at Dr. Benny's, our paths never crossed; still, in those brief moments, the boys took a disliking to little ol' me. How do I know they disliked me? Because at every given opportunity, they threw me to the ground. Hard. Really hard. I've blocked out the specifics of the attacks. The only things I know for certain were that a) they were unprovoked, and b) they hurt.[21]

Other reports have described the Emanuel household as a place of constant philosophical and political debate and one-upmanship, with the brothers competing intensely. Zeke described his parents lovingly but firmly pushing the boys to do better in sports and school. Their father taught them to play chess: "He would admonish us with two messages: 'Think three moves ahead!' and 'Remember what Napoleon said: "Offense is the best defense,"'" Zeke wrote.[22]

One can speculate that it was a rarified atmosphere of mutual self-confidence, based on liberal social values yet permeated with a sense of insular superiority. Bumiller's profile quoted Ari: "The pressure is that you were judged by the family.... Our family never cared about the kid down the block."[23]

Rahm was introduced to Democratic politics early on; as teenagers he and Ari joined their mother in volunteering for the successful congressional campaign of Abner Mikva, a popular liberal who later served as a federal chief judge and White House counsel.[24]

Despite the intellectual rigor of the Emanuel home, Rahm was an unexceptional student; a guidance counselor suggested he might consider other options besides college. (Ari, who is dyslexic, also struggled with schoolwork.)[25] Rahm had an after-school job at Arby's that ended up endangering his life and left him with one of his most celebrated physical characteristics. As a teenager he cut his finger at work and then took a late-night swim in Lake Michigan after the high school prom. The result was a life-threatening gangrenous infection, many weeks in the hospital, and the partial amputation of his middle finger.[26] Given his proclivity for literally or verbally giving people the finger, Emanuel's severed digit would become a lifelong source of amusement. President Obama would later joke that the accident left Emanuel "practically mute."[27]

THE EDUCATION OF RAHM EMANUEL

After high school graduation—having turned down the Joffrey Ballet scholarship—Emanuel headed to Sarah Lawrence College, a small and exclusive liberal arts school (formerly a women's college) north of New York City.[28] Emanuel studied dance, philosophy, and other social sciences at Sarah Lawrence, and he became heavily involved in politics.[29]

At age twenty he took a semester off to volunteer for the congressional campaign of Illinois Democrat David Robinson, who was seeking to unseat Paul Findley, a Republican viewed as unsympathetic to Israel because of his support for Palestinian rights.[30] Forrest Claypool—a lifelong Chicago politician who also worked for Robinson—told *Chicago Magazine* that this was the first prominent national campaign to use an opponent's purported anti-Israel stance as a major hook for fundraising.[31]

Emanuel started out volunteering as Robinson's driver, but he soon became the campaign's fundraising director.[32] He helped Robinson raise $750,000, and though the candidate ultimately lost the race, young Emanuel made an impression—notably on field director David Wilhelm, who later managed Bill Clinton's presidential campaign and became the youngest chair of the Democratic National Committee.[33]

After graduating from Sarah Lawrence, Emanuel worked for the Illinois Public Action Council, a large consumer advocacy group known for sending staff door to door to raise funds and enlist support for progressive causes. The council endorsed candidates and spent money on independent campaigns backing them. At the time Emanuel worked there, the council's program director was Jan Schakowsky, who would later become a long-serving congresswoman representing North Side "lake-front liberals" and the wealthy North Shore suburbs beyond."[34]

Emanuel also did fundraising work for Paul Simon's successful 1984 US Senate campaign, helping the liberal upset a three-term Republican incumbent. Though Emanuel was just twenty-four, famed Democratic strategist David Axelrod would later say, his tenaciousness and success in wringing money out of donors was striking.[35]

In the mid-1980s California congressman Tony Coelho was chairman of the Democratic Congressional Campaign Committee (DCCC), the campaign arm of Democrats in the House of Representatives. On a trip to Illinois he met Emanuel, who was working at the Illinois Public Action Council. Coelho was immediately impressed by the young politico, who he said "was organized, bang-bang-bang, knew the pros and cons" of every race. He recruited Emanuel to join the DCCC.[36]

Emanuel headed to Washington with the committee, then returned to Chicago to set up the DCCC's Midwest office, and he was named the committee's national campaign director for the 1988 elections.[37] While at the DCCC Emanuel notoriously sent a dead fish in the mail to pollster Alan Secrest, whose work he blamed for the loss of a congressional seat in Buffalo, New York. Secrest responded with a six-page letter excoriating Emanuel for arrogance, "lying," "star-fucking," and "hubris." Emanuel proceeded to fax the letter out to journalists and colleagues, very possibly to build his own reputation as someone not to be messed with.[38]

From 1984 to 1985 Emanuel earned a master's degree in communications at Northwestern University. He lived on the Evanston campus, not far from his parents' Wilmette home, and he impressed his fellow graduate students with his political rather than academic ambitions and his ceaseless appetite for lively debate.[39] His communications colleagues later speculated that Northwestern was where Emanuel learned the rhetorical techniques that helped him avoid answering tough questions from reporters and critics—for example, by taking a concrete question in a theoretical direction or answering a question about the past with a proclamation about the future.[40]

BECOMING RAHMBO

Harold Washington's election as mayor of Chicago in 1983 was a euphoric moment for many Chicagoans. A coalition of African Americans, whites, and Latinos came together to elect the independent African American congressman, who ran a massive grassroots campaign that registered more than one hundred thousand new African American voters.[41] Once in office Washington kept the momentum going, filling city agencies with progressive and multiracial staff; starting the city's first environmental affairs department; and striving to address economic, social, and environmental injustice in various forms. It wasn't easy—his tenure was characterized by the infamous "Council Wars." Washington backers in City Council constantly squared off against old-regime loyalists headed by Alderman Edward Vrdolyak. Racial tension boiled, and Vrdolyak's contingent blocked many of Washington's appointees and initiatives. But even with the bitter political standoffs, many saw a "new Chicago" emerging, and hopes were high. Washington easily won re-election against Vrdolyak in April 1987. So it was a devastating blow for many when Washington died of a heart attack on November 25, 1987, at the age of sixty-five.[42]

Washington's death cleared the way for the return of the Daley family, which would become a Chicago dynasty. In 1976 the twenty-one-year-term of Mayor Richard J. Daley had come to an end with the death of the "Boss," also by heart attack. His son Richard M. Daley ran in the 1989 mayoral election to replace interim Mayor Eugene Sawyer, an African American alderman installed by City Council, whose tenure was also characterized by bitter racial hostilities.

Though still not even thirty years old, Emanuel was already blossoming as a shrewd and powerful political operative, and he likely knew that allying with Daley could be a crucial move for his own career. Ben Joravsky of the *Chicago Reader* speculated:

> Emanuel was no dummy. He knew Daley would defeat Sawyer and, once in office, would probably rule for life—just like his father, the late Richard J. Daley. So Emanuel did what any bright and ambitious young politico would do—he signed on with Daley. By all accounts, he made himself indispensable to the boss as a fundraiser, badgering, bullying, or guilt-tripping the locals into giving money to Daley's campaign. It was then that Emanuel established his reputation as Rahmbo—the brash, arrogant, and tempestuous assistant that political bosses use to get things done.[43]

Emanuel honed his aggressive fundraising tactics for Daley. *Chicago Tribune* reporter and author Naftali Bendavid noted that Emanuel "told one donor that if he was not prepared to donate a certain amount he should keep his money, and he slammed down the phone." Apparently the approach worked: Emanuel raised $13 million in seven weeks for the man who would become Chicago's longest-serving mayor, and whose office Emanuel would later claim.[44]

RAHM EMANUEL MAY LACK BILL CLINTON'S CHARM, BUT HE SHARES
CLINTON'S NEW DEMOCRAT POLITICS. PHOTO BY KEVIN GEBHARDT.

2

THE ENFORCER—
THE CLINTON YEARS

Benjamin Emanuel thought his son was crazy.

It was November 1991, and Rahm was planning to leave Chicago for Arkansas, where he would work on the presidential campaign of William Jefferson Clinton, a Southern governor whom the elder Emanuel had never even heard of. "He thought maybe somebody needed to check the medication cabinet," Rahm later said in an interview.[1]

Since working on Daley's campaign, Emanuel had continued to do political advising and strategy out of Chicago.[2] He co-founded a company called the Research Group, which specialized in opposition research—essentially digging up information on political opponents or unearthing comments they'd made in the past that would be controversial or damaging in the current context.[3] These nuggets would be aired in the media and political ads or featured in direct-mail campaigns targeted to voters who would be particularly incensed by the news.[4]

Emanuel was recruited to join the Clinton campaign by David Wilhelm, with whom he'd worked on David Robinson's congressional campaign.[5] Emanuel had seen Clinton speak at events related to Chicago public housing in early 1991, and he had been highly impressed with the Arkansas governor's "New Democratic centrism."[6] The affection was mutual. Two decades later in Chicago, Clinton said he was taken with Emanuel right from the start and could tell he was "an executive by nature."[7]

"First of all, I liked him because our campaign was broke and he was a genius at raising money—even as a young person without any money himself," Clinton was quoted saying in the *Chicago Sun-Times*. "I liked him because people said I was too young to run for president and I was too ambitious and Rahm made me look laid-back and passive."[8]

Emanuel reportedly descended on Little Rock like a tornado, berating local advisers and fundraisers for their small-town ways. He once jumped on a table to lecture the staff for forty-five minutes about their practice of not working on Sundays and other failings.[9] When Emanuel arrived, the Clinton campaign had raised $600,000. Emanuel set up a whirlwind of twenty-six fundraising events in twenty days, and by the end of the primary season the take, not counting federal matching funds, was $17 million.[10] The final tally was a record $70 million.[11] *Esquire* magazine described Emanuel during that campaign as a "heat-seeking missile of a principal fundraiser, a brash wunderkind who collected millions for the candidate."[12]

As a senior adviser to Clinton at the age of thirty-two, Emanuel persuaded Clinton to prioritize fundraising, even to the extent of delaying campaigning in New Hampshire. The strategy proved sound, as Clinton's primary rival, Paul Tsongas, ultimately backed out of the race citing lack of funds.[13] Strong financial reserves helped Clinton ride out scandals over his relationship with Gennifer Flowers and his dodging the draft for the Vietnam War, because he was able to flood the airwaves with ads to mitigate the accusations.

A now-famous Emanuel moment came during the final stretch of Clinton's 1992 race, at a Little Rock restaurant and campaign hangout called Doe's. Emanuel performed a diatribe against prominent Democrats he thought had betrayed Clinton during the campaign. He called out each name one by one, in between stabbing a steak knife into the table and yelling, "Dead!"[14]

Once in the White House, Clinton appointed Emanuel to be his political director. Colleagues referred to him simply as "The Enforcer."[15] But Emanuel was forced out of the job after just six months because of conflicts with various staff and, perhaps most important, with First Lady Hillary Clinton.[16] As author Naftali Bendavid described it, on the day Emanuel's then-fiancée, Amy Rule, moved to Washington to join him, Clinton's chief of staff, Mack McLarty, told Emanuel he was fired. Emanuel simply refused to leave unless Clinton told him personally, and "the president, unable to fire the man who arguably had saved his candidacy, relented. Instead, Emanuel was knocked down to 'director of special projects.'"[17]

NAFTA

After his demotion, Emanuel had a chance to get back into Clinton's good graces with a formidable challenge: joining special counsel Bill Daley, brother of Richard M. Daley, in pushing Congress to approve the controversial North American Free Trade Agreement. Daley was dubbed the "NAFTA czar," and Emanuel would be his right-hand man in what *Businessweek* described as a "bloody fight" that "pitted friend against friend and allied the Administration with Republicans and Big Business."[18]

NAFTA had been signed by President George H. W. Bush, Mexican president Carlos Salinas de Gortari, and Canadian prime minister Brian Mulroney in 1992, but each country's legislative branch still had to ratify the agreement. Many Democrats opposed the trade agreement, as did an international movement of trade unionists, human rights advocates, and progressive economists. NAFTA was also unpopular among the general public, who worried about the impact on US jobs. So legislators in both parties feared consequences if they voted for it.

NAFTA backers said it would stimulate trade and bolster the Mexican and US economies by reducing and eliminating tariffs and breaking down other trade barriers. Among other things, the agreement was supposed to create massive demand in Mexico for US exports, which proponents promised would result in thousands of new manufacturing jobs in the United States.

Opponents were convinced that NAFTA would just mean profit for corporations while sending countless US jobs south of the border and undercutting labor and environmental protections in all three countries. Billionaire businessman Ross Perot, who had gotten a whopping 19 percent of the popular vote as an independent candidate in the 1992 presidential election, warned of a "giant sucking sound" of jobs going to Mexico.[19]

But Clinton was a strong supporter of free trade, and he was determined to implement the trade agreement, dubbed the "Lazarus Project" because it was so politically difficult.

"Nobody wanted to touch NAFTA," Emanuel told Chicago political writer Carol Felsenthal.[20] So he and Bill Daley threw all their political and rhetorical weight at the challenge. Side agreements were negotiated that were supposed to address concerns about labor and environmental issues, though these agreements proceeded in chaotic fits and starts and—critics argued—lacked strong enforcement measures. Republicans extracted from Clinton a promise that in the next election cycle, he would "personally repudiate" any NAFTA-related attacks on legislators of either party who had voted for the agreement.[21]

AFL-CIO president Lane Kirkland attacked Clinton for that promise, and warned that Democrats who voted for NAFTA would risk losing the support of state labor federations in future elections.[22] In turn, Clinton denounced organized labor for using "roughshod, muscle-bound tactics" to fight NAFTA—a notable attack by a Democratic president on a traditional Democratic power base.[23]

After thirteen hours of debate, the House of Representatives passed NAFTA on November 18, 1993, with a surprisingly wide margin of 234 to 200.[24] The Senate then passed it sixty-one to thirty-eight, and Clinton signed the bill on December 8. Tellingly, a majority of Democrats voted against the bill in both houses. (In the House, 156 Democrats voted against the bill versus 102 for it; and in the Senate, twenty-eight Democrats voted against it versus twenty-seven for it.)[25]

Years later, in 1997, Emanuel told a *Chicago Tribune* reporter that passing NAFTA was one of his proudest political moments, and his prized possessions included a photo taken with Clinton after the legislation passed.[26]

The White House seriously alienated organized labor by supporting the initiative. The AFL-CIO announced it would cut off funding Democratic campaign committees for at least three months in retaliation.[27] The respected progressive magazine *The Nation* blamed Clinton's "demoral[izing] his base with NAFTA" in part for the Republican Revolution that swept Congress in the 1994 midterm elections.[28]

The worst fears of NAFTA opponents were essentially realized over the next decade, as documented in numerous studies and as experienced in the lives of thousands of regular people in the United States and Mexico. Rather than increasing manufacturing jobs as promised, NAFTA led to the disappearance of good union jobs in the United States, as companies moved production to Mexico, where workers earned about one-tenth of US wages.[29] Often companies relocated just across the border in a booming maquiladora (factory) zone. The Carnegie Endowment for International Peace reported that about half a million jobs were created in Mexican maquiladoras in the five years following NAFTA. But Mexico's net job creation was "disappointing," as the agricultural sector lost many jobs in the wake of NAFTA. And a decade later, about 30 percent of those maquila jobs had moved to countries with even cheaper labor, like China.[30]

Nineteen months after NAFTA was instituted, a report by the watchdog group Public Citizen found that 90 percent of the promises made by its proponents had not come true. Companies that had pledged to create jobs if NAFTA passed—including General Electric, Mattel, Procter & Gamble, Scott Paper, and Zenith—had actually cut US jobs. The Department of Labor reported that thirty-eight thousand workers had lost their jobs because of NAFTA in just its first year and a half, and almost seventy thousand US workers had filed claims with the Labor Department to receive unemployment aid specifically related to NAFTA.[31]

The agreement would not redeem itself over time, either. By 2010 the trade deficit with Mexico had soared to $97 billion. US exports to Mexico had risen as expected, but imports from Mexico, which displaced US jobs, had risen even more. According to a report by the Economic Policy Institute, the ten hardest-hit states included Emanuel's native Illinois along with other already-struggling Rust Belt states like Ohio, Indiana, and Michigan.[32]

THE HANDSHAKE

Emanuel played a role in choreographing one of the iconic images of the twentieth century. That would be the famous handshake between Arafat and Israeli prime minister Yitzhak Rabin at the signing of the Oslo Accords in September 1993.[33] The accords called for Israeli troop withdrawal from the Gaza Strip and parts of

MEXICANS PROTEST THE KILLINGS OF WOMEN IN THE BORDER CITY JUÁREZ,
WIDELY SEEN AS AN OUTCOME OF THE SWEEPING ECONOMIC CHANGES
WROUGHT BY NAFTA—ONE OF EMANUEL'S CLINTON-ERA PROJECTS. PHOTO
BY KARI LYDERSEN.

the West Bank and affirmed a Palestinian right to self-determination. CNN re-marked upon the "uneasy, yet unforgettable handshake."[34] Emanuel, Clinton, and staffer John Podesta staged and meticulously rehearsed the handshake ahead of time. Emanuel studied footage of the 1978 Camp David Accords handshake where President Jimmy Carter oversaw an agreement between Egyptian president Anwar Sadat and Israeli prime minister Menachem Begin.[35] Emanuel put a new stamp on the moment by having Clinton spread his arms around the two Middle East leaders, bringing them together.[36]

Arafat and Rabin's clasp was a major international event signifying what many hoped would be a shift in Middle Eastern affairs. Meanwhile, for Emanuel, it was a relatively minor but interesting example of his ability to shift positions and allegiances as the political situation dictated, always with a keen eye to managing the image.

CRIME AND IMMIGRATION BILLS

Along with his work on NAFTA, Emanuel would frequently invoke with pride his role in the Clinton administration's law enforcement and crime-fighting efforts for decades to come. He helped Clinton pass bills cracking down on sex offenders, assault weapon ownership, street crime, and "terrorism"; and he staged photo opportunities with the president surrounded by police officers in uniform. Emanuel played a key role in Clinton's 1994 crime bill, the Violent Crime Control and Law Enforcement Act, which was signed into law in August 1994.[37] The act put one hundred thousand more officers on the street and allocated $9.7 billion in funding for prisons and $6.1 billion in funding for prevention programs. The bill also banned the manufacture of nineteen types of assault weapons, increased the reach of the death penalty, and created harsher penalties for immigration-related and gang-related offenses.[38]

Author Noam Scheiber described Emanuel as a driving force behind the crime bill: "Middle America thought Clinton was soft. And so Emanuel, from his perch as second-string White House counselor without portfolio, excluded from the action on health care, concocted an anti-crime campaign almost out of thin air."[39]

Clinton, Emanuel, and Democratic supporters often stressed aspects of the bill that were supported by many Americans across the political spectrum: gun control, domestic violence prevention, and officers on the ground. The assault weapons ban naturally infuriated the National Rifle Association and many powerful Republicans but was lauded by gun control and public safety advocates. The bill also increased penalties on repeat sex offenders, mandated financial restitution for rape and other sex crimes, increased funding for women's shelters and domestic violence prevention programs, and mandated that restraining orders be honored across state lines.[40]

These were logical, humane, and important reforms that aided the vulnerable and abused. But other aspects of the legislation were widely seen as draconian tough-on-crime measures that would have disproportionate impacts on people of color and low-income people. The Justice Policy Institute cited the bill in calling Clinton "the incarceration president" because spending on incarceration and the number of inmates behind bars—disproportionately African Americans—skyrocketed on his watch. The institute noted that the incarceration rate at the end of the Clinton administration was 476 per 100,000 citizens, compared to 332 per 100,000 at the end of President George H. W. Bush's term and 247 per 100,000 at the end of the Reagan administration.[41]

The 1994 act, the country's largest crime bill ever, expanded the scope of the death penalty to make more than sixty offenses punishable by execution.[42] In the *Chicago Sun-Times*, pundit Carl T. Rowan wrote, "Can Clinton be blind to the obvious truth that the death penalty is imposed mostly upon the poor, the black, brown and other minorities of America? Any law that adds to the unfairness of our judicial system will provoke more crime. And doesn't the president know that there is no credible evidence that electrocuting, gassing, shooting or hanging felons is a deterrent to criminal behavior?"[43]

The law aimed to crack down on gangs, including allowing up to ten years of additional prison time if a crime involved gang issues.[44] And it increased reliance on "boot camps" for juvenile offenders.[45] While arguably preferable to other types of incarceration, such boot camps would become the subject of many horror stories, including reports of abuse and youth suffering serious injuries and death after being forced to do hard physical exercise in extreme conditions.[46]

The crime bill also eliminated Pell grant funding for inmates pursuing higher education in federal and state prisons. Since the 1965 Higher Education Act, Pell grants had provided a way for many incarcerated men and women—often from poor communities with little education—to make productive use of their time be hind bars. Building more prisons while eliminating an important resource for those inside them was cruel and smashed the already-weak argument that US prisons were rehabilitative as much as punitive, prison reformers said.[47]

The crime bill also instituted a federal "three strikes" provision of the type later passed by various states. As a result, a third conviction for serious violent felonies or drug trafficking offenses would mean life imprisonment without the possibility of parole. Analysts said the provision was more posturing than substance, since relatively few violent crimes are federal offenses.[48] But perhaps the posturing worked. In early 1994, even before the final version of the crime bill was signed, a *Washington Post*/ABC poll found that 39 percent of Americans thought Democrats were doing a better job on crime than Republicans, compared to 32 percent with the inverse view.[49]

"The impact on the political climate I think was significant," Marc Mauer, executive director of the nonprofit justice reform group the Sentencing Project, told longtime Chicago journalist Curtis Black. "Here you have a Democratic administration saying we can be as tough as anybody on crime. You have a Democratic president supporting 'three strikes you're out.'"[50]

In 1995 Clinton outraged criminal justice reformers and civil rights leaders when he upheld the sentencing disparity between offenses involving crack and powder cocaine, wherein crimes involving one gram of crack received prison terms roughly equal to crimes involving one hundred grams of powder cocaine. Since African Americans were much more likely to be arrested on charges related to crack cocaine, the disparity had a blatantly racist effect. In spring 1995 the US Sentencing Commission decided the penalties should be equalized. This would have happened with no action from Clinton or Congress, but Congress soon passed a law (which Clinton signed in October 1995) perpetuating the sentencing disparity—arguing that crack was decimating inner cities and that a heavy hand was needed.[51] Furious members of the Congressional Black Caucus sent Clinton a letter saying the continued policy made "a mockery of justice."[52]

In 1996 Clinton signed another sweeping crime bill, the Antiterrorism and Effective Death Penalty Act (AEDPA), in which Emanuel likely also played a significant role.[53] Introduced after the 1995 Oklahoma City bombing, the AEDPA significantly curbed habeas corpus rights by severely limiting appeals. Defense attorneys said this created a greater chance that an innocent person would be executed. A prime example was the high-profile case of Troy Davis, who was executed in September 2011 for the 1989 killing of an off-duty police officer working security at a Burger King in Savannah, Georgia. An international movement supporting Davis's claims of innocence, including Amnesty International, former president Jimmy Carter, and Archbishop Desmond Tutu, argued that no physical evidence linked Davis to the crime, and noted that seven of the nine witnesses whose testimony had led to his conviction later recanted. Nonetheless, Davis was killed by lethal injection after the Georgia Board of Pardons and Parole refused to grant clemency and a last-minute appeal to the US Supreme Court was denied. Legal experts said that the AEDPA curbed Davis's legal recourse. *The Nation* described the bill as "greas[ing] the wheels of this death machinery by curtailing prisoners' rights to appeal their sentences."[54]

The AEDPA dovetailed with the 1996 Illegal Immigration Reform and Immigrant Responsibility Act (IIRIRA), also signed by Clinton and likely orchestrated at least in part by Emanuel. Immigrants' rights advocates decried the bill as inhumane and ineffective, saying it did little to solve larger problems with the country's immigration system. The combined effects of the two acts nearly doubled the number of immigrants in detention in just two years. The American Civil Liberties Union noted that the laws essentially created indefinite detention for immigrants who could not be deported to their home countries. And the laws' focus on deporting permanent residents with criminal convictions meant that many generally law-abiding people who had been in the country for years were placed in deportation proceedings because of relatively minor convictions like drug possession and statutory rape.[55]

WELFARE REFORM

Emanuel was also at Clinton's side as senior policy adviser for the sweeping welfare reform legislation that revamped an admittedly dysfunctional system but also eviscerated the whole concept of a guaranteed safety net.

In his 2006 book *The Plan*, cowritten with Clinton aide Bruce Reed, Emanuel described welfare reform as "an excruciating dilemma" for his boss. During his campaign Clinton had vowed to "end welfare as we know it."[56] But how to do it became a bitter battle both between Republicans and Democrats and among Democrats in the Clinton White House.

Republicans—who had taken over the House with their 1994 "Republican Revolution"—proposed bills that gutted numerous protections for the most vulnerable, including young women, children, and immigrants. Clinton vetoed two Republican bills that would have drastically cut food stamps and nutritional programs, benefits for documented immigrants, aid for disabled children, and other supports, while also imposing lifetime limits on benefits.[57]

In 1994 Clinton had proposed a bill that would have required welfare recipients to go to work but provided significant funding for job training and job creation and maintained safeguards if they couldn't find work. That bill was expensive; the cost, among other political considerations, killed the measure.[58]

As the 1996 presidential election approached, Clinton was under increasing pressure to keep his promise and pass some kind of welfare reform. In typical fashion Emanuel was central to making this happen, brokering compromises and pressuring not only Republicans but, perhaps more important, Democrats who objected to deep cuts.

By summer 1996 Clinton was considering a bill from Republicans that didn't include as many cuts as their previous proposals but still transformed the very nature of welfare by creating five-year lifetime limits on benefits.

Internal discussions over the bill pitted White House liberals against New Democrat conservatives. Cabinet opponents of the bill included health and human services secretary Donna Shalala, treasury secretary Robert Rubin, labor secretary Robert Reich, and housing secretary Henry Cisneros, as described in a book by Clinton's assistant secretary of health and human services, Peter B. Edelman.[59]

Another ardent critic of the proposed reform was New York senator Daniel Patrick Moynihan, a sociologist by training who predicted the bill would lead to desperately poor children "sleeping on grates."[60] *Fortune* magazine noted that Emanuel "had a very public run-in" with Moynihan, who suspected Emanuel was behind an anonymous quote that "we'll roll all over [Moynihan] if we have to."[61]

Emanuel's side ultimately won out. The reform bill Clinton signed in August 1996 fundamentally changed welfare into a temporary assistance program administered primarily through states, focused on moving people off public aid.[62]

For sixty years poor people had been guaranteed cash aid from the federal government. Clinton's Personal Responsibility and Work Opportunity Reconciliation Act changed that, incorporating several of the major tenets of the Republican bills Clinton had vetoed.[63] It created the Temporary Assistance for Needy Families (TANF) program, which gave block grants to states for services meant to move people to work. The bill placed a five-year lifetime limit on benefits while allowing states to set even shorter limits. TANF recipients also had to meet work requirements, and many ended up in low-paying jobs that left them in poverty or, down the line, again unemployed.[64]

Liberals were outraged at the reform law. Edelman and Mary Jo Bane, Clinton's assistant secretary for children and families, quit the administration in protest.[65] Edelman would spend the next few years studying the impact of welfare reform on the poor. He wrote that the bill "broke faith with America's children" and created a new class of "disappeared" people abandoned by the government and turning to desperate measures to survive.[66]

On the tenth anniversary of welfare reform's passage, Emanuel remarked in Congress that "I am proud to have played an active role in the passage of this legislation during my time in the White House." He recited numbers of people moving off public aid in Illinois and praised the legislation for "connecting a generation of children with a culture of work."[67]

During Clinton's presidency millions of families did indeed rise out of poverty and find work. "While Bill Clinton ended welfare as we had known it, America responded in heroic ways," Emanuel and Reed wrote in *The Plan*. "Businesses stepped forward to hire and train people. States overhauled their bureaucracies to help recipients find jobs. Most of all, people who had been trapped on welfare flocked to work in record numbers."[68]

But that was in the midst of a strong economy. In a 2012 report the Center on Budget and Policy Priorities noted that when poverty increased following the financial crash of 2008 the safety net that previously would have caught needy people and helped them get back on their feet was torn or nonexistent.[69]

"Because relatively few families receive TANF and benefits are very low, TANF plays a much more limited role in helping families escape poverty or deep poverty (i.e., income below half the poverty line) today," compared to the previous welfare program, the report explained. It noted that 2012 poverty levels exceeded 1996 levels, and "over the last 16 years, the national TANF caseload has declined by 60 percent, even as poverty and deep poverty have worsened. . . . These opposing trends—TANF caseloads going down while poverty is going up—mean that a much smaller share of poor families receive cash assistance from TANF than they did prior to welfare reform."

The center added that "many families left the welfare rolls *without* gaining employment, leading to a substantial increase in the number of families disconnected from both welfare and work."

In other words, Clinton's welfare reform may have looked good in the short term, but it contributed to the desperate poverty and instability that many families would later face nationwide—including in Chicago when Emanuel would take the helm.

POLITICAL SIGNIFICANCE

Welfare reform, NAFTA, and aspects of the 1994 and 1996 crime and immigration bills would for years to come be blamed for negative impacts on regular Americans—especially African Americans, who disproportionately were caught up in the criminal justice system, and poor people, who struggled to survive with reduced public aid options. Clinton's presidency would also be remembered as one of the most prosperous eras of the twentieth century, with low unemployment, a budget surplus, rising incomes and homeownership rates, national debt reduction, improvements in health indicators, and an overall expanding economy.[70] Emanuel surely deserves credit for his role in some of these achievements. But it is hard to know exactly how much his efforts or values were reflected in the policies and priorities of the Clinton White House—as it would be during his time as President Barack Obama's chief of staff.

Emanuel's advice and actions in the Clinton White House were likely based in large part on his own ambition and drive to succeed at the tasks assigned him, and also his arguably keen judgment about what stances were most expedient for his boss. Emanuel was well known for abandoning past positions and principles if they became politically inconvenient, so it is difficult to say how much his work on NAFTA, welfare reform, and draconian aspects of the crime bill reflected deep-seated ideologies. However, all three measures do fit with the known and consistent aspects of Emanuel's approach: his dedication to business interests and the free market; an emphasis on personal responsibility and choice; and his willingness to forge ahead with policies even in the face of intense opposition from labor unions, civil rights groups, and other interests that traditionally made up an important base of the Democratic Party.

RAHM EMANUEL'S CAREER AS A PRIVATE SECTOR BUSINESSMAN WAS BRIEF
BUT LUCRATIVE. PHOTO BY KAREN COOPER, AP.

3
CASHING IN

Though Emanuel had made his name fundraising for other candidates, as the millennium approached he was still young and "had political aspirations of his own, which necessitated some financial security," as Nina Easton explained in *Fortune* magazine. Easton quoted Rahm's brother Zeke saying, "Money is not the be-all and end-all for him. . . . But he knew he needed money so that wouldn't be a problem while he was doing public service."[1]

Hence in October 1998 Emanuel left the White House for the private sector. He had no formal business experience or even an MBA, but he did have a "golden Rolodex" from his days in the Clinton White House and all his political fundraising.[2] He was hired by the investment banking firm Wasserstein Perella and Company in Chicago in 1999. Bruce Wasserstein was a major Democratic donor, and according to the *New York Times* he called on John Simpson, the firm's Chicago manager, to meet with Emanuel in Washington. After a three-hour dinner Simpson made Emanuel an offer.[3] Soon the Emanuel family packed up and moved back to Chicago, where they bought a home in the leafy Ravenswood neighborhood on the city's North Side.

Demonstrating that connections, energy, and assertiveness can count for more than expertise in this field, Emanuel ultimately earned more than $18 million in just two and a half years as an investment banker. The *New York Times* broke it down: $900,000 his first year; almost $1.4 million the second year; and $6.5 million in another half year, plus about $9.7 million in deferred compensation, bonuses, and equity boosted when the firm was sold in 2001 to Germany's Dresdner Bank.[4] Even for the high-rolling world of investment banking, Emanuel was spectacularly successful; his earnings put him in the top 5 percent of the profession.[5]

Emanuel's major deals included the purchase of the home alarm company SecurityLink from SBC Communications, then run by his longtime friend and former White House colleague Bill Daley. In that nearly $500 million deal Emanuel represented the Chicago private equity firm GTCR Golder Rauner, whose chairman, Bruce Rauner, knew Emanuel through mutual connections and had encouraged him to try his hand at investment banking. Rauner would later become a key adviser and public backer when Emanuel became mayor of Chicago.[6]

Emanuel also worked on the $8.2 billion merger of the utilities Chicago Unicom and Philadelphia Peco, which created Exelon, the parent company of Commonwealth Edison and one of the country's biggest power corporations. Former Unicom and later Exelon CEO John W. Rowe knew Emanuel from his Clinton White House days and contacted him personally about the merger. Afterward, the new utility laid off 3,350 workers, more than a tenth of its workforce.[7]

Other companies headed by high-profile Democratic donors who became Emanuel banking clients included Slim-Fast, the aviation company Avolar, the Chicago Board Options Exchange, and Loral Space and Communications.[8]

Ron Suskind, a Pulitzer Prize–winning former reporter for the *Wall Street Journal*, described Emanuel's banking success in the 2011 book *Confidence Men*: "Insofar as it was always clear that he'd return to government, the compensation makes sense, said one former investment chief, a fan of Emanuel's, who now works in Washington: 'Paying someone who will be a future government official a lot of money for doing very little? On Wall Street we call that an investment.'"[9]

Emanuel also profited by serving on several boards of directors, including the Chicago Mercantile Exchange.[10] During Emanuel's mayoral campaign eleven years later, the exchange's parent group would give him $200,000, his biggest single campaign donation.[11] In 1999, the *Chicago Sun-Times* noted, Emanuel joined the boards of Rxdrugstore.com and Beautyjungle.com.[12] The *Sun-Times* also reported that Emanuel was paid more than $250,000 over two years in the early 2000s by the advertising agency Young & Rubicam, where he served on the board.

And in 1999 Mayor Daley appointed Emanuel to the board of the Chicago Housing Authority, the agency that oversaw the city's troubled public housing projects.[13] When Emanuel joined the board, the authority was in the process of launching a highly controversial overhaul known as the Plan for Transformation, which involved tearing down all the public housing high-rises and replacing them with "mixed income" developments that included a third each of market rate, affordable, and public housing.[14] Although most people agreed the high-rises had become extremely dilapidated and dangerous, there was great outcry among residents and fairhousing advocates over the plan. The city didn't comprehensively track whether residents displaced from the developments ever got new housing with the subsidized vouchers they were given.[15] Meanwhile, in some areas, the transformation was attractive to private developers, who were able to build market-rate housing on plots near downtown or the lakefront. The plan had already been crafted by the time

Emanuel joined the board, but it's likely that authority officials saw his business and real estate connections as an important asset while the authority was making deals with developers.

FREDDIE MAC

During his sojourn in the private sector, Emanuel also served on the board of Freddie Mac, the government-sponsored private mortgage company whose problems contributed to the economic crisis beginning in 2007.[16]

The colloquially named Fannie Mae and Freddie Mac were created by Congress to promote home ownership. Fannie was launched in 1938 to help fulfill the promises of the National Housing Act of 1934. The idea was that Fannie would purchase government-insured mortgages from lenders and sell those mortgages to other investors—in essence acting as a mortgage dealer. As it turned out, Fannie didn't always resell the mortgages. It soon became a major mortgage holder and was later authorized by Congress to build and maintain a portfolio by using federal and private funds and selling shares and bonds.

Freddie Mac was created in 1970 to purchase mortgages from Savings and Loan (S&L) institutions, and over time its operations basically dovetailed with those of Fannie Mae. In short, by decreasing risk for private lenders and by helping to create a secondary market for mortgages, Fannie and Freddie were meant to motivate lenders to offer mortgages to people who might not otherwise be able to get financing to buy a home.[17]

Freddie Mac started trading on the New York Stock Exchange in 1989. Like Fannie Mae, it was considered a private company even though it enjoyed closer ties with the government than other mortgage companies. Fannie and Freddie were known as government-sponsored entities, or GSEs, with federal charters. The government was not obligated to back the debt incurred by Fannie and Freddie, but they were exempt from taxes and regulations imposed on other private corporations, and the Treasury Secretary had the option of buying their debt and making it the obligation of US taxpayers.[18]

In February 2000, Clinton appointed Emanuel to Freddie Mac's board of directors for a term that expired in May 2001. In exchange, Emanuel got an annual payment and stock options. As the *Chicago Tribune* described it, Emanuel received "at least $320,000 for a 14-month stint at Freddie Mac that required little effort." The board met only six times a year and Emanuel was not assigned to any committees, so he did not have to do much legwork to earn his stipend. The *Tribune* quoted fellow Freddie board member Neil Hartigan, a former Illinois attorney general, noting that "Emanuel's primary contribution was explaining to others on the board how to play the levers of power."[19]

LOOKING THE OTHER WAY

During the time Emanuel and other board members were supposed to be keeping tabs on Freddie Mac's dealings, the GSE was carrying out behavior that government agencies would later deem illegal and unethical.

At the time Emanuel was on the board, Freddie Mac was profiting handsomely from the kind of risky investments (including subprime mortgage loans) that would later bring the financial system crashing down. Freddie Mac executives notified Emanuel and the other board members of a plan to misconstrue the nature of their profits to shareholders, with accounting tricks that would basically put current earnings on the books in future years, ensuring Freddie Mac would appear profitable and executives would get juicy bonuses for years to come even if the risky investments began to tank.[20]

The future of Freddie Mac was no small thing to gamble with. When the economic crisis started in 2007, Freddie and Fannie together had a stake in more than half of the nation's home mortgages, for a total value of more than $5 trillion.[21] Nearly every private mortgage lender in the United States depended on the GSEs to maintain liquidity in the market. Investors included countless US entities as well as foreign governments including China. So executives and board members knew well that jeopardizing the future stability of the institutions could have major economic and political ramifications across the globe.[22]

In 2007 the US Securities and Exchange Commission charged Freddie Mac with securities fraud for actions between 1998 and 2002 that included overstating its earnings by 30.5 percent in 2000 and 23.9 percent in 2001 to maintain its image as the consistently profitable "Steady Freddie." In a press release SEC enforcement director Linda Chatman Thomsen said, "As has been seen in so many cases, Freddie Mac's departure from proper accounting practices was the result of a corporate culture that sought stable earnings growth at any cost."[23]

A 2003 federal investigation yielded a damning report by Office of Federal Housing Enterprise Oversight director Armando Falcon Jr. that ordered Freddie to pay $585 million in fines and legal fees and restate $5 billion worth of earnings. Among many other things, Falcon said that presidential appointees to the lenders' boards—like Emanuel—played no "meaningful role" and should be eliminated.[24]

Falcon's report accused Freddie's board of directors (and senior management) of a "lack of attention" to the "corporate culture" and "tone at the top" that encouraged increasingly risky and deceptive maneuvers as a way to meet Wall Street expectations. The board and senior managers had "failed to establish and maintain adequate internal control systems."[25] And, Falcon said, the board "did not recognize red flags, failed to make reasonable inquiries of management, or otherwise failed in its duty to follow up on matters brought to its attention."[26]

In April 2006 Freddie Mac was fined $3.8 million by the Federal Election Commission for illegally using corporate funds for political fundraising, including during Emanuel's tenure on the board. Senior vice president for government relations Robert Mitchell Delk and head of congressional relations Clarke Camper had hosted eighty-five often lavish fundraising events that netted $1.7 million.[27] The commission noted that the board of directors reviewed documents outlining the illegal fundraising activities, which were framed as "political risk management." At the time, the fine was the commission's largest civil enforcement settlement.

Most of Freddie Mac's fundraising efforts were directed toward Republican candidates. An illegal $150,000 donation was made to the Republican Governors Association, and numerous fundraisers were held for Ohio Republican Michael G. Oxley, chair of the House Financial Services Committee.[28] But Freddie also hosted events to support Democrats, including a fundraiser for Emanuel's 2002 congressional campaign that netted a relatively paltry $7,000. Emanuel's campaign also collected $9,500 from a lunch hosted by Freddie Mac CEO Leland Brendsel, later ousted because of the fundraising scandal. During the 2002 election cycle Emanuel collected a total of $25,000 in donations from people connected to Freddie Mac—more than twice the amount Freddie Mac–linked donors gave to any other candidate, according to the *Chicago Tribune*.[29]

Freddie Mac officials likely concluded their fundraising for Emanuel and other powerful politicians paid off. Once in Congress, Emanuel was appointed to a subcommittee with responsibility for oversight of Freddie Mac.[30] His office has said he recused himself from any proceedings that would have raised conflicts of interest.[31] *Chicago Sun-Times* political correspondent Lynn Sweet argued that was not good enough:

> Emanuel told me he has no problem because he put his holdings into a blind trust and plans to recuse himself from any votes relating to Freddie Mac. "I chose to do something you don't have to do," he said, as if he deserved extra points. "I feel good about the actions I've taken to date," he added. Emanuel had no business getting on the Capital Markets, Insurance and Government Sponsored Enterprises subcommittee as long as he had the Freddie Mac options—in blind trust or not. It would have been better if Emanuel sold the Freddie Mac shares he already owned before being sworn in last January and told Freddie Mac to forget about any future options to which he may be entitled.[32]

Meanwhile, congressional disclosure documents showed that Emanuel had sold between $100,000 and $250,000 worth of Freddie Mac stock on February 21, 2003, a few days before the stock's value dropped by 10 percent and before revelations that Freddie was being investigated for possible criminal behavior.[33] The sale smacked of insider trading. At the time members of Congress were exempt from insider trading laws, a situation that changed in spring 2012, when President Obama, with strong bipartisan support, signed the STOCK Act, which prohibits congressional legislators from trading based on nonpublic information.[34]

The website *Business Insider* noted in 2011, before the STOCK Act was passed, that Emanuel's sales were "by no means illegal. . . . But the timing of the trades is certainly suspect, especially given Emanuel's service on the board during the time period for which the federal government was investigating the actions of Freddie Mac executives."[35]

FREDDIE AND THE ECONOMIC CRISIS

The federal government ultimately took over the floundering Freddie Mac and Fannie Mae in 2008, promising to insure up to $300 billion worth of their loans.[36] Emanuel was one of eighteen cosponsors of the Housing and Economic Recovery Act of 2008, which gave the government authority to do the takeover.[37]

In February 2009 the Obama administration committed to extend up to $400 billion to Fannie and Freddie to cover their losses.[38] The administration lifted that cap in December of that year, just weeks before the December 31 deadline, after which a new bailout would have required congressional approval.[39]

The debacle drew increased scrutiny to Freddie and Fannie, including the period when Emanuel served on the board. And it brought into the public eye the lashing Freddie Mac had taken at the hands of federal watchdogs. Risky investments of the kind made during Emanuel's board tenure were blamed in part for the collapse of Fannie and Freddie, meltdowns that played a significant role in the economic crisis.

In a letter written to Attorney General Eric Holder before the commitment of unlimited assistance to Fannie and Freddie, conservative pundit Grover Norquist, head of Americans for Tax Reform, and liberal *Firedoglake* blogger Jane Hamsher called for Emanuel to resign from the Obama cabinet and demanded that the Justice Department launch a federal investigation and empanel a grand jury. They wrote, "We believe there is an abundant public record which establishes that the actions of the White House have blocked any investigation into [Emanuel's] activities while on the board of Freddie Mac from 2000 to 2001, and facilitated the cover up of potential malfeasance until the ten-year statute of limitations has run out."[40]

Right-wing activists seized on Emanuel's involvement with Freddie Mac to bolster their narrative of widespread "Chicago-style" corruption within the Obama administration. But it was really just another example of Emanuel's longstanding ties to the financial sector, and of how his career had been built in part upon leveraging those ties for political and personal gain.

The ultimate takeaway of Emanuel's time in the private sector may be this: although he had the political savvy and financial smarts to earn some $18 million in investment banking in a few years, those same qualities didn't prevent him from standing by while people purportedly under his watch took a big gamble involving billions in taxpayer money and the homes of millions of Americans.

CONGRESSMAN RAHM EMANUEL MET CONSTITUENTS AT A CHICAGO SUPERMARKET. EMANUEL'S CONGRESSIONAL CAMPAIGN CAST HIM AS A CHICAGOAN LIKE HIS POLICE OFFICER UNCLE LES. PHOTO BY THE OFFICE OF U.S. CONGRESSMAN RAHM EMANUEL.

4
RAHM GOES TO CONGRESS

Emanuel's brief career in investment banking was clearly a great success. But he studiously avoided talking about his foray into the private sector when he made his next career move: running for Congress in Illinois's Fifth District.

The district represents more than half a million people, and stretches from lakefront high-rises on the east to unassuming blocks of typical Chicago bungalows further west, including several suburbs. It includes neighborhoods full of nightlife, such as the Boystown gay district; Wrigleyville, home to the Cubs' ball field; as well as quiet upscale residential enclaves like Emanuel's Ravenswood neighborhood. The median household income in 2000 was about $50,000.[1] The district was about three-quarters white and about a quarter Latino, with small African American and Asian populations.[2] The population logged as white by the Census was actually a prime example of ethnic Chicago, including a large number of Polish immigrants and Polish Americans, German Americans, numerous Bosnians and Russians, and a significant Jewish community.[3]

Emanuel reportedly decided to run for Congress almost on a whim after a certain Illinois politician jogged by while Emanuel was in the yard playing with his kids. Rod Blagojevich, who was then serving as congressman of the Fifth District, stopped his workout long enough to tell Emanuel he was thinking of running for governor.[4]

Two significant Democratic candidates had thrown their hats in the ring for Blagojevich's seat before Emanuel entered the race. They were Bernie Hansen, an alderman who'd been in City Council since 1983 and was a longstanding member of the famous Chicago Democratic "Machine"; and Nancy Kaszak, a state representative and lawyer of Polish descent.

Hansen dropped out of the race abruptly after Emanuel declared his candidacy; insiders speculated that Mayor Daley had pushed him to quit.[5] Such machinations are common in politics, but in Chicago they happen in the special context of the

Machine. By the turn of the twenty-first century, many experts considered the Machine defunct, yet its legacy and dynamics certainly played a role in Emanuel's political career—including in his congressional bid.

"The Machine" refers to the powerful Democratic Party organization that has controlled many of Chicago's political posts and other power structures since it was launched in the 1930s by Bohemian immigrant mayor Anton Cermak, who accumulated and maintained power in part by doling out thousands of patronage jobs with city agencies and appointments to political posts, demanding loyalty and legwork in return. Deciding which candidates will get party backing or even run at all was a hallowed Machine function. Machine support was long considered key to winning Chicago elections, because the Machine turned out patronage workers to campaign for and donate to chosen candidates while undermining opponents.

The Machine's grip on Chicago has loosened and tightened at various points over the years, with a defining figure being legendary Mayor Richard J. Daley, "the Boss," who served from 1955 to 1976. The 1983 election of African American mayor Harold Washington broke the Machine's traditional hold and launched the "Council Wars," with City Council split between aldermen loyal to Washington and powerful ethnic white South Side alderman Ed Vrdolyak. One of Vrdolyak's top lieutenants in the anti-Washington bloc was Irish American Alderman Ed Burke, who was still on the City Council when Emanuel took over.

Washington died in office after being reelected in 1987, and Daley's son Richard M. Daley was elected mayor in 1989. Although the Machine changed in structure and diminished in power from the days of the Boss, some saw its traces in the multiracial, multiethnic yet top-down coalitions that the younger Daley assembled. Rather than outright racial conflict, as had been seen during past decades, Daley's Machine formed mutually beneficial alliances with powerful African American and Latino leaders and groups including the Hispanic Democratic Organization. Patronage jobs were reduced by economic factors and a federal consent decree, but a modern if less omnipotent version of the Machine continued to deal in political clout, including in the awarding of city contracts to private businesses. So while many considered the Machine dead by the time Emanuel took office, others saw it in an altered state—still a formidable foe, and now with Emanuel very much a part of it.

A CHICAGO GIRL

Nancy Kaszak was a well-known and well-liked figure in the community, a populist and liberal who had grown up in the blue-collar south suburbs. Her father worked two jobs, at an oil refinery in northwest Indiana by day and at Sears by night. Kaszak was the first in her family to graduate from college, with a business degree from Northern Illinois University.[6]

She had worked as a consultant, fundraiser, and official for universities and non-profit organizations, including chief attorney for the Chicago Park District during Harold Washington's term as mayor.[7] She had a history of running as an independent against Machine candidates, including an unsuccessful bid for alderman in 1987, and the 1992 race where she unseated the Machine-linked incumbent to become a state representative.[8] In that campaign her co-chair was Abner Mikva—the congressman and future federal judge for whom both she and Emanuel had campaigned in the past.[9] In 1996 Kaszak ran against Blagojevich—also a state representative at the time—in the Democratic primary for the congressional seat then held by a Republican. Kaszak lost in a close race, with Blagojevich receiving an endorsement from Mayor Daley and help from his father-in-law, Richard Mell, a powerful alderman.[10] Blagojevich went on to beat incumbent Michael Flanagan with two-thirds of the vote in the general election.[11]

As a state representative, Kaszak gained attention for her campaigns against night baseball games at Wrigley Field, in which she argued that they were a disruption and a hassle for nearby residents. She generally compiled a liberal voting record, earning high marks from unions, women's groups, and community advocates.[12]

Kaszak was the granddaughter of Polish immigrants, and she worked her Polish roots. The Polish-language media and community leaders embraced her during her campaigns. She announced her Fifth District candidacy at the Copernicus Center, "surrounded by portraits of Polish kings," as reporter Chris Hayes noted in a profile.[13]

A MACHINE GUY

Emanuel announced his candidacy in November 2001. In a rare move, Mayor Daley—who usually didn't intervene in congressional races—gave his endorsement. He also helped Emanuel secure the backing of the all-important "ward bosses," who are key in Chicago elections because they use their clout and influence to turn out scores of volunteers and voters for Machine candidates. Former mayor Jane Byrne, a native of the area, supported Kaszak, saying, "I think it would be wonderful for the Fifth District and for the city of Chicago if Nancy beat the political machine. It would also be a breath of fresh air for the Democratic Party."[14]

So the Fifth District congressional Democratic primary matchup between Emanuel and Kaszak was a classic Chicago race pitting a Machine candidate against an independent with grassroots bona fides.

Kaszak was a local and a "regular Chicagoan" in a way Emanuel was not—given his Wilmette upbringing, East Coast liberal arts education, time in Washington, and millions of banking dollars. One of Kaszak's ads showed her driving her own Dodge Intrepid through a modest neighborhood, juxtaposed with Emanuel sitting in the back of a limo talking on a cellphone.[15] Early polls showed Kaszak ahead, with double-digit leads over Emanuel among women, independents, and blue-collar workers.[16]

Emanuel's campaign focused on rebranding him as a Chicago guy, kind of like the Daleys—who, for all their wealth and power, still oozed the South Side, rough-spoken Bridgeport neighborhood from which they hailed. The campaign played up the ties Emanuel did have to working-class Chicago: His life until fourth grade in an apartment in the Uptown neighborhood. Sunday evenings at his grandparents' Chicago home, in an unspecified location near a big park. His maternal grandfather, Herman Smulevitz, who came to Chicago as a child fleeing religious persecution. His Uncle Les, a twenty-three-year veteran of the Chicago Police Department. The *Chicago Reader* noted that a slick, lengthy campaign mailer mentioned Emanuel's investment banking not at all but devoted a full page to Uncle Les.[17]

Even a decade before "Wall Street versus Main Street" and "the 99 percent" became popular memes, Emanuel knew that voters might be turned off by the knowledge of his quick millions. So in November 2001, his staff conducted a focus group of male voters, paying them $75 each to describe how they felt upon hearing that Emanuel had become rich by "setting up deals."

Emanuel's wealth dwarfed that of Kaszak, who released tax returns showing she had earned $203,000 in the previous two years and had assets between $64,000 and $260,000.[18] Emanuel ultimately spent $450,000 of his own money on the campaign, along with generous contributions from his corporate and political backers. Kaszak got substantial support from the organization EMILY's List, which backs prochoice women candidates.[19] But she was still outspent by Emanuel: he would raise almost $2 million during the primary campaign, compared to Kaszak's $888,000.[20] The funding gap was especially damaging when it came to expensive television ads: Emanuel started airing them in mid-February, but Kaszak couldn't afford air time until the final week before the March 19 primary.[21]

As if his money and Machine backing weren't formidable enough, Emanuel also turned out to be a surprisingly effective campaigner in his first run for elected office. He had long been known as obnoxious, abrasive, and impatient—hardly qualities that lend themselves to kissing babies and empathizing with senior citizens. But reporters and pundits remarked upon his friendly, charming demeanor and his ability to connect with voters as he put in long hours at L train stations, senior centers, grocery stores, and other public places.[22] Perhaps Emanuel had picked up some tips from his former boss Bill Clinton, famed for the ease and enjoyment with which he moved among regular people.

Emanuel secured the endorsement of the Chicago Teachers Union, which would become his nemesis a decade later. The Illinois AFL-CIO also endorsed him after some nail-biting among Emanuel's people over whom the labor federation would choose. Emanuel found out he'd secured the AFL-CIO endorsement during a breakfast interview with *Reader* reporter Ben Joravsky, and the newly warm-and-fuzzy candidate was so happy he jumped up, hugged, and gave a noogie to "my new best friend," as Joravsky told it.[23]

Kaszak had a 94 percent approval rating from the AFL-CIO, but apparently Emanuel's clout and Washington connections trumped her more grassroots and state-level credentials. *The Nation* quoted Illinois AFL-CIO political director Bill Looby saying, "She had the good labor record, but he had the record of knowing his way around Washington. The feeling was, he could be more effective in Washington."[24]

Emanuel's role in NAFTA apparently didn't sway the AFL-CIO to support Kaszak. But EMILY's List spent $400,000 on Kaszak's behalf, funding ads that hammered Emanuel's central role in NAFTA and noted that the trade agreement had cost Illinois eleven thousand jobs.[25] (Emanuel media adviser David Axelrod, who would later serve as a top campaign adviser and then senior adviser to President Barack Obama, decried the ads as unfair attacks.)[26] Kaszak's campaign also spotlighted Emanuel's involvement with welfare reform and the controversial merger that created the energy company Exelon.[27]

Meanwhile, Emanuel lambasted Kaszak for being soft on crime, invoking several state legislative votes wherein she appeared to oppose stiffer sentences for criminals. Kaszak's campaign manager was Chris Mather, who would become Emanuel's communications chief during his run for mayor. Responding to Emanuel's line of attacks, Mather told the *Chicago Tribune*, "Anyone can take a vote or two out of context, out of thousands of votes taken, and try to distort someone's record.... Rahm is an opposition researcher at heart and this is the type of negative thing you're going to get from that type of individual."[28]

One endorsement Emanuel failed to get might have stung: his old employer the Illinois Public Action Council decided to endorse Kaszak. At the time Emanuel worked there, researcher and strategist Don Wiener worked for Citizen Action, the national group with which the council was affiliated. By 2002 Wiener was an Illinois Public Action Council board member. Wiener had been a leader of the grassroots national labor and community coalition opposing NAFTA when Emanuel shepherded it through during Clinton's presidency. He had promised to help secure the council's endorsement for Kaszak before Emanuel entered the race. Outside the Illinois Public Action Council board meeting where Emanuel made his pitch for endorsement, Wiener remembered him saying breezily, "Wiener, you're wearing the same clothes you were wearing last time I saw you"—which may have been more or less accurate, because Wiener was wearing his trademark jeans and leather jacket. Emanuel's words could be seen as a friendly signifier of familiarity, but Wiener took it as an intentional and clever jab that "you've stayed in the same place—you're still a community organizer—and look where I've gone." "He's a genius in insulting people," Wiener said.[29]

A SLUGFEST AND A SLUR

In early February 2002, Bill Clinton came to Chicago to campaign for Emanuel. Clinton headlined a $100-a-ticket fundraiser at the Park West auditorium and a $1,000-per-person reception at a private lakefront home. At that point Emanuel had almost $1 million in his war chest, while Kaszak had less than $65,000.[30] But Kaszak remained at least outwardly confident, saying, "The people of the Fifth Congressional District cannot be bought."[31]

Kaszak was still hanging on to her lead in mid-February; one poll showed her ahead of Emanuel 33 percent to 18 percent.[32] By early March, though, her lead had evaporated, and the two candidates were neck and neck. One poll found one in four voters still hadn't made up their minds, and Emanuel led Kaszak by a statistically insignificant margin of 35 to 33 percent.[33] A *Chicago Sun-Times* editorial called the race "a slugfest in the grand Chicago tradition, between grass-roots activist Kaszak and Washington insider Emanuel."[34]

So Kaszak could hardly afford the gaffe that occurred just two weeks before the election. Casimir Pulaski Day should have been a good one for Kaszak. It is an annual holiday commemorating the Polish-born Revolutionary War hero, usually celebrated with fairs and official events in Chicago's Polish neighborhoods. Ed Moskal, president of the Polish American Congress community group, ardently wanted Kaszak to win the seat. So Moskal presumably thought he was helping when he declared at a Pulaski Day event that Emanuel was an Israeli citizen who had served two years in the Israeli army. He took things even farther, decrying Polish American Emanuel supporters by saying, "Sadly, there are those among us who will accept thirty pieces of silver to betray Polonia."[35]

Both statements about Emanuel were false, and Moskal's address was viewed as virulently anti-Semitic, eliciting condemnations from Jewish groups.[36] Kaszak was in the crowd but didn't immediately comment; she later said she had been distracted and didn't hear much. Once she heard the full remarks, she denounced the speech and demanded Moskal apologize. He refused.[37]

Emanuel called Moskal's statements "deplorable," and he accused Moskal of orchestrating an anti-Semitic "whispering campaign" with Kaszak's knowledge and tacit support.[38] A spokesman for the Polish National Alliance made things worse by trying to justify Moskal's comments, saying they were just "born of frustration with Jews."[39]

The day after the festival the Emanuel campaign hosted a press conference of religious leaders to denounce Moskal's statements. A desperate Kaszak showed up pleading to make her case. Emanuel campaign staff reportedly tried to prevent her from speaking, even calling an abrupt premature end to the press conference. Eventually Kaszak was able to address the assembled reporters, and she again decried Moskal's remarks and said she and Emanuel were united in the cause of fighting anti-Semitism.[40]

Chicago Sun-Times political expert Lynn Sweet called Kaszak's crashing the press conference "a high-stakes strategy that would take nerves of steel to execute." Not only did it create an awkward moment; it risked alienating members of Kaszak's Polish American base.[41]

The Emanuel camp's original plan for the day had been to announce his endorsement by SEIU Local 1, the large and powerful union representing janitors, security guards, and other workers hired by private companies at city buildings. The planned endorsement statement by union president Tom Balanoff, a legendary Chicago labor leader, got drowned out by the excitement around the anti-Semitic remarks. A decade later Balanoff would become one of Emanuel's prime adversaries, spearheading a campaign to brand him a "job killer."

Kaszak ultimately lost by a wide margin, with the anti-Semitic remarks possibly playing a significant role, compounded by the impact of Emanuel's copious campaign funds and hardball tactics. Emanuel took 50 percent of the vote in the field of six, compared to Kaszak's 39 percent.[42] Emanuel's strongest showings came in two wards where his father had long practiced as a well-liked pediatrician—some voters had surely been treated by him in their childhood. Kaszak won in the most heavily Polish areas, but Emanuel beat her among Catholics as a whole and among Italian Americans and Irish Americans.[43] In other words, a Jewish candidate framed as an elitist outsider nonetheless won over the heart of ethnic middle-class Chicago.

The Fifth District is heavily Democratic, so after the primary the general election's outcome was nearly a foregone conclusion.[44] Emanuel got 69.3 percent of the final vote, compared to 26.3 percent for Republican candidate Mark Augusti, a bank executive and tax reform activist.[45]

CLOUT COUNTED

A few years later, details emerged about some of the "volunteers" who had helped Emanuel defeat Kaszak. In 2005 federal prosecutors indicted more than thirty city employees on fraud and corruption charges in a scandal dubbed "Hired Truck." Federal prosecutors alleged that city officials had taken bribes to steer city business to private trucking firms, which often did very little work, and that city officials had violated a longstanding court order known as the Shakman Decree, which barred patronage hiring—essentially the doling out of jobs for political reasons.[46]

Emanuel's name came up numerous times in the proceedings: many city workers allegedly spent time campaigning for him, in anticipation of raises, promotions, or other rewards, or simply to keep their jobs. *Chicago Tribune* columnist John Kass referred to an "illegal patronage army of hundreds of workers" pounding the pavement for Emanuel, many of them led by water department top deputy Donald Tomczak, who pleaded guilty to bribery charges in the investigation.[47] Kass coined a new nickname for Emanuel: "U.S. Representative Rahm Emanuel (D-Tomczak)."[48]

The *Tribune* quoted a retired Streets and Sanitation worker saying, "Daley made [Emanuel] a personal project. . . . Up until that time, I had never heard of Rahm Emanuel, but the Daley forces at City Hall said, 'We are going to support him,' so we did."[49]

Daniel Katalinic, the deputy Streets and Sanitation commissioner, told prosecutors that he organized a "white ethnic" patronage army of hundreds to work on campaigns for Emanuel and other candidates backed by Daley; and that he had met with patronage director Robert Sorich at Emanuel's campaign headquarters to set up work squads.[50] Names of workers who had volunteered for Emanuel's 2006 congressional reelection campaign also came up on a secret "clout list" of city employees earmarked for promotions and raises.[51]

Emanuel said that he had never met Katalinic and had no idea anything illegal was going on amid the thousands of people who had volunteered for his campaign.[52] Prosecutors never said Emanuel himself had done anything wrong. But the investigation highlighted that although his image was more Washington than Bridgeport, more pinstripes than patronage, Emanuel was still firmly entrenched in the Chicago Democratic Machine.

A DLC DEMOCRAT

The congressional seat was Emanuel's first elected position, even after more than a decade as a top politico. He was a consummate example of the "new Democrat," or "DLC Democrat." The acronym refers to the Democratic Leadership Council, a nonprofit organization founded in 1985 to move the Democratic Party away from its populist, left-leaning stances of the 1960s and '70s. The most prominent DLC chairman was Bill Clinton himself, who took the helm in 1990. And President Clinton's anti-crime, welfare reform and free trade initiatives—undertaken with Emanuel's help—epitomized the DLC political philosophy.[53]

In a January 1, 2001, document, the DLC described its "New Democrat Credo":

In keeping with our party's grand tradition, we reaffirm Jefferson's belief in individual liberty and capacity for self-government. We endorse Jackson's credo of equal opportunity for all, special privileges for none. We embrace Roosevelt's thirst for innovation and Kennedy's summons to civic duty. And we intend to carry on Clinton's insistence upon new means to achieve progressive ideals. We believe that the promise of America is equal opportunity for all and special privilege for none. We believe that economic growth generated in the private sector is the prerequisite for opportunity, and that government's role is to promote growth and to equip Americans with the tools they need to prosper in the New Economy.[54]

Reading between the lines, the DLC philosophy supported scaling back the role of government while emphasizing the principles of personal responsibility, liberty, and self-help. It proposed the private sector as key to helping people break their dependence on the government and pull themselves out of need and poverty. And it strongly advocated for charter schools and free trade agreements.[55] The DLC dissolved in 2011 after a failed attempt to recast itself as more of a think tank.[56] It had been struggling with identity and influence issues going back at least to the mid-2000s, when more liberal influences, including the "net-roots" movement Moveon.org, battled for power with the party's free-market moderates.[57]

But even after the council's demise, DLC philosophies would live on. Emanuel would be joined by other politicians with close links to the DLC in the Obama administration: Secretary of State Hillary Clinton, White House economic adviser Lawrence Summers, Agriculture Secretary Tom Vilsack, Interior Secretary Ken Salazar, and Homeland Security Secretary Janet Napolitano, among others.[58]

Emanuel would also carry the DLC philosophical torch into Chicago City Hall.

LAKES, VETS, AND VICTIMS

Even as a quintessential DLC Democrat, Emanuel sponsored many bills in Congress that were attractive by progressive or liberal standards. The Billionaire's Loophole Elimination Act made it harder for wealthy people in bankruptcy proceedings to hide their assets. Another bill funded electronic monitoring of adult sex offenders. The Great Lakes Restoration Act, hailed by environmental groups, provided a comprehensive framework for reducing pollution, combating invasive species, restoring degraded areas, and increasing community access to the lakes. One bill facilitated health insurance coverage for kids; another reined in unscrupulous life insurance agents targeting members of the military. The Welcome Home G.I. bill extended educational benefits for military members. Another bill allowed victims of Hurricane Katrina to get Earned Income Tax Credit payments earlier than usual. And yet another bill increased the tax credit for alternative fuel vehicles assembled in the United States.[59]

The nonpartisan project Govtrack.us, which tracks legislative data and trends online, described Emanuel as a "rank-and-file Democrat" based on his voting record. The website ranks legislators on leadership and ideology, in high-to-low and liberal-to-conservative continuums, respectively. Emanuel came in almost dead center among Democrats on ideology, and he ranked in the upper quarter on leadership compared to legislators of both parties. The leadership mark is based on rates of mutual bill cosponsorship—"It's a little like if you scratch my back will I scratch yours?" explains the group's website.[60] In other words, Emanuel was willing to play ball to get what he wanted.

The website OnTheIssues.org compiles highlights of legislators' voting records and scorecards from various organizations. Emanuel gained perfect or near-perfect marks for his records on reproductive rights, gay rights, and environmental issues. He got an 87 percent approval rating from the AFL-CIO and 100 percent from the National Education Association union, albeit both from December 2003, after less than a year in office. Overall his voting record indicated support for clean energy; a relatively tough approach to the oil and gas industry; a mixed bag on civil liberties, war, and national security issues; and strong support for free trade, though he did vote against the controversial Central America Free Trade Agreement (CAFTA), a sort of stepsister to NAFTA.[61]

Emanuel got extremely negative marks from anti-immigration groups for his congressional voting record; they saw him as staunchly pro-immigrant. He cosponsored immigration reform without amnesty for undocumented residents, an approach often opposed by both pro-immigrant and anti-immigrant forces. He voted against constructing a wall on the Mexican border and against forcing hospitals to collect information on undocumented immigrants.[62] Like most Democrats, he also voted no on the most notorious piece of federal immigration-related legislation in recent history: the Border Protection, Anti-terrorism, and Illegal Immigration Control Act (HR 4437), introduced in December 2005 by Wisconsin Republican congressman James Sensenbrenner.[63]

The draconian anti-immigrant bill would have criminalized a broad range of everyday interactions with undocumented immigrants. It would theoretically have made teachers, counselors, doctors, landlords, and other everyday people into criminals just for giving undocumented immigrants a ride, renting them a room, or providing them health or social services.[64] The House passed the bill 239 to 182 on December 16, 2005. In response, immigrants and their supporters marched by the tens of thousands in cities nationwide. The movement started right in Emanuel's hometown of Chicago, with the first march of more than one hundred thousand taking the nation by surprise on March 10, 2006.[65]

Democratic leaders, including Chicago congressman Luis Gutierrez and Mayor Daley, denounced the Sensenbrenner bill and joined immigrants' rights demonstrations. Many of Emanuel's Polish, Latino, and other immigrant constituents were among the marchers.

But in a 2010 speech during the Chicago mayoral campaign, Gutierrez said Emanuel put politics before immigrants' rights during the seminal fight. "Here's a fact Rahm doesn't want you to know but one he can't escape from," said Gutierrez, who was backing Emanuel's opponent Gery Chico in the mayoral race. "When the Sensenbrenner bill was on the floor of the House of Representatives, as chairman of the Democratic Congressional Campaign Committee, Rahm Emanuel told his colleagues to support Sensenbrenner. He told targeted Democrats in tough re-election fights that he wanted them to vote for this anti-immigrant bill. That's a fact, an irrefutable fact. . . . When he had a chance to step up as a leading member of Congress and do the right thing instead of the political thing, he refused to do it."[66]

Emanuel's votes often upset progressive, African American, and Latino elected

officials and constituents. He voted 128 times against bills or amendments supported by a majority of the ethnic minority members of the Congressional delega-
tion from Chicago, according to a report circulated by former Illinois senator Carol
Moseley Braun, who competed against Emanuel during the Chicago mayoral
race.[67] Many of those bills were backed by the Congressional Black Caucus and
Chicago congressmen Danny K. Davis, Bobby Rush, and Jesse Jackson Jr.[68] A
number of the bills involved free trade agreements, including those with Singapore,
Peru, Chile, and Morocco; Emanuel voted in favor of free trade, while African
American congressmen and unions opposed the agreements because of concerns
about their impact on US jobs.[69] Many of the contentious votes had to do with defense: Rush, Jackson, and Davis tended to take antiwar stances; but Emanuel supported defense spending, military options regarding Iran, and a resolution
affirming that the world was safer without deposed Iraqi leader Saddam Hussein.[70]
Emanuel also voted to make provisions of the USA PATRIOT Act permanent—
to the outrage of civil liberties groups, which denounced the act for allowing un-
warranted spying in the name of the war on terror.[71]

It was not clear what Emanuel's own thoughts were about the war in Iraq. He
took office after the initial vote to authorize the invasion, but during his congressional campaign he indicated he would have voted in favor of military intervention.[72] As a congressman he was relatively cagey about the increasingly unpopular
conflict, a stance that came through during his January 2005 appearance on NBC's
Meet the Press. Emanuel didn't definitively answer host Tim Russert's questions
about whether he would have voted to invade Iraq knowing there were no weapons
of mass destruction. He said, "I still believe that getting rid of Saddam Hussein was
the right thing to do, OK?"[73]

RECLAIMING THE HOUSE

In 2004, after the death of former chair Bob Matsui, Emanuel became chair of the
Democratic Congressional Campaign Committee.[74] Founded in the mid-1800s,
the DCCC is the official campaign arm of Democrats in the House of Representatives, a well-funded organization with a large research staff expert in Emanuel's
early forte, opposition research.[75]

Republicans had controlled the House since the "Republican Revolution" of
1994, featuring Georgia Congressman Newt Gingrich's "Contract with America."[76] Emanuel's major goal as head of the DCCC was to reclaim the House for
Democrats in the 2006 midterm elections. It was a major challenge: in January
2006, the House had 231 Republican members and just 201 Democrats (plus one
Democratic-leaning independent), and Republican George W. Bush was in the
White House.[77]

Emanuel pulled it off.

Several books and documentaries describe a strategically brilliant operation showcasing Emanuel's cutthroat style and stellar fundraising ability. *Chicago Tribune* reporter Naftali Bendavid's book *The Thumpin'* described Emanuel masterfully juggling the campaigns of candidates nationwide, down to the smallest minutiae. Candidates rose and fell in his favor based on their shifting political prospects.

That year Emanuel also released his book *The Plan: Big Ideas for America*, written with fellow Clinton aide and DLC president Bruce Reed.[78] *The Plan* outlined their political philosophy and their vision for "a new social contract." The authors indicated that politics should be driven by ideals rather than cynical pragmatism, denouncing Democrats who "bought into [Republican strategist] Karl Rove's logic that the most important challenge of our time is how to win an election." They decried a party driven by focus groups, consultants, and "second opinions," swaying without an ideological rudder.[79]

Ironically, the approach condemned in *The Plan* is very similar to what fans and critics alike describe as Emanuel's own approach to politics. A prime example would be the 2006 campaigns, where Emanuel pushed candidates to win at all costs. "He had no interest in a Democratic Party that was purer than the opposition if it lost," Bendavid wrote. "He did not care where a candidate stood on abortion or the Iraq war, or whether that candidate was displacing a 'better' Democrat, if such purity cost a House seat."[80]

Money had always been central to Emanuel's political strategy, and as the 2006 midterms geared up, he was only interested in candidates who could raise buckets of it. In their book *Winner-Take-All Politics*, political scientists Jacob S. Hacker and Paul Pierson noted:

> Emanuel spent more of his time courting cash than doing anything else. No matter how attractive a candidate or appealing his message, it meant little if he could not advertise on television, print brochures, or pay campaign workers to knock on doors.... In the 2006 campaign, Emanuel and his staff were judging candidates almost exclusively by how much money they raised. If a candidate proved a good fund-raiser, the DCCC would provide support, advertising, strategic advice, and whatever other help was needed. If not, the committee would shut him out.... Most of Emanuel's fundraising time was spent meeting with wealthy lawyers or financiers, telling them this was the year to give.[81]

One of the hot seats up for grabs in the 2006 race was Illinois's Sixth District. The district, which enfolds Chicago's western suburbs, was 78 percent white; relatively well off, with a $65,000 median household income; and politically moderate.[82] In both 2000 and 2004, 53 percent of voters had chosen George W. Bush for president.[83]

Since 1975 the Sixth District had been represented by Henry Hyde, a right-wing Republican who took a lead role in the effort to impeach President Clinton over the

DURING THE 2006 MIDTERM ELECTIONS, CONGRESSMAN EMANUEL BACKED CANDIDATES WITH MILITARY BACKGROUNDS—INCLUDING VETERAN MAJOR TAMMY DUCKWORTH (ABOVE), WHOM HE SUPPORTED OVER A POPULAR UNION-BACKED COMMUNITY ACTIVIST. PHOTO BY STAFF SERGEANT JON SOUCY, US ARMY.

Monica Lewinsky affair.[84] In the 2004 election, a likable software worker and community activist named Christine Cegelis made a decent showing against Hyde, getting 44 percent of the vote.[85] The eighty-one-year-old Hyde planned to retire after his term ended, so the 2006 race seemed ripe for Cegelis, a political outsider who could relate to the struggles of everyday people. She had campaigned for liberals Hubert Humphrey and George McGovern in her youth and got back into politics decades later as she saw her family and neighbors losing jobs and struggling to afford medicine. She opposed CAFTA and called for a rational timetable for withdrawal from Iraq. She had enthusiastic backing from high-profile left-leaning Democratic groups, bloggers, and leaders, including Democratic National Committee chair Howard Dean and the Independent Voters of Illinois-Independent Precinct Organization (IVI-IPO). She also had significant support among local residents.[86]

But rather than backing Cegelis, Emanuel recruited Tammy Duckworth, who didn't actually live in the Sixth District. Duckworth was a veteran who had lost both her legs and had her right arm shattered in Iraq in 2004, when her helicopter was shot down by a rocket-propelled grenade north of Baghdad. She was an impressive and sympathetic figure, determined not to be held back by her devastating injury. She came across as articulate, cheerful, and accessible. "Duckworth—be-spectacled, wearing an American flag on her lapel, her dark hair streaked with blond—was one of Emanuel's dream candidates," wrote Bendavid.[87]

Duckworth said the war was a mistake, but she stressed support for her military brethren and the idea that the United States must stay the course in Iraq. Cegelis and her supporters were at first shocked and then disillusioned when they learned that the Democratic Party was abandoning them for Duckworth.[88]

With Emanuel's backing, Duckworth earned the support of elected officials in-cluding Senators Dick Durbin and John Kerry and Congressman Mike Honda of California, who, like Duckworth, was Asian American. Barack Obama, then the junior senator from Illinois, also campaigned for Duckworth. The Illinois AFL-CIO endorsed her, though only Cegelis had been a union member—as a telephone operator with the Communications Workers of America.[89]

"It was an offensive outrage for Clinton, Kerry, Obama and other Senate Demo-crat insiders to foist Duckworth on the Sixth District, when they had a tough, strong campaigner in Cegelis," opined Philadelphia-based *Daily Kos* pundit Rob Kall.[90]

Despite all the big-time money and endorsements, Duckworth beat Cegelis in the Democratic primary by only 4 percent. Bitter, Cegelis didn't publicly con-cede until Duckworth called her, and she didn't endorse Duckworth for two weeks. Emanuel gloated that "we took on the Communists in the party," though in reality Cegelis's supporters were mostly regular residents who saw Cegelis as one of their own.[91]

In the general election Duckworth lost by two percentage points, or 4,810 votes, to Republican Peter Roskam.[92] The loss came despite the fact that Duckworth's campaign had raised $4.56 million, compared to Roskam's $3.44 million. (Cegelis, by contrast, had raised only $363,000 for the primary race.)[93]

Throughout the 2006 campaigns Emanuel had high-profile clashes with DNC chair Howard Dean, a former Vermont governor and doctor whose run for the presi-dency in 2004 had been propelled largely by his strong antiwar stance and pioneering online strategy. Dean criticized Emanuel for failing to back liberal and popular candi-dates like Cegelis. Meanwhile, Emanuel excoriated Dean for failing to put up more money for the races, especially because Republicans were greatly outspending Democ-rats overall. Emanuel demanded that Dean lay out $100,000 for each of forty key races in 2006, while Dean was more focused on a long-term strategy of building a Demo-cratic base in all fifty states. Details of the leaders' conflict were leaked to the press, and Dean supporters surmised that Emanuel was conniving to make sure Dean took the blame if Democrats did not reclaim the House.[94]

A few of the DCCC's favored candidates were defeated in the Democratic pri-maries by opponents with genuine grassroots support and clear antiwar positions, who went on to defeat Republicans in the general election. In New Hampshire, Carol

Shea-Porter, a social worker and community college teacher, won the primary by almost twenty percentage points, even though the DCCC had funded the campaign of moderate State House minority leader Jim Craig.[95] In the general election, Shea-Porter beat Republican incumbent Jeb Bradley by almost 3 percent.[96] Similarly, in New York's Hudson Valley, the DCCC eschewed John Hall—an environmental activist and former lead singer of the 1970s band Orleans—in favor of attorney Judy Aydelott, a former Republican and skilled fundraiser.[97] Hall got almost double Aydelott's votes in the primary and then won the general election to take the seat.[98]

Ultimately Democrats won the House in a near-landslide, ending up with 233 seats to Republicans' 202. They also retook the Senate, 51 to 49. California congresswoman Nancy Pelosi became the first female Speaker of the House.[99] Emanuel celebrated in typical fashion, jumping on a table and telling the crowd that Republicans "can go fuck themselves!"[100]

THE BAILOUT

Like most congressmen, Emanuel didn't face serious challenges to reelection once he was an incumbent, but donors still contributed generously to his campaign fund. He raised just shy of $9 million during his three-term congressional tenure. The political transparency organization Opensecrets.org listed the companies with which major donations were affiliated. (Donations didn't come from the companies themselves but rather from political action committees, employees, owners, their immediate family members, and others connected to the companies).[101] Madison Dearborn Partners, a Chicago-based private equity firm specializing in buyouts, topped the list. Next was the phone company AT&T, followed by the Swiss-headquartered global financial services company UBS AG, and then the New York–based global investment firm Goldman Sachs. Fifth on the list of donors was Emanuel's old employer Dresdner, Kleinwort & Wasserstein (the investment bank had changed its name from Wasserstein Perella and Company following a 2001 buyout by the German Dresdner Bank).[102]

Over the course of Emanuel's congressional career, the top five industries from which he received money were securities and investment ($1.7 million), lawyers ($756,768), the entertainment industry ($481,864), real estate ($370,460), and commercial banks ($265,500). Pro-Israel groups donated $169,700, and public sector unions—which would become his nemesis as mayor—donated $176,500. Other unions donated $109,500. Emanuel was consistently the first or second top recipient of donations from hedge funds and private equity firms for the entire House of Representatives.[103] He held seats on both the Ways and Means and Financial Services committees, positions of much interest to the financial sector.[104]

The year that turned out to be Emanuel's last in Congress featured legislation that showcased his deep ties to the financial sector. He played a key role in orchestrating and building political support for the controversial $700 billion bailout of banks and financial institutions including Goldman Sachs, Bank of America, and JPMorgan Chase, meant to prevent a total economic collapse and free up credit to stimulate spending and rescue home mortgages in the seizing-up economy.[105]

On October 3, 2008, the Emergency Economic Stabilization Act passed the House of Representatives 263 to 171, with Emanuel among the 172 Democrats voting for it.[106] Four days earlier, the bailout bill had failed in the House; as the Democratic Caucus chair (and fourth-ranking congressman), Emanuel played an important role in getting fifty-eight congressmen, including thirty-three Democrats, to change their votes. [107]

In the months and even years following the bank bailout, the public was largely furious with the maneuver and how it was carried out. Executives at many of the bailed-out institutions continued to give themselves multimillion-dollar bonuses and raises, and meanwhile the bailout did not result in notably increased lending or mortgage relief for regular people.[108] The anger over the bailout helped spark a major shift in public consciousness, a sudden spike in the awareness of class, and the concepts of "Main Street versus Wall Street" and "the 99 percent." It also motivated the rise of the virulently antigovernment Tea Party movement.[109]

"In no uncertain terms, our leaders told us anything short of saving these insolvent banks would result in a depression to the American public," said Josh Brown, a Manhattan investment adviser turned industry critic, on public radio's *Marketplace Money* in 2011. "We had to do it! At our darkest hour, we gave these banks every single thing they asked for. . . . We bailed out Wall Street to avoid Depression, but three years later, millions of Americans are in a living hell. This is why they're enraged, this is why they're assembling, this is why they hate you. Why for the first time in fifty years, the people are coming out in the streets and they're saying, 'Enough.'"[110]

Though Emanuel was about to leave Congress, this new paradigm would be a defining factor of his tenure in the Obama White House and even more directly in Chicago's City Hall.

RAHM EMANUEL WITH PRESIDENT OBAMA IN THE OVAL OFFICE, WHICH HE WOULD LEAVE TO RUN FOR CHICAGO MAYOR. PHOTO BY PETE SOUZA, WHITE HOUSE.

5
THE OBAMA WHITE HOUSE

Chicago erupted in all-out celebration on November 4, 2008. As the results of the presidential election came in and Obama made his stirring acceptance speech in Grant Park, the downtown streets were packed with people wearing campaign T-shirts, smiling broadly, and giving high fives to complete strangers.

In a city famous for segregation and racial tension, there was a notable coming together of people from different races. For several days after the election, the feeling lingered that a cloud of positivity and camaraderie had settled over Chicago, that past wrongs and slights had been forgotten as the city prepared to move forward under its new mantle as the hometown of the most popular man in the world.

Two days after the election Obama made his first announcement about his cabinet: his chief of staff would be "my good friend, Congressman Rahm Emanuel."[1] It was well known in Chicago circles that Emanuel and Obama had never been close.[2] But the president-elect likely thought Emanuel's skills and personality could be just what he needed for the challenges that lay ahead.

"No one I know is better at getting things done than Rahm Emanuel," said Obama. "In just six years in Congress, he has risen to leadership, helping to craft myriad important pieces of legislation and guide them to passage. In between, Rahm spent several years in the private sector, where he worked on large and complicated financial transactions. That experience, combined with his service on the committees on Ways and Means and Banking, have given Rahm deep insights into the challenging economic issues that will be front and center for our administration."[3]

Emanuel said that he was "humbled by the responsibility" Obama had given him and quoted Abraham Lincoln: "The dogmas of the quiet past are inadequate to the stormy present. The occasion is piled high with difficulty, and we must rise with the occasion. As our case is new, so we must think anew, and act anew."[4]

But many people who had been elated by Obama's election were skeptical of and disappointed in his choice of a right-hand man. "The selection rankled many in the greater Obama orbit," wrote Peter Baker in the *New York Times Magazine*. "For all the work they put in electing an apostle of hope to clean up Washington, now they were handing over the keys to a crass, cynical operator? Even if it was a sensible decision, what message did it send?"[5]

On the world stage, Israeli and Palestinian leaders speculated about what the choice meant for the Middle East. Emanuel kept a low profile on this front, but his father created a headache for his son with his own speculation about what Rahm's role in the White House would mean for Israel.

"Obviously he'll influence the president to be pro-Israel. Why wouldn't he? What is he, an Arab? He's not going to be mopping floors at the White House," Benjamin Emanuel told the Israeli daily *Ma'ariv*. Emanuel apologized for his father's remarks and offered to meet with Arab American leaders in the future.[6]

Emanuel had been offered the chief of staff job several weeks earlier and had reportedly "agonized" over whether to take it. He enjoyed his role in Congress and aspired to be the first Jewish Speaker of the House, and with kids ages nine, ten, and eleven, he was reluctant to move his family again from Chicago to Washington.[7]

In his book *Obama's Wars,* veteran reporter Bob Woodward described Emanuel's internal dilemma: "Emanuel, who was known for his bluster, confided to associates that the driving force in his life was fear of failure. It was as if he knew his entire career was a dangerous high-wire act and he was being forced to take the wire to new heights, requiring that he move faster and not look down. Despite his misgivings, he finally said yes."[8]

Obama's decision for chief of staff had reportedly come down to Emanuel versus Obama's good friend Tom Daschle.[9] The former Senate majority leader from South Dakota was later nominated for secretary of health and human services—until questions over his failure to pay taxes and his lobbying-related work forced him to withdraw.[10] Obama had known Emanuel for years, and Emanuel's famous pugnacious style was an interesting contrast to Obama's measured, calm, even remote demeanor. Emanuel's profane, sarcastic outbursts and tight smirk were quite different from Obama's beneficent smile and lofty proclamations about hope and dreams.

At a 2005 fundraiser in Chicago, Obama had riffed on Emanuel's dancing background, saying he had adapted Machiavelli's *The Prince* as a dance "with a lot of kicks below the waist."[11]

It's entirely likely that Obama sought out this approach as a complement to his own style; he probably sensed what a hard road lay ahead and figured someone like "Rahmbo" was just what he needed to muscle through sweeping changes.

But as it turned out, Emanuel may have been a big reason Obama did not successfully pass or forcefully advocate for key things he had promised or proposed during the campaign: namely, a climate bill that put a price on carbon emissions, comprehensive immigration reform, and sweeping health-care reform with a "public option."

"The paradox of the current situation for Obama and Emanuel has not been lost on Washington," wrote Peter Baker in March 2010. "A visionary outsider who is relatively inexperienced and perhaps even a tad naïve about the ways of Washington captures the White House and, eager to get things done, hires the ultimate get-it-done insider to run his operation. . . . But if picking the leading practitioner of the dark arts of the capital was a Faustian bargain for Obama in the name of getting things done, why haven't things got done?"[12]

THE STIMULUS AND THE BAILOUTS

President Obama and his chief of staff did get off to a quick start. Within his first month in office, Obama signed three major bills. The Lilly Ledbetter Fair Pay Act addressed pay discrimination against women.[13] A week later Obama signed a significant expansion of the State Children's Health Insurance Program.[14] And on February 17 he signed the $787 billion American Recovery and Reinvestment Act (ARRA), a landmark stimulus bill meant to create jobs by funding infrastructure projects, energy efficiency, broadband expansion, and numerous other undertakings, especially "shovel-ready" tasks.[15]

Many progressives criticized the stimulus for being too small and including too many tax cuts, while conservatives attacked it as wasteful and unsuccessful. For years to come, pundits would debate how much good the stimulus did and how it could have been better.[16] The Congressional Budget Office estimated the stimulus created or saved between half a million and 3.3 million jobs. There had been heated debate among Obama's economic team over how big to make the stimulus. Emanuel consistently took the more conservative side of this debate, and won. When Christina Romer, chair of the president's Council of Economic Advisers, argued for a larger package—to the tune of $1 trillion—Emanuel reportedly said, "What are you smoking?"[17]

Emanuel also was at Obama's side for the bailout of the auto industry, a move credited with saving it from collapse and preventing the mass outsourcing of jobs.[18] During the negotiations, according to a book by former administration "car czar" Steve Rattner, Emanuel responded flippantly regarding concerns of the United Automobile Workers, the labor union representing the tens of thousands of workers who risked losing their jobs: "Fuck the UAW."[19] Interviewed after the book came out, UAW president Bob King said he was not offended. "I appreciate the Obama administration," he told CNBC. "I appreciate what they have done for workers in general. Did they do good for the auto industry? Yes, they did. Did Rahm Emanuel play a role in that? Yes, he did. I appreciate him."[20]

And of course Emanuel was one of the main voices—along with economic adviser Larry Summers and Treasury Secretary Timothy Geithner—counseling the president on how to deal with the financial institutions that were on the verge of collapse. He had played a lead role during his last months in Congress in passing the un-popular bank bailout. Early in Obama's presidency, Romer was enthusiastic about the idea of taking bold action to break up some of the banks whose reckless behavior had played a major role in causing the economic crisis. Romer was an expert in the Great Depression and the New Deal, and as Ron Suskind explained in *Confidence Men*, she saw an opportunity for Obama to make a bold "Rooseveltian" move that would tele-graph his willingness to stand up to these financial titans. Cracking down on the banks would, she indicated, show that Obama had cast his lot with the common peo-ple. Summers also supported the idea that the big banks should be broken up by the government, and Suskind reported that Obama liked the idea. But Emanuel was stri-dently opposed, saying it would be politically impossible to get such a move through Congress, especially since it could cost about $700 billion on top of the bailout funds already doled out. Suskind described a long and contentious meeting from which Obama ultimately left to have dinner with his family and told the debating staff to come to a decision. Emanuel took the opportunity, as Suskind described it, to get his way and keep the big banks intact—nixing the idea of breaking them up.

"Everyone shut the fuck up," Suskind quoted Emanuel as saying. "Listen, it's not going to fuckin' happen. We have no fucking credibility. So give it up. The job of everyone in this room is to move the president, when he gets back, to a solution that *works*."

Suskind quoted Romer saying that Rahm "killed" and "crushed" the idea of breaking up the big banks. When Obama returned, the group agreed to a much more modest plan of focusing first on Citigroup and conducting "stress tests" on other banks, essentially leaving the status quo intact. "The president," Suskind con-cluded, "had been well managed."[21]

CLIMATE CHANGE

Although Emanuel helped beat down conservative opposition to pass the job-creating stimulus bill, he seemed to cave to industry and right-wing think tank cries about "job-killing" in relation to a climate bill that would have put a price on carbon emis-sions through a cap-and-trade system or carbon tax.

Environmental leaders including Al Gore said it was important to pass a cli-mate-related resolution before the December 2009 United Nations climate summit in Copenhagen if the United States wanted to take a leadership position in the cru-cial talks around a successor agreement to the Kyoto Protocol.[22] International coop-eration was considered essential to reducing global emissions enough to avoid the most catastrophic effects of climate change, and a number of countries had made sig-nificant progress since Kyoto was adopted in 1997, promoting cleaner energy sources and passing domestic legislation addressing the issue.[23] Developed nations like the United States, which had already reaped the lion's share of economic and social benefits from their disproportionate energy use, were supposed to take the lead in reducing emissions and guiding the global process. But without a domestic policy of its own, the United States—whose per capita carbon emissions dwarf those of most other countries except China—would have a serious deficiency of moral authority.[24]

In *The Plan*, Emanuel and Reed discussed the threat of climate change and stressed the importance of weaning the country from imported oil. They criticized President George W. Bush for withdrawing from the Kyoto Protocol, calling it a "foreign policy blunder" that "hurt America's cause on other fronts."[25] But the Kyoto Protocol required each country to pass its own climate legislation—something Emanuel reportedly urged Obama not to do.

Obama promised during his campaign to address climate change, and after taking office he even created the position of "climate czar," filled by Carol Browner, a highly respected Clinton-era EPA administrator. In June 2009 the House passed the Waxman-Markey bill (the American Clean Energy and Security Act) by a vote of 219 to 212.[26] At the crucial moment Obama and Emanuel pushed hard for the bill, which would have created a cap-and-trade system and could have led to significant emissions reductions. But the legislation was doomed in the Senate; the bill died, and soon the whole idea of cap and trade or a carbon tax largely dropped off political radar screens.[27]

Emanuel was reportedly a major reason for the failure. Instead of muscling the bill through, he seemed to cave to pressure from industry parties, who howled that such legislation would lead to mass factory closings as power and production costs soared. Climate change was also a hot-button topic in the "culture wars," with conservative pundits and citizens groups denying the existence of man-made climate change and framing climate legislation as an attack on freedom. The science by this point left no doubt that human-induced climate change is real, escalating, and posing a serious global threat. Experts declared that fears of dire economic consequences from putting a price on carbon were overblown, and that a carbon tax could actually help create clean energy and technology jobs and fund social programs.[28] But even as the Obama administration promoted "carrots" such as tax breaks and other incentives for energy efficiency and clean energy generation, the "stick" of a price on carbon had apparently become taboo.

Eric Pooley, author of *The Climate War: True Believers, Power Brokers, and the Fight to Save Planet Earth*, blamed Emanuel. "The chief of staff was an obstacle to climate action," Pooley wrote. "Climate and energy were agenda items to him, pieces on a legislative chessboard; he was only willing to play them in ways that enhanced Obama's larger objectives. He saw no point in squandering capital on a lost cause. The White House could claim victory if Congress passed a beefy energy bill without a cap—and never mind that doing so could torpedo Copenhagen and delay serious greenhouse-gas reductions, perhaps for many years."[29]

An unnamed inside source told Pooley, "You had this incredible green cabinet of really committed people, but the only thing that really matters is what the president says—so everyone was trying to get words into his mouth. And Rahm was trying to keep the words out of his mouth."[30]

The Copenhagen conference came and went without a US domestic climate policy, as did the next major UN climate conference, in Durban, South Africa, which took place after Emanuel had left the White House.

Ironically, some of the same right-wing, climate-change-denying fossil fuel interests Emanuel had essentially protected on the climate front later pounced on him for his role in a $535 million federal loan guarantee to Solyndra, a California-based solar energy company that went bankrupt. Emails indicated that Energy Department officials and others were pressured to rush the loan through without a thorough vetting process, in part because Emanuel wanted Obama involved in a publicity event that had already been scheduled.[31] Throughout the 2012 presidential election campaign season, Republicans pointed to Solyndra as a supposed example of Democratic waste, blunder, and corruption. Such accusations were clearly a stretch, especially given the fact that the Solyndra loan and government support for renewable energy in general pale beside longstanding financial and political support for fossil fuels. But on a relatively minor yet interesting level, the debacle may indeed have been an example of Emanuel's misbehavior—not his corrupt pandering to the solar industry, but his famous penchant for rushing into things while steamrolling over others' concerns and established processes.

HEALTH CARE

Emanuel reportedly "begged" Obama not to pursue health-care reform early in his term, saying instead that the president needed to focus on jobs and the economy.[32] Once the president had committed to a health-care bill, Emanuel zealously devoted his efforts to making something happen.[33] But in keeping with his image as a narrowly focused pragmatist, Emanuel's vision of health-care reform greatly angered and disappointed many who had hoped for a true overhaul.

Emanuel is often blamed for the fact that the Affordable Care Act, as the bill eventually came to be known, was more "health insurance reform" than comprehensive "health-care reform."[34]

Obama, House Speaker Nancy Pelosi, and other, more progressive leaders initially said they felt strongly about offering a "public option"—government-sponsored insurance that would offer coverage to needy people without the profit motive, and would compete with private insurance companies. They also called for cutting health-care costs, which would theoretically make health-care more accessible to a wide range of people (though it would likely cut into profits for hospitals, drug companies, and doctors).

Obama promoted the idea of cutting costs in part through evidence-based medicine—making decisions based on studies showing which procedures and drugs really yielded the best results, and ferreting out instances where surgeries or other expensive treatments were widely used despite showing little or no better outcomes than less expensive and less invasive options. Among the leading advocates of this approach was Zeke Emanuel, Rahm's brother, who was advising the White House on health care.[35] But as described in various books and articles based on inside sources, Rahm Emanuel pushed back against comprehensive health-care reform, trying to dissuade Obama from tackling health care during the economic crisis and then advocating strenuously against a public option and in favor of a much narrower version of reform.

Emanuel was a key liaison to pharmaceutical companies, hospitals, and Republican leaders during the debate. He reportedly promised pharmaceutical companies that the law would not include price controls on drugs and would not allow cheaper drug imports from Canada and Europe—measures that could have been beneficial for low-income people struggling to afford medication.

As Jodi Kantor explained in her book *The Obamas*:

> Rahm Emanuel and Jim Messina, a deputy chief of staff, had cut a quiet deal with pharmaceutical industry lobbyists: in exchange for supporting the legislation, the administration would guarantee that it would cost the companies no more than $80 billion. Many White House aides were surprised and alarmed: Obama had campaigned as a reformer who would fight lobbyists and pharmaceutical companies, and now he was cutting a backroom deal with them that looked like a giveaway?[36]

Emanuel tried to push Obama to agree to a smaller health-care program that would add only about ten million Americans to the insurance rolls. It was dubbed "the Titanic Strategy" because it would primarily expand coverage for single women and children.[37]

According to Ron Suskind, Emanuel tried to shield Obama from outside advice on health-care reform, including from his friend and health-care expert Tom Daschle. Suskind quoted a longtime Washington manager saying Emanuel "convinced Obama that 'all Rahm, all the time' was all he needed. . . . Obama didn't know how things were supposed to work, and Emanuel, running in every direction, wasn't going to tell him."[38]

Meanwhile, some critics argued that despite Obama's early statements in favor of a public option, the much less comprehensive bill that eventually passed was what he "wanted in the first place," in the words of Wisconsin Democratic senator Russ Feingold.[39]

"Contrary to Obama's occasional public statements in support of a public option, the White House clearly intended from the start that the final health care reform bill would contain no such provision and was actively and privately participating in efforts to shape a final bill without it," wrote pundit Glenn Greenwald in *Salon*. "Engineering these sorts of 'centrist,' industry-serving compromises has been the modus operandi of both Obama and, especially, Emanuel."[40]

One of the issues that stalled and nearly killed health-care reform was the debate over the use of government funds for abortion. On this point, Emanuel brokered a crucial compromise. Obama agreed to sign an executive order saying federal funding would not go to abortion in order to get congressmen to drop an amendment proposed by Michigan Democratic congressman Bart Stupak that would have included such a prohibition in the actual bill. While many abortion rights advocates decried the compromise, mainstream prochoice organizations supported it as the lesser of two evils. The right-wing blogosphere crowed that Emanuel was "pro-abortion" and that the executive order had loopholes that would allow federal funding in some situations. Emanuel later explained that the compromise was necessary to get the fourteen congressional holdout votes that were crucial for the bill to pass.[41]

The health-care bill hammered out during a torturous year-plus process was eventually signed by Obama on March 23, 2010. It offered significant gains for regular Americans: insurance companies could no longer bar people with pre-existing conditions, young adults could remain on their parents' insurance until age twenty-six, and about thirty-two million more Americans would be covered.[42] As noted on the White House website, 105 million Americans were relieved of lifetime dollar limits on their coverage, and insurance companies could no longer drop people when they got sick or made a mistake in paperwork.[43]

Watered down as it was, the bill qualified as a historic achievement, and Emanuel surely deserves some credit for making it happen. It's impossible to know if a wider-ranging bill could have passed with more political will and a different strategy. But for people left angry and disillusioned that the reform didn't go further, perhaps the question shouldn't be so much about Emanuel's approach but rather about the larger system supported by corporate influence and poisonous rhetoric—a system that meant the chief of staff could have been correct in betting this was the best the government could do.

IMMIGRATION

Immigrants' rights groups and immigrant community leaders turned out in force to campaign for Barack Obama, including by helping people become citizens and registering new voters likely to cast their ballots for him. The alliance made sense given Obama's family history and home base in Chicago, with its rich immigrant communities, pro-immigrant politicians, and powerful immigrant organizations. Immigrants' rights advocates pushed Obama to promise he would tackle immigration reform within his first hundred days in office. The candidate responded in an interview with ABC that he would make immigration a priority and address it within his first year. But a year came and went, with no reform bill in sight.[44] The Obama administration ultimately ended up deporting immigrants at a faster clip than President Bush had.[45] Many law-abiding, hard-working immigrants were ensnared in the controversial Secure Communities program, which was supposed to remove serious criminals but instead targeted many people with traffic or minor drug offenses.[46]

As with climate change and the public option, the buzz on immigration was that Emanuel had dissuaded Obama from tackling it. During his time in Congress—when he reportedly advised Democrats in close races to vote for the stridently anti-immigrant Sensenbrenner bill—Emanuel had labeled immigration the "third rail of American politics."[47]

Comprehensive immigration reform during Obama's first year—or at any time—was a tall order, to be sure. But during Obama's first two years there was no significant progress on smaller and more urgent pieces of the immigration puzzle, like the DREAM Act, which would offer legal residency to undocumented students who came to the country as children, or legislation to prevent undocumented parents from being deported and separated from their citizen children. (In June 2012, in the midst of his reelection campaign, Obama issued a directive blocking the deportation of youth who would have been covered by the DREAM Act.)[48]

During Emanuel's mayoral campaign, his opponents would hammer him for his stance on immigration during his time in Congress and the White House. Emanuel responded that he did not "kill" the DREAM Act, as some had phrased it, and declined to discuss his private interactions with President Obama.[49]

The *Los Angeles Times* quoted Arizona Democratic congressman Raúl Grijalva saying, "There's always a sense that no matter how hard we work, to get through the White House, we have to get through Rahm. . . . I would like immigration not to be part of the chief of staff's portfolio. It would make our ability to convince and access decision-makers in the White House a lot easier."[50]

That story also quoted New Democrat Network president Simon Rosenberg saying, "It's going to be much easier for this issue to move after Rahm Emanuel leaves the White House. . . . Rahm has a long history of a lack of sympathy for the importance of the immigration issue."[51] Indeed, in June 2013, a wide-ranging immigration reform bill—including a path to citizenship for undocumented immigrants—passed the Senate, though its fate in the House remained uncertain.[52]

LIBERALS ATTACK EMANUEL

In August 2009, during a confidential White House strategy session, Emanuel met with liberal activists upset with the administration's failure to push aggressive health-care reform. The activists were planning to run ads attacking conservative

Democrats, trying to hold the party to more progressive ideals. Emanuel told them the planned ad campaign was "fucking retarded." Months later, he apologized for the statement, acknowledging that it showed insensitivity to people with developmental disabilities.[53] Though he regretted the terminology he had used, Emanuel clearly did not apologize for the attitude he'd taken with the liberal leaders. Author Jonathan Alter described Emanuel responding to the flap: "Rahm's voice dripped with disgust for those dainty Democrats who imagined they were above politics. 'I'm sure there are a lot of people sitting in the shade at the Aspen Institute, my brother being one of them, who will tell you what the ideal plan is,' he said. 'Great, fascinating. You have the art of the possible measured against the ideal.'"[54]

By this point, increasingly fed-up liberals and progressives were calling for Emanuel to resign.[55] "The Rahm Emanuel strategy was to cut deals with power brokers in Washington and ignore what liberals wanted," wrote Cenk Uygur, co-founder of the popular Internet show *The Young Turks*, who dubbed Emanuel "Barack Obama's Dick Cheney."[56]

THE "WOMEN PROBLEM"

Many insider accounts described the Obama White House as a place where highly accomplished, spectacularly intelligent, and strong-willed people worked in an atmosphere characterized by disorganization, backbiting, jealousy, and insularity; where the potential of the immensely talented team Obama had assembled was greatly diminished by a chaotic and sometimes poisonous office culture.[57]

Several high-profile books and numerous articles chronicled how key initiatives, including health-care and financial reform, were bogged down by infighting among Obama's top cabinet members and advisers, a lack of clarity over roles, and the tendency of several top staffers to steamroll over or even ignore the president's wishes.[58]

Various reports said Emanuel's mercurial and demanding personality was a constant source of tension within the White House, though also something other cabinet members and officials learned to live with. In *The Escape Artists* Noam Scheiber said that Emanuel demanded Treasury Secretary Timothy Geithner do a "rewrite of 75 years' worth of financial regulations" in a few weeks for a Wall Street reform bill, but "fortunately for Geithner, the dirty little secret of life under Emanuel was that if you just wait him out, his attention would soon drift to the next major obsession."[59]

There was also a chronic issue dubbed the "women problem." Obama had hired a number of highly accomplished women for top posts. Council of Economic Advisers chair Christina Romer, "climate czar" Carol Browner, health-care reform chief Nancy-Ann DeParle, EPA administrator Lisa Jackson, UN ambassador Susan Rice, and chief domestic policy adviser Melody Barnes were among the prominent women in Obama's administration. But many of them complained they felt silenced and sidelined by a "boys' club" culture. They said they were not asked to speak in free-wheeling debates on economic and policy issues and were left out of inner-circle socializing that revolved around basketball and golf games—even though a few of the women were top athletes in their own right. Regarding both the general office culture and the particular complaints of White House women, Emanuel and economic adviser Larry Summers were frequently named as the main culprits.

Emanuel's role in the managerial and organizational problems was often attributed to his personality—highly competitive, impulsive, rushed, unwilling to admit errors or take the time to hear others out, and focused on political gamesmanship and "winning" above all else. A controversial February 2010 piece in the *Financial Times* said that "the Obama White House is geared for campaigning rather than governing,"[60] and attributed that orientation to the "Fearsome Foursome" of Emanuel, senior advisers David Axelrod and Valerie Jarrett, and press secretary Robert Gibbs.

On its surface the idea that an office is "campaigning" rather than "governing" might not sound like a serious problem. But the criticism got to the heart of a recurring and potentially serious critique of Emanuel, one that would become central during his time as mayor of Chicago: that he was fixated on "getting points on the board" and defeating political enemies.[61]

It is hard to say if Emanuel's central role in creating and refusing to address the "women problem" was related to concrete sexism or his personality more generally. The former explanation could be bolstered by comments like one he made to a male staffer stammering over an answer: "Take your fucking tampon out and tell me what you have to say."[62] When Emanuel was asked during an interview about the women's complaints, Suskind reported, "He was succinct. The concerns of women, he said, were a nonissue, a 'blip.' As to the fact that the White House's women rather strongly disagreed with him on that point, he said, 'I understand,' and then laughed uproariously."[63]

"This, to be sure, was the sort of problem that chiefs of staff were generally left to handle," Suskind wrote. "In this case, the chief of staff was at the center of the problem."[64]

MOVING ON

The never-loving relationship between Obama and Emanuel reportedly soured irreparably after a February 2010 *Washington Post* column by Dana Milbank, headlined "Why Obama Needs Rahm at the Top." Milbank attributed Obama's first-year failures to not listening to his chief of staff, and said that Emanuel's hard-nosed, "earthy and calculating" attitude was crucial to grounding Obama's "airy and idealistic" approach. Milbank blamed Obama for not accepting Emanuel's proposal for very narrow health-care reform from the start; Milbank thought

Emanuel's "Titanic Strategy" would have passed easily and cleared the way to move on to other issues.[65]

Suskind wrote that Obama was "livid" about the column and confronted Emanuel in a tense private meeting where the chief of staff tried to smooth the waters. The larger implication was that Emanuel had a hand in the column and was trying to bolster his own image—to score points for himself—at the expense of his boss, the president of the United States. (Both Milbank and Emanuel denied this.) Suskind indicated that the incident marked a permanent rupture between the two, and that afterward the jokes and banter that had once seasoned the men's rocky relationship were gone.[66]

It was widely reported that Obama wanted Emanuel out by mid-2010, if not sooner. Suskind noted that Emanuel was such a thorn in Obama's side, his impending departure left the president feeling "oddly buoyant" on an otherwise difficult day in September 2010:

"In the past few days, he's caught a break. The mayor of Chicago decided not to run for reelection. That means his chief of staff, Rahm Emanuel, will be seeking 'other opportunities' and the president won't have to worry about firing him."[67]

RAHM ON A JUMBOTRON: OTHER MAYORAL CANDIDATES DROPPED OUT OF THE RACE AS THIS LARGER-THAN-LIFE FIGURE RETURNED TO CHICAGO. PHOTO BY C. SVEN.

6
THE RACE FOR CITY HALL

On September 7, 2010, the news hit Chicago like a strong gust of late summer wind, leaving a trail of chaos and reporters and pundits momentarily short of breath. After six terms in office, Mayor Richard M. Daley announced he would not run for reelection in the coming year. Either Daley or his father, Richard J. Daley, had ruled Chicago for forty-two out of the past fifty-five years, and the family name had become synonymous with the Windy City and its Democratic Machine.[1]

The idea that Daley would call it quits was not a total shocker. It had been a rough few years for the mayor, between the failure to secure the 2016 Olympic Games; the budget crisis; and the debacle surrounding his leasing of the parking meters, a notoriously bad and rushed deal that could remain one of his major legacies. Additionally, Daley's wife, Maggie, was suffering from breast cancer. (She died on November 24, 2011, just thirteen months later.)[2]

But the abruptness of Daley's announcement came as a surprise to political watchers, elected officials, and residents alike. Emanuel had previously floated the idea that he longed to be mayor of Chicago, perhaps laying the groundwork for a White House exit. But immediately after Daley's announcement, both Emanuel and David Axelrod, the famous Democratic media strategist from Chicago, said they were caught off guard by the news.[3]

Chicago has a nonpartisan mayoral election held every four years. Anyone who gets enough signatures and meets other relatively modest requirements can run. But aside from a daring yet ill-fated campaign by congressman and former Black Panther Bobby Rush in 1999—he won only 28 percent of the vote and barely took the African American vote—no one else had launched a serious challenge against Daley in recent times.[4] Though Daley's retirement announcement took people by surprise, plenty of prominent Chicagoans had toyed with the idea of running for mayor over the years. A field of colorful potential candidates quickly emerged, including at least ten out of the city's fifty aldermen.[5]

There was Tom Dart, the handsome and engaging Cook County sheriff, who had gained national attention and local popularity for his 2008 refusal to evict renters in foreclosed apartment buildings.[6]

There was Carol Moseley Braun, the first African American woman elected to the US Senate (in 1992, as a Democrat for Illinois)—a flamboyant and outspoken woman who had also run for president in 2004.[7]

There was the well-connected lawyer and politician Gery Chico, who had served as Daley's former chief of staff and also held top posts with the school board, park district, city colleges, and the Public Building Commission.[8]

There was Danny K. Davis, the African American congressman representing West Side neighborhoods, who had a reputation as a civil rights leader and the oratorical skills of a preacher.[9]

City Clerk Miguel del Valle, an easygoing technocrat and longtime community leader in the Puerto Rican Humboldt Park neighborhood, was backed by many progressive and grassroots groups.[10]

Luis Gutierrez, another prominent Puerto Rican leader, was briefly counted in the race. The congressman was known as a national leader on immigration reform and a champion of popular movements; he had been arrested occupying the US Navy bombing range off the Puerto Rican island of Vieques in 2001.[11]

There was State Senator James Meeks, a fiery South Side pastor known for his crusades against violence and school segregation, as well as his antigay views.[12]

There was even talk of three different candidates from one powerful African American family: Jesse Jackson Jr., the hardworking congressman and son of the renowned civil rights leader; his wife, Sandi, an alderman; and even his brother Jonathan.[13]

And then there was Rahm Emanuel, still in the White House as chief of staff.

Roland S. Martin, a Chicago resident and political commentator for CNN, predicted Emanuel would have an "uphill battle," largely because of the divisive racial politics of Chicago neighborhoods and the lack of affection for Emanuel among African American leaders. Martin wrote:

> It is an open secret in Washington that the Congressional Black Caucus despises Emanuel. A longtime caucus member told me that normally when they meet with the president, the chief of staff attends the meetings. But in the time Obama has been in the White House, Emanuel didn't attend one meeting, and has always given a cold shoulder to black members of Congress. And if you ask black political operatives, pollsters and insiders, they all have a 'why-I-can't-stand-Emanuel' story.[14]

Others felt Emanuel's victory was almost predetermined.

In the days after Daley's announcement, Emanuel's people were polling residents about his prospects and those of other potential mayoral candidates. Respondents were asked about Emanuel's achievements and also about potential sore spots, including his lucrative investment banking career and his ties to infamous former Governor Rod Blagojevich.[15]

During September and October 2010, the race was often framed as one between Emanuel and Dart, with Chico and Moseley Braun possibly nipping at their heels. Things changed in late October, when Dart announced he would not run, citing his young children. Some speculated Emanuel's money and clout had "scared him away."[16]

On November 13 Emanuel made the formal announcement—now old news—that he was running for mayor. In the packed auditorium of John C. Coonley, a Northwest Side elementary school, Emanuel told the cheering crowd, "Only the opportunity to help President Obama as his chief of staff could have pried me away from here. . . . And only the opportunity to lead this city could have pried me away from the president's side."

He had visited the same school a month earlier as part of the Principal for a Day program. With a special program for gifted students and a majority white, less-than-a-third-low-income student body, Coonley was not at all representative of the majority of Chicago public schools—starved for resources, with mostly poor, black, and Latino students—which would be at the center of Emanuel's biggest political battles.[17]

In his announcement Emanuel foreshadowed the battles over layoffs and service cuts that would characterize his administration—by pledging to aggressively cut spending. "Our first responsibility is to make the tough choices that have been avoided too long because of politics and inertia," he said.[18]

A REAL CHICAGOAN?

The Emanuel family had moved to Washington after Emanuel was appointed Obama's chief of staff. Robert Halpin, an industrial real estate developer with a wife and two kids, found a notice online about the house for lease on North Hermitage Avenue, a spacious and attractive though not ostentatious home with a wide front porch on the city's North Side. The Halpins, who had never met Emanuel, moved into the four-bedroom home in September 2009. Coincidentally, Emanuel had extended Halpin's lease through June 2011 just six days before Daley announced he would retire. When Emanuel decided to move back to run for mayor, Halpin told him he was not leaving—even after Emanuel offered to reimburse three months' rent and compensate him for the rest of the lease extension. Halpin reportedly even refused to let Emanuel live in the basement.[19] So Emanuel ended up leasing a condo in the tony River West neighborhood near downtown, while his wife and three kids planned to remain in Washington to finish the school year.[20]

The fact that Emanuel could not move back into his own home fueled the fire of opponents who said he did not meet the residency requirements to run for mayor. State election rules require candidates to maintain a residence in the city for at least one year prior to the election, a requirement Emanuel appeared to have fulfilled by keeping the house as his registered address and voting absentee in the February 2010 city election.[21] The rules say that a resident can be away for "business of the United States," including military service and seemingly governmental service. Whether one liked Emanuel or not, it appeared he was qualified to run for mayor.

But in Chicago candidates are famous for trying to kick each other off the ballot for any number of obscure and arcane reasons.[22] The twenty people who turned in petitions seeking to run for mayor included Halpin himself. "As a lifelong Chicagoan, I considered a mayoral run because I am passionate about the city, its residents and its future," he said.[23] A homeless man with a criminal record had collected almost four thousand signatures to get Halpin on the ballot; the man had also collected more than three thousand signatures for State Senator Meeks. There's nothing illegal about this, and it is common practice to pay people to canvass for signatures. But the situation got fishier when it turned out that several of the people certified as signature collectors for Halpin were bogus, and a Republican strategist previously convicted of forging signatures acknowledged that he had recruited people to fill petitions for Halpin.[24]

Widespread speculation held that powerful veteran Machine alderman Ed Burke had launched the residency challenge, likely based on old political feuds and Burke's fear that Emanuel would try to strip him of his powerful post heading the finance committee.[25] Burke, who had represented the heavily Irish-turned-Latino Fourteenth Ward since 1969, was backing Chico.[26]

In December 2010, officials on the city elections board went through their ritual of hearing challenges seeking to toss people off the ballot. They weeded out a number of candidates based on problems with their petitions and nominating signatures. But they didn't have to bother with Halpin, who had dropped out of the race before the hearings began.

On December 14, Emanuel spent eleven hours in a windowless basement room at the city board of elections, answering questions from people who had objected to his candidacy, including queries both irrelevant and bizarre. An attorney hired by Emanuel's opponents showed slides of empty rooms in the Emanuel house and of his lease agreement with Halpin. Emanuel emphasized that the family always intended to move back into their house, noting they still kept Amy's wedding dress, family photos, china, and other prized possessions in boxes in the basement.[27] A representative of a group of public housing residents asked why Emanuel would need to rent out his house, saying, "You're a millionaire."[28]

Just before Christmas the city's election commissioners ruled that Emanuel could indeed run for mayor.[29] The attorney representing objectors appealed to a county judge, who also ruled in Emanuel's favor. Then the attorney appealed to a state appellate court. On January 24, 2011—a month before the election—the Illinois appellate court ruled two to one that Emanuel did not meet the residency requirements and could not run for mayor. The *Chicago Tribune* noted that the judges who voted against Emanuel owed their jobs to appointments by the county Democratic Party, which was chaired by Ed Burke.[30] The city began printing ballots without Emanuel's name, and three hundred thousand of them were inked before the Illinois Supreme Court ordered the ballot-printing to stop while it reviewed the appellate court's decision.[31] Emanuel backers pointed out that Burke's wife, Anne, was one of the justices on the Supreme Court, and demanded she recuse herself.

In an expedited ruling on January 27, the State Supreme Court cleared Emanuel to run.[32] Anne Burke had not recused herself, but the decision was unanimous. Emanuel got the news while on one of his trademark L train campaign stops—at the Clark and Lake station downtown. He triumphantly shared the news with voters and also made a call to Obama.[33]

AND THEN THERE WERE FIVE

The drama of proving he was a legal resident likely helped Emanuel's campaign, as he handled the rambling and often wacky citizen questions with uncharacteristic patience and humor, and also got a chance to give citizens a humanizing window into his family life. But the outcome didn't stop his opponents and critics from trying to paint him as an outsider, a wealthy "carpetbagger" from Washington and suburbia who didn't really understand Chicago or the needs of its citizens—especially the poor, black, and brown ones.[34]

African American leaders had decided early on that they needed a "consensus candidate" to make sure their vote was not diluted among multiple contenders. By December they decided that Moseley Braun would be the one.[35]

As typically happens, deals were cut, alliances were formed, and promises were made. Soon the field of serious candidates was narrowed down to Emanuel, Chico, del Valle, and Moseley Braun. Some public attention also went to Patricia Van Pelt-Watkins, a community organizer and cofounder of a South Side development agency; and William "Dock" Walls III, former national political director for Jesse Jackson's Rainbow/PUSH organization.

Emanuel had started with $1.2 million in campaign funds, left over from his congressional war chest. He began fundraising promptly after Daley's announcement, and by the end of January he had already raised more than $11.8 million. (Chico came next, with just $2.5 million.[36]) Emanuel's donations included seventy contributions greater than $50,000. Three-quarters of his overall funds came from within the county, but some of the biggest donations came from out of state. He got $50,000 each from Apple CEO Steve Jobs and right-wing zealot developer Donald Trump; and $100,000 and $75,000 from Hollywood moguls David Geffen and

Steven Spielberg, respectively—Emanuel's Hollywood agent brother, Ari, helped with such connections. Emanuel was lucky that his big donations came in before January 1, 2011, when new campaign finance laws kicked in that limited individual contributions to $5,000, corporations to $10,000, and PACs to $50,000.[37]

Emanuel used the money in part to blanket the airwaves with ads, starting early on, and he hired AKPD Message and Media, the consulting firm founded by David Axelrod, to manage the ad buys.[38] Chico did not start airing TV ads until early January, and by late January Moseley Braun had still not bought air time.[39]

Chico's donations reflected his status as a Machine insider and raised some eyebrows. He got $25,000 from Symon Garber, head of a taxi company that was employing Chico's law firm to fight massive city fines for operating previously wrecked cars as taxis. In the face of media attention Chico returned Garber's donation. He also received $20,000 from Dan Walsh, head of a major construction firm known for its City Hall contracts and connections.[40]

Chico, whose father was a Mexican immigrant, emphasized his Mexican heritage and had the support of prominent Latino developers and politicians. including Congressman Gutierrez after he dropped out of the race. But Chico was not especially known for getting involved in local Latino community issues or for taking on issues affecting immigrants; rather, he was seen as part of the largely white Democratic Machine, and known to represent its interests.[41]

TARGET TOWN HALLS AND L STOPS

In the victory speech he ultimately ended up giving, Emanuel boasted that he visited 110 L train stops during the mayoral campaign. He said that despite frigid weather, "because of the people of Chicago" the L stop was the "warmest place in America."[42] (The L is Chicago's elevated—and sometimes underground—public light rail system, with a "Loop" around downtown and arms extending to different sectors of the city.)

Critics pointed out that with all that time at train stations, Emanuel couldn't seem to find the time to attend community meetings and debates with the other candidates—he turned down nearly all such invitations. Maybe he didn't have the appetite for the extended engagement that such forums would entail; he preferred the frenetic, ultimately shallow venue of L stops, where everyone is on the move. Maybe it was a reflection of how Emanuel viewed the other candidates—not worth his time or effort. He apparently felt comfortable enough in his impending victory that in December 2010—in the heart of campaign season—he took a weeklong vacation in Thailand with his family.[43]

Chicago author Scott Turow described one of Emanuel's train station campaign stops:

> On a brutally cold morning in mid-December, Rahm Emanuel, hatless and wearing a
> glove on only his left hand, stood for an hour in front of the turnstiles at the Paulina L

station, which sits in his old congressional district on Chicago's north side. As the trains slammed and screeched overhead, he offered his hand to the mostly young and professional commuters heading downtown. Emanuel's manner seemed more studied than spontaneous. He employed standard lines—"nice hat," "good book"—and relied on the logos on riders' head wear and jackets for conversation starters. He addressed both sexes as "man," and when a woman asked about his plans for the Chicago Transit Authority, he was characteristically a trifle abrupt—"Here's the deal," he said to start—and egocentric. As he did with me, he told her the elevated line right above us was something "I built," before saying "we," apparently realizing he was discounting the work and leadership of many others. He hardly seemed like an irresistible force.[44]

Chicago Sun-Times columnist Mary Mitchell described Emanuel campaigning in impoverished African American neighborhoods on the South Side. She noted that he went to the Ninety-Fifth Street station (the final stop on the red line) four times, another South Side intersection three or four times, and a South Side Target store once (he hosted several "Target Town Halls").[45] Mitchell wrote that what Emanuel saw on the L train platforms "haunts him," and she quoted him saying, "I saw too many kids on those platforms with not a thing in their eyes. That is the only thing about this job that gives me pause about my abilities."[46]

Emanuel would reiterate this image a number of times. After the teachers union strike in September 2012, he would say, "Too many times I have met kids, whether on the [L] or on the street walking to school, who have a look of emptiness in their eyes that no one would accept in their own child."[47]

Emanuel obviously meant to convey his emotional intuition and his deep empathy with African American kids in poor neighborhoods. But when actually riding trains or buses or walking through a school in these same neighborhoods, one hardly sees scores of ashen-faced youth with vacant and hopeless stares. As dire as their circumstances may be, youth in poor South and West Side Chicago neighborhoods are typically laughing, chatting, arguing, teasing, gossiping, and sometimes fighting, just like kids anywhere. It's possible their eyes convey anger, fear, or pain more frequently than the eyes of kids in wealthier neighborhoods, but even these expressions could hardly be described as "emptiness." Emanuel's touchstone phrase could be seen as meaningless rhetoric or a sign of unfamiliarity with the people living in the neighborhoods whose train stations he frequented.

Like his congressional run, Emanuel's mayoral campaign offered plenty of fodder for observers to parse and evaluate his public and personal style—his ease or lack thereof with people, his ability to relate, his fluency in the everyday routines and concerns of the 99 percent. Conclusions varied. Many described Emanuel as socially awkward, aloof, and defensive even with his own peers, not to mention the "less fortunate." Others described him in senior centers and classrooms working the crowd with relaxed charm and cheer.

Like most modern political candidates Emanuel had a Twitter account, allowing him (or his staff) to send messages (Tweets) of 140 characters or less over the social media service. Over two long days of campaigning Emanuel visited "50 Wards in 50 Hours," as the stunt was dubbed, and a Twitter message was sent from each one.[48]

But Emanuel's Twitter presence was eclipsed by a mysterious Tweeter with the handle @MayorEmanuel, who amassed several times more followers than the real Emanuel. @MayorEmanuel's profanity-laden Tweets created an image of the candidate as a hard-drinking, coffee-swilling, obnoxious jerk careening through Chicago with David Axelrod, "Carl the Intern," and hapless staffers in tow.

One typical offering had Emanuel attending the Joffrey Ballet's *Nutcracker,* judging his fellow ballet dancers quite harshly: "Seriously, Clara may as well just pull down her tutu and take a shit on the stage. Would be more elegant than her dancing."[49] And @MayorEmanuel's opinion of his opponents wasn't much higher: "All [Carol] Moseley Braun's signatures and two bucks will buy her is a Coke. No idea how much it'd cost her to buy a fucking clue."[50]

The real Emanuel offered to donate $5,000 to charity if the impostor would reveal himself. After five months and two thousand Tweets that were later collected in a book, journalism professor and former *Punk Planet* magazine editor Dan Sinker came forward, and the group Young Chicago Authors got the cash from Emanuel.[51]

LAYING THE GROUNDWORK: SCHOOL REFORM AND CITY WORKERS

During his meetings with regular voters during the campaign—even before he officially announced his candidacy—Emanuel stressed his focus on school reform and spending cuts. His promises to make schools more competitive, lengthen the school day, and introduce "parent choice" immediately raised the hackles of union teachers, progressive parents' groups, and other veterans of the battle over "school reform" that had been raging for some years on the national level and had become highly contentious in Chicago under Daley.

During an early November 2010 swing through the Little Village neighborhood, a largely Latino bastion of community organizing and activism, Emanuel was talking about school reform when he was distracted by a tossed egg, which hit a cameraman behind him.[52] The egg thrower may not have known a thing about Emanuel's school reform plans, but the move was symbolic of how the candidate's attitude was being received in many neighborhoods like Little Village.

During his campaign Emanuel stressed his commitment to efficiency and getting the city budget under control. The budget deficit clearly had to be addressed, but many city workers and public sector union leaders feared that serious belt-tightening and privatization of public jobs would be in store under an Emanuel administration.

The two largest and most outspoken unions representing city workers, AFSCME and SEIU, declined to endorse anyone in the mayoral race. The powerful Chicago Firefighters Union Local 2 and the Fraternal Order of Police union endorsed Chico, as did the operating engineers, laborers, sheet metal workers, electrical workers, and other trades. Emanuel was endorsed by some unions, including the Teamsters Joint Council 25 and the plumbers, bricklayers and one local of the ironworkers, all of which probably imagined Emanuel would launch a lucrative construction boom.[53]

In early February the Emanuel campaign ran an ad saying, "City government is not an employment agency. It is delivering a service to the residents and the taxpayers of the city. I want that mind-set to be different. We're going to deliver a service to the taxpayers. We're going to give them the best price for what they pay for, whether that's protecting a street, cleaning a street, plowing a street."[54]

City employees and union leaders saw it as a not-so-subtle attack, tapping into stereotypes of lazy city workers with an entitlement mind-set. The pledge implied cuts and possibly privatization to come and pitted city workers against taxpayers while seemingly ignoring the fact that city workers are also taxpayers and their salaries play an important role in sustaining their communities.

The police and firefighters unions and AFSCME demanded Emanuel apologize for the ad. *Sun-Times* columnist Mark Brown noted that it was no surprise unions endorsing Chico would lash out at Emanuel. "What stands out," Brown wrote, "is that Emanuel appears to have willingly supplied the provocation in his own bid to capture the votes of those with anti-public employee sentiments."[55]

Emanuel was the most specific of the candidates in his proposals for closing the budget gap. He said he could reduce it by $500 million through a number of measures. These included saving $65 million by transforming garbage collection routes and $110 million by cutting through red tape bureaucracy.[56] He also proposed raising $25 million by putting ads on city property like garbage trucks and the vehicle stickers mandatory for all residents. City Clerk Susana Mendoza rushed to point out that she had proposed the ads on vehicle stickers a few weeks earlier. She posted a press release on her website titled "Susana Mendoza Praises Rahm Emanuel for Backing Her City Sticker Idea."[57]

THE DEBATES

On January 14, 2011, Emanuel, Moseley Braun, Chico, and del Valle met with the *Chicago Tribune* editorial board in an event that became more like a debate than an interview. All three opponents attacked Emanuel mercilessly, invoking his weak White House record on immigration, his hostility toward city workers, his animosity toward public school teachers, and his abrasive personality. Moseley Braun brought up the tampon comment, which Emanuel denied having made. "Tampons, let's talk about tampons," she said. "This is about tampons and how women would feel about somebody who said that in the workplace."[58] Chico insinuated that Emanuel was unfamiliar with how to run a city, saying, "Are we gonna have snow picked up? Are we gonna have the garbage picked up? Are we gonna have the buses and trains running?"[59] And del Valle highlighted the fact that he himself had been to eight community forums, including large events sponsored by important social service and advocacy groups, while Emanuel had largely skipped such gatherings. "When are you going to start talking to the neighborhoods?" he asked.[60]

The first official mayoral debate took place January 27—a little more than three weeks before the election. There Moseley Braun accused both Chico and Emanuel of being in public service for the money and exploiting their power for personal gain, while she boasted that she had never profited from holding elected office. Emanuel was polling with a two-to-one lead over any opponents at this point, and the other candidates knew their only shot was to force him into a runoff by making sure he got less than 50 percent of the total vote.[61]

Chico attacked Emanuel on his plans for increasing revenue, including by taxing services that had not previously been taxed. He railed that the new taxes would hurt independent companies like car washes and child-care providers. Chico's campaign had sent out a large color mailer trumpeting what he dubbed "The Rahm Tax," claiming that "everyday services like car repair, haircuts and pet care would be taxed—costing working families even more."[62] Emanuel said this was not the case; the new tax would cover "luxury services" like tanning parlors, limos, private club membership, and dog grooming.[63] He also defended his plan to end free water for nonprofit organizations, including big-budget churches and hospitals as well as small grassroots and social service groups, for whom a water bill could be a significant expense.[64]

Whatever chance Moseley Braun may have had was torpedoed during a January 30 debate at Trinity United Church of Christ (the same South Side church Obama had attended until Pastor Jeremiah Wright's fiery sermons became a political liability).[65]

Van Pelt-Watkins, a former public housing resident, steelworker, and union steward who'd founded a respected community organization, repeated her frequent criticism that Moseley Braun had withdrawn from the African American community and social activism in recent years.[66] "Carol Moseley Braun hasn't been around for twenty years," she said, as audience members began to clap. "We haven't seen her, we haven't heard from her. . . . I didn't even know the woman lived in the city of Chicago, because I have not heard her voice out on the street. . . . We do not need people who have been missing in action and lost somewhere for twenty years to wake up one day and decide they want to be mayor of the city of Chicago."

"Patricia, the reason you didn't know where I was the last twenty years is because you were strung out on crack," said Moseley Braun, as gasps rose from the audience.

She and Van Pelt-Watkins stood at the table as Chico and del Valle sat between them awkwardly keeping their eyes straight ahead. Emanuel was not there. Moseley Braun leaned toward Van Pelt-Watkins and continued: "I was not strung out on crack. I don't have a record. I, in fact, have spent years of my life working and fighting for this community as the only black United States senator from 1992 to 1998, as the only ambassador. So I don't want to hear it from you, sweetie."[67]

Van Pelt-Watkins emphasized in interviews in the following days that she had never used crack, and had never even seen the drug. She had long been open about the fact that she used alcohol, marijuana, and powder cocaine between the ages of eleven and twenty-one, but by the time she entered the mayoral race she said she had been clean for thirty-two years.[68] While Moseley Braun's political career appeared over, Van Pelt-Watkins was elected in 2012 to a seat in the State Senate.[69]

ELECTION DAY

The big question going into election day was not whether Emanuel would win but whether he would win outright, with the majority vote needed to avoid a runoff. In the end, it was hardly a race at all. Emanuel got 55 percent, Chico 24 percent, del Valle 9.3 percent, Moseley Braun 9 percent, and Van Pelt-Watkins 1.6 percent.[70]

Emanuel carried 59 percent of the African American vote and won in all but one majority African American precinct. This was remarkable, columnist Mary Mitchell pointed out, given his lack of support from local African American leaders.[71] Emanuel likely was aided by his endorsements from Obama and, perhaps even more important, from Bill Clinton. Moseley Braun had called Clinton's endorsement a "betrayal" of Chicago African Americans, who still harbored great loyalty and affection for the former president.[72] Chico, meanwhile, won in several neighborhoods home to many police, firefighters, and city workers. This was not surprising, given his deep Machine connections.[73]

"Chicago residents are an interesting bunch," said one Chicago elected official. "While they say they don't want a dictator, they vote for a strong hand. Miguel [del Valle] was the soft-spoken, nice guy—nice guys always finish last. Gery [Chico] was the connected lawyer. Rahm was the boss, the doer."[74]

Overall voter turnout was considered low—41 percent.[75] Past municipal elections had been even lower, but during Daley's reign the mayor's office was never considered up for grabs.[76] Hence pundits had originally expected the 2011 turnout to be higher. Many saw the low turnout as an expression of frustration with the choices offered, and the feeling among many that Emanuel's victory was preordained.

Emanuel gave his victory speech in the Plumbers' union hall surrounded by his family and a multiracial group of students holding cardboard signs signifying their neighborhoods: Beverly, Lincoln Square, Portage Park. He pumped his fist and beamed at the crowd, though his voice sounded hoarse and tired as he stumbled over words. He proclaimed his love for Chicago and all its people, and pledged a new beginning and a break from past troubles, even as he praised Mayor Daley for making "Chicago a world-class city." He invoked his familial connection to the public sector—Uncle Les—while foreshadowing the public cuts that lay in store:

> As we move forward we face serious new challenges, and overcoming them will not be easy. It requires new ideas, cooperation, and sacrifice from everyone involved. . . . I look forward to working with tens of thousands of dedicated public servants, those like my Uncle Les, who patrolled our streets, who teach our children and fulfill so many vital functions to meet our current challenges; and to do it in a way that is fair to them and fair to the taxpayers who pay all of us.

FOR A BETTER CHICAGO

Emanuel's involvement in campaigning didn't end with the election. Though he easily avoided a runoff, many aldermen weren't so lucky. Emanuel endorsed seven incumbents in the April 5 runoff, and one new challenger—Debra Silverstein, an accountant who ended up defeating longtime alderman Bernard Stone in a heavily Jewish North Side neighborhood.[77]

Emanuel's support may have been crucial to the runoff victory of Danny Solis, a onetime community organizer turned loyal Machine politician who had long represented the Near Southwest Side, including the Mexican immigrant neighborhood of Pilsen. Solis was a cofounder of the United Neighborhood Organization (UNO), which ran thirteen charter schools. Two decades earlier Solis's sister Patti had, like Emanuel, worked on Bill Clinton's presidential campaign in Little Rock; she would later become Hillary Clinton's campaign manager during the 2008 Democratic presidential primary. Solis rebuffed Emanuel's request for an endorsement during the mayoral race; he said he was committed either to Congressman Luis Gutierrez or Gery Chico. But the night of Emanuel's election Solis called to congratulate the new mayor and cement an alliance.[78]

Solis was forced into a runoff by a community activist and former juvenile probation officer named Cuauhtémoc Morfin. Morfin's strong showing was due in large part to Solis's longstanding silence on the coal-fired power plant in Pilsen. For a decade local activists had been demanding the coal plant and another one in nearby Little Village shut down or greatly reduce their emissions. Like Daley, Solis had refused to take a stand on the issue. Leading up to the runoff, with Emanuel's backing, he reversed course and backed stringent emissions limits for the coal plants.[79] Within a year Emanuel would negotiate a deal closing the coal plants, though energy experts noted that competition from cheap natural-gas-fired power would likely have forced the plants to close regardless.[80] Meanwhile, Solis would become one of Emanuel's most loyal followers in City Council.

Solis and other aldermen favored by Emanuel received support from a Political Action Committee called For a Better Chicago. The PAC grew out of a nonprofit organization formed the previous fall; the nonprofit had donated $855,000 to the PAC a few days before state campaign finance reforms that would curtail such donations took effect.[81] For a Better Chicago's founders included Greg Goldner, Emanuel's 2002 congressional campaign manager and CEO of the PR firm Resolute Consulting.[82] Resolute had done much work for Daley and would help orchestrate Emanuel's controversial plan to close public schools.[83] The PAC's formation and the aldermanic runoff showed that Emanuel was quickly cementing his power and taking over the controls of the old Daley Machine.

MAYOR RAHM EMANUEL PROMISED TO BRING ORDER AND DISCIPLINE TO
CHICAGO'S FINANCES—EVEN IF IT MEANT PAINFUL CUTS. PHOTO BY C. SVEN.

7

GETTING DOWN
TO BUSINESS

INAUGURATION DAY

Rahm Emanuel was inaugurated as mayor of Chicago on May 16, 2011. Richard
M. Daley pounded the gavel in one last symbolic City Council meeting before the
inauguration, which was held in the Jay Pritzker Pavilion, the graceful bandshell in
Millennium Park designed by architect Frank Gehry. A host of political luminaries
were on hand, including Emanuel's former allies and adversaries. Vice President Joe
Biden and his wife, Jill, were there, as was Illinois senator Dick Durbin, whose campaign Emanuel had worked on three decades earlier. There was Daley's brother Bill,
who had worked with Emanuel in the Clinton White House and taken over as
Obama's chief of staff upon Emanuel's departure. A host of congressmen were in
attendance, including Luis Gutierrez and Jesse Jackson Jr.—both of whom had been
considered potential rivals for the mayor's office. Emanuel was sworn in by Timothy
Evans, the chief judge of the Cook County Circuit Court. He was flanked by wife,
Amy Rule; his daughters, Ilana and Leah; and son, Zach. Emanuel's parents hugged,
and his brother Ari smiled. The trademark dark circles surrounding Emanuel's eyes
did nothing to diminish the aura of agility, energy, and power he exuded as he
beamed at the crowd and delivered a forceful thumbs-up.[1]

"We must face the truth," Emanuel told the crowd. "It is time to take on the
challenges that threaten the very future of our city: the quality of our schools, the
safety of our streets, the cost and effectiveness of city government, and the urgent
need to create and keep the jobs of the future right here in Chicago. The decisions
we make in the next two or three years will determine what Chicago will look like
in the next twenty or thirty."[2]

He focused first on the schools, declaring his determination to institute the longer school day. "As some have noted, including my wife, I am not a patient man. When it comes to improving our schools, I will not be a patient mayor." Then he talked about epidemic gun violence in the streets and asked for the public's help in solving crimes. After that, he vowed to get the city's "financial house in order."

"From the moment I began my campaign for mayor, I have been clear about the hard truths and tough choices we face: we simply can't afford the size of city government that we had in the past. And taxpayers deserve a more effective and efficient government than the one we have today. Our city's financial situation is difficult and profound. We cannot ignore these problems one day longer. It's not just a matter of doing more with less. We must look at every aspect of city government and ask the basic questions: Do we need it? Is it worth it? Can we afford it? Is there a better deal?"[3]

Without saying the words "union" or "labor," he alluded to the looming battles and essentially promised not to replicate the vicious attacks on public sector unions being waged in other states, while also warning unions to expect some serious changes. "I reject how leaders in Wisconsin and Ohio are exploiting their fiscal crisis to achieve a political goal. That course is not the right course for Chicago's future. However, doing everything the same way we always have is not the right course for Chicago's future, either. We will do no favors to our city employees or our taxpayers if we let outdated rules and outmoded practices make important government services too costly to deliver."[4]

Later in his remarks Emanuel said, "I reach out a hand of mutual respect and cooperation, and I welcome your ideas for change," referring to City Council members, large and small businesses, and labor unions. He invoked the city's rich history and diversity, noting that the day's inauguration included the son of an Israeli immigrant (himself); Treasurer Stephanie Neely, whose African American family had come north in the Great Migration; and City Clerk Susana Mendoza, the daughter of Mexican immigrants. (Mendoza gave the new mayor a bizarre welcome gift: a bottle of Midol for premenstrual cramps, a reference to his notorious "tampon" comment in the White House.)[5]

Emanuel called for passing the Illinois DREAM Act, which would make scholarships and other college financial assistance available to undocumented immigrant students graduating from Illinois high schools.[6] And he announced his intentions to bolster the city colleges to train young people for jobs. He highlighted the accomplishments of high school students at both charters and neighborhood public schools: Kenwood Academy, Simeon Career Academy, Ralph Ellison High School, Urban Prep Academy, and Whitney M. Young Magnet High School.

After finishing at the park, Emanuel moved into his new office on the fifth floor of City Hall. Mayor Daley had taken his desk home. So Emanuel adopted a desk used by Anton Cermak, the former Chicago mayor who had been killed in 1933 by a bullet intended for President-Elect Franklin D. Roosevelt (the shot was fired by an Italian immigrant with a "ferocious hatred for politicians").[7] Cermak, a Bohemian immigrant firewood seller turned politician, was known as the creator of the notorious Chicago Democratic Machine.[8] Eight decades later, pundits would describe Emanuel as reshaping the Machine, dismantling some pieces while retaining others and grafting onto it his own brand of neoliberal, New Democrat power politics.

A BLAST FROM THE PAST

Nine days after the inauguration, Emanuel was in federal court testifying in the second corruption trial of former governor Rod Blagojevich.

Two and a half years earlier, on December 9, 2008, as Emanuel was preparing for his role in the Obama White House, Blagojevich was arrested by federal agents in the early morning, escorted out of the house in his running clothes. He was indicted and removed from office based on charges he tried to "sell" Barack Obama's Senate seat to the highest bidder and otherwise personally profit from his position as governor. Blagojevich's wiretapped, profanity-laced phone calls included his assertion that the vacated Senate seat—which the governor is allowed to fill under state law—was "fucking golden."[9]

Prosecutors said the phone calls indicated that Blagojevich had hoped to pressure Emanuel, then newly slated as chief of staff for President-Elect Obama, to help Blagojevich set up a lucrative gig running a nonprofit organization if he appointed Obama's friend Valerie Jarrett. The wiretaps indicated that Blagojevich aide John Wyma relayed a message from Emanuel to the governor that Obama would "value and appreciate" a Jarrett appointment—offering no quid pro quo. Blagojevich responded, "Fuck them!"[10]

Emanuel reportedly wanted Jarrett placed in the Senate seat for personal reasons. Author Jonathan Alter noted, "He wanted her out of the White House, where he worried that her long and close relationship with the Obamas would threaten his authority."[11]

Prosecutors also said that when Emanuel was in Congress in 2006, he asked Wyma to prod Blagojevich to release a $2 million state grant that had already been awarded to a school in Emanuel's district. The school was run by the Academy for Urban School Leadership, known for taking over troubled "turnaround" schools. A Blagojevich staffer allegedly told Wyma that Blagojevich wanted Emanuel's Hollywood agent brother Ari to host a fundraiser for him before he would release the grant.[12] If such a request was indeed made, Ari apparently ignored or denied it, and no such fundraiser ever happened. Wyma, formerly a friend of both Emanuel and Blagojevich, ended up cooperating with the prosecution.[13]

Emanuel had been subpoenaed but never called to testify in Blagojevich's first trial, in August 2010, which ended in a hung jury on twenty-three of twenty-four counts. As the second trial approached, speculation had been swirling over whether Emanuel would be called to the stand. Just weeks before the mayoral election, Blagojevich's lawyers demanded federal prosecutors release what they said was a wiretapped phone conversation in which Emanuel tried to broker a deal to put Illinois attorney general Lisa Madigan in the Senate seat.[14]

Prosecutors never alleged Emanuel did anything illegal; they didn't even allege he was aware of the attempted shakedowns. Still, pundits considered Emanuel lucky that the second Blagojevich trial was delayed from a scheduled January 2011 start to after the mayoral election, given the stain of any appearance of wheeling and dealing with Blagojevich.

National media filled the federal courtroom for Emanuel's testimony on May 25, 2011. It was ultimately anticlimactic, lasting all of three minutes. But the event showcased Emanuel's brash confidence and even smugness: he smirked, with a ramrod yet relaxed posture, and gave terse answers to the defense's questions. He answered negatively to questions about whether he had been asked to get his brother to hold a Hollywood fundraiser, and whether he had been asked to set up a nonprofit for Blagojevich to run in exchange for a Jarrett Senate appointment. He betrayed no anxiety about being potentially mired in one of the juiciest political scandals in state history. Rather, he appeared breezy and in control, with a whiff of annoyance at having his day interrupted by trivial proceedings.

By the second week of his mayoral term, Emanuel had essentially cleansed himself of one of the political scandals that had dogged prominent Chicago Democrats for the past few years. He was ready to charge full speed ahead.

TICKING OFF SUCCESSES

After thirty days in office, Emanuel held a press event featuring two tall posters listing his goals for his first hundred days in office. He flamboyantly checked off the twenty-three he said he'd already accomplished.

The top box on one poster said, "Put an additional 500 cops on the street": check—though critics, including the police union, said Emanuel's reassignment of cops in specialized units to high-crime beat patrols didn't actually count as "more" officers on the street but was just a reshuffling of the existing force.[15] Other goals accomplished: selecting a location for two miles of separated bike lanes, convening a food desert summit, and launching the One Summer Chicago program to provide summer jobs for youth. On his first day as mayor, Emanuel had signed as an executive order an anticorruption measure banning city employees from taking jobs where they would lobby the city.[16] He also posted information about lobbyists online, allowing citizens to track potential conflicts of interest.[17] Other goals "accomplished" were squishier and had more to do with meetings than action, including "develop public health goals" and "accelerate development" of a water management plan.[18]

Chicago Reader journalist Mick Dumke called the media stunt "a very Rahm thing. . . . This is a guy who obviously is very focused on the whole scorecard approach of checking things off."[19]

Some of the "accomplishments" laid the groundwork for the battles that would plague Emanuel in coming months: "Push for state legislation enabling CPS [Chicago Public Schools] to lengthen the school day," "Engage stakeholders in a new teacher evaluation process," and cut $75 million from the current budget.[20]

The state education law known as SB 7 was passed by the Democratic state legislature and signed by Governor Pat Quinn on June 13, 2011, a month after Emanuel took office. Emanuel's quest for a longer school day was among the main reasons for the law, and he reportedly lobbied hard for it. The law mandated that the teachers union could go on strike only if 75 percent of the membership voted to authorize it. This bar was considered by both pro-union and antiunion types to be quite high, and was seen by national school reformers who backed it as a de facto ban on teachers strikes. The bill also mandated that schools base teacher evaluations heavily on student performance on standardized tests, and made it easier for schools to dismiss teachers—both concepts the union stridently opposed.[21]

For Emanuel's hundredth day in office, the posters were back, and so were some of the same catch-phrases, like the idea that improving schools was one of his "north stars." He touted continuing progress and checked off more boxes on his scorecard.[22] He announced that he'd "secured more than 4,000 private-sector jobs in neighborhoods across the city." He slashed the number of city-issued credit cards and reined in the use of petty cash by city employees. He "championed" a strong curfew ordinance, and "launched Internet Essentials, a public-private partnership that will provide access to high-speed, reliable Internet service for families of 330,000 students across the city."[23] He also instituted a program to deal with foreclosed properties in areas hard-hit by the economic crisis, taking a community-wide rather than house-by-house approach.[24]

UNION BATTLES BEGIN

Emanuel's book *The Plan* devoted much space to the importance and needs of the middle class. The book celebrated the golden age of the middle class after World War II, and noted that employees at General Motors and elsewhere could expect a lifelong job followed by a comfortable pension-funded retirement. Yet the book never mentioned the word "union," despite the central role of labor unions in the creation and security of such jobs. Experts across the political spectrum agree that labor unions were central to the creation of an American middle class with job security and benefits after World War II. Yet Emanuel and coauthor Reed didn't reference unions either in the historical context or in their discussion of current and future American politics. Unions clearly didn't figure into what they proposed as a "social contract for the twenty-first century."[25]

Though he had gotten high marks from labor organizations during his time in Congress, Emanuel had never been seen as a particular friend of organized labor, especially given his role during the NAFTA negotiations. So it was not surprising that the mayor got off to a rough start with Chicago labor unions—which had indeed played a central role in making the city an economic and social powerhouse.

Emanuel began working to cut city spending almost immediately upon taking office. Payroll made up more than three-quarters of the city's spending, so he looked to public jobs—about 90 percent of them unionized—as a major place to slash costs.[26] Emanuel knew a budget deficit of up to $700 million was looming in 2012, and he also planned to cut spending in 2011.[27] One of the first major actions of his newly appointed Board of Education was a vote to rescind 4 percent annual raises that were scheduled as part of the Chicago Teachers Union's contract.[28] And the mayor made clear that other city workers would also have to make sacrifices.

There was extra urgency for immediate spending cuts because an agreement worked out under Mayor Daley wherein city workers would take unpaid furlough days expired at the end of June. The 2011 budget had been based on an understanding that the agreement would be extended for the remaining six months. But Emanuel wasn't a fan of furlough days, so he let the agreement expire and pledged to find another way to cut the roughly $30 million that would have been saved had the furlough program continued.[29]

Emanuel said about $10 million could be saved by leaving unfilled positions vacant and about $10 million more could be saved by turning over health-care services at seven city clinics to private providers working under federal programs. He also wanted unions to agree to $10 million or $11 million worth of "work rules" changes.[30]

The term "work rules" covered a complex and largely secret range of agreements in city union contracts, including how overtime was calculated, the schedules of various union workers, and which tasks must be done by certain unions. Developed over years in a city where many unions had enjoyed cozy ties with the Democratic Machine, some of the work rules could be seen as ways to pad union workers' paychecks with unnecessarily inefficient or bureaucratic requirements.

The specifics of work rules in the existing contracts and Emanuel's proposed changes were largely not public knowledge, though Emanuel eventually announced a list of changes that sounded reasonable for a budget crisis. They included reducing paid holidays from twelve to nine annually, changing the pay rates for vehicle operators based on experience, paying time and a half instead of double for overtime hours, and eliminating extra pay for drivers working alone on a truck as opposed to with a crew.[31] Emanuel singled out the city's two hundred hoisting engineers as an example of the fat in union contracts signed under Mayor Daley, who had especially close ties with that union. The hoisting engineers, who operate cranes, made on average $93,808 a year plus tens of thousands of dollars in over-time, including being paid $90 an hour—double their usual rate—for "grease time" spent prepping their heavy equipment.[32]

Even though the work rules were arguably a valid place for Emanuel to cut costs, his bid to do so outside normal contract negotiation structures was seen by unions as an attack on rights and policies they held sacred.

Starting early in his term, Emanuel made a habit of holding press conferences to announce new jobs coming to the city. He usually joined a CEO or other corporate officials in announcing that a given company was moving its headquarters to Chicago, adding another shift, or otherwise expanding its workforce. He held one such event in late June 2011 with Greg Wasson, president and CEO of Walgreens, announcing the drugstore chain was bringing six hundred more jobs to the city.[33]

Emanuel also chose this moment to publicly pick a fight—as many city workers saw it—with Chicago unions, particularly the tradesmen who typically make up an important base of support. Unions would have to agree to work rule changes, he announced, or he would make 625 layoffs. "It is not necessary to do the layoffs if you agree to these reforms. If you don't, that will be the choice left to me on behalf of the taxpayers," Emanuel said. "If they [unions] don't agree to it [work rules reforms], 625 people and their families will lose that job."[34]

Union leaders resented this public ultimatum, saying it subverted the channels through which such negotiations were supposed to take place. In a joint statement, Chicago Federation of Labor president Jorge Ramirez and Tom Villanova, president of the Chicago and Cook County Building and Construction Trades Council, said: "There have been absolutely no negotiations between the city and the unions representing the city's workforce."[35] Similarly, Henry Bayer, executive director of AFSCME Council 31, said the Emanuel administration had not asked his union to negotiate the work rule changes: "The fact that he has never done so is clear evidence that his attempt to blame union work rules for the city's massive deficit is mere public relations gimmickry."[36]

Two weeks after Emanuel's threat to cut jobs, the unions still had not agreed to the changes. So the mayor's office said up to 625 pink slips would be sent to employees, including call center staffers and seasonal transportation workers.[37] Union leaders were furious. They said the mayor had never given them a deadline for agreeing to the changes, and that he still hadn't negotiated with the heads of unions or even contacted union leaders until several days prior. In a statement on behalf of the Coalition of Unionized Public Employees (COUPE),[38] Ramirez and Villanova indicated that the mayor expected union leaders to agree to the changes even though he had not given them comprehensive details about what the changes would actually entail.[39]

Meanwhile COUPE, which included about 6,400 members of various city unions, commissioned a study by a well-known Pennsylvania policy firm to identify alternate ways the city could cut costs. The study, released in late July 2011, said Chicago could save a full $242 million by laying off unnecessary middle managers rather than front-line union workers; adopting more efficient scheduling and contracting procedures; and replacing some private contractors with city workers who, the coalition argued, could do the jobs more cheaply.[40] Some of the efficiency measures were common-sense ideas like streamlining expensive equipment rentals and replacing workweeks of five eight-hour days with four ten-hour days, which would reduce time spent setting up and breaking down equipment. The report recommended thinning the ranks of management in departments including family support services, where there were as many as one supervisor for every 1.6 front-line employees.[41] And most significant, it said the city could save up to $40 million by reversing the privatization of some services, ending contracts with private firms for things like airport snow removal equipment maintenance and emergency management communications.[42] Private contracts were "padded for profit," the report argued, and the city could save money by bringing back in-house many services that had been privatized.[43]

Ramirez and Lou Phillips, business manager of the Laborers Local 1001 union, said the mayor's office never directly responded to them after the report was released. "We're saying we can save you more than $200 million and they don't even read it!" was Phillips's initial impression.[44] But as negotiations progressed, Phillips and Ramirez felt the mayor's office did take some of the recommendations to heart.

Ultimately union leaders reached an agreement with Emanuel on cost-saving work rule changes, and the threatened 625 layoffs never happened. In October 2011 unions also agreed to work rule changes at the McCormick Place convention center, where union contracts had long been a sticking point (officials said they inhibited Chicago's ability to compete with other cities for lucrative conventions and trade shows). The Chicago Regional Council of Carpenters and Teamsters Local 727 agreed to drop a federal lawsuit challenging 2010 state legislation that undercut union work at trade shows—a battle that had started and festered under Mayor Daley.[45]

"The mayor came in like most wanting to fix things and solve problems; he had set ideas of what he wanted to do," said Ramirez, taking a diplomatic tone a year and a half after the contentious negotiations. "As we dialogued with him he's been able to see our viewpoint."[46]

THE GREAT GARBAGE CHALLENGE

Collecting garbage may not be glamorous, but in Chicago the Department of Streets and Sanitation is an important, almost sacred institution. It has long been known as a bastion of patronage jobs, and it provides a crucial service that if interrupted or carried out poorly would leave residents desperate and furious. "Streets and San" is the city's third largest department, after police and fire, with the Laborers Local 1001 union representing about 1,900 workers.[47]

Longstanding tradition had dictated that aldermen personally oversee garbage collection in their wards, with the idea that their local offices were best equipped to respond to complaints and crises. The stereotypically burly men who man garbage trucks and eat Polish sausages or roast beef sandwiches in classic Chicago diners on their lunch break make good money. When Emanuel took office, a Teamster making $33 an hour would drive each city garbage truck, and a Laborer making $34 an hour would tip the bins into the back of it.[48]

But this two-union, ward-based garbage system was clearly inefficient, as it meant the trucks would follow streets within the strangely shaped, heavily gerrymandered ward boundaries, skipping over some blocks and frequently doubling back on themselves. Under traditional policy the Teamsters driver would pick up his Laborers teammate at a separate location, which meant perhaps a half hour of driving before a single bin was emptied. Chicago's trash pickup costs were considered the highest in the nation, more than 50 percent above most cities.[49] Emanuel campaigned on a promise of instituting a more logical and efficient "grid-based" garbage collection system. Labor leaders generally supported the grid, but they worried what other changes Emanuel had in mind.

Meanwhile, the city had never gotten a comprehensive curbside recycling program off the ground—common practice in many municipalities nationwide—even as boosters dubbed Chicago a nation-leading "green city." Under Mayor Daley, only 241,000 out of 600,000 Chicago households had curbside recycling.[50] Reporters revealed that the city had spent $1 million on 22,000 blue recycling bins, which were being stored in a South Side warehouse because the city had run out of money to implement a wider recycling program.[51] With the publicly run recycling program a shambles, Daley quietly put out a request for proposals seeking to privatize recycling. The Laborers Local 1001 filed actions under labor law trying to block the privatization, but arbiters ruled in the city's favor.[52]

Overwhelmed with budget problems, Daley never did privatize recycling pickup. But even before taking office, Emanuel picked up the baton. He talked about privatizing not only recycling but possibly garbage pickup as a whole. Phillips was dismayed and wondered if his endorsement of Gery Chico during the mayoral race would hurt the union garbagemen going forward.[53]

Emanuel essentially challenged the union sanitation workers to a duel. In an example of "managed competition," union teams employed by the city would compete against two different private contractors in picking up recyclables. The private companies were Waste Management and Metal Management Midwest, which in July 2011 were awarded recycling contracts in a process not subject to

City Council approval.[54] (Waste Management, a politically connected national behemoth, had a much larger contract than Metal Management Midwest.)[55]

The two companies and the city workers were given different sectors of the city in which to pick up recycling. Time would tell who did the work most cheaply and efficiently, and it was implied that the results would determine longer-term recycling contracts and the likelihood of privatizing all garbage pickup. The private companies had promised they could do the work at about half the price of city workers.[56] Union leaders argued that the private companies should be required to pay equivalent wages and benefits, otherwise private contractors could undercut public workers with substandard pay. At the time, Waste Management paid its drivers—also Teamsters members—$25.56 an hour, according to the *Chicago Tribune*, and those drivers worked solo, tipping the bins themselves. By contrast, the city drivers made $33.85 an hour, and the city workers who tipped the bins made $34.37 an hour.[57]

Emanuel's administration made it clear that "managed competition" was a concept that would be carried out in other realms as well, and that union city workers should be prepared to essentially bid on their own jobs in order to prove they could do the work as efficiently as private contractors. Union leaders said they were all for competition, but they wanted to make sure that the playing field was fair and that the indirect but important benefits of city employees were figured into the equation.

Union members worried that the competitions could be a way to justify slashing city jobs, and also a chance to pressure unions for concessions when contracts were negotiated. Basically, they suspected city officials would rig the competitions to make sure the private contractors won. As Bayer told the *Chicago Tribune*, "Competition is supposed to be when you don't know what the result is going to be. ... With these efforts you already know the outcome."[58]

Lou Phillips could be seen as the quintessential Chicago public union member from a quintessential Chicago family of a certain era. He grew up in Bridgeport, the Daley family's neighborhood, with an Italian mother and an Irish father. His mother lived her entire life in the house she was born in, watching as the neighborhood changed from an insular white ethnic enclave where outsiders weren't welcome to a diverse mix of Chinese and Mexican immigrants and artsy hipsters. As adults Phillips and his siblings all lived within blocks of their parents, practically in the shadow of their beloved White Sox ballpark. In his early twenties, Phillips got a city job the way most people did in those days: he went to his alderman and asked for one.[59] The alderman got him a position as a garbageman and "told me to take it for six months until things got better," Phillips remembered. The alderman never offered Phillips anything else, and the young man never pushed the issue.

"I loved the job," Phillips said. It offered the kind of security and solid middle-class wages that allowed him and thousands of other Chicagoans to comfortably

GARBAGE PICKUP BECAME A PROVING GROUND FOR THE VALUE OF PUBLIC
VERSUS PRIVATE WORKERS. PHOTO BY JOHN W. IWANSKY.

raise a family, never worrying where their health care or retirement funds would come from. After being transferred to a far-flung West Side neighborhood, Phillips ran for union business manager in 2005 and won. From then on, instead of spending his days on a truck plying the streets and alleys, he worked in the Laborers' inconspicuous headquarters on Ashland Avenue's "Union Row," in an office decorated with family photos and White Sox memorabilia.

Phillips is a firm believer in unions, and as he saw the job security and power of union members eroding he became increasingly fixated on making sure regular Chicagoans could continue to enjoy a stable job and comfortable living serving the city they loved. He was dedicated to making this happen however necessary, which in his view meant fighting the mayor's proposals when necessary but also working with him and offering public support. Members of more activist unions, including the teachers, would often criticize Phillips for being "in bed" with Emanuel. Phillips shrugged off the insults, saying he was doing what was best for his members. "It's his bat and ball," he said of Emanuel. "As long as I can stay to play another day, I'm happy."[60]

With the recycling pickup competition, Phillips was determined to show the mayor that it was smarter to employ city workers than private contractors. That would mean shaking things up a bit within the city workforce, who hadn't necessarily faced such scrutiny before. "I said to the guys, 'We have to step up our game,'" noted Phillips. With the aid of scores of maps, his own three decades in the business, and the computer acumen of the union's assistant business manager, Phillips and his colleagues devised more efficient routes and other ways their crews could pick up recycling more cheaply. Phillips knew they could not beat the price offered by Waste Management. Echoing a common complaint with privatization, he argued that the huge company's bid would not reflect its true costs and that it would use its vast coffers to absorb any losses on the city contract in hopes of locking in city work for years to come. But if the union workers could cut their costs considerably from past levels, they figured they could keep their jobs.[61]

By the end of 2011, all sides were declaring victory. The city crews had cut their cost per recycling bin from $4.77 to $3.75, doing the work much more efficiently than before.[62] "I think we opened the mayor's eyes," said Phillips. "I showed him I'm a hands-on, no-bullshit-type guy."[63]

Meanwhile, the private contractors said they were meeting their promise of $2.70 a bin. In a press conference at a city fleet garage, Emanuel touted the benefits of competition, saying the real winners were the taxpayers, with a savings of about $1 million in three months.[64] Because of the savings, he said, recycling would be expanded to twenty thousand more households immediately and all households in buildings of four units or less would get recycling pickup by the end of 2013. A year later, recycling pickup was still being done by a mix of city workers and private contractors, a situation that seemed to satisfy all sides.[65]

Jorge Ramirez stressed the reasons beyond cost-per-bin that recycling pickup and garbage collection should stay in-house, including factors not immediately obvious to a number cruncher who has never manned a garbage truck. For one thing, the labor federation president said, keeping recycling public would guarantee that the city would benefit from the resale value of the recyclables. The July 2011 COUPE report estimated the city could earn $3.7 million from selling recyclable materials in 2011.[66] Ramirez also noted that city workers could switch tasks and coordinate with other city agencies more easily than a private contractor could. City garbage trucks can double as snow plows in the winter; in the summer, the workers can do rodent control.

"Cities need people who understand how these departments work and interact," Ramirez said. "And city workers take pride in their city, they know their neighbors, they *are* the city themselves."

THE MILLIONAIRE CLUB

In the standoff over the work rules changes, union leaders had denounced Emanuel's failure to meet with them even as he demanded they agree to significant contractual changes. Emanuel's approach must have been particularly insulting given the close if often testy relationships many union leaders had enjoyed with Mayor Daley. In fact, examining the types of people Emanuel found time to meet with offered a notable contrast between him and his predecessor.

Emanuel was known for packing a lot into his day—a day that typically began with a workout in the pool or gym followed by a quick succession of rapid-fire meetings, public appearances, and decision-making sessions where he never lingered on one topic or stayed in one place for too long. The mayor's work schedule is supposed to be public under freedom of information laws, and the mayor's office typically publishes a brief schedule each day. But the *Chicago Reader* wanted a closer look at how Emanuel spent his time, beyond the official documents that often noted no public events for the day. The weekly alternative newspaper spent months tussling with the mayor's press office to obtain his detailed "in-house" schedules so reporters could map out exactly how Emanuel spent his twelve- to fourteen-hour workdays.[67]

Eventually the *Reader* received Emanuel's in-house schedules for June, July, and August 2011. The documents the paper posted online showed the mayor's day sliced up into blocks of thirty to forty-five minutes, with travel times and distances noted down to the minute and the tenth of a mile. There were meetings with state legislators and aldermen, county officials and top appointees like schools CEO Jean-Claude Brizard and police superintendent Garry McCarthy. There were numerous public announcements of various initiatives and a handful of media interviews and off-the-record talks with *Chicago Tribune* and *Sun-Times* reporters.[68]

Chicago Reader reporters were particularly interested in Emanuel's meetings with private citizens. After analyzing the schedules, they concluded that Emanuel spent a disproportionate amount of his time with a group they dubbed "the Millionaire Club"—very wealthy and powerful people, including those who had donated generously to Emanuel's campaigns. Notables included Larry Fink, CEO of the global money management firm BlackRock; Marc Lasry, billionaire CEO of the Avenue Capital Group hedge fund; and Howard Gottlieb, retired general partner at Glen Eagle Partners. The three had donated $25,000, $50,000, and $100,000, respectively, to Emanuel's mayoral campaign. Emanuel also met with Bruce Rauner, the friend who had helped launch his investment banking career and would become one of his right-hand men in his fight against the Chicago Teachers Union.

"It's a scary set of relationships—those folks don't have much respect for the public sector," said Robert Bruno, a professor in the School of Labor and Employment Relations at the University of Illinois. "At the same time, if you don't have [city] revenue, you can turn to those sources. All of these diffuse sources of institutional power need to be fed."[69]

The *Reader* cited Emanuel's hour-long lunch in late July 2011 with two banking CEOs: Bill Downe of the Bank of Montreal and Mark Furlong of BMO Harris

Bank. "That might not seem like much time," reporters Mick Dumke and Ben Joravsky wrote. "But it amounted to one of the longest meetings of the week in the
dusk-to-dawn schedule of the mayor who can't sit still. In fact, Downe and Furlong
are the kind of guys Mayor Emanuel often makes time for: rich, influential, and frequently at odds with organized labor and other progressive groups that historically
made up the base of Emanuel's Democratic Party."[70]

Emanuel's schedules also included frequent meetings with political operatives,
top federal officials, and elected officeholders from other states. He hosted such visitors in Chicago and also made frequent trips to Washington, DC. On balance,
Emanuel's deep connections with politicos in the nation's capital and in other states
was likely a good thing for Chicago, indicating his power to bring federal funding and
attention to the city's needs and issues. Likewise the mayor's connections with the
very wealthy could lead to private investment and philanthropic dollars to nurture
important community programs and create jobs and opportunities in Chicago.

But as the *Reader* pointed out, Emanuel's meeting schedules underscored a complaint that became common among regular citizens and community leaders even in
the mayor's first few months in office: that he was focused primarily on the wealthy
and powerful, and devoted too little attention or time to the needs and opinions of
the majority of Chicagoans who were not wealthy or politically connected.

"Daley was a lunch-bucket Democrat," said one elected official who knew both
mayors well.[71] "Daley made decisions off his gut, he knew the streets, he knew the drivers of the garbage trucks, he knew the tree trimmers, he knew their parents. Rahm has
no clue who the drivers are, and he doesn't care. You ask Rahm to describe a 'T alley' or
a 'permeable alley,' and he has no idea. But you ask him who the head of the Chicago
Mercantile Exchange is, and he'll have him on speed dial. The concern is who he listens
to. Daley knew what it meant to have lunch with workers. Rahm doesn't."

By the time Emanuel took office, political scientist Dick Simpson had spent al-
most four decades studying Chicago politics from the inside and the outside.
Simpson is an author and political science professor at the University of Illinois at
Chicago; he had served two terms as an aldermen; and he had advised mayors
Harold Washington and Jane Byrne.[72] Simpson had become well known for his
political acumen and his advocacy on issues including universal health care, civil
rights, government transparency, and services for the needy. He said the goals
Emanuel laid out in his inaugural address were laudable ones but questioned the
efficacy of Emanuel's private-sector-centric approach.[73]

"What he articulates constantly is some vision about good schools, a safe city
where everyone has jobs with good pay," said Simpson. "But he sets out to do that
differently than Harold Washington did with affirmative action or Richard M.
Daley did with patronage.... What Rahm doesn't do is consult with people. He's
like an effective CEO with a new program every day, but he is short on democ-

racy. He doesn't know how to mobilize the public so they'll accept the decision. This is at the heart of a problem of the Emanuel administration."[74]

Emanuel's apparent distaste for engaging with a critical public would be put on display during a Chicago tradition: meetings around the proposed budget. The struggle to find $30 million in cuts earlier that summer had not been pretty, so addressing a 2012 budget deficit more than twenty times greater would be quite a drama.

"THE FREE RIDE IS OVER"

For years the process had been roughly the same: in the late summer or early fall the Chicago mayor announced the proposed budget for the coming year; public hearings were held in the evenings in several parts of the city; some changes were made based on public and aldermanic feedback; and then the City Council voted to approve the budget. When Emanuel took office the city was facing a $637 million deficit.[75] It was also facing an unfunded pension liability of $26.8 billion.[76]

Emanuel attacked the problem with trademark efficiency, and proposed a 2012 budget that included deep service cuts, numerous layoffs, and significantly increased fees and fines. The mayor's press office said the proposed budget would shrink the deficit by $417 million, in part through savings "realized by cutting spending, increasing efficiencies, and additional innovations or government reforms."[77]

The budget called for 517 layoffs of city workers and the elimination of more than two thousand vacant positions. It also noted a new infrastructure initiative slated to create eighteen thousand jobs in ten years, but that promise did little to alleviate the anxiety caused by immediately looming cuts.[78]

The city's 911 emergency response office, the public libraries, and health and social services would take major hits. Police and fire dispatchers and radio technicians for the emergency office would lose their jobs, and several police district stations would be closed. The library system would suffer $10 million in cuts and about three hundred layoffs, including about sixty librarians and all the pages responsible for reshelving books. As many as two hundred positions would be cut among social service staffers who dealt with domestic violence victims, the elderly, and at-risk youth.[79]

There would be no property tax or sales tax increases in the 2012 budget.[80] But residents would face increased fees for standard things like vehicle stickers and water service, and increased fines for a range of infractions were projected to bring in $26 million.[81] In his budget address Emanuel framed the fines as demanding "greater accountability by cracking down on those who put our communities at risk."[82] He continued:

> We all share the goal of collecting what's owed to us. The more we collect, the less we have to cut. So, with this budget, we are sending an important message: To the banks who hold property and aren't keeping it up; to city employees who owe millions in

parking fines and water bills; to people advertising on billboards that haven't been paid for; to suburbs not paying the City for water it provides; to those who've skipped out on city ambulance fees; and to every nonprofit that has received free water. To everyone who has not paid their fair share: Ladies and gentlemen—the free ride is over![83]

The idea that the proposed new fines would target people causing a hazard for their neighbors or getting a "free ride" was in many cases questionable. In general, flat fees and fines disproportionately impact lower-income people. And lower-income people in certain neighborhoods could be more susceptible to the increased fines Emanuel proposed—for example, people without a garage or the money to pay for a parking spot would be more likely to get parking-related tickets. And those without the time or money to take care of their yard could be penalized for uncut weeds. Given cultural differences and varying levels of police scrutiny in different neighborhoods, lower-income African Americans and Latinos could also be more likely to be fined for loud radios, spray-paint, storing things in a yard, or drag-racing.

Union analysts figured there would be racial inequity in the effects of the proposed job cuts, too. This would add insult to injury, or perhaps injury to insult, given that African American and Latino aldermen and community leaders were already upset with Emanuel for disproportionately appointing white people to his cabinet. Soon after Emanuel's inauguration, aldermen began complaining about the lack of African Americans in top city positions, especially considering Emanuel had gotten 59 percent of the African American vote.[84] Emanuel picked white men to head the Fire Department, Police Department, and Office of Emergency Management. A *Sun-Times* investigation later revealed that of his top thirty appointees, only five were African American and three Latino, while white appointees were responsible for almost 80 percent of City Hall's operating budget.[85] This was especially grating in a city where neither African Americans, Latinos, nor whites made up more than a third of the population. Emanuel stressed that he appointed African Americans to head the city's three powerful "sister agencies"—the schools, Chicago Housing Authority, and the City Colleges. He said he was looking for a "diversity of experience," apparently as opposed to ethnic diversity, in his appointees. African American leaders countered that schools chief Brizard was Haitian and the housing chief had been recruited from outside the city, indicating a lack of respect for homegrown African American leadership.[86]

BOOS FOR THE BUDGET

As part of his stated commitment to transparency, Emanuel launched a new city budget website, www.chicagobudget.org, where residents could offer their own ideas on cutting costs. Within a week the site got 1,800 submissions.[87]

On August 29, 2011, about seven hundred people crowded into Kennedy-King City College for Emanuel's first community hearing on the proposed budget. The college is in the South Side Englewood neighborhood, which had become nationally infamous for shootings, gang violence, foreclosed homes, high rates of lead poisoning, and other problems. The auditorium filled up and an overflow room opened. During Mayor Daley's tenure, anyone who attended a budget hearing was allowed to line up behind microphones and offer a brief statement. Emanuel's office tweaked the format, asking attendees to submit questions on note cards and then choosing which ones to read. When a note card was selected, the person who had written it was invited to step up to a microphone and recite the question.

Matt Ginsberg-Jaeckle from the Mental Health Movement submitted a question about Emanuel's vision for public health. When he got to the microphone, he politely requested to ask a follow-up question. In a calm voice that belied the highly charged topic, he asked, "I wonder where you got the idea it would be a good idea to privatize health services?"[88]

Ginsberg-Jaeckle also asked a question about how street violence—one of Emanuel's top priorities—might be linked to a dearth of mental health services. As he remembered it, Emanuel replied that he took mental health concerns seriously, and that contracting health services out made sense when private providers could offer equivalent care more cheaply.[89] Ginsberg-Jaeckle's questions brought up sore subjects, and the tone of the hearing quickly built into a crescendo of discontent.

Along with a crowd from the Mental Health Movement, the audience included numerous members of SEIU Local 73—most notably traffic control aides facing layoffs.[90] Laid-off traffic aide Maria Randazzo asked in a steady, tired yet determined voice: "I don't have insurance, I don't have money to pay my bills, how can you answer that?" She interrupted Emanuel as he started to stammer out a reply. "I don't think you understand," she said, "I'm not sure you heard me."[91]

Emanuel's retort sounded patronizing: "There's parts of your union leadership, my dear friend, that were involved in conversation, so to act like they weren't involved or discussed, is not level."[92]

With seemingly each new question, the crowd erupted in cheers for the citizens and boos for the mayor. "I'm responsible to the city taxpayers and the city residents," explained Emanuel, speaking in a slow voice and gesturing as if to calm a roomful of kindergarteners.[93] He noted that more job losses would be coming, and he pointed out that aldermen were taking a 10 percent pay cut and members of various city commissions and boards would take pay cuts as well, for a total savings of about $314,000.[94]

"We have real changes, real reforms, they're going to hit close to home. I don't have a problem with that," Emanuel said. "We've been doing some smoke and mirrors on the budget and avoided taking control of our own future as a city," he continued. "And we have to take control of our future. That moment of reckoning [a long dramatic pause] is here."[95]

READ OUR LIPS

Two days later, union workers headed to Malcolm X City College on the West Side for the second community budget hearing. Groups of SEIU Local 73 members arrived wearing purple T-shirts and holding big cardboard lips painted purple and pink, saying, "Read our lips. Let us work." It was a show of solidarity with the seventy-two union traffic control aides laid off to save $2.3 million.[96] The lips were confiscated at the door, so the union members were already agitated as they got inside. The sports arena quickly filled up, and several hundred people were channeled into an overflow room.[97]

For the mayor, the second budget hearing didn't go any better than the first. Boos from the audience were so loud that Emanuel had to wave his arms and ask people to quiet down so schools CEO Jean-Claude Brizard and police superintendent Garry McCarthy could speak.[98] "I want ideas, not insults," Emanuel told the restive crowd. "Insults don't close a $637 million deficit."[99]

Despite the public outcry, Emanuel surely had no doubt his budget would pass the City Council. In his first six months in office, there were only five votes where any alderman voted against his wishes—that's out of fifteen to twenty votes per month.[100] Mayor Daley saw nineteen divided votes for the same period in 2010, according to political scientist Dick Simpson, who said, "It's still a rubber-stamp council."[101]

Some aldermen did raise concerns about the 2012 budget proposal. Twenty-eight of them signed a letter opposing the library cuts. Robert Fioretti said the city would suffer in the long term if citizens were hammered with "nickel-and-dime increases" to close the budget hole. Nick Sposato, a former firefighter, worried about potential tragedies and lawsuits because of planned cuts in the 911 call center that would leave remaining employees overstretched.[102] The week before the final budget vote, Emanuel agreed to some amendments: he restored $3.3 million in library funding and about one hundred library jobs, returned $1 million in funding for graffiti-removal and weed-cutting services, and scaled back his demand that nonprofit institutions start paying full price for their water.[103]

When the full council voted on the budget on November 16, 2011, it passed unanimously. Numerous aldermen rose to make speeches praising the budget, the mayor, and the tough choices the council had made. They spoke of the necessity of "spreading the pain" and avoiding the city's previous tendency to "kick the can down the road."[104] "We have a bright future, we have a strong future, this budget does not run away from that, it shapes it," Emanuel said after the vote.[105]

PEOPLE'S LIBRARIES

Beginning in 2012, city libraries were closed on Mondays following a budget cut that reduced the total weekly hours from forty-eight to forty and put almost two hundred library staff out of work. This came on top of steep reductions in library hours, services, and staffing during the previous Daley administration. Mary Dempsey, the longtime and highly respected commissioner of the library system, resigned in January 2012, shortly after the cuts took effect. "She was apparently unwilling to preside over the dismantling of a library system she helped to build," wrote *Sun-Times* City Hall reporter Fran Spielman. Dempsey felt Emanuel had treated her and the whole library system with "contempt"; Emanuel had railed at her for talking to aldermen about the cuts and barred her from talking to reporters, Spielman reported.[106]

Thirty-year-old library page Sara Doe was among those laid off at the end of 2011. She had gotten her job in 2007, and immediately fell in love with the work. It wasn't particularly well paying or challenging—she earned $11.18 an hour without benefits for shelving books, directing customers, and other basic tasks. But she relished the interaction with residents and she had adored libraries since she was a kid. Her mother worked in a city library, and growing up Doe spent many happy hours there helping stamp due dates in books.[107]

After losing her job, Doe applied for other positions—"anything and everything," including food service at Wrigley Field—but she had no luck. She was qualified for disability payments and applied for unemployment, but she said she would rather be working at the library. "It's not just a job, it's something I really enjoyed," she said a few weeks after being laid off. "Even though it was low-status, I felt really good and made some good money.... Now I feel like I'm work-sick. I'm one of those people who like to work their butts off."[108]

Like most Chicago library staff, Doe was a member of AFSCME Council 31. The union fought hard against the library cuts as soon as Emanuel's proposed budget was announced. The day before the vote, hundreds of people rallied outside the mayor's office and delivered a petition with four thousand signatures opposing library cuts.[109] The union activism along with outcry from aldermen and regular residents ultimately persuaded the mayor to reduce the plan for roughly 350 layoffs by about half.

That didn't mollify AFSCME. After the cuts took effect the union organized "people's library hours" outside the shuttered libraries on Mondays. Among the attendees was Natasha Nicholes. Far from being a knee-jerk activist or union militant, she is a cheery, vivacious African American mother whose widely read blog, *Houseful of Nicholes,* normally focused on her loving relationship with her husband and the accomplishments and foibles of their adorable children. As a child in Chicago, Nicholes had spent almost every Saturday at the library with her younger sister. She had made the local library a second home for her four children, and because she homeschooled them the resources and social outlet were particularly important. She said her children were in tears upon hearing about the library cuts, and she was afraid that with the staff reduction her preschooler's beloved story hour would be axed. She took to her blog to demand the city restore the services. "I won't let this pass without saying something, especially since libraries played such a large role in my growing up," Nicholes said.[110]

AFSCME Council 31 spokesman Anders Lindall noted that as with teachers and nurses, Chicagoans like Nicholes felt much loyalty to and connection with their local library staff. And the feeling was mutual.[111] "People don't give their working lives to public service to get rich," Lindall said. "Library employees love their communities, their patrons and the role of their libraries as hubs of learning, research, culture, community, and much more."

Like other layoffs resulting from city budget cuts, the library cuts disproportionately impacted minorities and women. Lindall said 72 percent of the staff initially laid off were women and 77 percent were people of color, including seventy-eight African Americans and forty Latinos. The reduction in services and hours surely hit harder in low-income, minority neighborhoods, where people rely more heavily on public libraries as places where they can use the Internet to look for jobs and keep in touch with family, do research or homework, and even find a peaceful haven from dangerous streets and substandard housing conditions.

"Any reduction in hours is a barrier to access," said Lindall. "Weekday morning hours are especially popular with families and caregivers for preschool-aged children, seniors, shift workers, and the unemployed. Monday mornings are the most crucial time for people looking for work, as new job postings come out in the Sunday paper. Unemployed folks line up at the branches waiting for the libraries to open on Monday morning."[112]

Emanuel eventually restored service on Monday afternoons at libraries and hired back sixty-five laid-off workers, balancing the move in part by making other cuts at the main downtown library. The move was described as an end run around the union: by hiring back part-time clerks and other nonlibrarian staff, the mayor was able to avoid negotiating with AFSCME. "They were notified I was going to take independent action," Emanuel told the *Chicago Tribune*. AFSCME Council 31 executive director Henry Bayer countered that he knew nothing of the plan and hadn't heard from the mayor in more than a week.[113]

One alderman said he resented the way Emanuel dealt with the library situation. "He insisted we need to make these cuts, then in mid-January he polled and found that middle-class white women with kids were protesting," so he "walked back" his planned cuts and looked like a good guy in the process. "He asks [the aldermen] to do tough things, then he pats himself on the back for restoring part of the cuts that were made. He pushes the envelope to see how far he can go, then he pulls back."[114]

AFSCME also represented the staff of the mental health clinics that were being closed down, and members of the Mental Health Movement joined AF-

CITY WORKERS PROTESTED BRUTAL CUTS IN MAYOR EMANUEL'S INAUGURAL
BUDGET. PHOTO BY BARTOSZ BRZEZINSKI.

SCME members in protesting and chanting during a meeting Emanuel held at a South Side library about the library cuts. Margaret Sullivan, a patient at one of the mental health clinics and a former university English professor, remembered members of the group smuggling picket signs into the library under their coats. "I have to do things like interrupt, or else we'll never be heard," she explained. "We crept up, brought out the posters, and started chanting, 'Talk to us!'" She said she remembered Emanuel commenting, "I thought this was about the libraries, but no, it's about the nuts."[115]

During a late January 2012 "Facebook town hall meeting" focused on education, Emanuel answered a question about the library cuts with a dig at the union: "I had to work something out with AFSCME, the union, after six weeks of discussion that went nowhere because they were trying to use the libraries to achieve other things in the budget . . . the libraries are not for anybody but our children and our residents . . . they are not the—I don't want to say playground—but they are not for the control of an individual element of our city."

It was a theme Emanuel would hone during his battle with the teachers union nine months later: unions were manipulative special interest groups putting their goals ahead of the greater good, and he was a public servant fighting to protect regular residents from their machinations. Union leaders would likely see a similar drama playing out with the roles reversed: union members representing and constituting the general public, fighting to protect public goods and services from the mayor's bottom-line approach. In any face-off between government and public sector unions, there is bound to be self-interest, politics, and ulterior motives on both sides. But within months of taking office, Emanuel had made a serious error—pundits said—in alienating organized labor, casting them as the enemy rather than playing ball.

"Rahm lost the support of unions except for the construction trades that depend on him for jobs," noted Simpson. "He destroyed the coalition with unions that the Daleys had built. He undermined a tradition."[116]

THE HISTORIC WOODLAWN MENTAL HEALTH CLINIC BECAME THE SITE OF A
SHOWDOWN OVER THE FUTURE OF PUBLIC MENTAL HEALTH SERVICES. PHOTO
BY SARAH JANE RHEE.

8
THE MENTAL HEALTH MOVEMENT

CLOSING CLINICS

The Woodlawn Mental Health Clinic was opened in 1962 as a joint project between the city and the University of Chicago in the impoverished, violence-plagued, largely African American neighborhood that borders Hyde Park. The contrast between the two neighborhoods could hardly be more striking. The University of Chicago campus in Hyde Park features soaring Gothic stone towers, ivy-covered walls, lovely gardens. Wide leafy streets are lined with quaint court-yard apartment buildings and beautiful stately homes, including President Obama's residence. Woodlawn, by contrast, is peppered with vacant lots, broken-down and boarded-up buildings, and corners where jobless young men loiter. Gunshots and other signs of violence are a daily occurrence.

The Woodlawn clinic was founded by three Yale psychiatrists devoted to the idea that a holistic, community-centered approach is crucial to not only healing but preventing mental health crises. As reporter Steve Bogira explained in the academic journal *Health Affairs*, local residents were involved with shaping the Wood-lawn clinic from early on and successfully pushed the medical staff to increase their focus on prevention and community participation, including an early intervention program working with young children, their families, and teachers.[1]

By the 1970s Chicago had twenty-two public mental health centers, which provided care to thousands of residents and jobs to scores of counselors, therapists, clerks, and other staffers. These were often jobs awarded through the Chicago patronage system, which was known as corrupt but also an important source of stable employment for residents of minority, working-class neighborhoods.[2]

In the 1980s President Ronald Reagan slashed federal funding for mental health services, and at clinics around the country the emphasis on prevention fell by the wayside, forcing providers to prioritize those with chronic and severe mental health issues.[3]

Through the ensuing decades the Chicago public mental health clinics soldiered on, supported by state and city funds. Clinics closed and consolidated along the way. By 2008 there were twelve—three on the North Side, one on the Near Southwest Side, and eight on the sprawling, largely impoverished South and Southwest Sides.[4] In January 2009 the Daley administration announced that up to five clinics would have to be closed because of budget shortfalls.[5]

Four of the five clinics singled out for closure were on the South Side, including the one in Woodlawn.[6] Since 2004 a grassroots group of Woodlawn residents, university staff, students, and other supporters had been running energetic, vocal campaigns on neighborhood issues, including the loss of affordable and subsidized housing—a problem linked to the university's expansion, private development, and poor management of affordable housing complexes. They also focused on health issues, including changes in the University of Chicago's health system that, they said, were making it less accessible to the poor. The group called itself Southside Together Organizing for Power, or STOP. Members launched several tenant organizations at embattled housing developments and an affiliated neighborhood youth organization called Fearless Leading by Youth. FLY's many creative protests included delivering underwear to the county juvenile detention facility in Chicago (young people incarcerated there complained of horrible living conditions, including a lack of clean underwear).[7]

STOP and FLY leaders realized that the closing of the Woodlawn clinic would pose a serious threat to the well-being of their community. The group's website said, "If we did not fight to save the services that make the community stable, then we might as well throw in the towel on our campaign against housing displacement." STOP joined up with patients at the clinics (whom the group refers to as "consumers") and embarked on a citywide Mental Health Movement campaign to preserve the clinics.[8]

The clinics were scheduled to close in April 2009, coinciding with a visit by representatives of the International Olympic Committee, part of the city's effort to host the 2016 Olympic Games. While Mayor Daley and other officials were trying to put the city's best face forward for the Olympic visitors, the Mental Health Movement staged a sit-in. The *Chi-Town Daily News* revealed that glitches with a new city computer system had contributed significantly to the clinics' funding crisis—the city had failed to properly bill the state for $1.2 million worth of reimbursement.[9] The clinics were shuttered in April—furniture tossed out, doors locked—but they were reopened a few months later thanks to an influx of federal stimulus dollars.[10]

In August 2009, the clinics were put back on the chopping block.[11] At a community budget hearing, Mental Health Movement member Carol Smith confronted Daley about the city billing error that contributed to the debacle, asking, "Why should people who have mental health problems suffer because the administration screwed up?"[12]

NBC Chicago blogger Steve Rhodes described a "remarkable scene in which a citizen confronted the city's powerful leader and made him look like a weak, weaselly child. It was a moment that would kill lesser political careers. . . . Daley sat silent, mouth closed with eyes straight ahead. He would not answer."[13] Eventually he promised that the clinics would stay open, though with lower staffing levels than before.[14]

Though the battle to save the clinics had apparently been won for the time being, clinic consumers and STOP leaders realized that the future of city mental health services would continue to be precarious.

A NEW MAYOR, A NEW BATTLE

When Emanuel announced his proposed budget for 2012, Mental Health Movement members were outraged but not shocked at the proposal to close six of the city's twelve mental health clinics, including the one in Woodlawn. The other facilities to be closed were in Auburn Gresham, not far from Woodlawn; Back of the Yards, a largely Latino immigrant neighborhood on the Southwest Side; Beverly Morgan Park, further southwest; the Northwest Side Logan Square neighborhood, serving largely Latino and African American patients; and Rogers Park, serving a diverse community on the far North Side.

The Emanuel administration said the city would save between $2 million and $3 million annually by closing the clinics. The plan was referred to as "consolidation," because patients would be directed to the remaining clinics or private clinics that would receive a total of $500,000 from the city to augment their federal funding.[15]

"These changes allow us to increase our psychiatry services and improve efficiency at our sites," said an overview of the plan on the city's website.[16] Staff would monitor transitions for individual patients for ninety days after the closings, the city promised, and would offer subsidies for transportation to the remaining clinics.

Cook County sheriff Tom Dart, who had briefly competed with Emanuel in the mayoral race, stridently opposed the plan. He told the Chicago News Cooperative that the county jail had already "become the largest mental health provider in the state of Illinois." He predicted the clinic closings would have "direct consequences for us in my general jail population," and he noted that jailing mentally ill people often costs taxpayers two to three times more than the typical cost of $143 per inmate per day. "And then there's the humane side of it," he said. "Not treating people with mental illness is bad enough, but treating them like criminals? Please, what have we become?"[17]

Clinic supporters also argued that closures would disproportionately affect people of color. A report by the Mental Health Movement and AFSCME Council

31 found that 2,549 out of the 5,337 city residents listed as clinic patients would see their clinic closed. The customers at the clinics slated for closure were 61 percent African American and 17 percent Latino, and many of them lacked access to sufficient health care, according to the report. The report also cited state and national health data in arguing that even without the closures there was already a vast unmet need for mental health services, especially among low-income people. [18]

On November 15, 2011, Mental Health Movement members held a ten-hour sit-in outside Emanuel's office in City Hall. "We were reading Shakespeare sonnets, chatting, we got to know everything and anything about each other," remembered clinic consumer Margaret Sullivan. "We were laying around, sprawled out with no shame, fighting over the last cough drop. And we're wearing hospital gowns with a sign that says 'Rahm's Psych Ward.'"[19] They left around 10:30 p.m., because guards had blocked access to the bathrooms and water fountains, and there were several diabetics in the group who needed to take medication.

The next day the City Council passed the proposed budget unanimously, including the mental health clinic closings.[20]

"ERIC'S OLD LADIES"

For clients of the Beverly Morgan Park Mental Health Center, about nine miles southwest of the Woodlawn Mental Health Clinic, the modest building was an oasis in a hectic and sometimes terrifying world, a place they could drop in to see friendly and sympathetic faces and talk to therapists they knew and trusted. Margaret Sullivan was one of those people.

Sullivan had earned a doctorate in literature from the University of California at Los Angeles in 1993, and she had taught college English. Her thesis, titled *From Queens to Housewives to Richardson's Pamela*, explored the domestication of women in medieval times.[21] Sullivan had been plagued by mental illness throughout her life. She once suffered a bipolar episode that left her so despondent she spent two years barely leaving her home. She was on the verge of suicide when a friend persuaded her to visit the nearby Beverly Morgan Park clinic. That's where she met therapist Eric Lindquist and a group of fellow patients who would become closer than family.

"I'm manic depressive, I see black and white, I felt like if the world doesn't want me alive, then fine," said Sullivan, a fifty-eight-year-old with bright blue eyes, freckles, bouncy shoulder-length red hair, and biting quick wit, which she warns gets even sharper when she's changing her meds. "Eric talked me into living another week. He taught me how to stay alive, he told me you go out into the community. He said, 'You'll feel a lot less helpless if you do something.'"

Lindquist persuaded Sullivan to start volunteering with special-needs kids and tutoring at a home for girls, activities that made all the difference in bringing her back to the world of the living. "I told him he got me off my suicide plane, he made me throw away my Dramamine."

Jeanette Hansen, another patient of Lindquist's at the Beverly Morgan Park clinic, is one of Sullivan's best friends. Short of stature and known for her beatnik fashion sense, Hansen had studied art at a college in London for several years in the 1970s and still practices ceramics and other disciplines. She was diagnosed with mental illness at age fifteen, but had always been determined to overcome it. As a youth she was so shy she couldn't look someone in the eye without blushing, so she forced herself to conquer her fear, studiously making eye contact even if she turned crimson. "I knew I couldn't live like that," she said.[22]

Hansen got a job checking parking meters through the Mayor's Office for People with Disabilities, under Mayor Daley. She was raised Republican but developed a loyalty to Daley because of her job, even as he tried to close mental health clinics. Sullivan, meanwhile, had never been a fan of Daley until Emanuel took over and she saw the contrasts. "It used to be I would never say a kind word about Daley. Now I love him like a father!" she said with a laugh.

Sullivan and Hansen were both very close to Helen Morley, the woman who rushed Emanuel at Chicago's 175th birthday party warning that if the Beverly Morgan Park clinic closed, she would die. They called themselves "Eric's Old Ladies." They described Lindquist as a tirelessly dedicated and caring worker, who took their phone calls at any time of day or night and moved from his North Side home to the Far Southwest Side—"across the alley" from the clinic—so he could more easily stay late into the evening meeting with patients.

When Sullivan heard in 2009 that the Beverly Morgan Park clinic would be closed, she was devastated and terrified. But Lindquist persuaded her and other distraught patients to channel their anger and fear into action. "Eric's Ladies are the activists," said Sullivan proudly. They hooked up with the Mental Health Movement and became veterans of sit-ins and protests. Sullivan delighted in making up ditties and derogatory nicknames for the mayor. To the tune of a religious hymn, she liked to sing:

Oh go on, Emanu-El,
Do not any more of our assets sell.
You don't come from our part of town;
We don't need any Wilmette boys around.

Sullivan grew up in the heart of Chicago's South Side, attending Fenger Academy High School, in a neighborhood then home to many middle-class and working-class white ethnic families. "People are so afraid of the mayor, but what can he do, take away my Fenger diploma?" she asked. A tall, powerfully built woman, she liked to mock Emanuel's height, calling him a "malicious midget." And she got a kick out of watching the mayor dodge confrontations with the Mental Health

Movement activists, including at the Chicago birthday party where Morley approached him.

"You can't catch this guy," she said. "I emailed him one time and asked, 'Why are you afraid of a bunch of crazy people?' Taxpayers are paying for all his police and bodyguards and decoy Humvees, and most of us are either old ladies, university students, or loonies."

CHUY CAMPUZANO FOUND HIS CALLING AS AN ACTIVIST THROUGH THE MENTAL HEALTH MOVEMENT. PHOTO BY KARI LYDERSEN.

CHUY CAMPUZANO

The sit-in before the budget vote is where Eric's Old Ladies bonded with Jesus "Chuy" Campuzano, an energetic young activist who would become a central part of the Mental Health Movement.

Campuzano grew up in Southeast Chicago, a once-vibrant neighborhood in the shadow of the city's famous steel mills. After the mills closed the neighborhood deteriorated: slumping vacant buildings and weedy lots mixed with a few remnants of industry. Campuzano had always been gregarious and friendly, and not afraid to speak his mind. At Washington High School, on the Far South Side, he led a student walkout to protest plans to close the swimming pool.

But in high school Campuzano also struggled with depression and despair. He considered ending his life, and he says that if it weren't for caring and dedicated school social workers, he wouldn't be alive today. After graduating in 2000, he continued living with his parents and did work with his church.

In late summer 2011 Campuzano kept hearing about the Occupy movement on the news, and he became curious about the way the group was often vilified and mocked. "I had to check this out for myself," he said. Once he got involved with a few Occupy Chicago actions, he decided he had found his "true calling" in activism and "fighting injustice." Campuzano realized he had always been a born community leader, going at least back to that walkout over the swimming pool. He dove head first into the Chicago activism scene, jumping at the chance to learn about any new group or political event. Through other Occupiers, he found out about the City Hall sit-in organized by the Mental Health Movement.

"I was like, 'What the hell is a sit-in?' I went there and saw for the first time the level of energy I was looking for," he remembered.[23] "At the time I was going to a therapist about mental issues—I was like, 'This ties in with me—what else can I do but fight for these people!'"

Campuzano had already decided he was not a fan of Chicago's new mayor, and the Mental Health Movement quickly cemented his views. "I think he needs to go back to Washington," he said. "We need a mayor who's going to listen to the people, not his pockets. I see the mayor as a greedy person who just thinks about money and not the people."

Campuzano also became active with STOP; the group sent him to a community organizer training hosted by the Midwest Academy, which he described as a transformative experience. He also joined the Chicago Anti-Eviction Campaign, which had much overlap with the Mental Health Movement. He even spent two months living inside a foreclosed home in Woodlawn—to make a statement about the inhumanity of foreclosures and also to prove to himself that he could survive in substandard conditions, depending on community solidarity.

"We're like a family," he said of STOP and the Mental Health Movement. "We're from different backgrounds, but we're all fighting for a cause. They've invested in me, and I'm there for them."

HELEN MORLEY

In December 2011, the Mental Health Movement visited City Hall to do some Christmas caroling. As aldermen filed into the chambers, a group of activists sang popular tunes with lyrics revised to invoke the mental health clinics.[24]

Helen Morley took the floor, wearing a colorful gauzy scarf, overcoat, and big fuzzy black hat. She waved a piece of paper as she expounded in her scratchy voice about the crisis facing her and other patients.[25] "I'll be a hell of a disaster and a mess if they take [the Beverly Morgan Park clinic] away," Morley told reporters and the other protesters. "People look at us on the street like we're nuts,

HELEN MORLEY'S CRY BECAME LEGENDARY WITHIN THE MENTAL HEALTH COMMUNITY: "IF YOU CLOSE MY CLINIC, I WILL DIE!" PHOTO BY ALLEN MCNAIR.

we're crazy, we don't know what the hell we're doing, just put us in a closet some-where, put us in a corner."

Morley grew up in a close-knit Chicago family challenged by health and men-tal health issues. Her mother relied on Social Security disability benefits and wel-fare, as Morley's close friend and sometimes boyfriend Allen McNair remembered. "Her mother was illiterate, so Helen was always helping her navigate the social service system. Helen was raised as an advocate," McNair said. Morley had also struggled with serious bipolar disorder throughout her life, and relied on govern-ment assistance to survive while keeping busy in her self-proclaimed role as advo-cate for the less fortunate.

"She just wanted something better for herself and other people, she couldn't un-derstand why things couldn't be different," said McNair, an artist and poet who suf-fers from bipolar disorder himself. As he described in an essay called "This Is What a Hero Looks Like—Remembering Helen Morley," McNair met Morley in 1985 at a mental health clinic they both attended on the Northwest Side, shortly after she'd had surgery on her left foot.

"I remember fondly that she would go everywhere wearing that bulky plaster cast. It would not stop her at all," he wrote in his essay, a rambling, poignant reminiscence with perceptive insights mingled with mundane details. "Though she was not what I would call a looker, I admired her fortitude so much that I wanted to know her well. I might even say that seeing her on crutches made me fall instantly in love with her."[26]

McNair and Morley became close friends, even soul mates. He once had a powerful dream about a woman named "A'maresh," a being from another planet who died of a mysterious illness even as they were falling in love. He decided "Helen was my A'maresh" and that he was destined to marry her. But Morley didn't believe in marriage, and she clung to affection for Angel, an emotionally fragile re-covering addict and former boyfriend she'd met at the Northwest Side clinic. Mc-Nair dated a woman named Maria, who was jealous of Morley.

The two continued a largely platonic but intense partnership. They watched TV and ate pizza together. Morley went to Baha'i devotional services with Mc-Nair; even though she considered herself Lutheran, she appreciated tolerant faiths and his involvement with the Baha'i. "She especially liked the Baha'i rule about not gossiping," McNair remembered. "She felt comfortable with them, she sensed they didn't judge her."

When Morley fled one city housing authority apartment traumatized by an in-festation of bedbugs, McNair helped her find a new apartment. Then she per-suaded him to move in nearby. McNair put up with Morley's insistence on constantly playing country and western music on the radio, and she put up with his hobby of drawing "scantily clad women," as he described it, in magic marker.

The two were drawn even closer together by deaths in their families. Morley

lost her mother and brother to illness.
She told McNair's family members that
along with one sister, McNair was the
only family she had left. Morley .was
there for McNair when his beloved
twenty-year-old calico cat Kit Kat was
put to sleep. And she joined McNair at
the 2010 funeral for his brother Roger.
McNair drew a portrait of Morley based
on a photograph from Roger's memorial
gathering, taken on a warm day in a
backyard. The photo captured Morley's
signature and contradictory auras of vul-
nerability and feistiness. Her face bore an
expression of loneliness, confusion, and
even fear. Yet her stance was that of a
fighter: a fist clenched, feet set stolidly
apart, her posture implying a readiness to
meet any threat or challenge. McNair's
portrait transformed Morley's tight-
lipped frown into an easy red smile. He
added a hint of feminine grace to her
pugilistic pose and colored her eyes, hat
band, and dress the same cheerful turquoise.

ALLEN MCNAIR'S PORTRAIT OF
HELEN MORLEY. COURTESY OF
ALLEN MCNAIR.

McNair was traumatized by hearing his parents constantly argue as a child, and he tried to avoid confrontation at all costs. Morley, by contrast, never shied away from a fight. McNair was sometimes the target of her ire, including when he failed to repay $30 he owed her—she filed a lawsuit in small claims court and pestered him so much that he sought a restraining order. "Helen was a warm and fiery person all of her life," McNair wrote. "She would plainly speak her mind at times that made me cringe."

In 1995, Morley contacted Access Living, a progressive, outspoken disability rights group known for brave direct actions and concrete victories including forcing the city to increase accessibility of public transportation. Morley hoped Access Living could help her with problems in her public housing unit. Among her various battles was one to get a new bed during the bedbug infestation, as Jeanette Hansen remembered it. Hansen said that housing authority maintenance staff removed Morley's bed but failed to bring her another, so Morley raised hell during the day and slept in a chair at night.

"She was mentally ill and she knew it, but she knew her rights," said Hansen, some months after Morley's death. "Boy, did she!" chimed in Margaret Sullivan.[27]

Beto Barrera, an organizing director at Access Living and a veteran of struggles for Chicano rights and other issues in Chicago, recognized Morley's tenacity and recruited her to lobby elected officials and otherwise join Access Living's campaigns.

"It was easy to label Helen as wholesome and benign," said a tribute on Access Living's website. "However, on the inside, she was full of ardent passion for a cause she knew affected so many more than just herself.... Helen was also a constant presence at sit-in and sleep over protests. When others tired or got bored, she was relentless, sitting as long as it took to get her point across."[28]

Indeed, Morley was determined to attend every meeting, rally, protest, or sit-in, even when she was seriously ill. Glaucoma marred her vision, and she suffered excruciating chronic back pain—McNair figured from lugging around heavy bags of documents to plead her case at different agencies.

Although many patients were prevented by physical, emotional, financial, or other logistical barriers from visiting different sites after the clinic closures, Matt Ginsberg-Jaeckle noted that the distance was never an issue for Helen. "She was capable of making her way anywhere in the city, even if she got lost and it took her a while. It was the trauma of not knowing whether her therapist would be kept on staff, the loss of a physical space where she felt safe" that devastated her.[29]

Morley ended up at the Beverly Morgan Park clinic because other therapists were unable to work with her, Hansen and Sullivan remembered. Lindquist, by contrast, made her feel special. He would talk on the phone with her for long stretches, and when he couldn't reach her he'd call McNair out of concern.

At the December 2011 City Hall sit-in, Morley told the crowd what Lindquist meant to her. "He's just one of the best guys in the world that you could ever know," she said, as Hansen and Sullivan nodded energetically. Morley couldn't imagine becoming comfortable with a different therapist. Switching therapists might not seem like a big deal for many people, but for someone hanging by a thread emotionally and physically it could be the final straw. If her clinic closed, Morley said at the City Hall sit-in, she would end up in the emergency room or worse.

"I'm going to crack up here, something's going to go wrong up here," she said, hitting her soft hat with the paper in her hand. "I don't want to go to no hospital like they said I've got to ... it costs more to be in the hospital ... if people don't have insurance, don't have money, how are they going to go?... We're all going to die, that's the way I see it."[30]

THE OCCUPATION

On April 12, 2012, about two weeks before the scheduled closing of the Woodlawn clinic, the Mental Health Movement planned a party to commemorate the clinic and its consumers. Movement members wheeled in garbage barrels filled with soda and collapsible barricades on which to hang artwork. They brought snacks. Every-one was in a festive mood. Sullivan and Hansen took the bus there together. Hansen took a bad fall as she was getting on the bus, both of them overloaded with bags. A passerby tried to persuade her to go to the emergency room, but she stridently refused. "I'm on the way to a party!" she said.

About two hours into the celebration, members of the movement announced to the revelers that people should leave if they didn't want to get arrested. The clinic was being occupied with help from members of Occupy Chicago. As it turned out, they had brought much more food than needed for an afternoon celebration; there was enough for about twenty people to survive for a month. The barrels weren't filled with soda and ice, after all—under a few drinks and a layer of ice cubes were bags of quick-dry cement. The occupiers would add water and then fasten barri-cades into the mixture, creating immovable obstacles to cordon off the clinic from the adjacent county primary care clinic, which would remain open. Sullivan's "party preparations" included bathroom cleaning supplies and reams of toilet paper—"the things the boys never think of."

At the moment the occupation started, movement members also dropped two large banners from the clinic's roof—the furled fabric had been stowed there before sunrise. One listed the group's main five demands; the other said, "Stop Stealing Our Health—Save Our Clinics."

The occupiers settled in for the long haul, passing the time playing cards and Scrabble and cooking spaghetti, washing the Styrofoam plates afterward because they figured they might be in there for a long time.[31]

Soon enough, the police arrived, and an officer in a police department ball cap stood in the county clinic on the other side of a folding barricade, which the activists had fortified with a vending machine and about a dozen overturned office chairs. He talked through a small opening in the makeshift barrier with N'Dana Carter, an outspoken community leader, STOP member, and mental health clinic consumer. Officers tried to persuade the group to leave the clinic and join protesters who were gathered outside, but they refused.

"Let me tell you, for three years we have been negotiating with the other mayor," said Carter. "This mayor, we gave him four thousand letters from citizens that live in the city and visited the city. He did not acknowledge it—"

"What is your plan?" interrupted the officer.

"Our plan is for you to get the mayor here to negotiate in good faith and stop being a bully."

"OK, I don't think the mayor is going to come under *these* circumstances," said the officer flatly.

"What circumstances will it take?" asked Carter with a laugh. "This guy, we have followed him . . ."

The officer again tried to persuade the occupiers to move outside where others were protesting, saying that the police presence in the clinic would mean neighborhood 911 calls going unanswered. Carter countered that keeping the clinics open would be crucial to making sure police could spend their time "fighting crime," not dealing with the mentally ill.

"We're not just fighting for us. We think it's unfair the police are forced to be babysitters for the mentally ill. . . . You are being shot at by people who are struggling with mental health issues," she told the officer.[32]

Ultimately the occupiers demanded that Emanuel cancel the plans to close six mental health clinics. Two North Side ones, in Rogers Park and Logan Square, had recently been closed, and four more were slated for closure by the end of the month, including the Beverly Morgan Park clinic.

Around midnight, more than nine hours into the occupation of the Woodlawn clinic, a police SWAT team arrived. They used chain saws and bolt cutters to break through the barricades and arrested twenty-three people. The activists were taken to the local police station lock-up, where they spent the night. Sullivan took it upon herself to keep people's spirits up, leading a cappella versions of Marvin Gaye songs and persuading the women to get up and do the hokey pokey to keep their blood flowing. Police released Hansen early on, possibly because she had an abscess on an infected tooth. But she refused to leave without Sullivan. By morning all the protesters were released; about half of them faced charges of trespassing, which would result in fines totaling about $1,000 and several suspended jail sentences. Sullivan struggled to walk, as she hadn't gotten her shoelaces back and her loose sneakers were flopping. Hansen, on the other hand, had planned ahead, intentionally wearing stylish boots without shoelaces.[33]

THE OCCUPATION CONTINUES—OUTSIDE

The morning after the occupation, the arrestees held a press conference outside the Woodlawn clinic. The next day, a Saturday, movement members had planned a community health fair in the empty lot across the street. Even though the occupation had been broken up, the health fair went on as scheduled. Nurses and therapists offered free blood pressure readings, depression screenings, and educational sessions about mental health. Congressman Danny K. Davis dropped by to have his blood pressure tested. Local alderman Willie Cochran also paid a visit. People who had been arrested and other clinic consumers and supporters held a speak-out, offering a litany of stories and testimonials about the importance of the clinics.

"I received lifesaving care at a mental health clinic," said a wiry woman with glasses. "But we saw what Rahm has in store for us. We were put in jail and handcuffed, which intensifies psychosis, anxiety, and other things we have to deal with."

"You're going to have an increase in incarceration and more visits to emergency rooms," said an older African American man leaning on a walker.

"I can guarantee you there will be a surge in arrests of people with mental health issues, so the new mental health clinic will be Twenty-Sixth and California," added a young man, referring to the county jail.

"It's not a question of whether the city is broke," said a young woman. "It's a question of who the city thinks is valuable."

A post on a blog by Occupy Chicago member Rachel Allshiny captured the mood at the outdoor occupation:

> If I didn't know better, my first impression would not have been that this was the site of an embattled protest. As we approached the camp we saw people sitting together— talking, laughing, and sharing a bite to eat. A long table was overflowing with food donated throughout the day and a makeshift grill gave off the scent of fresh barbecue. Music played, people danced. It had all the makings of a great block party—plus, of course, some large protest banners and a few police vehicles idling nearby.[34]

As Allshiny was finishing up the blog post on her laptop, police squad cars surrounded the encampment and threatened everyone with arrest. No arrests were made, however, and the occupation continued. Within the following days police tore down tents and arrested eleven people who refused to leave. Two of the arrestees would later become notorious in activist circles when it was revealed that they were police informants, known as "Mo" and "Gloves." Matt Ginsberg-Jaeckle spent about six hours in the Woodlawn police lockup handcuffed to Mo. He remembered the young man making lots of jokes and occasionally talking in more serious tones about "taking things to the next level." Ginsberg-Jaeckle told him it wasn't wise to talk that way in a police station.[35]

Despite the arrests, the occupation continued for weeks. People were still camping there (albeit without tents) on June 5, the day Helen Morley died. That afternoon Allen McNair got a call from a caseworker at Thresholds, a private mental health provider where Morley received medication. The caseworker told McNair that after Morley had missed several appointments, she was found dead in her apartment, from what turned out to be a heart attack. McNair was overcome with shock. He couldn't believe it; he couldn't even react. He was wracked with guilt; he'd been meaning to call her but was preoccupied by preparing to be photographed for a documentary project. He kept grief at bay by fixating on mundane details, like the recliner he was planning to buy from Morley. It wasn't until the next day, when McNair heard Tracy Chapman's song "Fast Car" on the radio while driving to his afternoon shift at a grocery store, that he broke down and cried.

A few days after Morley died, the Mental Health Movement held a memorial service at the occupation site outside the Woodlawn clinic. In keeping with Morley's insistence on speaking out whenever and wherever the need arose—and for as long as she had something to say—friends and supporters gave long, sometimes rambling ruminations about her life and the meaning of the Mental Health Movement. Morley's therapist, Eric Lindquist, was there, as were advocates for disability rights, universal health care, and fair housing—all issues Morley had adopted as her own. McNair read a long poem he had written in Morley's honor, "Another Wave of Change." A blind preacher and accomplished soul singer performed. The memorial service also doubled as a baby shower complete with gifts: one woman who had been camping outside the clinic while very pregnant gave birth right around the time of Morley's passing. "We commemorated the cycle of life and death," noted Ginsberg-Jaeckle.

The previous summer, members of the youth activist group FLY (who were also involved with the Mental Health Movement) had built a full-size coffin out of scrap wood to commemorate the death of eighteen-year-old Damian Turner. Turner perished after being shot nearby and transported to the nearest Level 1 trauma center, which was miles away on the North Side. The FLY activists launched a campaign demanding that the University of Chicago open one for South Side residents. After Morley's death, the group repainted Turner's coffin to say "RIP Helen Morley," and used it in a similar way as a prop in their campaign for social justice. They hauled it downtown for a protest outside the health department offices, and then kept it in silent testament at the ongoing outdoor occupation.

Campuzano continued his own one-man occupation outside the clinic for some weeks, even after the others moved on. He slept outside in the weathered van known as STOP's official vehicle. He was determined to make his own personal and political statement, by living in conditions similar to what he envisioned people with mental illness would experience after being cut off from their care: homelessness, cold, anxiety, loneliness. "My point was that by the mayor closing the clinics, this is how you leave people—out in the streets begging for money," he said. "How many people are homeless here in Chicago, people who had jobs, had medication, were doing well and leading productive lives, and now they are out on the streets? In Woodlawn, in almost any neighborhood you can walk down the street and you see why you need a clinic—you see people asking for money to buy their medication."[36]

"I amaze myself sometimes by the things I do," he continued. "Nine weeks in a neighborhood where there were gunshots and violence every night, risking my life. My parents would call me crazy—they were considering calling the police to arrest me to bring me back home. But all the cops knew me around there, they knew what I was doing."

Sometimes N'Dana Carter stayed with Campuzano in the van, but usually he was alone. On some days he would see former clinic patients distraught, wandering. "I got to experience how messed up a neighborhood can be," he said. "That's the way you leave people when you take away their medicine, take away their services, take away their livelihood. A lot of people depended on their social workers and therapists—to see that go away is heartbreaking."

LONG MILES

Under the city's plan, patients at the six closed clinics were supposed to travel to one of the six clinics that remained open or to one of the nonprofit private clinics that received modest city funding. Woodlawn patients were supposed to go to the clinic in Englewood, which was two and a half miles west, accessible by bus. It didn't sound like an unrealistic requirement, but to draw that conclusion would be to misunderstand the importance of the clinics in the communities and the harsh conditions and fragility of the lives of people struggling to survive emotionally, financially, and physically in a world where mental trauma, violence, poverty, and racism were ever-present.

The shuttered clinics were not simply places to check in and out and receive care. They were true community centers: even when people were not seeking treatment, they would hang out in the lobby, chatting with friends and participating in informal group therapy sessions. "If someone was hungry, they'd go to the clinic and someone would get them food. They knew not only their therapists but the secretaries, the security guards. It was a community," said Ginsberg-Jaeckle.

Taking a city bus the few miles from Woodlawn to Englewood was no easy matter, either. Bus fare of several dollars could be prohibitive for many patients, and many were not healthy enough to walk so far or eager to face the risk of mugging or gunshots. The trip required crossing gang lines and entering unfamiliar and violence-plagued territory, a very real danger both physically and mentally for many patients, including those who had lost family members to violence, suffered violence themselves, or developed post-traumatic stress disorder because of it.

For people who live in relatively safe neighborhoods, it can be hard to understand the high risk level of riding a bus, waiting for a bus, or even walking a few blocks in an impoverished, gang-infested area. That risk was something Debbie Delgado knew all too well. In November 2006 she was on the phone with her twenty-one-year-old son, Jeremiah, who was walking with his nineteen-year-old brother, Joshua. Jeremiah told Delgado, "Mommy, I'm on my way home." Then she heard gunshots over the receiver, followed by silence. Delgado frantically dashed out of the house and found her sons on the street. Joshua had been shot in the knee; Jeremiah was fatally wounded. "He died in his brother's arms," Delgado would explain countless times at different meetings and events, her voice always cracking.

Delgado had long struggled with depression and suicidal thoughts, and in the 1990s she started therapy at the mental health clinic in Logan Square. It was the same clinic where Morley and McNair had met. Delgado would often take her four kids, including Joshua and Jeremiah, to therapy with her. After Jeremiah's death, Joshua and Debbie relied on the clinic for their very survival as they struggled mightily to deal with the grief and trauma. "When the mayor closed the clinic, my son shut down," Delgado said of Joshua. "He said the system had failed him. I said, 'The system didn't fail you, the mayor failed you.'"[37]

Under the city plans, Delgado and her son were reassigned to a public clinic about seven miles northwest. It took her more than an hour to get there on the bus, compared to a five-minute walk to the old clinic. Riding the bus the first time, she couldn't help but realize that they passed by three cemeteries. It made her think of Jeremiah. "By the time I got there I was a wreck, I couldn't talk about anything else," she remembered. Joshua likewise refused to visit the new clinic.

After he stopped getting therapy, Joshua tumbled deeper into depression and isolation. "He is unable to go out, he has shut himself off from society, he's always looking over his shoulder, and now that he's not on his medication, he's getting into alcohol," Delgado said at a meeting nine months after the clinic closures. "He's literally dying at home."[38]

HIDDEN COSTS, "DISAPPEARED PATIENTS"

The $2 million to $3 million a year that closing the clinics was supposed to save was a minor amount compared to the city's gaping budget hole of more than $600 million and the health department's $169 million budget.[39] Critics figured the savings would be offset by other costs to taxpayers caused by the clinic closures. In January 2012 AFSCME Council 31—the union representing the clinic staff—released a report in conjunction with the Mental Health Movement detailing these "hidden costs." For one thing, it concluded that diverting up to 1,100 patients (by the union's calculations) eligible for Medicaid to private providers would be "effectively giving away federal reimbursement for their services."If the plan was budget-driven, the report concluded, "it is illogical to turn away patients with the ability to pay."[40]

The authors cited national studies indicating that visits to emergency rooms and jails are likely to increase if affordable mental health services are cut, and made the case that these effects are more expensive in the long run than keeping clinics open. The study also determined that the Department of Public Health's budget had increased $1.67 million from 2011 to 2012. These increases included three new deputy commissioner positions paying each more than $100,000 a year, and more than $500,000 spent on surveys and advertising.[41] AFSCME and the Mental Health Movement said the city should eliminate or reduce these new expenditures rather than closing clinics.[42]

In April 2012, the month of the clinic closings, thirty-eight public mental health patients were hospitalized, according to AFSCME and the Mental Health Movement. That was a notable spike from the monthly average of twenty-two in 2011 and 2012.[43] Advocates figured that the stress of the closures contributed to the hospitalizations, and that patients might continue to be hospitalized at higher rates. In general, a hospital visit costs a lot more than ongoing therapy, monitoring, and preventive care, all of which can help avoid emergency situations. Because many city mental health clinic patients were uninsured, their hospital visits would ultimately be covered by public funds.

A July 2012 report by the Department of Public Health spelled out a seemingly smooth transition after the six clinics closed. It noted that in November 2011, therapists began meeting with patients about the change and helping them adjust. Therapists made first appointments for each patient at their new clinics, the report said, and gave them four-day public transit passes to help with travel. A team from the department monitored patients who transferred to private clinics for at least sixty days.[44]

A follow-up report in August 2012 noted that 355 of the 429 patients who had gone to private providers had already attended their first appointment, and fifty-four had chosen to return to the public clinic system. "All clients have individual transition plans and are monitored to ensure they are receiving care, they are making it to their first appointments and they are getting their medications," the authors wrote. "We are following up with these clients to make sure they are satisfied with their care."[45]

But AFSCME and the Mental Health Movement analyzed city statistics and came to a less rosy conclusion. They found that between fall 2011 and August 2012, at least 484 and as many as 2,200 patients had left the city mental health system—"disappeared," in their words.[46]

AFSCME's report noted that in October 2011 the Department of Public Health had 5,337 mental health patients on its rolls. By February 2012 that number had dropped to 3,282; in May it was 2,932, and in August it was 2,798. Documents that AFSCME obtained with a Freedom of Information Act request showed that the department considered many of the 5,337 cases "inactive," hence the 3,282 number logged two months before the clinic closures was arguably an accurate baseline. By August 2012, after the six clinics closed, the city reported it was seeing 2,369 patients at the remaining public clinics, and 429 former city patients had been transferred to private providers, for the total of 2,798. That meant that 484 patients had stopped receiving services in the course of a few months.

City records noted 278 cases closed in that period and fifty-two "transfers pending," apparently accounting for much of the difference. The union argued that the sudden closure of so many cases raised doubts: did these people really all of a sudden stop needing services or find new services on their own? And how well had the city continued to track the pending transfers or the people who had already transferred to private clinics?[47]

AFSCME also noted that nearly half the therapists in the system had been laid off, which put an unfair and unworkable burden on remaining staff, who already had heavy caseloads. The union's analysis of city data showed that the shift could lead to an increase of 58–80 percent more patients at some of the remaining clinics, with no increases in staff.[48] AFSCME Council 31 special projects director Jo Patton would later testify that in the months after the closures, some therapists were responsible for one hundred patients.[49] The city's own transition report said that the average therapist caseload would be fewer than ninety patients, a threshold the union called unworkable.[50]

Just as the patients at the closing clinics were disproportionately African American and Latino, so were the clinic staff who lost their jobs. In fact, all the African American male therapists were laid off, according to AFSCME, and so were half of the bilingual Spanish-speaking therapists.[51]

"The city of Chicago made a hit on the African American community when they decided to fire every African American male therapist," said STOP leader N'Dana Carter. "Who are the first to be arrested in the city of Chicago? African American males. And upon release from prison, there's often a requirement to seek mental health therapy. Therapy is successful because you develop a healthy relationship with your therapist. These are people who have been displaced, disrespected, locked up for some years; do you really think they'll be able to relate to white women, white men?"

By closing the clinics, Carter said, the mayor was turning his back on the African Americans who had played an important role in electing him. "Emanuel is an enemy of people of color," she said bluntly.[52] "Some of the therapists who were laid off had been on the job twenty or twenty-five years. They had substantial relationships with their patients. It wasn't a casual relationship; they were loving, intense relationships. To tear up those relationships, to tear up people's lives—that's just wrong."

PROTESTERS AT CITY HALL STAGED THE REPRESSION THEY FEARED WOULD HAPPEN DURING THE UPCOMING NATO SUMMIT, AS CITY COUNCIL DEBATED ORDINANCES IMPOSING NEW LIMITS ON DEMONSTRATIONS. PHOTO BY KARI LYDERSEN.

9
NATO AND THE GLOBAL CITY

"There are about 100 cities in the world that are the economic, cultural and intellectual energy of the world today. Chicago is one of those cities. Look around the world and look at this time. The cities are Paris, Berlin, London, Chicago, Shanghai, Rio, New York. There's no guarantee that 20 years from now Chicago's here. Nothing is certain. So what you do today determines whether it's a viable city. What I do today as mayor—attract talent, build industry, strengthen our schools, support our businesses, expand our broadband and the rail—determines whether the city of Chicago stays on the level of Shanghai and New York and London."

—Rahm Emanuel, quoted in *DuJour Magazine*[1]

Sixty-three years after the founding of the North Atlantic Treaty Organization military alliance, there had been twenty-five major international NATO summits. Most of them had been held in Western European capitals symbolic of political, financial, and cultural power: Paris, Brussels, London, Madrid, Rome. Until 2012, the only summit in the United States had been in Washington, DC, in 1999.[2]

Meanwhile, a club of countries representing the world's largest economies has been holding annual summits since 1975. The original members of the Group of 6, as it was called back then, were France, Germany, Italy, Japan, Britain, and the United States. The group later expanded to include Canada and Russia, becoming the Group of 8, or G8.[3] The G8 summits have been held in major cities like Venice, Versailles, and Tokyo; and they are often held in more isolated (yet luxurious) locations like Sea Island, Georgia, and Auchterarder, a small town in the hills of Scotland.[4]

When Emanuel took office, the NATO and G8 summits hadn't been held in the same city at the same time since 1977, in London, and they'd never been held in conjunction in the United States. On June 22, 2011, President Obama announced that both summits would be held in Chicago in mid-May 2012. The selection process was not an open competition, and Emanuel's lobbying of Obama, Vice President Joe Biden, and then–Chief of Staff Bill Daley reportedly was central to Chicago's garnering the summits.[5]

For Emanuel and civic boosters and business leaders intent on positioning Chicago as a "global city" on par with European and Asian metropolises, the summits were a major coup. "This will be an opportunity to showcase what is great about the greatest city in the greatest country," Emanuel said the day after Obama's announcement. "It's an opportunity for the city of Chicago economically, but also a message internationally about why Chicago is a city that's on the move and, if you're thinking of investing, Chicago is a place to invest."[6]

There are, of course, different ways one can define "global city." Mayor Daley, who invoked the term frequently, made an effort to transform Chicago into a global city by fostering close business and cultural relationships with China—he instituted a Chinese program in public schools, visited China often, and hosted Chinese leaders in Chicago. Daley also gave Chicago a European feel, adding lovely parks, sidewalk cafes, and overflowing flower boxes downtown.

If one were judging Chicago on its high-level financial, artistic, and aesthetic achievements, it was well on its way to becoming a "global city" when Emanuel took office—though it was still no Paris or London. But many people would argue that Chicago has always been a global city, from the days when scrappy European immigrants labored in meatpacking houses and steel mills to the modern era, with its vibrant ethnic and immigrant neighborhoods where one could almost be in Mexico, India, or Poland. It is these immigrants and their descendants who make Chicago inherently cosmopolitan, infusing all its achievements, eccentricities, and inequities with a global nature. Both Daley and Emanuel as mayors were seen as supporters of immigrants, including undocumented immigrants. Daley signed a 2006 ordinance that declared Chicago a "sanctuary city" where police would not turn undocumented immigrants over to federal officials.[7] As mayor, Emanuel became a close ally of the major immigrants' rights groups that had criticized him during his time heading the DCCC and in the White House. He was a consummate political animal, and although he had called immigration a "third rail" and reportedly lobbied against federal immigration reform for political reasons, once in City Hall he found it politically expedient to advocate for immigrants' rights.

But when it came to defining the city's identity on the national and international stage, Emanuel, like Daley before him, seemed more interested in providing a sanitized showcase for businesspeople and tourists rather than channeling public and private resources toward the daily needs of Chicago's regular citizens, however "global" they might be. And as Emanuel prepared to host the global coming-out that would be the NATO and G8 summits, he didn't want these regular citizens to crash the party.

Since at least 1999, when massive protests by labor unions and antiglobalization activists disrupted the World Trade Organization (WTO) meeting in Seattle, all major international summits could be expected to draw crowds of protesters from around the world. At high-powered global gatherings like those in Washington, DC, during the International Monetary Fund and World Bank meetings in 2001, Cancun during the WTO meeting in 2003, and Genoa during the G8 summit in 2001, mass protests and the issues they raised became inextricable parts of the story line. When Pittsburgh, a city fairly analogous to Chicago, hosted the G20 summit in 2009, police reported eighty-three arrests and $50,000 in property damage.[8] Chicago police were among the officers from other cities sent to Pittsburgh to aid in crowd control and security.[9]

Emanuel and police superintendent Garry McCarthy knew from the start that the G8 and NATO summits would be a magnet for national and international protesters, and they immediately began developing a battle plan that included training thirteen thousand officers and sending Chicago cops to Pittsburgh and Seattle to learn from those cities' protest experience.[10]

CANG8

Joe Iosbaker grew up an Iowa farm boy in the 1960s and '70s. A self-described "patriotic kid," he was nominated for the US Air Force Academy by his senator. Instead he headed to the University of Iowa in 1977, and there his whole worldview changed.

"My first friends were Iranian students who told me the story of the CIA coup that overthrew democracy in their country and reinstalled the Shah," Iosbaker remembered. "They described the torture that was commonly practiced by the secret police. It was shocking to me. The Iranians started my lifelong opposition to US imperialism."

At the university he also met a student activist named Stephanie Weiner, who would become his wife. The two had friends in Chicago and were inspired by the multiethnic "rainbow coalition" they'd seen come together to elect Mayor Harold Washington. In the mid-1980s the couple moved to Chicago specifically to be part of that movement.

Iosbaker got a job at the University of Illinois at Chicago, first as a clerical worker and then as the recycling director. He also became a member and then a union steward and executive board representative for SEIU Local 73, the labor union that represented more than twenty-five thousand public employees in Illinois and northwest Indiana. He and Weiner, an adult educator at the City Colleges, devoted their lives to organizing and activism on a range of issues. They are deeply involved in solidarity efforts for justice in Palestine and Colombia. Weiner also expresses her artistic side with her Revolutionary Lemonade Stand, where she sells handmade clothing, crafts, and trinkets with social justice themes. Iosbaker played a central role in organizing the national protest during the Republican National Convention in Minneapolis-St. Paul in 2008.

At 7 a.m. on September 24, 2010, FBI agents raided Weiner and Iosbaker's home, apparently because of the couple's involvement with the Republican convention protests and also because of their work related to Palestine and Colombia. (Federal agents raided other homes of activists in Chicago and Minneapolis at the same time.)[11] Weiner's passport was confiscated, and the couple was called to testify before a grand jury looking into clandestine material support for foreign terror groups, a charge their friends and acquaintances found both ludicrous and highly disturbing. Along with computers and files, FBI agents seized photos of Martin Luther King Jr. and Malcolm X, a postcard from Iosbaker's old girlfriend, and their sons' childhood drawings.[12]

Lawyers, activists, and friends formed the Chicago Committee Against Political Repression to support the targets of the FBI investigation and more generally to protest civil liberties violations under the mantle of the war on terror.

The FBI investigation was still open though seemingly dormant almost nine months later, when President Obama announced the G8 and NATO summits would be held in Chicago. That evening, Iosbaker was walking into a meeting of the Committee Against Political Repression when he got a call from a national organizer saying the United National Antiwar Coalition wanted to hold big protests during the summits and asking if Iosbaker would take a central role. Iosbaker immediately saw the parallels between NATO and the G8 and the issues on which he'd long been working, as did the other members of the committee. The next day he applied for permits to hold rallies at Daley Plaza and Federal Plaza, and over the following weeks he helped pull together a coalition of antiwar activists, religious leaders, labor union members, and other Chicagoans with the goal of holding major peaceful protests during the summits.[13]

On July 15, 2011, the *Chicago Sun-Times* reported that Iosbaker was scouting locations for a march to the McCormick Place convention center, and four days later activists posted an online petition asking Emanuel to grant the permits.[14] Iosbaker described the group's persistence:

> On July 28, our coalition delivered petition signatures with union officials, faith leaders, and community groups. We asked for a meeting with the mayor at a press conference outside his office. We continued our online petitioning, garnering 1,500 signatures, asking for permits, an end to threats of mass arrests and the vilification of protesters. On August 5, we sent a follow-up email to Vanessa Hall, the assistant to Emanuel to whom we had handed our letter on July 28. She never dignified us with a response.[15]

On August 28, more than eighty groups from around the Midwest came together for the official founding of the Coalition Against NATO/G8 War and Poverty Agenda, or CANG8 (pronounced "Cangate"). Meeting at Chicago-Kent

College of Law, they agreed to organize a "family-friendly," legally permitted march and protest during the summits, along with a "People's Summit" the preceding week.[16] CANG8 was officially housed under the auspices of the 8th Day Center for Justice, a Christian organization known for nonviolent civil disobedience and social justice campaigns. The founding meeting featured Kathy Kelly, a Chicago peace activist who'd traveled to bear witness in war zones including Iraq, Bosnia, Egypt, and the Gaza Strip; Hatem Abudayyeh, an Arab American community leader whose home had also been raided by the FBI the previous September; and N'Dana Carter from the Mental Health Movement.

Another speaker at the meeting and a key CANG8 organizer was Andy Thayer, a veteran of countless struggles, from protesting nuclear power in the 1970s to apartheid in the '80s to police brutality and the death penalty in the '90s—not to mention a lifelong focus on gay rights and antiwar campaigns. Raised in a small town in upstate New York with a father who built missile parts and a mother who helped Vietnam War draft dodgers escape to Canada, Thayer became a rabble-rouser as a high school journalist and never looked back.[17] He cofounded the Gay Liberation Network and helped force conservative Chicago Cardinal Francis George to apologize for comments comparing the gay rights movement to the Ku Klux Klan.[18] Thayer had significant experience organizing mass protests involving diverse groups and objectives, so the summit protests were right up his alley.

CANG8's launch roughly coincided with the birth of the Occupy movement, which started in New York City and soon spread to cities and towns nationwide. Occupy Chicago activists convened downtown near the Chicago Board of Trade and in Grant Park. The movement pressed Emanuel to allow a long-term twenty-four-hour occupation site, as had happened in many cities, to no avail.[19]

Iosbaker and Thayer were frequent Occupy participants. On October 15, Iosbaker spoke to about two thousand people at a rally in Grant Park, announcing the plans to march during the summits. Early the next morning, Chicago police broke up the lakefront Occupy encampment and arrested 175 people, invoking city curfew rules. The arrests were billed as a practice run for the summits, and media praised the police for carrying it out in an orderly and efficient manner.[20] The following weekend, police again arrested more than a hundred Occupiers minutes after the 11 p.m. curfew kicked in. Arrestees—including union nurses who'd set up a first aid tent—said they were treated much more harshly than the previous weekend; many saw it as an intentional escalation strategy meant to punish those who refused to stop protesting. They complained of harassment and bad treatment in lockups, including being held in a crowded cell without toilet paper for thirty hours.[21] A year later, a Cook County judge ruled the arrests illegal, saying the curfew ordinance had been selectively enforced—especially considering the night of the 2008 presidential election, when people celebrated Obama's victory in the same park late into the night.[22]

Activists said Emanuel's handling of the Occupy movement did not bode well for the NATO and G8 summits. Elected officials all over the country were trying to walk a fine line, dealing with the Occupy encampments and the threat they posed to the status quo while trying not to seem dismissive of the growing and undeniable frustration and anger of regular people. Emanuel said as much in a meeting with the *Chicago Tribune* editorial board, where he voiced opposition to Occupy tactics but added, "If you can't hear the anguish in people's lives, which they're literally living on a razor's edge, you're too callous for public life."[23]

Emanuel's claims of sympathy for regular people rang hollow to most protesters. Those participating in the Occupy movement and planning to protest the NATO and G8 summits didn't see Emanuel only as an authority trying to limit their free speech rights, as mayors in many other cities. They also saw him as the embodiment of the very concepts they were rising up against.

"He was perfect as a symbol of everything that's coming down on working people," Iosbaker said. "He's wealthy, he's arrogant, he's disdainful of the needs of the vast majority of humanity, and he's also a militarist. We could not have dreamed up a more suitable opponent for our movement."[24]

That fall, "Mayor One Percent" became a popular nickname for Emanuel among Occupy protesters, labor and community activists, and progressive journalists. Edward McClelland, a blogger for NBC Chicago's *Ward Room*, took credit for coining the term, saying he first used it in an October 13, 2011, headline.[25] More than a year later, it would still be synonymous with Emanuel—emblazoned on countless protest signs, stickers, buttons, and patches.

ORDINANCES AND INSULTS

Emanuel was in an especially sensitive position in the lead-up to the summits thanks to Chicago's handling of the 1968 Democratic National Convention, often described as a "police riot" in which city officers beat and tear-gassed antiwar protesters and spied on and arrested popular movement leaders.[26] The world would again be watching during the NATO and G8 summits, and Emanuel could not risk a messy, violent, attention-grabbing confrontation on the world stage.

Iosbaker noted that in the lead-up to the 2008 Republican National Convention protests, organizers communicated frequently with the mayors' offices in St. Paul and Minneapolis. Dealing with the Emanuel administration in Chicago was a different story. Organizers felt city officials were intentionally setting up a conflict narrative pitting radical protesters against upstanding citizens, in an attempt to marginalize the protests and frighten people away.

"It was a vilification campaign. They could not refer to protesters without using the word 'violent,'" said Iosbaker. "Their intention was pretty clear: to frustrate our efforts to get permits and to create this climate of fear in the city such that most people would be afraid to go anywhere near the protest. So we had to assert our right to march, but do it in such a way that it didn't feed into this fear they were fomenting. We made it clear we were planning a permitted march, a family-friendly event."

On December 14, 2011, Emanuel asked City Council to pass two ordinances that would amend city code in preparation for the summits. One of the proposals, which did not mention the summits specifically, would have changed an ordinance governing "parades, public assemblies and athletic events." Among other things, the proposal would have required that all amplification devices and props be registered with the city at least a week in advance, that the organizers obtain a $1 million insurance policy and promise to reimburse the city for any damages, and that marches be limited to two hours. It also would have mandated a parade marshal for every hundred participants.[27] The fines for violating a parade permit would be increased from an existing range of $50 to $1,000 up to a minimum fine of $1,000 and a maximum penalty of $2,000 and/or ten days in jail.[28]

CANG8 and Occupy Chicago organizers were unsettled and furious, envisioning that they could face serious fines and even jail time for violating impossibly specific permit requirements. They interpreted the registration requirement as meaning that every protest banner, sign, and bullhorn would have to be described and registered ahead of time. It eventually became clear that the proposed new ordinance was not greatly different from the parade ordinance already on the books, which was rarely enforced to the letter of the law. But given the high stakes of the summits, organizers feared city officials would invoke and enforce the ordinance more strictly than ever before. That way, organizers figured, the city could virtually ensure multiple permit violations at any given protest and potentially dissuade many groups from applying for them.

The other proposal was specifically framed as preparation for the summit protests. It would more than double the fines for resisting arrest and aiding escape from police, common charges during antiglobalization protests, to as high as $1,000. It would allow the city to enter no-bid contracts with private security firms for video surveillance and other services without City Council approval—a major concern, especially in a city with a long history of patronage and corrupt deal-making. It would allow Chicago police to deputize out-of-town and federal officers with local authority, and it would let the police form agreements with other federal and state law enforcement agencies.[29]

Emanuel described the proposal to reporters as a temporary provision necessary for the summits, but critics pointed out that the ordinance as written would allow increased fines and no-bid security contracts for the indefinite future.

At that same council meeting, Northwest Side alderman Margaret Laurino introduced a resolution inviting the police department to testify before the City Council's public safety committee about the possibility of using sound devices for crowd control during the summits. She touted the idea of "a tactical weapon that

COMMUNITY LEADERS DECRIED "SIT DOWN AND SHUT UP" ORDINANCES
MAYOR EMANUEL ASKED CITY COUNCIL TO PASS IN ADVANCE OF THE NATO
SUMMIT. PHOTO BY KARI LYDERSEN.

emits harmful, pain-inducing tones over long distances . . . developed for the Pentagon by a military contractor, LRAD Corporation, after the September 11th terror attacks as a sonic weapon to help control unruly crowds, thwart hijackers and keep other potential threats at bay."

Laurino's resolution gave historical context: "Sound has long been used as a weapon, from the Biblical story of rams' horns bringing down the walls of Jericho to sirens on dive bombers in World War II to the US Army blasting rock music to torment former Panamanian dictator Manuel Noriega." And it said that "experts have stated that [the summits] will be a security challenge that no other American city has ever faced."[30]

It's not clear if the city ever investigated or purchased cutting-edge sound control equipment, but Laurino's resolution showed the fever pitch reached in the lead-up to the summits and the protests—even bringing discussion of epic historical battles and military technology into the City Council chambers.

"A TREMENDOUS OPPORTUNITY"?

The preamble to the ordinance allowing no-bid security contracts noted that "hosting the NATO and G8 summits will be a tremendous opportunity for the

City of Chicago to showcase what it can offer to the world, including its beautiful lakefront, world-class airports, spectacular architecture, modern convention and meeting facilities, and broad spectrum of fine hotels and restaurants."[31]

Emanuel and civic boosters promised the summits would result in huge economic ripple effects, as people around the world would see what Chicago had to offer and presumably come visit and invest. Chicagoans had heard similar arguments a few years earlier when the city was bidding for the 2016 Olympics, and many people didn't buy it then, either. Olympics visitors wouldn't be roaming the neighborhoods spending money at mom-and-pop shops, and they wouldn't be especially likely to come back to Chicago in the future, academics and community leaders argued.[32] The high-powered, high-security leaders coming to Chicago for the summits would be even less likely than Olympic visitors to stimulate the local economy. And as with the Olympics, people wondered what the cash-strapped city administration was doing spending huge amounts of time, money, and other resources on a flashy but brief international event while basic public services were being cut.

In a statement Emanuel said, "Hosting these summits puts the spotlight on Chicago as a city on the move and an unparalleled destination for travel, tourism and business." Whether that was true was debatable. Regardless, the promotion of travel, tourism, and business raised resentment for familiar reasons: as with plans for the Olympics and other major events, low-income and regular working people felt like they were not a priority for the city.

REFORMS AND REVOLTS

Based on discussion at the December 14 City Council meeting, it appeared Emanuel and aldermen figured there would be little opposition or controversy around passing the two proposed ordinances at the next meeting. But CANG8 and Occupy Chicago quickly showed them otherwise. The timing was bad—the ordinances were introduced just a week and a half before Christmas, and they could be passed by a full council vote just a few weeks after New Year's Day. Activists naturally had their own family plans for the holidays, and aldermen would also be out of the office and hard to reach. Nonetheless, CANG8 members worked hard to spread the word about the proposed ordinances, meeting with aldermen and encouraging residents to contact City Hall. Alderman Joe Moreno—a relatively young, new addition to the council who liked to speak his mind—received two thousand emails demanding he vote down the ordinances. Iosbaker and other CANG8 organizers helped convince union leaders that the ordinances could threaten their ability to picket over labor disputes. SEIU Local 73 dedicated staff time to calling all fifty aldermen.[33] "It became a pretty enormous pressure campaign," Iosbaker said.

Joe Moore, a Far North Side alderman representing an area known for "lakefront liberals," took the lead in designing and promoting revised ordinances that addressed some of the concerns. Fines for parade permit violations were scaled back, the insurance mandate was relaxed, and the requirement of a parade marshal for every hundred participants was scrapped, among other changes.[34] Cultural affairs commissioner Michelle T. Boone promised during a hearing that, as in the past, the most specific components of the parade ordinance were unlikely to be enforced.[35] Increased fines for protest-related offenses were eliminated, and the revised ordinance mandated that no-bid contract provisions would expire after the summits.[36]

CANG8 leaders were not appeased. They issued a press release saying that "the concessions are relatively minor" and that "major civil liberties issues remain in the proposed ordinances."[37] On January 17, 2012, the day before City Council was scheduled to vote on the revised ordinances, opponents held a press conference. "If the ordinances pass tomorrow, all bets are off," Andy Thayer said.[38] "If you cancel people's constitutional rights, the onus is on you for what happens."

As the council debated the revisions the next day, a diverse mosaic of several hundred community activists gathered outside the mayor's office for a protest convened in part by Stand Up! Chicago, a coalition of community, faith, and labor groups: Adam Ballard, a member of the disability rights group ADAPT, in a wheelchair. Eighty-five-year-old activist Ruth Long, with her long gray dreadlocks and dignified, weathered face. Mental Health Movement leader N'Dana Carter. And the Reverend Calvin Morris, executive director of the faith-based Community Renewal Society and a prominent veteran of civil rights struggles.

"I was deployed to the wrong war," said Iraq Veterans Against the War member Aaron Hughes. "My fight is here at home for democracy and civil rights. . . . Here we are seeing democracy erode, even as my brothers and sisters are sent to Iraq and Afghanistan to supposedly fight for democracy there."

As more and more people stepped off the elevators into the lobby, the speakers were periodically drowned out by chants of "This is what democracy looks like!" The crowd got especially noisy with the arrival of a slender woman wearing a larger-than-life bobbling papier-mâché mask of Rahm Emanuel, accompanied by a man dressed as a riot cop. The riot cop began beating seated protesters with their hands bound in plastic cuffs as the papier-mâché mayor looked on. Protest signs proclaimed "RIP Bill of Rights: 1789–2012" and "Rahmageddon."

People had started lining up early to get into the City Council chambers for the votes. Soon a folding table was placed in front of the metal detector leading to the chambers, and no one else was allowed in. Protesters pressed against the table, chanting "Let us in!" They pumped their fists and stomped their feet. Guards met their gazes impassively. African American aldermen attempted to hold a press conference at the other side of the lobby about ongoing redistricting, which threatened to undercut the power of leaders in wards with big minority populations. A few journalists struggled to hear them as chaos erupted.

After about an hour, several protesters came out of the council chambers, swiftly ducking around cordons toward the elevators, calling out, "It passed!" The crowd went wild. A skinny young man with long hair got in a tussle with guards and was arrested, while a female police officer looking nervous held her baton horizontally against the protesters pressing toward the elevators. "One-term mayor, Rahm's got to go, we just thought we'd let you know!" they chanted, and called out to the police: "We vote no!" "Join us!" "We are the 99 percent!" "Who do you serve?"

"WE *ARE* THE PUBLIC"

On the ground floor of City Hall, SEIU Local 73 division director Wayne Lindwall was leaving the protest to go back to work. He shook his head in frustration and dismay about what he saw as Emanuel's latest attack on organized labor. SEIU Local 73 was fighting with Emanuel over city worker layoffs, and it was planning to join other unions at the NATO-G8 protests. Lindwall saw the new ordinances as a direct affront to hard-working union members.

"The mayor is using a scare tactic. Local 73 is one of the oldest unions in the country. We aren't out there breaking bottles and messing with the public," Lindwall said. "We *are* the public."[39]

"I miss Daley," Lindwall added. "I didn't drink his Kool-Aid, but I was a Daley fan. Daley grew up with labor. Rahm just expects everything to be handed to him because he says so. By walking out on the stage with President Obama he had a free ride with labor. Nobody believed he would attack unions like he has. Now we believe he's really antiunion and all about his connections to big business. The mayor's using the whole G8-NATO summit as a blank check to get what he wants and to muffle the voice of labor."

The Occupy movement denounced the ordinances and the aldermen who voted for them, decorating their headquarters in a warehouse near the Chicago River with a poster of "King Rahm" dangling four puppets from his fingers, including Aldermen Joe Moore and Joe Moreno.[40]

Moreno defended his vote immediately after the City Council meeting, writing in the *Huffington Post*, "The ordinance itself is not as extreme as many, with their own agendas, have made it seem. . . . There is definitely a reality gap between the perception and reality of this ordinance."[41]

Although the revised ordinances did not look much different from the ordinances that were already on the books, activists railed against City Council both for not improving troublesome provisions of the previous ordinance and for allowing changes that may have seemed small but that had great significance. For example, the revised ordinance allowed the denial of a parade permit if there were not enough "on duty" police officers to maintain order. The previous ordinance had just referred to police officers, period. Thayer said the addition of the "on duty" caveat would make it even easier for a permit to be denied.[42] And the fight over the ordinances had come to symbolize issues much larger than the city code, namely the view of Emanuel as an autocratic mayor manipulating even progressive aldermen and trying to silence the public.

NURSES AND THE NIGHTWATCHMAN

With the ordinance fight over, the opposition movement focused wholly on preparing for the summits and the People's Summit the preceding week, which would feature former Afghan Parliament member Malalai Joya, Code Pink leader Medea Benjamin, and retired Air Force colonel Ann Wright—all outspoken critics of NATO operations.[43]

The CANG8 organizing was locally based, supplemented with endorsements and planned participation from major national activist, labor, and civil rights groups. One of the national groups, National Nurses United, was planning its own protest during the summits, with the enthusiastic support of many Chicagoans. NNU is a labor union representing more than 180,000 registered nurses nationwide.[44] It grew out of the California Nurses Association, a militant union famous for taking on California governor Arnold Schwarzenegger in 2005 over hospital staffing levels and state budget cuts.[45] The nurses saw the G8 as a perfect venue for their message that health care and the nurses who provide it are victims of the global economic crisis caused by greedy and unregulated financial institutions. Along with other labor groups, the NNU had been calling for a financial transactions tax, which could help curb uncontrolled speculative financial trading and fund public services.[46]

A battle with Schwarzenegger under its belt, the activist nurses union was hardly afraid of another tough, swaggering politician like Rahm Emanuel. An affiliate of the NNU represented nurses at Cook County's John H. Stroger Jr. Hospital in Chicago, one of the nation's largest public hospitals and the inspiration for the TV series *ER*.[47] Emanuel had no direct role in the Chicago nurses' ongoing struggle to maintain their jobs and serve the poorest patients with increasingly tight budgets and smaller staffs at the county hospital. But nurses in the county system expected to see their patient loads increase following the mental health clinic closures and the privatization of city primary care clinics; and they saw their situation as emblematic of the gutting of public services and safety nets from local to global levels.

As plans were falling in place for the summits and the protests, both sides were hit with a surprise that upended everything. On March 5, news spread that the G8 summit would not be held in Chicago after all, but rather at the president's retreat at Camp David. Obama's former chief of staff heard the news only about an hour before the general public. It was a big blow for the mayor: his efforts to control every aspect of the summits were undermined in one fell swoop by the president himself. And it was a signal that perhaps the White House didn't trust Chicago to offer top-flight security and logistical support for the meeting of world leaders. Adding insult to injury, Obama had not called Emanuel personally to deliver the news.[48] White House spokespeople stated that the G8 summit was being moved to a more "intimate" setting.[49]

Many activists saw the pulling of the G8 as a victory, figuring Obama was afraid of the opposition that awaited him. "It's clear Obama pulled the plug because he saw it as a total PR disaster," said Thayer.

Despite a feeling of victory, protest organizers were thrown for a loop. All of the largest international protests since the Battle for Seattle had been based around free trade, globalization, and the growing inequality between rich and poor. Economic forums like the G8 offered a perfect focus for protests against capitalism run amok. The NATO summit would still be held in Chicago. But while NATO represented militarism and the highly unpopular wars in Iraq and Afghanistan, it was a trickier peg for protests about privatization, poverty, and the evils of the financial industry.

CANG8 announced that its plans for a massive march would proceed. The nurses briefly considered moving their protest, but then announced their march would stay in Chicago as well. The yanking of the G8 messed with the protesters' schedules. Now no summit action would be happening on May 18 or 19, the dates for which the nurses and CANG8, respectively, had gotten permits. The nurses decided to stick with May 18. CANG8 submitted a new permit application for the first day of the NATO summit, May 20. "We would look like fools marching on an empty building," said Thayer, who had already worked for months to get what he called the "magical piece of paper" allowing people to legally protest on May 19.

Thayer submitted the identical permit application that had been approved before with only the date changed, but it was denied because of a provision allowing the city to prohibit a march if there are not enough police officers on duty to monitor it.[50]

City officials also began raising concerns about the nurses' permit to march and rally, citing the participation of Tom Morello, formerly of the political rock band Rage Against the Machine and more recently an acoustic troubadour playing under the name Nightwatchman at protests and strikes around the country.[51] The administration canceled the nurses' permit for a rally and concert in Daley Plaza, in the heart of downtown, and instead said the concert would have to be in Grant Park.

"My first reaction was one of surprise, because let's get this straight—NATO, the defender of the free world, is afraid of a musician and a few nurses?" said Morello.[52] He told *Rolling Stone* magazine that "Chicago is my hometown and the mayor is making me feel mighty unwelcome. . . . I don't care what they say or do, I'm coming to rock out and speak my mind. We won't be silenced and we won't be stopped. If Rahm Emanuel is so afraid of my popularity in Chicago maybe I should run against him in the next election. See you in the streets."[53]

THE WHOLE WORLD IS WATCHING

Just five days before the planned May 20 march, CANG8 got its permit. The
next night, police officers broke down the door of an apartment in Bridgeport
and took away nine residents and visitors, including a sixty-six-year-old man with
heart trouble.[54]

Bridgeport is one of Chicago's iconic neighborhoods. Mayor Richard J. Daley was
among the Irish Americans who forged the area's hardscrabble white ethnic identity:
he was part of a Bridgeport gang called the Hamburgs, who were involved in infamous 1919 race riots.[55] Ringed by stockyards and heavy industry, Bridgeport was
home to hardworking, hard-drinking, big-shouldered Chicagoans, particularly Irish,
Poles, and Italians. As recently as the late 1990s it was clear that African Americans
were not welcome to pass through the neighborhood, especially from the public
housing projects on the other side of the expressway. In 1997, thirteen-year-old
Lenard Clark, a public housing resident, stopped in Bridgeport to put air in his bike
tires and ended up being beaten into a coma by local young toughs.[56] In more recent
years Bridgeport attracted a growing Latino and Chinese working-class population
and became a magnet for hipsters, students, and artists drawn by the cheap rents, raw
warehouse space, and urban charm. These newer residents were among the many
young people planning to turn out in force to protest the NATO summit, and their

THOUSANDS TOOK TO THE CHICAGO STREETS AS WORLD LEADERS GATHERED
FOR THE NATO SUMMIT. PHOTO BY SARAH JANE RHEE.

spacious apartments were also crash pads for out-of-town activists who arrived in significant if not staggering numbers before the People's Summit.

Zoe Sigman, a member of Occupy Chicago, lived in one such apartment in Bridgeport and had guests from around the country staying with her before the NATO summit. Around 11 p.m. on May 16, there was a loud bang as police officers with guns drawn broke down the door of Sigman's second-floor unit. According to the residents, the officers entered Sigman's apartment and also the third-floor unit above. One resident said officers mocked him and his roommate with antigay slurs and called them Communists.[57]

The officers detained nine people after finding what the department later said were the makings of Molotov cocktails. Sigman and the others said the officers had seized innocent home-brewing equipment—beer caps and bottles—along with a cellphone.[58] The nine were held for thirty hours or more, and said they were denied access to bathrooms or medication. Ultimately six were released without charges and three were charged under the state's antiterrorism law, passed after the September 11 attacks. Prosecutors alleged that three young men—a twenty-year-old from Ft. Lauderdale, a twenty-four-year-old from a smaller Florida town, and a twenty-four-year-old from New Hampshire—filled bottles with gasoline and made fuses out of bandannas. The prosecutors later said the three identified as anarchists and had other weapons on hand including a mortar gun, swords, a hunting bow, throwing stars, knives, and brass knuckles. They said the men planned to attack targets including Obama's Chicago campaign headquarters and Emanuel's home.[59] It was the first test of the state's antiterrorism law, and some legal analysts skeptically noted that if there was a legitimate terrorism risk, the federal government would have been involved.[60]

The young men had been stopped by police a week earlier as they made a turn in a private driveway in Bridgeport. They captured shaky cellphone video showing three officers badgering them while searching their car, asking, "You guys got something planned for next week?"[61]

"You guys know all about '68," said one officer with a thick Chicago accent. "What did they say back in '68?" goaded another officer. "Billy club to the fucking skull," finished a third cop.[62]

Thursday brought two more arrests that would result in terrorism-related charges. Prosecutors said that Sebastian Senakiewicz, a twenty-four-year-old Polish immigrant and self-described anarchist, boasted about plans to blow up a Chicago bridge and hide explosives in a hollowed-out Harry Potter book. He was charged with falsely making a terrorist threat. Twenty-eight-year-old Mark Neiweem was charged with (unsuccessfully) seeking explosives and materials to make a pipe bomb.[63] Neiweem allegedly wrote down a list of bomb ingredients and noted that the necessary model rocket engines were available at Hobby Lobby stores.

Defense attorney Sarah Gelsomino and other activists noticed that the Florida and New Hampshire men had all spent time with two visitors who turned out not to be who they seemed.[64] "Mo" and "Gloves" (also known as "Nadia") were a charismatic pair who showed up in the weeks before the summits. Mo had been arrested in April at the protest outside the Woodlawn Mental Health Clinic, where he ended up handcuffed to activist Matt Ginsberg-Jaeckle.[65] And they were among the people arrested at the Bridgeport apartment, where police claimed they found the makings of Molotov cocktails and other gear. But people noticed that after the NATO arrests, Mo and Gloves inexplicably disappeared.[66] In the week following the protests, video and photos were circulated online of the two, who had befriended the men arrested in Bridgeport and numerous other activists in advance of the protests. Emanuel and the Chicago police refused to address whether the two had been informants or agents provocateurs, and police superintendent Garry McCarthy and Emanuel denounced the Internet and social media chatter for unmasking them.[67] Later, pretrial documents in the case of the "NATO 3" arrested in the Bridgeport apartment would reveal that Mo and Gloves were indeed undercover cops, contracted for a ninety-day assignment to spy on Occupy Chicago and anarchists in advance of the NATO summit.[68]

Anti-NATO activists had been highly suspicious of McCarthy and his plans for the summit all along. McCarthy had risen up through the police ranks in his native New York City and was serving as deputy commissioner of operations during the 2004 Republican National Convention, when police arrested and fingerprinted hundreds of protesters after boxing them in and preventing them from leaving the area. A federal judge later deemed the mass arrests and fingerprinting illegal, saying it unfairly targeted people based on their political views.[69]

In 2006 McCarthy was hired as police chief in violence-plagued Newark. The murder rate dropped by 30 percent under his watch, but he was dogged by complaints of rampant misconduct by officers.[70] After a scathing report by the American Civil Liberties Union, issued as McCarthy was preparing to move to Chicago, the US Justice Department announced its own investigation into allegations of excessive force, discrimination, and poor conditions in holding cells in Newark.[71] The ACLU said about two-thirds of the incidents cited in the report occurred before McCarthy's tenure, but it blamed him for allowing the abuses to continue and for failing to reform the department.[72]

NATO AND THE NEIGHBORHOODS

Leaders of a group called the Grassroots Collaborative figured that the expected influx of international journalists for the summit would be a perfect opportunity to offer up some stories of a different type—about everyday Chicagoans in the struggling areas that would not be visited by NATO delegates. The collaborative offered to take visiting reporters on tours to meet with community leaders, calling its campaign "A Global City Takes Care of Its Neighborhoods."

As it turned out, there wasn't much interest from foreign reporters, who were apparently overwhelmed with coverage of the summit itself; though the British *Guardian* published a piece noting, "The dissonance between the global pretensions of the summit this weekend and the local realities of Chicago could not be more striking. NATO claims its purpose is to secure peace through security; in much of Chicago neither exists."[73]

The grassroots tours did draw substantial interest from local reporters, though. One of the tours covered Little Village, a largely Latino and immigrant neighborhood on the Southwest Side that was often in the news for gang shootings. The collaborative introduced reporters to Pastor Victor Rodriguez, who ran a ragged boxing gym out of La Villita Community Church. Rodriguez wished that after the city had raised tens of millions of dollars for the summit, officials would have offered his gym at least a modest subsidy. The pastor noted that a mere $700 would allow him to get new boxing equipment and attract more young members. Little Village residents also talked of their longstanding push for more parks and green space, showing journalists a run-down park that locals said was taken over by gangs and unsafe for families. (That tour also highlighted one of the closed mental health clinics, in the Back of the Yards neighborhood, an impoverished immigrant enclave formerly home to Chicago's stockyards.)

Another Grassroots Collaborative tour brought journalists to Brighton Park and Englewood, two low-income South Side neighborhoods rife with vacant lots and deteriorating foreclosed buildings. The journalists got a firsthand taste of the insecurity in Brighton Park, as a young man came by and made threatening comments while they were looking at graffiti and memorial shrines on the street. That same evening, fourteen-year-old Alejandro Jaime was shot dead in Brighton Park while riding his bike with an eleven-year-old friend.[74]

"If you step outside downtown, the city is burning," said Grassroots Collaborative executive director Amisha Patel.[75]

[City officials'] idea was this focus on downtown would trickle down to the neighborhoods, but that's not happening. As there are fewer and fewer jobs and lower and lower wages, and public services are cut, these neighborhoods are literally crumbling. The city figures out how to raise all this money when they need it, while we have Pastor Vic saying he just needs $700 to keep kids off the street. Think about what we could do with just some of the money that is being spent downtown, the transformative effect it could have.

146 MAYOR 1%

A CITY ON LOCKDOWN

During the summit, downtown streets, beaches, parks, and other facilities were closed. Bomb-sniffing dogs paced the L trains. Sharpshooters were positioned on rooftops along Michigan Avenue. In a secret location somewhere outside the city, the Multi-Agency Communications Center housed members of forty-three federal, state, and local law enforcement agencies.[76] About thirteen thousand Chicago police officers were on the clock, collecting much overtime that would later be the subject of disputes between the mayor and the police union.[77]

For downtown business owners, residents, and workers, the city outreach and media coverage leading up to the summit must have seemed schizophrenic. City officials trumpeted the expected $130 million economic infusion and the spotlight that would be shone on Chicago.[78] At the same time, warnings and rumors flew about the impending violence and mayhem. People were advised to work at home and not to wear business suits if they came downtown, to avoid being targeted by anticorporate protesters.[79] Scores of businesses closed their doors, often fortifying their storefronts against attack. Twenty-two Starbucks locations coated their windows with shatter-proof film.[80] The company Midwest Solar Control put out a press release advising companies to buy its "3M Security and Safety Blast Window Film" to keep broken glass in place. The release said, "Rahm Emanuel, the city's mayor, has put restrictions on all public activities" during the summits. "It therefore follows that confrontation is imminent since protestors are not backing down."[81]

ROBIN HOODS IN SCRUBS

On Friday, May 18, Daley Plaza was filled with thousands of nurses in bright red scrubs, their typical gear for protests and strikes. For this occasion they'd added green felt hats with red feathers, an allusion to the financial transactions tax they were calling for, often dubbed the "Robin Hood Tax." They kept their message tailored to the G8 summit happening at that moment in Camp David: NNU executive director RoseAnn DeMoro called on the rich nations and corporations that caused the global financial collapse to do more to "heal the world" by revoking austerity measures and expanding health-care and public services. Thousands of Chicagoans mingled with the Robin Hood nurses, including many members of the Chicago Teachers Union. Tom Morello called out praise for the nurses and other union members during his rousing concert, his guitar emblazoned with the phrase "Whatever it takes." He applauded the nurses for persevering with their protest and concert plans after Emanuel tried to cancel them. "They looked the mayor dead in the eye and they said, in the words of the old 1990 spiritual, 'Fuck you, I won't do what you tell me!'"[82]

On Saturday, Emanuel greeted the Obamas on the tarmac at O'Hare International Airport, then joined them in a helicopter to Soldier Field, near the convention center that would host the summit.[83] Meanwhile, protesters marched through

PROTESTERS DREW CONNECTIONS BETWEEN U.S. FOREIGN POLICY AND
LOCAL ECONOMIC IMPACTS. PHOTO BY SARAH JANE RHEE.

downtown and held a sit-in outside the Board of Trade. In the afternoon they turned their attention to the fight to save the mental health clinics. Several thousand people, organized through word of mouth and social media, converged at an L train station on the Northwest Side and donned hospital gowns emblazoned with the slogans "Healthcare Not Warfare" and "Clinics Not NATO." Jeanette Hansen made the trek in her motorized wheelchair, a fluorescent yellow safety vest draped over the back. The protesters took over the streets and marched two miles to Emanuel's house, chanting, "Whose clinics? Our clinics!" "They say cut back, we say fight back!" and "Fight fight fight, health care is a human right!"[84]

When they got close to the mayor's residence, the streets were lined with officers in riot gear. Emanuel was not at home—he was at the Hotel Sax downtown, at a gathering for the Young Atlanticist group, which identifies "future leaders."[85] Chuy Campuzano knocked on Emanuel's neighbors' doors. "Do you know where I can find a mental health clinic?" he asked. "Because your neighbor just closed mine."[86]

THE BIG DAY

On Sunday, NATO leaders walked down a red carpet for photos with President Obama, and the summit officially began. They discussed the future of Afghanistan, including pending troop withdrawals, and Obama described the war-ravaged country as poised on the edge of a "transformation decade."[87] Emanuel gave British prime minister David Cameron a tour of City Hall's acclaimed rooftop garden,

and First Lady Michelle Obama visited a South Side youth center with other spouses of world leaders.

Meanwhile, CANG8 held its antiwar rally under a blistering sun in Grant Park. Afterward thousands of protesters, some in playful outfits, marched south on Michigan Avenue to the intersection with Cermak Avenue, a few blocks from the McCormick Place convention center. A group of about forty military veterans in fatigues and formal dress led the procession, encircled by a yellow ribbon. When they got to Michigan and Cermak, they threw down their military medals in a statement against the Iraq and Afghanistan wars. They were followed by thousands of protesters from around the country, including nuns, black-clad anarchists, and prominent community leaders like the Reverend Jesse Jackson.

In the evening, just after the parade permit expired, police officers surrounded the protesters and funneled them away from the summit, demanding they leave. Some did, but others stayed in place or tried to push toward the convention center. Many people, including out-of-town visitors, were confused about how to exit the area. They said they were hemmed in and blocked by police as they tried to get out.

Tension escalated as people milled around, tired, hot, and confused, and as more militant protesters tried to break through police lines toward the convention center. Some threw bottles, wooden sticks from protest signs, and even a small fence at police. Tussles erupted. Officers put on their gas masks, shoved protesters down, and hit some with batons. People chanted, "The whole world is watching!"—an allusion to the 1968 convention. A *Chicago Tribune* photo showed a beefy officer sticking out his tongue as he punched a protester with his bare fist; behind him officers had protesters on the ground.[88]

Other press photos showed numerous protesters with bloody faces, arms, and backs. At least seven people were taken to hospitals and more received first aid from street medics. Andy Thayer grabbed a megaphone to plead with police and protesters for calm, saying the coalition had worked hard to organize a peaceful march.[89]

Eventually people dispersed from the area around the convention center. Many moved north and west into the heart of downtown, chanting and dancing in the streets, a light rain washing off the day's sweat. Small clashes with police continued to break out until late at night. About forty-five people were arrested, many of whom were held at a makeshift detention area near the protest and then transported to a North Side police station. Most were released during the night or the following day without charges, as tired supporters and lawyers waited outside.[90]

THE RECAP

On Monday, protesters held one last march interspersed with rallies. They started at Union Park, on the Near West Side, then walked downtown to Boeing's corporate headquarters, where they held a "die-in." Boeing had advised employees to work from home, so only a few dozen people were in the building to see the "dead" protesters sprawled on the pavement below. The protest ended with a festive atmosphere in a downtown park, and those who still had energy discussed taking public transportation to a North Side beach to celebrate.[91]

NATO officials likewise deemed the summit a success, though hoped-for agreements over reopening supply lines in Pakistan and securing financing for Afghanistan operations were not reached.[92] President Obama and Afghan president Hamid Karzai affirmed their plan for the United States to withdraw troops over two years.[93] And NATO members adopted a "Chicago Summit Declaration on Afghanistan," enshrining Chicago's name in the faraway country's historic saga.[94]

Emanuel declared victory, saying that "this was a world-class event, held in a world-class city, by people who showed the character and qualities which also captured all the world leaders' imaginations."[95] He praised the police for their "resolve, their self-discipline and professionalism." He said meetings with the Dutch and British prime ministers and the German foreign minister could lead to more business opportunities for Chicago, including the possibility of making O'Hare airport the North American hub for the Dutch flower industry. Overall, he dubbed the summit "another milestone in Chicago's history."[96]

"As the Columbian Exposition in 1893 showed the world that Chicago was a city on the move at the end of the nineteenth century, the NATO summit showed

Chicago is once again a city on the move at the start of the twenty-first century,"
Emanuel continued. "By hosting the NATO summit, we have reinforced, reaf-
firmed, and revitalized Chicago's role on the world stage."[97]

Less than two weeks after the summit, Emanuel announced his intention to
bring the Super Bowl to Chicago, never mind that the city's Soldier Field stadium
is outdoors, right on the lakefront, and frigid temperatures and blizzards are common in February.[98] Pundits even speculated that Emanuel should make another attempt to bring the Olympic Games to Chicago, perhaps in 2024.[99]

COSTS AND BENEFITS

In his remarks at the end of the summit, Emanuel apologized that businesses had to
close but reiterated that it would benefit the city in the long run.[100] With the summit
over, journalists, community leaders, and city officials alike began tabulating the more
direct costs and benefits. Critics figured local businesses had taken a financial hit, as
predicted. "It wasn't just the mom-and-pop burger stands getting hurt; it was the posh
restaurants," said Thayer.[101] "Downtown was a ghost town." Ina Pinkney, longtime
owner of Ina's, a trendy restaurant west of downtown, posted a video on Facebook
titled "What NATO Did to Us." She lamented that during the summit hardly anyone
set foot in the restaurant, and international delegates were not eating out because they
were occupied with organized meals and events.[102] Grassroots Collaborative leader
Amisha Patel remembered walking down Congress Avenue in the heart of downtown
a day before the summit, "thinking I could literally just lay down on the street here."

Ultimately the summit cost $27.5 million, about $20 million of which was covered by the federal government. About $33 million raised from private donors was
used to reimburse the city for police and transit worker overtime, security, and other
costs; and for hotels, dinners, and insurance for dignitaries. Donors included powerful
companies with close ties to Emanuel: JPMorgan Chase, BMO Harris Bank, Boeing,
Exelon, and CME Group (parent of the Chicago Mercantile Exchange). More than
$10 million was left over from the private donations.[103] The mayor's office announced
the surplus funds would be spent on "NATO legacy" projects, including park improvements and $150,000 donated to a fund for college scholarships to undocu-
mented immigrants. One million dollars would be spent to create sixty "learning
gardens" adjacent to public schools; another million would support a youth jobs program; and substantial grants would help fund cultural programs in low-income
African American and Latino neighborhoods.[104]

As the Grassroots Collaborative had demanded, significant funds were indeed
doled out to important projects and programs in needy neighborhoods. But critics
asked, If the powerful and well-connected mayor could tap his contacts to raise
tens of millions of dollars to host world leaders in Chicago, couldn't he raise a few
million to keep the mental health clinics open?

MAYOR EMANUEL WAS CAST AS THE VILLAIN ON COUNTLESS HAND-
MADE PROTEST SIGNS DURING THE TEACHERS STRIKE. PHOTO BY
KARI LYDERSEN.

10
RAHM GETS SCHOOLED

"WORST IN THE NATION"

There was no doubt that Chicago Public Schools had serious problems, and had been coping with them for quite some time. In 1987, US education secretary William Bennett called Chicago's public schools "the worst in the nation."[1] About 15 percent of Chicago youth don't graduate from high school. For African American and Latino young men, the number is nearly one in three.[2] Gang problems and violence are a daily occurrence.

When Emanuel took office, the roughly four hundred thousand students in the Chicago Public Schools were 41 percent African American, 44 percent Latino, and 9 percent white; 87 percent were low-income.[3] Despite the efforts of countless dedicated and energetic teachers and many eager, hard-working students, Chicago classrooms often had an atmosphere of chaos, crowded with too many students distracted by too many things. The schools were so strapped for funding that teachers regularly bought their own supplies, and students made do with outdated equipment and battered books while sweltering in stuffy rooms without air conditioning.

Many teachers and parents say the disparities within the system are perhaps even more disturbing than the challenges at individual schools. Some of the schools—particularly on the North Side—are among the best in the state and offer a wealth of extracurricular activities and electives. By contrast, "schools on the South Side are so decrepit and poor, it's like a different universe," said Chicago Teachers Union vice president Jesse Sharkey.[4]

Chicago has been a national testing ground for various strategies meant to improve schools, from the creation of Local School Councils made up of community members to the controversial trend of replacing public schools with privately run charters. Former Chicago Public Schools CEO Arne Duncan went to the Obama

White House along with Rahm Emanuel in 2009, bringing Chicago experience to his role as education secretary.

Throughout his mayoral campaign and after his election, Emanuel repeatedly promised to overhaul the city's public school system. His main solution would be a longer school day. At five hours and forty-five minutes when Emanuel took office, Chicago's school day was the shortest of the country's fifty largest districts, according to a 2007 study by the National Council on Teacher Quality, which placed it a full hour below the national average.[5] Emanuel promised to keep students in the classroom longer, and indicated that student achievement and well-being would increase accordingly.

Not everyone agreed. The Chicago Teachers Union said the national report was misleading and that Chicago teachers and students actually did spend as much time in the classroom as many of their peers nationwide. More important, many parents and teachers said the obsession with time spent in class was missing the point. Sure, it might help students perform better on tests and be a boon to working parents. But given all the serious problems facing students and teachers during the school day, not to mention the social and economic crises students struggled with outside school, it seemed that tacking more hours onto the day without addressing more fundamental challenges would hardly do the trick. "It is not the length of time, but the quality of time that truly matters here," said Chicago Teachers Union president Karen Lewis, who would become Emanuel's nemesis.[6]

One could argue that Emanuel's fixation on a longer school day revealed his failure to understand the everyday realities of Chicago students in environments so different from the Chicago private school he attended as a child or New Trier, his high school in suburban Wilmette.

Emanuel proposed increasing the school day by up to an hour and forty-five minutes and expanding the school year by ten days. But he wasn't planning to increase teacher pay accordingly; in fact, his handpicked school board had canceled teachers' scheduled raise in 2011 and proposed small 2 percent annual raises after that.[7]

In recent years powerful Republicans had engaged in high-profile battles with union teachers. Republican New Jersey governor Chris Christie seemed to enjoy crassly berating teachers at town forums as the 2012 Republican presidential primary loomed.[8] And in 2010, Republican California governor Arnold Schwarzenegger fought with the state teachers union over his plans to tie teacher pay and evaluation more closely to student test scores.[9]

Some observers posited that Emanuel likewise intentionally picked a fight with Chicago teachers; at nearly thirty thousand members, they made up the third-largest teachers union in the country.[10] Whether Emanuel sought a public showdown with the union or not, his cavalier attitude toward the teachers indicated that, famed as he was for knowing his adversaries, he did not understand what he was getting into.

Maybe Emanuel didn't understand the drama that had played out starting in the summer of 2010. That's when the union—often described by disgruntled members as incompetent, apathetic, or in bed with the city administration—was suddenly taken over by a new wave of young, energetic, progressive leaders based in close-knit activist communities. Many of these teachers had grown up organizing against the war, launching youth media projects, protesting police brutality, and teaching "people's history." They saw the Chicago public schools in the context of a nationwide battle over the future of public education, and they saw their contract negotiations as part of a larger fight to protect workers' rights and the vitality of organized labor.

SCHOOL REFORM IN CHICAGO

In 2004, Chicago schools CEO Arne Duncan unveiled a plan called Renaissance 2010 that aimed to create one hundred high-quality schools by 2010.[11] The schools would be charters and "contract schools" falling under the public system but operated by private entities including community organizations, universities, foundations, and corporations. They would be free from most of the requirements and processes governing the regular public schools, including the Chicago Teachers Union contract.[12] The new schools would also include "performance schools" staffed by Chicago Public Schools employees but not subject to other standard requirements and policies.[13] While opening these new schools, the city would be closing schools deemed as "failing" and under-enrolled.

Renaissance 2010 and the attendant school closings lined up with the national "school reform" movement promoted by well-funded national groups—many of them "Astroturf" organizations with pretensions of grassroots spontaneity masking the involvement of right-wing think tanks and big business groups.[14]

The prevailing wisdom among school reformers was that mediocre public schools should be replaced by charter schools, free from most bureaucratic requirements and union contracts and run by private entities. School reformers trumpeted the market concept of "parent choice": charter schools would compete to show the best results on standardized tests, and parents would choose where to send their kids accordingly. The idea was that charter schools, funded with public money but run by private actors, have the flexibility and freshness to offer things the regular public schools can't: smaller classes, innovative curricula, longer school days, extra-strict discipline, and special programming for subjects like urban farming and performing arts. Charters also have much more flexibility in hiring and firing teachers, unbound by union contracts and standard tenure provisions.

Teachers in charter schools are often entitled to organize unions, though relatively few have in Chicago or across the nation. They generally earn much less than union teachers in regular public schools—in Chicago, $15,000 to $30,000 less per year. And they have much less job security and fewer benefits than their unionized counterparts.[15]

The subtext of the national school reform movement is clearly anti-union and hostile to unionized teachers, promoting the narrative that public education has been taken over by lazy, selfish tenured teachers who are not held accountable for student performance, coasting along in well-paid jobs from which they cannot be fired.

Some of Emanuel's closest advisers were prominent school reform advocates, including venture capitalist Bruce Rauner and Juan Rangel, head of the United Neighborhood Organization (UNO), which runs multiple charter schools in Chicago.[16] Ideologically, school reform was a neat fit for Emanuel—emphasizing the preeminence of the market and the private sector, the concept of competition, and the use of standardized metrics to determine winners and losers.

Critics of the school reform movement saw a profit motive at work: with government funding, private donations, and the ability to charge fees and do their own fundraising, the people running charters could claim generous salaries and significant profits. In August 2012, Reuters reported that venture capitalists made $389 million worth of transactions in the public education sector in 2011, up from just $13 million in 2005. "Indeed, investors of all stripes are beginning to sense big profit potential in public education," Reuters reported. "Traditionally, public education has been a tough market for private firms to break into—fraught with politics, tangled in bureaucracy and fragmented into tens of thousands of individual schools and school districts from coast to coast. Now investors are signaling optimism that a golden moment has arrived. They're pouring private equity and venture capital into scores of companies that aim to profit by taking over broad swaths of public education."[17]

"It's a hustle and a way to make money," said Jitu Brown, education organizer for the Kenwood Oakland Community Organization (KOCO), a longstanding South Side neighborhood group. "They don't have to pay union wages to the teachers, the custodians, the lunchroom workers. They are making a profit by taking advantage of underserved communities, rather than working to get public education right."[18]

CORE BELIEFS

As the Renaissance 2010 plan was getting under way, Jackson Potter was teaching American and world history and coaching the debate team at Englewood High School, in a rough, mostly African American neighborhood on the South Side. Potter was hired because of a staff reshuffling following the fatal shooting of eighteen-year-old school basketball star Maurice Davis. Davis's seventeen-year-old sister had gotten into an altercation with another boy, apparently an ex-boyfriend, during the school day. After school that teen and another boy confronted her across the street from school grounds; Davis was killed when he rushed over to defend his sister.[19] Potter said the murder and an increased but, in his view, badly organized focus on security at the school just exacerbated the tensions and challenges that had already existed.

"General chaos, mayhem, and trauma permeated the halls," Potter remembered. Students didn't perform well on standardized tests, a fact that was hardly surprising given everything else going on in their lives. "Was it bad personnel decisions, policy, teachers who didn't care enough?" asked Potter. He continued:

> My students absolutely needed a lot more therapeutic services, much more intensive intervention, more robust social programs. I was certainly not equipped to adequately deal with these problems. I tried to hook them up with services and professionals who could help, but I was completely out of my league. We're trying to teach and dealing with sexual abuse, physical and psychological abuse, random violence.[20]

Not to mention the lack of resources. While the school invested heavily in security cameras and metal detectors after Davis's death, students and teachers still lacked the most basic supplies. For example, more than eight hundred students had to share about fifteen computers in the outdated library.[21]

Englewood High was labeled as failing; Arne Duncan referred to it as having a "culture of failure."[22] The school was closed in 2008, and the students were dispersed to several other high schools in the area. The result was even more disorder and tension. Potter and other teachers described students dropping out rather than crossing into enemy gang territories; many who stayed saw their academic performance plummet as familiar routines and relationships were shattered.

The closing of Englewood High motivated Potter to become more involved in the Chicago Teachers Union. A union representative had visited him when the closing was imminent, telling him to get his résumé ready. Potter was disgusted that the union did not try to fight or negotiate around the closing. "They dealt strictly with contractual issues," he said. So he and some other teachers took it upon themselves to form alliances with community groups, pastors, and parents to address school closings and other big-picture issues affecting the future of public education in Chicago. They formed a progressive, proactive caucus within the union and held their first meeting at the United Electrical, Radio and Machine Workers of America (UE) mural-covered union hall on Ashland Avenue. Thus began the Caucus of Rank and File Educators in the spring of 2008. CORE set out to recruit specific teachers, and also launched a book club and study group. The group's first selection was Naomi Klein's *The Shock Doctrine*, a popular screed against neoliberalism, global capitalism, and privatization.[23]

One of the first people contacted by the founding CORE members was Karen Lewis, a chemistry teacher who'd grown up with civil rights activist parents in Hyde Park, the Obamas' neighborhood. Lewis had gravitated toward teaching after stints doing standup comedy at a local tavern and attending medical school in hopes of becoming a doctor in Barbados. She was looking forward to retiring and spending time in Hawaii, where her retired husband had a time-share. But reading and discussing *The Shock Doctrine* and connecting with other politically active teachers persuaded her to keep her commitment to Chicago classrooms.[24]

Xian Barrett, another early CORE convert, was a young law and history teacher who had grown up around the labor movement. His mother was a National Education Association organizing director in Urbana-Champaign, Illinois, and his father was a labor historian. Barrett got his first taste of teaching in the JET program in Japan, where he taught English and human rights. He started at the Chicago Public Schools in 2006, and was disillusioned with the union leadership at the time. After Potter invited him to participate, Barrett was excited that "I had found a group of troublemakers who could offer something new to students."

Barrett's local colleagues weren't the only ones who recognized his dedication to his students: in 2009 he was chosen as a Classroom Teaching Ambassador Fellow by the US Department of Education. A bio on the department's website noted that Barrett had founded a citywide youth-led social justice organization, brought students to New Orleans for service learning trips, and organized sister city events with Japanese schools. It also noted his philosophy of teaching: "Before the students lose interest in your instruction, ask them what they are passionate about and work with that—their learning belongs to them."[25]

Over the next few years the group Teachers for Social Justice, which included members of CORE, held public workshops and teach-ins for parents, teachers, and students concerned about Renaissance 2010 and the direction of the public schools. CORE based its model in part on the teachers union in British Columbia, Canada, which successfully forced the government to mandate smaller classes and other improvements.[26]

CORE members became increasingly vocal in teachers union meetings. They didn't actively oppose the existing union leadership, as Barrett remembered it, but they proposed ways the union could be more proactive and progressive. In return, Barrett said, "we were viciously attacked" by union leaders.[27] Potter noted that entrenched union leaders seemed particularly threatened by the way CORE members were coordinating with community and parent groups, and a union community outreach initiative was canceled—Potter thinks because union leaders were upset about CORE's growing influence.

Such dramas generated more support for CORE and its way of thinking, members recalled. So in 2010 they decided to run a CORE slate in the union election, challenging incumbent president Marilyn Stewart. Karen Lewis would be CORE's candidate for president. In the union election on May 21, 2010, Stewart's slate won 32 percent of the vote, just 2 percent ahead of CORE, with two other caucuses running. In a June 11 runoff, 12,080 teachers voted for CORE and 8,326 for the slate headed by Stewart.[28]

Lewis's acceptance speech was a declaration of war on the school reform movement. "Today marks the beginning of the end of scapegoating educators for the social ills that all of our children, families, and schools struggle against every day," she proclaimed. "This election shows the unity of thirty thousand educators standing strong to put business in its place, out of our schools. Corporate America sees K–12 public education as a $380 billion trust that up until the last ten or fifteen years they haven't had a sizable piece of. So-called school reform is not an education plan. It's a business plan."

This was right around the time Emanuel—still at the White House—told talk-show host Charlie Rose that he'd long dreamed of being mayor of Chicago.[29] He still might not have known that he'd be running for mayor in just a few short months. But viewed in retrospect, Lewis's acceptance speech could be seen as the opening sally of a major battle to come.

XIAN BARRETT WAS AMONG THE PROGRESSIVE YOUNG LEADERS TAKING THE CHICAGO TEACHERS UNION IN A NEW DIRECTION. PHOTO BY KARI LYDERSEN.

SB 7 AND THE RIGHT TO STRIKE

Even as Barrett was riding high on the union victory, things were getting difficult for him at Julian High School. Violence and family trauma were everyday occurrences for Barrett's students, and they affected him personally. "You have to have a lesson plan for the Mondays when one of your students was lost over the weekend," he said, noting that six students in his classes were killed within several years. Barrett also talked to his students about current events, and the ongoing controversy over school closings and charter schools was a hot topic. He took students on field trips to school board meetings, figuring that the process was an important civics lesson. Some of them got so interested that they skipped classes to attend school board meetings or protests on their own, he said. Barrett thinks his students' activism and his contemporary lessons ultimately led to losing his job at Julian. In early summer 2010 he got notice that his job was eliminated through "redefinition," and he said that a school district middle manager had brought up his outside activities in discussions with the principal.

Without a classroom job, Barrett took the opportunity to work as the union's political director in Springfield, the state capital. One of his main assignments involved work on the proposed sweeping education legislation known as Senate Bill 7 (SB 7). Even in the afterglow of the progressive faction's takeover of the Chicago Teachers Union, SB 7 created serious tension among union leaders and members, and between the Chicago Teachers Union and state education unions.[30] Karen Lewis and officials with the two statewide education unions (the Illinois Federation of Teachers and the Illinois Education Association) participated in months of secret negotiations around the bill, which was supported by national conservative school reform groups like the Oregon-based Stand for Children.[31] Though Emanuel had no official capacity during the bulk of the negotiations—he was a mayoral candidate and mayor-elect at the time—he made sure his interests were represented.[32]

The bill would make it much more difficult for teachers to strike and would tie their evaluations—and their job security and pay—closely to student performance on standardized tests. Everyone involved knew the bill could have major ramifications for public education in Chicago, and that it was being closely watched by teachers unions and school reform groups nationwide. Given the high stakes and the complicated maneuvering such legislative battles always entail, Chicago Teachers Union leaders struggled with how much to compromise, how much to trust key legislators, and how to best protect their members. Eventually Lewis and the state union leaders agreed to support a draft bill. But many members of the Chicago Teachers Union considered it an abhorrent antiunion measure, and blasted Lewis for signing off on it.[33]

Most notably, the bill mandated a strike could happen only if 75 percent of the union membership authorized it. This was considered an extremely high threshold in any sector, and Chicago teachers had never before voted to strike by such a wide margin. The bill also included bureaucratic processes and requirements that the administration could leverage to delay a strike; it also mandated that a certain percentage of teachers' evaluations be based on students' standardized test scores, and it changed the process for determining tenure.[34]

The State Senate passed the bill fifty-four to zero on April 15, 2011.[35] Lewis wrote her membership a letter saying that though the bill was not ideal, the union had beaten down much worse proposals. "Yesterday a legislative compromise between 20 different parties became a bill," her letter said. "It is far from perfect, but it is far superior from where we started. Everyone at the table swallowed more than one bitter pill."[36]

The union's House of Delegates, its governing body, uniformly rejected the bill in both an executive committee vote and a vote of the full body in early May. The delegates called on Lewis to reject the bill and demand that it be renegotiated, ultimately to no avail.[37]

The State House passed the legislation on May 12, by a vote of 112 to one—just four days before Emanuel's inauguration.[38] The bill was signed by Governor Pat Quinn on June 13. Showing the bill's national significance, Quinn was joined by Stand for Children CEO Jonah Edelman and a senior aide to Arne Duncan.[39]

STANDING FOR CHILDREN?

It was common knowledge that national school reform groups played a role in shaping and lobbying for SB 7. But still many were shocked when video went viral showing Edelman speaking at the summer 2011 Aspen Ideas Festival, a high-profile and prestigious gathering for intellectuals and pundits from various disciplines.

In the speech Edelman candidly described the strategizing, back-room deals, and complicated negotiations that made the legislation a reality. He bragged about slyly persuading unions to agree to deals not in their best interest, in part by appealing to what he described as their purported concern primarily with dues and collective bargaining rights. He described Emanuel as a key ally in the campaign. "That was another shoe that dropped. It put a lot of pressure on the unions, particularly the Chicago Teachers Union because they didn't support him," he said. "To our surprise, and with Rahm Emanuel's involvement behind the scenes, we were able to split the IEA [Illinois Education Association] from the Chicago Teachers Union."[40]

Edelman revealed that his group "hired eleven lobbyists, including four of the absolute best insiders and seven of the best minority lobbyists, preventing the unions from hiring them." And he described how securing union agreement, albeit coerced, allowed school reformers to steamroll any opposition from Democratic legislators.

"Now it makes it hard for folks leading unions in other states to say these types of reforms are terrible because their colleagues in Illinois said these reforms are great," Edelman concluded. "Our hope is to use this as a catalyst to very quickly make change in other very entrenched [union] states."

Once the video circulated, members and supporters of the Chicago Teachers Union and unions across the country saw the speech as a deep insult and a disturbing window into the increasingly polarized and high-stakes fights over the future of public education and public sector unions. But if Edelman and other reformers thought that SB 7 had taken away the teachers' ability to strike and gutted their power, the union would ultimately have the last laugh.

KAREN LEWIS (LEFT) BECAME A NATIONAL POPULIST HERO DURING THE
TEACHERS STRIKE. PHOTO BY KARI LYDERSEN.

A NEW BOARD, A NEW CEO, A NEW BEGINNING?

Starting in 1995, the Chicago mayor began appointing the members of the city's Board of Education, which oversees the public education system and bargains with the Chicago Teachers Union. The vast majority of school districts nationwide have an elected school board, but Illinois legislators who passed state legislation giving board appointment power to the mayor argued that it would make the bureaucracy more efficient and effective.

Emanuel appointed his new school board immediately after taking office. They were an illustrious and diverse bunch, with impressive credentials in the business, nonprofit, and education worlds. Among them was Penny Pritzker, a billionaire developer, investor, major Democratic donor, and member of the prominent Pritzker family—who, among other things, founded the Hyatt hotel chain. In March 2013 Pritzker would resign from the school board, and soon after President Obama nominated her to be US commerce secretary. Like Emanuel, the board members were determined to implement a longer school day. The teachers union, however, was adamant that Emanuel could not legally impose a longer school day without negotiating pay and other contract issues. The teachers contract would expire in June 2012, and negotiations typically start months in advance; the longer school day should have been part of those negotiations, the union argued.

In summer 2011 Emanuel launched private negotiations with individual princi-pals, pushing them to accept ninety extra minutes in the school day starting that fall. Teachers union vice president Jesse Sharkey said the mayor enlisted aldermen to talk directly with principals, urging them to agree to the longer school day without going through union channels. Principals and teachers were offered incentives: an extra $150,000 to schools that complied in September, $75,000 to those that started in January. Participating teachers would get $1,250 bonuses. Some principals re-portedly offered teachers comp time and iPads to vote for the deal.[41] And some schools held votes, including with nonunion staff, on whether to agree to the longer school day. The mayor's office was essentially making an end run around the union, offering incentives and seeking commitments without going through processes mandated in the union contract.[42]

"The implication was that if two hundred schools voted to side with Rahm against their union, Rahm effectively would have broken the union before the con-tract talks had even begun," said Sharkey.[43] "The union was furious. You have to think about what collective bargaining is—that's what a union does. For Rahm to go around the union and develop political influence with the members so they side with the boss instead of the union, that's union-busting."

Ultimately only a handful of schools agreed to adopt the longer day, which some saw as a victory for the union. And the union filed a complaint with the Illinois Ed-ucational Labor Relations Board, which agreed that the administration had violated teachers' bargaining rights, and prohibited school-by-school negotiations.[44]

After taking office Emanuel had appointed Jean-Claude Brizard as the CEO of the Chicago Public Schools, making him the fourth chief executive of the trou-ble-plagued district in just three years. Brizard was born in Haiti, the son of educa-tors, during the brutal dictatorship of François "Papa Doc" Duvalier. When Brizard was twelve, the family fled to New York City, where they lived in public housing in Brooklyn.[45] Brizard attended public school and became a physics teacher; he later rose to regional superintendent of New York City schools and then became superintendent of the school district in the upstate city of Rochester.[46]

Though many praised Brizard as charismatic, energetic, and inspiring, he also left anger and discontent in his wake in both those districts—for spearheading school closures, teacher layoffs, and a shift to nonunion private charter schools. Be-fore going to Rochester, Brizard was a fellow at the Superintendents' Academy of the Broad Center for the Management of School Systems, a program known for its emphasis on "school choice," "teacher accountability," a business-driven approach, and other conservative reforms detested by public unions. In Rochester test scores rose under Brizard's watch.[47] But he alienated parents and teachers by aggressively instituting private charter schools even as he laid off teachers.

In February 2011 Rochester parents and community members gave Brizard a vote of no confidence, and then the Rochester Teachers Association union held its own vote of no confidence in which 80 percent of members participated and 95 percent voted against Brizard.[48] Two federal lawsuits were filed regarding Brizard's tenure in Rochester, and the union charged him with discrimination in the firing of an older African American teacher. Brizard and his wife, a teacher with a doctorate in cognitive studies in education who had started an all-girls charter school, were considering a move to Cleveland or Newark when Emanuel called offering the Chicago job.[49]

Talking with *Chicago Magazine* a few months into his Chicago tenure, Brizard described his relationship with union president Lewis and his views of union teachers:

> I really do think that teachers unions have evolved. They were created for good reason. When you look at what happened to teachers in the '50s, '60s and even '70s—it's unjust. [But] we have overcorrected. What we are doing not just in Chicago but across the country is discouraging a lot of young people from coming into education. They don't want to see themselves being vilified by people who [see] teachers unionized as blue-collar workers. They want to be treated as professionals.[50]

Brizard described going to dinner with Lewis and both of their spouses, and noted that Lewis called him a liar in French. That spring Lewis also had a dinner date with Emanuel. Shortly before he took office, Emanuel invited her to the fancy French restaurant Henri and to a dance performance, since they shared an interest in ballet. Like Emanuel, Lewis is Jewish, having converted as an adult, and she recognized similarities between herself and the mayor. "We should be best friends. We have way more in common than we don't," she told *Chicago Magazine*, noting that they both ordered Malbec wine and lamb.[51]

UNO CHARTER SCHOOLS

There were ninety-six charter schools in Chicago as of the 2012–13 school year.[52] Thirteen of them were run by the United Neighborhood Organization, the community organization formed in 1984 by churches and community groups, which became known for deep and sometimes controversial ties to powerful Democratic Machine politicians.[53] UNO CEO Juan Rangel served as Emanuel's mayoral campaign cochair and continued as a close adviser after the election. Rangel was born the son of undocumented immigrants in the border town of Brownsville, Texas. He moved with his large family to Chicago as a child and launched his political career when he was elected to a Local School Council with UNO's backing in 1989.[54]

Over time, Rangel gained significant clout with city and state officials and capitalized on their embrace of school reform. In January 2013, state legislators proposed a bill that would have given all the public schools in Chicago $35 million for building acquisition and construction while giving UNO the same amount. The teachers union argued that "UNO currently has 13 schools and serves approximately 6,500 students. The rest of CPS [Chicago Public Schools] has more than 600 schools and serves 395,000 students. UNO's share works out to $5,415 per student, while the rest of the district's share works out to $89 per student."[55]

In 2009, UNO got a $98 million state grant, the largest to a charter school network in state history.[56] In February 2013 the *Sun-Times* revealed that millions of those taxpayer dollars were going to companies owned by people with close political and familial ties to UNO, including two brothers of UNO top official Miguel d'Escoto; two brothers of State Representative Ed Acevedo, a big UNO supporter; and Gery Chico, the Machine-connected lawyer who had run for mayor against Emanuel. UNO had signed multimillion-dollar contracts for security, zoning work, construction, new windows, and other goods and services with these firms, without competitive bidding. Meanwhile, the organization was paying its own nonprofit spinoff for school janitorial service.[57]

In April 2013 the grant was suspended by Governor Quinn for alleged misuse of funds. Although $84 million had already been disbursed, the remaining $14 million in payments were halted.[58] Apparently as a result, construction on UNO's Soccer Academy High School on the Southwest Side was stopped.[59] In late May, Rangel stepped down as chair of the boards that oversee the organization and its schools, but kept his $250,000 a year post as CEO.[60]

"A TALE OF TWO MISSIONS"

Emanuel also forged close ties with another prominent charter school operator, Noble Street, a chain started in Chicago in 1999 by two public school teachers. Noble Street's philosophy centered on high expectations, strict discipline, long school days, and long school years. Its students turned in relatively high test scores, and many who came from overcrowded, chaotic public schools said they thrived in the rigid and demanding atmosphere.[61]

In early 2012 Emanuel and Noble Street were showcased in an online teaser for a forthcoming feature film called *A Tale of Two Missions*.[62] The film was produced by the Michigan-based Education Action Group, headed by Kyle Olson. Olson was a blogger for Breitbart.com, the website founded by brash right-wing pundit Andrew Breitbart, who gained notoriety for deceptively edited "gotcha" videos targeting Democrats.[63] Breitbart was linked to blatantly misrepresentative pieces that led to the downfall of the national community organization ACORN, and that helped force the resignation of Shirley Sherrod, an African American official in Obama's Agriculture Department. His protégées had manipulated video to make Sherrod sound prejudiced against white people.[64] So one would not have expected to see a former top Obama staffer like Emanuel working with a Breitbart devotee.

Olson and former National Public Radio host Juan Williams, who narrated *A Tale of Two Missions*, billed it as a "documentary." But it was actually a vicious and sensational attack on the Chicago Teachers Union, casting school reformers as selfless idealistic upstarts "rattling the cages of the education system's traditional power brokers."

"What you're about to witness is a tale of two cultures," Williams intoned, "one intent on maintaining its power and influence" (footage shows Karen Lewis marching and talking to reporters) "and one intent on preparing our children for life" (a dreadlocked teacher interacts with students in a calm charter school classroom). "One obsessed with the mechanics of contract negotiations, and one obsessed with graduating all of its students. This is the story of a Chicago miracle, and the people who would kill it."

Footage of protests against antiunion Wisconsin governor Scott Walker was interspersed throughout the film, even though those protests had no direct relevance to the narrative, which was otherwise about Chicago. The film came off as a not-so-subtle hint that the battle against teachers unions, and the Chicago Teachers Union in particular, was part of a much larger culture war. "Ultimately the more choices you have, the more freedom you have," concluded Williams in the film's teaser. "And freedom always works."

FACEBOOK TOWN HALL

On January 23, 2012, Emanuel held a "Facebook town hall" to talk about his plans for the schools. Addressing the public via live video, he answered a handful of questions culled from about 150 submitted earlier on Facebook. The questions were read by an adult moderator and two student journalists at George Westinghouse College Prep, a beautiful new school on the West Side.

Emanuel briefly mentioned the union contract negotiations that had recently kicked off. He said Chicago teachers were "among the best paid in the nation, and they deserve it." The mayor followed that curt praise with a veiled dig at the union, saying, "I will not allow another contract to occur that leaves our kids on the side of the road. No one can point to the shortest school day in the country and say that's in the interest of our kids." He described his main criteria in evaluating a new contract: "Is that contract good for children? Everyone knows what the last contract got for adults."[65]

The questions Emanuel chose to answer were softballs that helped the mayor paint a rosy picture of the school system's future. The teachers and parents commenting in the Facebook chat room were not buying it. "What a strokefest," said one. Participants complained that Emanuel was not answering tough questions like, "How can you expect to keep quality educators in CPS when they see you blatantly violate their contract by refusing to implement a contractually negotiated raise?" and "Doesn't closing schools add instability to children's lives?"

Commenters also attacked Emanuel's plan for more summer school, noting that temperatures got dangerously hot in old city schools because many didn't have air conditioning. They questioned whether there was air conditioning at the private University of Chicago Lab School that Emanuel's kids attended.

Frustrated parents who stayed on Facebook after the town hall concluded discussed organizing for the next school board meeting. They complained that the meetings were always held during daytime work hours, and people had to get in line before dawn just to speak for a few minutes. They also chatted about boycotting the public schools and protesting the longer day.

"The only thing that stops the longer day is a huge parent uproar, and I mean big," said one commenter. "No one has a voice with Rahm," said another. "It's his way or the highway. Very sad."

CLOSING SCHOOLS

A key component of Chicago's Renaissance 2010 plan and school reform movements more generally is closing regular public schools that are deemed failing or underenrolled and redirecting students to other, presumably better schools—including new charters. In Chicago and around the nation, closing public schools has proved highly controversial and led to countless protests.

Troubled as these schools may be, they are ingrained parts of the communities they serve. Often multiple generations from the same family have attended, and students have a strong sense of identification with and pride in their school. Switching schools can be emotionally traumatic as well as highly problematic for working parents and even dangerous for students. Chicago does not provide school bus service, and many parents and students don't have cars. So traveling to and from a new school often requires a commute on public transit, including long waits at bus stops that increase the risk of being jumped or shot.

Many Chicago parents' worst fears were embodied in the 2009 tragedy of Derrion Albert, who was beaten to death by a mob of students at Fenger Academy High School, where he had transferred after his local high school on the Far South Side was changed into a military academy.[66] Although closing troubled neighborhood schools could theoretically create better opportunities for students at another venue, many parents and students simply see increased stress, risk, inconvenience, and a larger signal that their neighborhoods and their local schools are not considered a priority by downtown power brokers.

During Emanuel's first year in office, the administration proposed closing down seven schools and putting ten more into "turnaround" proceedings, in which new leadership takes over and most or all of the teachers are laid off. No charter schools were on the list to be closed or turned around, despite the fact that, according to a *Chicago Tribune* analysis, "some had students performing nearly as badly on state exams as those at neighborhood schools targeted for closing." In fact, the *Tribune* noted, UNO and the charter organizations LEARN and Catalyst were being awarded the right to open new schools despite their failure to meet district average scores on state exams.[67]

The plan brought a sense of déjà vu to Jackson Potter and other teachers who'd already seen their schools close. Potter noted that Emanuel was even "more aggressive" than Mayor Daley about school closings. "Daley was much more sensitive to upsetting labor—a natural constituency for him," said Potter. "At least he had a sense of Chicago and some of the third rails in terms of politics and community. Rahm doesn't have any of that. He looks at how we get things done from a business perspective—how do we use power and money to help us shape everything?"[68]

Public meetings about the plan were held in various neighborhoods. Reporters revealed that many of the "community members" holding signs or speaking out in support of school closings were actually paid $20 to $25, doled out in white envelopes as they stepped off buses afterward.[69] The payments were orchestrated in part by the Reverend Roosevelt Watkins, a longtime ally of Mayor Daley who continued to receive city money to run social service programs after Emanuel took over. Alderman Robert Fioretti told the *Chicago Tribune* he was disturbed when some of the protesters indicated they were paid. He said one man tapped him on the shoulder and told him as much, and two others said they were ordered to read speeches in favor of the administration's plans—and refused. Some paid protesters were confused about what they were supposed to be supporting, and some disobeyed orders and spoke their mind—*against* closing schools. Media photos showed many hiding their faces behind their protest signs.[70]

The *Tribune* reported that Watkins's HOPE Organization was one of three groups that received a one-month grant totaling $1 million for programming to keep kids off the street during the summer. Watkins's church was also one of ten to which the city paid a total of $6.3 million to escort kids safely to school. According to the public radio station WBEZ, Chicago Public Schools paid Watkins's organization $1.4 million over a year and a half. It was not surprising, then, that Watkins was a loyal supporter of the administration's plans. In August 2011, for example, he sat beside schools CEO Brizard at a breakfast at the White Sox ball field where Emanuel asked pastors to sermonize about the value of a longer school day.[71]

When Emanuel was confronted about the paid protesters at a January 2012 press conference, he answered, "I'm not speaking on it. I'm speaking about the fact that the ministers care about their schools and care about their community."[72] The *Chicago Tribune* reported that the public relations firm Resolute Consulting had orchestrated funding for pastors supporting school closings and had also written press releases, produced a video, and helped organize meetings in support of the school closings. Resolute was headed by Greg Goldner, who had run Emanuel's successful 2002 campaign for Congress.[73]

DEFENDING DYETT

During the Facebook town hall Emanuel had said, "It's easy to get isolated in the mayor's office. My job is to make sure I continue to hear the voices of the people, the optimism, what's troubling to them, do they have a solution to a problem that I can carry into the office and make it happen."

In early January 2012, a group of parents had visited City Hall offering just that. For about two years parents and community leaders from the South Side neighborhoods of Kenwood and Oakland had worked with university experts to craft a proposal for a program called Global Community Achievers, which would bring together five elementary and middle schools and a high school in an educational "village" focused on math, science, engineering, international studies, and leadership. Each elementary school would have a certain focus, and students could continue these specialized studies at the local high school, Walter H. Dyett—one of the schools to which many Englewood High students went when their school was closed.

Under the educational village scenario, a full-time social worker and nurse would be on call. Parents would staff a "safe passage" program helping kids get to and from school. And students would have the opportunity to take field trips and hear from expert speakers. The proposal was based in part on community efforts that had already resulted in significant improvements at Dyett. Parents had worked with teachers to offer supplemental programs and incentives for students, explained Jitu Brown, the education organizer for KOCO. In 2007 and 2008 a "restorative justice" program was instituted at Dyett, along with "wraparound services" to help students deal with issues in their lives outside school and a program called "Life after Dyett" for graduating seniors. Schools CEO Arne Duncan had praised the efforts, and school officials nationwide looked at the programs as models. The number of Dyett graduates going to college spiked, and the school won various awards; a few students qualified for the prestigious Gates Millennium Scholarship Program.[74] "The culture had changed, the school began to soar," said Brown.

But in 2009, 2010, and 2011, Dyett suffered severe budget cuts that ended or gutted most of these programs and left Dyett with only one honors class.[75] By 2012, Dyett's very existence was precarious: it was on the list of schools to be closed.

The school board called a vote on the school closings and turnarounds on February 22. In early January parents, pastors, and students affiliated with KOCO camped out in the lobby of Emanuel's office for two consecutive days, demanding he meet with them and read their Global Community Achievers proposal.[76] On the first day of the sit-in, some people brought folding chairs. The next day, guards told them chairs were not allowed. So teenagers, middle-aged parents, and elderly grandparents sat on the floor with two fuzzy red blankets and a few yoga mats for padding. One older woman curled in the fetal position. A box of Dunkin' Donuts and bottles of hand sanitizer were scattered around. Finally, on the second afternoon, a member of Emanuel's staff emerged from his office and agreed to meet with some of the KOCO members. The others talked quietly while waiting to hear the results.

When the KOCO members emerged from the meeting, the others pulled themselves off the floor to hear the news. One of the leaders announced that the mayor's deputy chief of staff for education, Elizabeth Swanson, had agreed to meet with them later that month. It was not clear if Emanuel would attend. Sixteen-year-old Dyett student O'Sha Dancy wasn't impressed. "It's not a meeting because the mayor wasn't there," he said. "He's the one who makes the decisions. Rahm has the power to get things done." Dancy was right to be so skeptical. Neither Swanson nor anyone from the mayor's office ever got back to KOCO about the proposal. Brown said they sent two letters and made three more calls to the mayor's office asking for a meeting with Emanuel, but never got a response. Emanuel's refusal to meet with, or even respond to, one of the city's oldest civil rights organizations about an issue of dire importance to their members, Brown believed, was a slap in the face to the African American community.

PICCOLO PARENTS

Parents of students at Brian Piccolo Elementary School and Pablo Casals Elementary School in the largely low-income African American and Puerto Rican neighborhood of West Humboldt Park also developed a plan for improving their struggling schools. Like the KOCO members, they wanted to present their ideas to Emanuel but had no luck getting an audience.

Both schools were slated to potentially become "turnaround schools" and be taken over by the private Academy for Urban School Leadership. Chicago Public Schools chief administrative officer Tim Cawley and school board president David Vitale had been top officials at the academy, which ran nineteen schools in Chicago.[77]

On February 17, 2012, parents and supporters began a sit-in demanding that Emanuel listen to their plan to save Piccolo and Casals from being "turned around."[78] In chilly weather, they pitched tents to spend the night in front of Piccolo and held signs in Spanish and English.[79] The next evening they ended the occupation after getting an audience with school board vice president Jesse Ruiz, who promised that other members of the board would meet with them.[80]

Two nights before the scheduled school board vote, parents and supporters dressed in heavy coats against the winter chill and marched outside Emanuel's house.[81] Protesters also marched to Cawley's sprawling Tudor home, on a private drive in Winnetka, one of the country's wealthiest suburbs. They rang the door-

CHICAGO STUDENTS, PARENTS, AND TEACHERS PACKED COMMUNITY HEARINGS
BEGGING THE MAYOR NOT TO CLOSE THEIR SCHOOLS—LIKE COOPER
ELEMENTARY, IN THE PILSEN NEIGHBORHOOD. PHOTO BY KARI LYDERSEN.

bells of neighbors and handed out play money, a jibe at the paid protesters at the public hearings.[82] The next night, hundreds rallied downtown outside the school board offices.

Before sunrise on February 22, the day of the vote, parents who had taken off work were already lined up outside the Board of Education for the big meeting.[83] When the doors opened, the relatively small conference room filled up quickly, and many who wanted to speak could not get in. After hours of impassioned testimony about saving the schools and retaining teachers and principals, the board voted unanimously to close or turn around all seventeen schools identified as failing, including Dyett, Piccolo, and Casals.[84]

"Mayor Rahm Emanuel, you said you were going to give us change," said activist Carolina Gaete, who had helped lead sit-ins at several schools over the years. "You've changed things for the worse. And the board? This is a dictatorship!"

"EDUCATIONAL APARTHEID"

The school closings vote happened during Black History Month, a fact not lost on those who saw it all in the context of racial inequity and segregation. The Rev. Jesse Jackson preached about injustices in the school system and threatened to file a federal complaint about what he called "educational apartheid." Not only would African

American and Latino students be affected most by the school closings, he noted, but African American and Latino teachers would be disproportionately laid off.

Schools CEO Brizard took to the pulpit himself to respond, telling the crowd at the Apostolic Church of God, in the South Side Woodlawn neighborhood, "Ninety percent of our kids are black and brown, 90 percent of the resources go to kids who are black and brown. How can that be educational apartheid?"[85]

Of course, 90 percent of the children in Chicago are not black and brown, so the elephant in the room was the fact that people who can afford it—including most white families—send their kids to private school or move to the suburbs.

The disparities within the system were indeed severe. Reverend Jackson noted that 160 South Side schools lacked a library, in contrast to the superior selective-enrollment and magnet schools on the city's North and Near West Sides that the relatively few white students in the public system were more likely to attend.[86] KOCO compiled a report documenting class offerings at Dyett High School and Lakeview High School and Northside College Prep, two schools in wealthier North Side neighborhoods. The comparison was stark; in every subject category, the North Side schools' offerings dwarfed those at Dyett. Rather than closing the subpar schools in their neighborhoods, parents argued, the city should invest enough resources and attention to make them as good as the schools attended by wealthier, white students.

CONTRACT NEGOTIATIONS

The school board and the teachers union had started contract negotiations months before their contract expired in June 2012. But progress was slow or even nonexistent.

On May 23, about four thousand union members in red shirts filled the historic Auditorium Theater to listen to Karen Lewis recite a litany of abuses by the administration. "Fight, fight!" and "Strike, strike!" they chanted before spilling into the streets to join several thousand supporters in a march through downtown. As dusk fell they clogged the wide street in the financial district in front of the Chicago Mercantile Exchange, brandishing signs saying, "I AM a Teacher" and "Yes to Respect."[87]

By June, the union and the board were still deadlocked on numerous issues. So the teachers union decided to vote on whether to authorize a strike in the coming school year. A "yes" vote would not necessarily mean a strike would happen, but it would give Karen Lewis the authority to call for one if negotiations hit a wall. The SB 7 legislation had set the threshold very high—75 percent of members would have to vote yes to authorize the strike. "We'd done our homework," Jonah Edelman bragged at the Aspen Ideas Festival. "We knew the highest threshold of any bargaining unit that had voted one way or another was 48.3 percent. . . . In the end game the Chicago Teachers Union took that deal misunderstanding, probably not knowing, the statistics about voting history."[88]

Regardless of whether teachers knew the voting statistics, the school reformers had clearly underestimated how well the union was organized and how angry members were about Emanuel's plans. Almost 90 percent of them voted to authorize a strike.[89]

SB 7 also mandated that an "independent fact-finder" do a study and make recommendations in the case of contentious contract negotiations. In July 2012, the independent report was released. Fact-finder Edwin Benn called the negotiations "toxic," and recommended teachers get a raise totaling 35.7 percent over four years because of the longer school day. "The board cannot realistically expect that it should not have to compensate employees" for the longer day, wrote Benn.[90]

The school board unanimously rejected Benn's nonbinding recommendations, saying they would be too expensive: the raise alone would cost $331 million in just the first year.[91] The teachers union's house of delegates also unanimously rejected the recommendations, arguing that Benn had failed to address important issues including class size, teacher evaluations, and job security for teachers laid off at closing or turned around schools. The union argued that teachers who lost their jobs at such underperforming schools should be first in line for new openings anywhere in the district. All the administration had offered was that laid-off teachers would be placed in a pool of potential hires for new jobs and guaranteed at least one interview with a principal.

Teachers argued that without job protection in the case of a school closing, they would be forced to avoid working at the most challenging schools. In other words, the best teachers with the most potential to be hired elsewhere would tend to leave the struggling schools that needed them most.

TEMPERATURES RISING

July 2012 smashed records for heat in Chicago, leaving grass parched brown and teenagers prying open fire hydrants so often that city workers apparently gave up trying to close them. Many apartments and homes—like the public schools—lacked air conditioning, and families in neighborhoods like Pilsen, Back of the Yards, North Lawndale, and Brighton Park spent long hours sitting on sidewalks and stoops. Among parents, speculation about the coming school year was a frequent topic of discussion. With both the teachers and the city rejecting Benn's recommendations, a strike in coming weeks seemed imminent.

The last time Chicago teachers had gone on strike was in 1987, for nineteen days, during the tenure of Mayor Harold Washington. That was also a time of budget crisis, and the teachers union was demanding 10 percent raises while the school board was proposing a 1.7 percent pay cut and shortening the school year by three days. Washington blamed previous mayors for giving teachers too much without taking responsibility for the cost down the road. The two-year contract the parties eventually negotiated gave teachers a 4 percent raise the first year and reduced some class sizes but allowed more than five hundred layoffs.[92]

Though Washington clashed with teachers during the strike, he was generally known as a supporter of organized labor—albeit in the complicated context of Chicago politics, where many established unions had ties with his opponents' Democratic Machine.[93] In contrast, by summer 2012 Emanuel was widely seen as an opponent of organized labor, and people expected a strike could be a protracted and ugly showdown.

After more than a year of bitter fighting over the proposed longer school day, the issue was resolved with the kind of compromise that many said could have been achieved early on if the mayor had been willing to work with the union. The administration agreed to rehire almost five hundred teachers in exchange for the union accepting a longer school day structured so that teachers' total hours would be the same or only slightly increased. The day was lengthened by thirty minutes for high schools and seventy-five minutes for elementary schools, less than Emanuel had wanted but still a significant change. By eliminating prep time and moving the lunch period, teachers' schedules were supposed to remain similar.[94]

But even with that issue somewhat laid to rest, the union and the city were still miles apart on important aspects of the contract: recall rights for laid-off teachers, teacher evaluation methods, and other issues. About a third of the student body was scheduled to start classes on August 13. Would school doors be open? The union was required to give notice ten days before striking. The first week in August ticked by with no notice of a strike, but the union ramped up preparations. Teachers gathered to make signs and held informational pickets before and after classes at the schools in session. A teachers solidarity group held regular meetings, ready to join the union on the picket lines. Teachers marched in the annual Bud Billiken Parade, a longstanding ritual in the African American community. Though many parents were undoubtedly nervous about what their kids would do in the case of a strike, teachers said they got an overwhelmingly warm and supportive response during the parade. A network called the Chicago Teachers Solidarity Campaign brought together labor unions, parent groups, community organizations, and others to support the teachers and keep the general public updated.

The administration was also gearing up for battle. A memo from public schools administrative officials was circulated advising principals to report activities including work slowdowns, "sick outs," and "other job actions that undermine supervisory authority and deleteriously affect the mission and goals of the Chicago public school system."[95] Though the memo was careful to mention that certain union activities are legal, teachers and union staff saw it as asking principals to "spy" on teachers. On Au-

gust 22, the school board voted to authorize spending $25 million on student serv-
ices and meals to be offered by libraries, churches, and other nonschool institutions
in case of a strike.[96] The idea was to provide students safety and nourishment even if
there were no classes in session. But many teachers saw the authorization as a public
relations move—trying to make it look like the board was dedicated to caring for
students while teachers were putting their own interests first and wasting taxpayer
money.

That same afternoon, at the union's delegates meeting, union representatives from
schools across the city voted on whether to authorize Karen Lewis to give the ten-day
notice. The first day of school for the majority of students would be the day after
Labor Day—thirteen days away. Considering almost 90 percent of union members
had already voted to authorize a strike, the results were not much in doubt. Still, there
was palpable tension in the air as teachers in red union T-shirts streamed into the formidable stone and brick structure that is Lane Tech College Prep, a selective enrollment high school on the North Side. The possibility of a strike seemed much more
concrete than it had during the authorization vote back in June. Worried about their
students and their own finances, teachers said they were not looking forward to being
on the picket lines. But they felt it might be necessary, and they were ready.

"From day to day working with kids, I hope there's not a strike," said Xian Barrett, a founding CORE member. "But in terms of caring about these students' long-
term futures, and the future of their kids and their kids' kids, I think a strike is a
necessary step in taking the schools back." Barrett had started a new job teaching at
Gage Park High School on the South Side. He wasn't a union delegate, so he wasn't
allowed into the meeting. But he came to soak up the atmosphere and convene with
teachers at a bar called Pete's afterward. He made the trek up north even though he
had gotten food poisoning from eating lunch in the school cafeteria earlier that day.

After about two hours, teachers started coming out of the building, looking
fired up. They had voted to allow Lewis to give notice to strike. As Lewis exited, the
red-shirted crowd surrounded her and cheered. Teachers refrained from discussing
what had happened in the meeting, but they were eager to talk about the person
they saw as responsible for their battle: Mayor Emanuel.

"He is ridiculous," said Jeanine Trize, a teacher's aide who had worked in the
schools for twenty-two years. "How can you come into a system you know nothing
about and, without working with the teachers and students, just start changing
things? We don't have money to put our kids in private school like he does. We
should be the ones deciding what goes on in the public schools."

POLITICKING

The City Club of Chicago was founded in 1903 as a nonpartisan forum for debate
about current issues among top policy-makers, businessmen, journalists, and other

civic leaders. More than a century later, it was still a venerable forum for movers and shakers to hear speakers and ask questions in a collegial atmosphere. The invited speaker for the club's August 29, 2012, meeting was Juan Rangel—Emanuel's adviser and CEO of the charter school organization UNO.

Rangel's less-than-eloquent speech was all about the strike and school reform. He urged attendees to support "billionaire philanthropists" and stand up to the teachers union. "Do we have the resolve to embrace Chicago's wealthy community—the Rauners, the Pritzkers, the Searles, the Crowns, and support them as a focus source of energy that fuels the school reform movement with their money? Or will we shy away from them and allow the silly talk that currently passes for debate about the so-called 1 percenters privatizing our schools?"

"Will we cave to the hate-mongers and their heightened rhetoric and public actions against school reformers," he continued, "or will we instead hide our heads in the sand from the name-calling, the protests, the pickets, from shortsighted individuals who see their immediate self-interests as job preservation first—over the self-interest of our city and its future?"[97]

While Rangel and other Emanuel supporters were making the administration's case on the local level, Emanuel had commitments on the national political stage. He was scheduled to give a speech at the Democratic National Convention on September 4, the first day of school. Karen Lewis had not given the ten days' notice required to start a strike, so it was clear that teachers would not strike the first week of school. But contract negotiations were still highly contentious, and a strike the following week looked very possible. Prominent Republicans called on Emanuel to skip the convention altogether, saying with obvious self-interest that jetting to North Carolina would show skewed priorities. Top Chicago Democratic leaders said Emanuel's presence was needed at the convention, but they hoped he would hurry back.[98]

The imminent strike had become national and even international news at this point, and the stakes were high. With the presidential election approaching and President Obama in a relatively tight race with Republican candidate Mitt Romney, a massive teachers strike in the president's hometown, overseen by the president's former chief of staff, would not look good. Emanuel risked appearing weak to school reformers and those antagonistic to unions by failing to contain the teachers. But he was alienating national organized labor interests, whom Obama needed. Teachers and their supporters grew increasingly angry that Obama and Education Secretary Arne Duncan remained virtually silent on the issue, offering no meaningful words of support for teachers or their collective bargaining rights.

On Labor Day, Chicago teachers and supporters held a rowdy protest outside the Board of Education and City Hall, where Karen Lewis called Emanuel a "liar and a bully."[99] The following Tuesday morning, Emanuel oversaw the start of classes

THE TEACHERS STRIKE WAS CLEARLY ABOUT LARGER ISSUES LIKE THE
FUTURE OF PUBLIC EDUCATION. PHOTO BY KARI LYDERSEN.

and then flew to Charlotte to deliver his speech at the Democratic National Convention. He strode onstage to Michael Jackson's music, and said, "From President Obama's hometown of Chicago, it is my honor to speak to you about the president I served." He touted President Obama's commitment to hard-working middle-class families "fighting tooth and nail to hold onto their jobs." He praised the auto bailout and the stimulus for saving and creating jobs.

"Today, our economy has gone from losing 800,000 jobs a month to adding 4.5 million private-sector jobs in the last twenty-nine months. Banks are slowly but surely lending again, and never again will taxpayers foot the bill for Wall Street's excesses," he said to loud cheers. "In case we forgot, that was the change we believed in. That was the change we fought for. That was the change President Obama delivered."[100]

Emanuel sat up front during Bill Clinton's speech on Wednesday, wherein the former president—looking svelte and dynamic—referenced Emanuel's leadership. "Ask the mayors who are here—Los Angeles is getting green and Chicago's getting an infrastructure bank because Republicans and Democrats are working together to get it!" proclaimed Clinton.[101] A camera zoomed in on Emanuel leaning forward in his seat with a cheek-splitting laugh as Clinton praised bipartisan cooperation and said that "nobody is right all the time and a broken clock is right twice a day." But even in this overwhelmingly adulatory atmosphere, Emanuel could not escape his standoff in Chicago. "Support public school teachers!" called out a Midwestern union official who had been picked by organizers to sit behind Emanuel. The next day, his seat was changed.

After Emanuel left the convention, Obama aides confirmed that he had resigned his post as cochair of the president's reelection campaign to head up fundraising for the Democratic Super PAC Priorities USA Action.[102] But just a few days later, Emanuel suspended all his fundraising activities. That's because on the night of September 9, the announcement came: the teachers would go on strike the next morning, the first day of the second week of school.

THE STRIKE

Teachers who had spent the weekend in a frenzy of preparation rose at 5 a.m. or earlier to convene at schools throughout the city by 6:30 a.m. As promised, the school board would be operating drop-in centers for students at about 140 schools, where nonteaching staff would offer activities like games and movies for four hours a day. And many parents, including teachers whose children attended public schools, had organized "strike schools" and "solidarity camps," where parents took turns supervising students and leading activities.

It was impossible to avoid seeing teachers that Monday morning. People wearing red T-shirts surged through the streets, pounding drums, shaking maracas, strumming guitars, chanting, cheering, pumping fists, and waving picket signs. There were almost six hundred noncharter public schools in Chicago, and it would be the rare morning commute or shopping trip that would not pass one. Horns blared nonstop in solidarity. In the early afternoon the rivulets of red flowed toward downtown. The bridges that cross highways and the Chicago River on the edges of downtown were taken over by waves of teachers and supporters whose chants and footsteps built in a crescendo. The crowd converged outside the Board of Education on Clark Street, and with impassioned speeches and raucous cheering the teachers declared their intention to fight for their rights and the best interests of their students.

Exhausted teachers finally began to make their way home in the late afternoon, lingering on corners and bus stops downtown, prolonging the impression that the city had been totally taken over. Some teachers, volunteers, and supporters mustered the energy to go to the strike headquarters in a spacious auditorium at Teamster City on the Near West Side. Here was the war room, where picket signs were delivered by the thousands and strategy was mapped out on butcher paper taped to walls.

With sore feet yet riding high on adrenaline, many teachers hardly slept that night. Early Tuesday they were back at it again. Outside the Cooper bilingual elementary school in the heavily immigrant Pilsen neighborhood, teachers' signs and chants filled the streets in both Spanish and English as protesters marched beneath tile mosaics of labor leaders and resistance figures from the Aztec times to the present. School librarian Colleen Herman described the litany of challenges that faced teachers and students at a school like Cooper. Many parents in the neighborhood worked long hours at low-wage jobs and didn't speak English. Local gang violence had claimed young children in cross fire and would likely become a bigger problem for them as they got older. Herman said that if job security was based on standardized test scores at schools like Cooper, many teachers would move to schools in wealthier neighborhoods—even outside the district—where fewer factors would impact how kids did on tests.

At 10 a.m. on September 11, the teachers outside Cooper paused for a moment of silence in memory of the terrorist attacks eleven years earlier. Then it was time for more noise, and plenty of it. The union members and parents in red T-shirts marched two blocks to Ashland Avenue, a busy north-south thoroughfare, where they took over several corners and the concrete median. Local residents joined them with conga drums, guitars, and chants. That afternoon another mass rally was held outside the Board of Education.

A few blocks away from the board headquarters, teachers spotted Karen Lewis and crowded around as if she were a rock star: jostling to get close and hug her, lifting cellphones high to snap pictures. Colorful homemade signs bobbed above the crowd. "This strike approved by Rahm Emanuel." A doctored photo of a grinning Emanuel in a tutu: "You've been dancing around the issues since November." "Rahmold Reagan."

In front of the board offices a giant inflatable "union rat" swayed in the breeze, its red eyes and bared fangs dipping forward as if to take a bite out of the building's statuesque columns. (The inflatable rat has long been a common prop at union pickets across the country.) Above the rat danced a skeleton in silky royal blue graduation robes, held aloft on a stick, with a sign saying, "Don't Kill Public Education."

Randi Weingarten, president of the American Federation of Teachers, gave an impassioned speech. Then came Karen Lewis. She placed the strike in the larger context of battles for public union rights. She seemed to be speaking off the cuff, rambling a little but with genuine conviction. It was the board's policies that had created the current situation in the schools, she said. "But who do they blame?" "Us!" the crowd cried.

As the protest was winding down Tuesday evening, other union leaders held a press scrum outside the Board of Education to voice their support for the teachers. Among them was Tom Balanoff, president of SEIU Local 1, which was engaged in its own fight with the mayor's office over contracts for janitorial services at public buildings. Balanoff announced that SEIU Local 1 had given the forty-eight-hour notice mandated for them to honor the teachers' picket lines. That meant by Friday, 1,500 janitors working in the Chicago Public Schools could also be on strike.

THE MENTAL HEALTH MOVEMENT JOINS IN

The teachers union also included school counselors, social workers, teacher's assistants, school nurses, and other "paraprofessionials." Lewis made sure to give a shout-out to "the paras" during her speech.

Outside the mayor's office on Tuesday, school counselors and social workers joined members of the Mental Health Movement to decry the lack of adequate mental health services in public schools. They demanded that rather than cutting staff at unionized schools, the administration should hire more counselors and other mental health professionals. Two school social workers said that there were only 370 counselors for 400,000 students and most moved between multiple schools throughout the system in the course of a day.

"Social work services take place in old bathrooms, in hallways, in dingy closets," said David Temkin, a public schools social worker for fourteen years. "How would Mayor Emanuel feel if the only therapy he had was held in one of these locations? How would he feel if it was his child?" Chuy Campuzano, who had spent the past day and a half on picket lines around the city, told the crowd that school counselors and social workers were to thank for his very survival. "I'm a former CPS special ed student," he said, beads of sweat trickling down his round face, his big brown eyes glistening and earnest. "I know the importance of having a social worker by your side. If I didn't have my social worker I wouldn't be here right now. There were times I felt depressed, down, sometimes I even felt like killing myself. If Rahm Emanuel really cared, he would open more mental health clinics in our communities and hire more social workers in the schools."

As the press conference wrapped up, Mental Health Movement organizer Matt Ginsberg-Jaeckle broke out with a call and response chant: "Whose schools?" "Our schools!" the crowd responded vigorously. Campuzano didn't waste a moment jumping in, bouncing and pumping his fist. "Whose clinics?" "Our clinics!" the crowd responded even more loudly.

THE STRIKE STRETCHES ON

As the negotiations dragged on over the course of the week, with the teachers and supporters continuing to man the picket lines in force, a war over public perception gained intensity. On September 10, Republican vice-presidential nominee and ultra-right-wing Wisconsin congressman Paul Ryan crossed party lines to announce his support for Emanuel.[103] His true intention was obvious: putting Obama on the spot during the presidential campaign, trying to force him to take a position that was bound to alienate him from one camp or another. "Where does President Obama stand?" Ryan asked coyly. "Does he stand with his former chief of staff Mayor Rahm Emanuel, with the children and the parents, or does he stand with the union?"[104]

On Thursday the respected politics blog *Capitol Fax* released a survey showing strong parent support for the teachers. Editor Rich Miller reported that 55.5 percent of Chicagoans supported the teachers. Sixty-three percent of African Americans and 65 percent of Latinos supported the striking teachers. Support was even higher among parents of public school students, at 66 percent. Whites were the only ethnic group who registered majority disapproval of the strike, at 52 percent.

The numbers were a blow to the administration's depictions of working-class parents afraid of losing their jobs because their kids were out of school. Rather, the more likely Chicagoans were to have a child in the public schools, the more likely they were to support the strike. "With overwhelming poverty in black and Latino neighborhoods, parents simply can't afford to send their kids to private schools," Miller wrote.

Teachers union vice president Jesse Sharkey was pleased but not surprised when he saw the survey. "The poll numbers were scientific confirmation of what you could see—the public was siding with the teachers," he said. "It showed the more directly affected you were by the strike, the more working class you were, the more black and Latino, the more you had kids in public schools, the more you supported the strike."

A DEAL

Finally, on Friday afternoon came word that a tentative deal had been reached. Union delegates would meet to discuss it and possibly vote on it Sunday afternoon. School might be back in session by Monday if the delegates decided to call off the strike, though the full membership would still need to ratify the new contract. A summary of the tentative agreement released by the union over the weekend described notable progress on contract issues and a vow to keep fighting on larger bedrock themes like school closings, "merit-based" evaluation, and racial inequities in the school system—things that were only partially or not at all subject to contract negotiations.[105]

The deal stipulated that half the teachers laid off from closed or "turned-around" schools would get priority in the hiring pool for new positions. Teachers would also "follow their students" from closed schools and get first recall rights for ten months if a new position opened up at a school from which they'd been laid off.[106] The agreement also stipulated that only 30 percent of a teacher's evaluation, the minimum required by SB 7, would be based on student test scores; the administration had pushed for a higher proportion. And the union said it had defeated the concept of "merit pay," or "differentiated compensation"—a central tenet of the school reform movement, which allows some teachers to be paid more than others based on criteria unions described as unclear and unfair.[107] The proposed contract would include a 3 percent raise the first year and 2 percent raises for the next two years. That was not much different from what the administration had originally offered, but pay had never been the main issue for the union.[108]

The board promised to hire 512 music, art, physical education, world language, and other "special" teachers, and it agreed to hire more nurses, social workers, and counselors if new revenue sources were identified. The agreement also included an unusual "no bullying" provision. Such measures typically address students harassing each other, but this one prohibited principals and administrators from bullying teachers, particularly in retribution for their outspokenness or union involvement.[109]

As a union summary of the agreement described it, "For the first time, the new contract will guarantee all CPS students and educators have textbooks on day one and [they] will not have to wait up to six weeks for learning materials." It also promised to reimburse teachers up to $250 a year for buying supplies out of pocket.[110] Such provisions showed just how dire things were financially and bureaucratically, and what odds teachers were up against.

The union's house of delegates met on Sunday, but they did not call off the strike. Delegates said they would not make such a weighty decision without time to consult their members. Some teachers felt the deal wasn't good enough. They said Lewis should have pushed for more, and they distributed leaflets calling her a "sell-out."[111]

Emanuel was furious. He charged that students were being held hostage to an "internal conflict" within the union. He promised to go to court for an injunction to force the teachers back to work, alleging that they were striking over issues not subject to collective bargaining and that they were endangering students. Lewis and the leadership essentially dared him to do it; they would not be rushed.

On Tuesday, after long hours of meeting with members and discussing the contract proposal, union delegates voted to suspend the strike. On the morning of Wednesday, September 19, after seven days without class, students and teachers were back in school. The full union membership still had to vote to ratify the contract; in early October, 79 percent of members supported it.[112]

THE "CAMPAIGN" CONTINUES

With class back in session, the postmortems began. The strike was widely seen as a victory for the teachers, who gained significant concessions on major bargaining points and some smaller gains, and enjoyed strong public support. Labor leaders not surprisingly bashed Emanuel's handling of the strike, and so did some school reform advocates and right-wing pundits, who said he'd given in to the teachers.[113] The school reform group Education Now funded TV commercials, reportedly at a cost of $1 million, in which Emanuel touted the administration's gains, namely the longer school day and greater authority for principals over new hires.[114] The ads gave the feeling of an electoral campaign, an odd move for a sitting mayor who presumably should have been buckling down to carry out the contract, not continuing to fight the battle of public opinion over who had "won."

One of Emanuel's key advisers and proxies in the public relations battle was Bruce Rauner, the billionaire investor who had helped launch Emanuel's banking career. Rauner, a prominent school reform advocate and philanthropist who billed himself as a "free-market conservative," savagely attacked the teachers union in various public venues and interviews. In an editorial in the *Chicago Tribune* he wrote, "Let's recognize the CTU strike for what it is. Plain and simple, it is about the union's drive to protect Chicago's incompetent teachers at the expense of students and good teachers. We must not be fooled by the rhetoric that teachers are striking in the interest of students. Baloney. This strike is about protecting political power."[115]

Rauner also faced off with Sharkey on the television show *Chicago Tonight*, where he told host Carol Marin, "This is a war with huge stakes, and the taxpayers and the parents have got to win." Rauner refused to answer Marin's questions about whether his attitude toward the teachers represented his view on unions in general. Sharkey said, "I think it's ironic to hear someone who's a billionaire—whose interests in the schools aren't based in his longstanding work in that school system—talking about how what's ruining the schools are the very people who go in those schools every day and pour their heart and soul into the public education system. Frankly, if you want to know what's wrong with the public education system, it's been a series of efforts at corporate top-down reform that don't take the opinions of the actual educators into account."[116]

The whole debacle demanded a scapegoat, and it would be schools CEO Jean-Claude Brizard. For weeks rumors had swirled about his impending firing or resignation. A month after the strike, Marin asked Emanuel flat-out whether Brizard was "a goner." Emanuel responded dismissively about this "rumor du jour" and said Brizard "has my confidence." A day later Brizard's resignation was announced, and it turned out his replacement had already been selected even as Emanuel was denying the "rumor" on Marin's show.[117]

Karen Lewis charged that Emanuel had set Brizard up for failure, denying him

STRIKING TEACHERS FIGURED MAYOR EMANUEL AND THE SCHOOL BOARD
AIMED TO BUST THE UNION THROUGH PRIVATE CHARTER SCHOOLS. PHOTO BY
KARI LYDERSEN.

the chance to choose his own staff and—she thought—preventing him from work-ing with the teachers union.[118] Regardless, Brizard would get a generous extra full year's salary of $250,000 and a year of health benefits to cushion the blow.[119] The new schools CEO would be Barbara Byrd-Bennett, a former teacher who'd held top administrative posts in Detroit, Cleveland, and New York City, and generally had positive relationships with teachers and union leaders.[120] Some local education ex-perts had recommended Emanuel hire her in the first place, and some saw her ap-pointment as a signal that Emanuel had become a little better at listening to advice. One of the first phone calls Byrd-Bennett made after taking office was to Lewis, and the union president said she felt good about the pending relationship.[121]

AN ELECTED SCHOOL BOARD?

On the November 6, 2012, ballot—along with the choice between Barack Obama and Mitt Romney for president—voters in about one-sixth of Chicago's precincts were faced with a referendum asking whether they supported an elected school board.

When the Illinois state legislature gave the Chicago mayor control over the school system in 1995, the mayor was granted the power to appoint the schools

CEO and a five-member board of trustees, later renamed the Board of Education and expanded to seven members.[122] Proponents of the move argued that centralized control would lead to more cooperative and efficient decision-making. Critics said that allowing the mayor to appoint the school board was not democratic and unfairly took power away from parents and other residents. Chicago was the only district in Illinois that did not have an elected school board; in all, 96 percent of cities nationwide elected their boards.[123]

A *Chicago Tribune*/WGN poll taken during the 2010 mayoral race found that 77 percent of residents wanted an elected school board and only 17 percent wanted the mayor to keep appointing members.[124] As in many states and cities, Chicago voters can place a referendum on the ballot if they get enough signatures. So in spring 2012, a coalition of education and parent groups decided to get a question about the school board on the ballot. Only three citywide ballot referendums are allowed in each election, and clean energy advocates had already laid the groundwork for one regarding whether the city should ditch its monopoly electricity provider and buy from independent companies. At its June 27 meeting, the City Council voted to include two other referendums on the November ballot. *Chicago Reader* reporter Ben Joravsky painted this as a move by the mayor to keep a citywide referendum about an elected school board off the ballot.[125]

Chicago aldermen could also seek to place nonbinding referendums on the city ballot in their wards, so aldermen in ten of the city's fifty wards decided to request the school board referendum themselves. As required, they turned their requests in to a council committee to be placed on the agenda for the next full meeting. But the head of that committee, Alderman Joe Moore, said the applications were filed three minutes too late.[126] "In other words, the mayor avoided a potentially embarrassing referendum in 10 wards, just as he avoided a potentially even more embarrassing setback citywide," wrote Joravsky. "All in all, it was a great three minutes for the mayor."[127]

Voters were left with one last option—to place referendums in individual precincts by collecting enough signatures within the smaller precincts that make up each ward. Once again, parents, teachers, and supporters pounded the pavement, and they ended up getting the referendum on the ballot in 327 precincts (accounting for about one-sixth of the city).[128]

Only state legislation could actually institute an elected school board in Chicago, but strong Chicago voter support could set the stage for a shift. And the referendum passed overwhelmingly, with about 85 percent in favor, in precincts from ritzy Lincoln Park on the North Side to the Altgeld Gardens public housing projects on the Far South Side.[129]

ANOTHER BATTLE BEGINS

Byrd-Bennett's honeymoon did not last long. By November the administration and the union and parents were again at loggerheads, this time over the planned closings of public schools for the upcoming 2013–14 academic year. The administration said school closings were even more necessary after the strike, to help cover the costs of the new contract.[130]

The administration declined to specify how many schools would be closed, but it indicated that up to half the district's schools were underenrolled.[131] School officials said there were about one hundred thousand empty seats in Chicago schools, with about 140 schools only half full and about 10 percent of schools overcrowded.[132] The schools chief financial officer said each closed school could save $500,000 to $800,000 per year, after expenses involved in the closure.[133]

"We have more buildings, chairs, tables and desks than we have students in our district," said a statement from the mayor's press office.[134] Lewis said the union's calculations indicated up to two hundred schools could be closed; the *Chicago Tribune* reported an estimate of eighty to 120 closings, and the *Sun-Times* cited an estimate of about one hundred.[135]

Critics said the administration's definition of "underutilized" was subjective and that its statistics didn't necessarily add up. The number of "empty seats" was based on a fairly arbitrary formula that might count any "nonancillary" classroom with less than thirty students as underutilized, even if it was being used as an extra science lab or special reading room.[136] Further, the experiences of other districts indicated that closing schools often didn't save as much money as expected, especially because a vacant aging school building in a poor neighborhood could easily become a liability rather than a sellable asset.[137]

Under state law, the list of Chicago schools to be closed had to be included in a master plan by January 2013. The administration had said it would announce closures by December 1, 2012.[138] Community groups had long been pushing for a moratorium on school closings, and in January 2012 state legislators introduced a bill that would have blocked school closings during the 2013–14 school year. But now parents and teachers in low-income African American and Latino neighborhoods on the South and West Sides feared that their local schools would be closed.

Anticipating the move, in June 2012 KOCO joined groups in New York; Detroit; Washington, DC; Boston; Atlanta; Wichita, Kansas; and Eureka, Mississippi to file federal civil rights complaints with the US Department of Education based on the effects of school reform and school closings.[139] "Regardless of the reason given, when you close a school you are disinvesting in the population," said Jitu Brown, the KOCO education organizer. "To us that is the killing of a neighborhood."

Earlier that year, school officials had made a proposal to the Bill and Melinda Gates Foundation seeking funds for sixty new charter schools over five years. The school district did not get the grant, but the request revealed the intention to open many more charters. Byrd-Bennett said the push was unrelated to school closings, but many teachers and parents didn't believe her.[140]

The *Chicago Tribune* reported that in recent years charter schools "began taking up a larger share of the CPS budget, in no small part because they operate more cheaply by hiring nonunion teachers. The amount of money going into charters grew eightfold between 2002 and 2011, from $47 million to nearly $380 million." Meanwhile, the *Tribune* noted, the number of union teachers in the system declined by 1,700 between 2009 and 2012.[141]

On November 2, 2012, a Friday afternoon, about a hundred teachers, parents, and supporters staged another sit-in outside Emanuel's office to protest school closings. Earlier that day Byrd-Bennett had said in a speech that she would ask the state legislature to give the district a few more months—through March 2013—to announce which schools would be closed. She also appointed an independent commission to study the issue.[142] Karen Lewis responded that an extension on announcing school closings would only make the problem worse: if schools were going to close, then teachers, parents, and students needed as much lead time as possible to prepare.[143] School closings announced at the end of March would be especially problematic because that would be after the deadline for applying to charter, magnet, and selective enrollment schools.[144]

At the City Hall sit-in, Jesse Sharkey proclaimed that the union was putting the board "on notice" that they would fight any school closings. As protesters sat and sang on the floor outside Emanuel's office, Jitu Brown announced that the group would not leave until they got a meeting with Emanuel. Police officers said the mayor was out of town, and the group was offered a meeting with Emanuel's top education deputy. They declined, saying only the mayor would do, and around 10 p.m. police cleared the lobby. Ten people were arrested.

"We've given the mayor a proposal, we've asked to meet with the mayor, we've done everything and way more than citizens are supposed to do," said Brown. "We've had to scratch and claw and fight and become researchers. All we're asking for is a right to shape and protect the schools our children are going to."

A MORATORIUM?

Three weeks after the sit-in, a new wrinkle developed in the school closing drama. Byrd-Bennett was still asking the state legislature for an extension until March 2013. The teachers union said that only a flat-out moratorium would do. In late November Emanuel's office announced that he too supported a five-year moratorium on school closings, with one important caveat—it would start after the round of 2013–14 closings. On her blog, parent activist Julie Woestehoff likened the mayor's position to saying, "I promise to stop beating you after I get in this last round of punches."[145]

The state legislature ultimately voted to grant the board an extension until March. Parents and advocacy groups had charged that Emanuel and school officials were already deciding which schools to close. The administration repeatedly denied the charge. In November the *Chicago Tribune* quoted Byrd-Bennett saying, "Unless my staff has a hidden drawer somewhere where they've got numbers in there, we don't have a number."[146]

In mid-December, though, the *Tribune* obtained an internal document describing plans to close up to ninety-five schools and consolidate others or turn them into charters. Most of the closings would happen in impoverished, largely African American and Latino South and West Side neighborhoods, the document indicated. It also discussed strategies for tamping down expected public opposition: creating "a meaningful engagement process with community members" and a "monitoring mechanism to ensure nimble response to opposition."[147]

The school closings commission that Byrd-Bennett had appointed came out with its recommendations in early January 2013. They fell more on the side of the union's and community groups' wishes than the administration's plans, saying that no high schools should be closed because of concerns about forcing students to cross gang lines. The commission also said that no schools that had already undergone upheaval in the form of "consolidation" or a "turnaround" should be closed. But the recommendations were not binding, and it remained to be seen what the administration would decide to do.[148] Residents could air their concerns over the course of twenty-eight public hearings to be held throughout the city from late January to March. After that the administration would come up with a list of schools to close.[149]

"LET US IN!"

The journal *Catalyst* revealed that the Walton Family Foundation, affiliated with Walmart and known for backing charter schools, had awarded city officials a $478,000 grant to host the public hearings.[150] *Catalyst* also noted that the city had hired a consulting firm, the Civic Consulting Alliance, which was housed in the same offices as the procharter organization New Schools for Chicago. The consulting firm, which would advise the city on school closings, had received a separate $220,000 grant from the Walton Family Foundation.[151] Union supporters could not ignore the link with Walmart, famous for its antiunion stance and allegations of mistreating workers.

Residents thronged to each meeting, in many cases filling up the main auditoriums and forcing overflow rooms to be opened. On February 6, at a meeting on the Southwest Side to discuss school closings in Pilsen and Little Village, hundreds of parents, students, and teachers clustered in groups according to their school. Kids wore T-shirts celebrating the Cooper Jaguars and Jungman Eagles, among others, and waved signs with slogans like "Jungman Eagles Are Endangered."

TEACHERS AND PARENTS POINTED OUT THAT MAYOR EMANUEL'S KIDS WENT TO A PRICEY PRIVATE SCHOOL. PHOTO BY KARI LYDERSEN.

Administration officials sat at a table in front of the auditorium. The plan was for three representatives from each school to speak for two minutes each. Great pains had been taken to prepare for an orderly two-hour event, but the format couldn't contain the passion in the room.

Chuy Campuzano, in his trademark orange hooded sweatshirt, stood up and tried to start a chant: "Whose schools? Our schools!" But the crowd loudly shushed him; they were anxious to make their points. One after another the speakers argued why their schools should not be closed; many also attacked the whole policy of closing schools and opening charters. People went on past their allotted two minutes, words tumbling out in torrents of distress. Spanish and English were intermixed. Some people spoke fluently in both languages. Other times the Mental Health Movement activist Matt Ginsberg-Jaeckle—who made his living as an interpreter—provided translation. The testimony was periodically drowned out by pounding on the auditorium doors and loud chants from people in the hallways angry that they were barred from the overcapacity auditorium.

"We're counting on you!" diminutive middle-school student Marcos Reyes told the schools officials, pivoting to point a finger at them. Dressed in his formal ROTC uniform and wiping tears from behind his glasses, Reyes pleaded with the officials not to close his school. "My parents have been here for seven years, working hard for me so I can have a better future . . . and you guys can stand here and close my school. I don't really think that is fair!"

Emanuel had frequently described Chicago Public Schools students as being robbed of their futures by a poor education system, of having empty eyes devoid of hope. But the hearing presented an entirely different view. Students like Reyes expressed deep love for their schools and their teachers and terror that these institutions would be taken away. There was nothing passive or hopeless about them.

Alderman Ricardo Muñoz—who represented the Little Village neighborhood—was cheered as he took the floor and promised to "fight arduously against any closings or consolidations, because we deserve our community schools." Pilsen Alderman Danny Solis, a close ally of the mayor, was booed loudly at first but then received applause when he promised to oppose closings.

Sarah Chambers, a special education teacher in Pilsen and a CORE member, noted that neither Byrd-Bennett, Emanuel, nor the school board members were attending the community meetings. "If they are not here, what does that say about how much they value our input?"

"The board is not asking us whether or not school closings are a valid option," Chambers continued. "They're asking us which schools should we close. They're asking us to plan our own funeral. Are we going to let them do this?"

"No!"

COMMUNITY AND UNION ACTIVISTS RAILED AGAINST TAXES GOING TO PRIVATE DEVELOPERS THROUGH THE TIF PROGRAM. PHOTO BY KARI LYDERSEN.

11
TIFS, JOBS, AND THE
INFRASTRUCTURE TRUST

The Chicago building known as River Point slices cleanly and gracefully into a blue sky, its sleek mirrored sides reflecting a dusting of clouds. It doesn't actually exist yet, except as a rendering on a website, which also promises a "sophisticated exterior and interior" and "extraordinary views of the Chicago River, Wacker Drive and the Central Business District."[1]

At the building's base, a verdant plaza planted with native trees and flowers looks out over the Chicago River. The proposed indoor-outdoor plaza includes spacious lobbies, underground parking, and a tunnel to nearby Union Station. The building's forty-five stories offer ample office space for rent, and full-length glass walls on the ground floor showcase the plaza and river. The edifice is on Lake and Canal Streets in the West Loop, at a picturesque confluence of two branches of the river. Across the street is the sprawling French Market, offering boutique cheeses and wines. Across the river is the historic Merchandise Mart, billed as Chicago's "premier business address," with showrooms full of "high design and luxury goods."[2]

The area could hardly be described as "blighted." But as of summer 2012, up to $29.5 million in property tax dollars was earmarked to build River Point's plaza through a tax subsidy program—tax increment financing (TIF)—meant to spur development and create jobs in blighted areas.[3] The planned plaza is part of the LaSalle-Central TIF district, which covers a slice of the western edge of downtown. The Lyric Opera and the headquarters of United Airlines[4] and MillerCoors[5] were among the institutions within the TIF boundaries that had received millions of taxpayer dollars through the program.[6] Those property taxes would otherwise have gone to fund schools, libraries, and parks.[7]

On August 7, 2012, shortly before the lunch rush, a stream of people holding picket signs crowded the sidewalk of a bridge crossing the Chicago River, not far from the proposed location of River Point Plaza. A bottleneck formed as they pressed onto the narrow walkway and down the stairs leading to the riverfront dining terrace of Fulton's on the River. This was part of the upscale restaurant empire Larry Levy had started three decades ago with his brother and mother; and Levy would be a developer of the River Point Plaza. Protesters acting like maître d's handed out an elegantly printed menu. The offerings included:

"River Point Plaza: A generous portion of useless private space, drizzled with the sweat of working families. Served with a side of your tax dollars." Price: $29.5 million.

"United Airlines: A flight of public money." Despite the $30 million price tag, "peanuts and beverages are not included with this flight."

The protesters chanted, "Whose money? Our money!" and "We're hungry, we're broke, we can't pay the rent. We must not be part of the 1 percent!"

TIF TROUBLE

Emanuel is not the first Chicago leader to promise millions of taxpayer dollars to wealthy developers in prosperous parts of town through the TIF program. Mayor Daley was famous for using TIFs to reward politically connected operatives in often tony areas; this has long been a favorite topic of dogged *Chicago Reader* reporter Ben Joravsky. By the time Emanuel took office, there were 163 TIF districts in Chicago covering a full 30 percent of the city.[8]

In a nutshell, when an area is designated a TIF district, the amount of property taxes going to schools, libraries, parks, and other public uses is capped at the current level, and any increases in property taxes over the next twenty-three years—the life of a TIF—are doled out for public and private projects at the mayor's discretion, with the aim of improving an area's economic fortunes. In a perfect world, it would create a positive feedback loop where new investment would raise the area's property values and tax base, and reinvesting that extra tax money would continue the cycle. At the end of the twenty-three years, the area would be more prosperous and the TIF could be retired, with local residents enjoying improved surroundings and the increased tax base benefiting the public.[9]

In Chicago, TIFs often don't work that way. The city's TIF funds have been spent roughly evenly on public and private projects. In both cases critics often charge favoritism and politics in terms of where and how the money is spent. They also say that Chicago schools, parks, and libraries suffer because TIFs divert millions of property tax dollars that would otherwise fund these institutions. The consumer watchdog group Illinois PIRG said in a 2012 report that Chicago TIF revenue "is spent outside of ordinary city budgeting processes, allowing for unsupervised spending, political horse-trading and a concentration of spending authority in the mayor's office."[10]

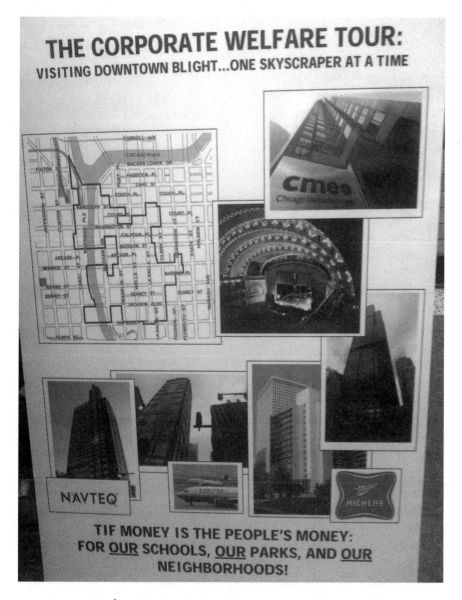

AS A PROTESTER'S SIGN POINTED OUT, MAJOR CORPORATIONS RECEIVED
TAXPAYER MONEY THAT OTHERWISE WOULD HAVE GONE TO PARKS AND
SCHOOLS. PHOTO BY KARI LYDERSEN.

Emanuel promised early on to reform the TIF program, and after taking office in May 2011 he convened an expert task force and asked for recommendations on how to ensure that TIFs were really creating jobs and fostering economic development. In August 2011, the task force said that each TIF should be evaluated every five years and subjected to strict analytical metrics—provisions that the task force said would likely mean multiple cancellations.[11]

A year later, Illinois PIRG released its report saying basically none of the recommendations had been implemented. The report looked at TIFs that were supposed to create more than two hundred jobs each between 2000 and 2010. These TIFs were instituted and mostly administered by Daley but fell under Emanuel's purview after he took office. None of the TIFs complied with a 2009 ordinance demanding certain documents be posted online, Illinois PIRG said, and fifteen of twenty-one relevant TIFs could not show they'd met job creation promises.[12]

In 2011, $471 million was set aside from property taxes within Chicago TIF districts.[13] This was not unusual: $520 million was set aside in 2009, and $510 million in 2010. Typically about 10 percent of the city's property tax base is diverted into TIFs.[14]

Emanuel did cancel a number of TIFs and collected TIF money back from some corporations—a total of $34 million in 2011.[15] But he also continued to use TIFs in questionable ways. In an October 2012 press release announcing the cancellation of eight TIFs, the mayor also announced the proposed creation of the 51st/Lake Park TIF near the lakefront and the University of Chicago.[16] Local residents and watchdogs had been protesting the use of TIFs in this area for months, saying the attractive location meant development would proceed without taxpayer subsidies.[17]

THE GOLDEN TOILET

On January 24, 2012, members of Stand Up! Chicago, the Grassroots Collaborative and other groups marched through downtown Chicago carrying aloft a golden toilet. They were protesting the allocation of $15 million in TIF funds to the CME Group, parent company of the Chicago Mercantile Exchange and Chicago Board of Trade. The institutions were created more than a century ago to trade agricultural products like eggs and pork bellies, and grew to deal in commodities along with complicated financial products like derivatives, currency, and equities. The Daley administration had promised the TIF money to the CME Group for building upgrades including a new fitness center and new restrooms. The City Council approved the grant in 2010. Stand Up! Chicago saw the private financial institutions as hardly deserving of taxpayer funds for luxury upgrades to their gym and bathrooms—hence the golden toilet.

The stunt gained significant media attention, and soon the CME Group said it was renouncing the TIF dollars, which had never actually been received or spent and were to be doled out over ten years if the exchange maintained 1,750 jobs in Chicago and created 638 jobs.[18] Renouncing the money was probably not too painful considering the state legislature had recently passed a law granting the CME Group tax breaks worth $77 million or more—cutting its state tax bill roughly in half. CME had threatened that without such tax breaks the operation would leave Illinois. Emanuel

AFTER THE "MARCH OF THE GOLDEN TOILET" THROUGH DOWNTOWN, THE CHICAGO
MERCANTILE EXCHANGE RENOUNCED PLANS TO SPEND TAXPAYER "TIF" MONEY ON
NEW RESTROOMS. PHOTO COURTESY OF THE GRASSROOTS COLLABORATIVE.

pushed for the state legislation on the grounds that it would protect Chicago jobs, and he was considered to have played an important role in its passing. Emanuel was formerly on the CME Group board, and CME made the single largest donation to his mayoral campaign, $200,000.[19] Critics accused the trading institution of making empty threats and said it should have to pay its fair share of taxes.

"It's like toothpaste out of a tube. You squeeze it one place and it comes out somewhere else," Grassroots Collaborative executive director Amisha Patel said of the tradeoff between city and state subsidies for the CME Group. "This is an example of how Rahm is as smart or smarter than Daley when it comes to leveraging Springfield."[20]

Leaders of Stand Up! Chicago and other critics noted that Emanuel never addressed their protests or demands about the CME Group. CME officials likewise would not comment on the protests or whether the outcry motivated them to renounce the TIF dollars.[21] So on February 8, the golden toilet made a trip up to the fifth floor of City Hall. Public school teachers and supporters of the mental health clinics were among the lively crowd hoisting the toilet, demanding Emanuel spend TIF funds—including those renounced by the CME Group—on schools, clinics, and other public services.[22]

EMANUEL TOUTED NEW BIKE LANES AND A BIKE SHARE PROGRAM AS WAYS TO
ATTRACT THE "CREATIVE CLASS" TO CHICAGO. PHOTO BY KARI LYDERSEN.

BIKE LANES AND DOT-COMS

Aside from direct subsidies in the form of TIF funds or tax breaks, Emanuel focused on creating a business-friendly climate to lure new companies. That included
making Chicago the kind of trendy, attractive "global city" where corporations could
lure top staffers and woo clients. For example, the mayor and civic boosters often
pointed out that the miles of "protected" bike lanes Emanuel installed early in his
term were not only good for the environment and the bike commuters already plying the streets, but would help attract hot tech companies whose employees prized
such things.[23] "You talk to the CEOs we're recruiting, and having a bike lane helps
them recruit the types of employees they want," Emanuel said during a January
2013 event where *Chicago Tribune* editorial page editor Bruce Dold interviewed
him in front of an adoring crowd.[24]

The public-private, city-funded booster group World Business Chicago said
that in 2011 there were 128 new digital high-tech startups launched in Chicago,
and such companies had raised $689 million in venture capital.[25] Additionally, the
company Red Sea Group announced it would create a five-hundred-thousand-
square-foot, multimillion-dollar data and advanced trading center downtown—
conveniently, as Emanuel told Dold, right near the first protected bike lane.[26]

World Business Chicago noted that along with the high-tech boom, other sectors of the Chicago economy also grew under Emanuel's watch—including exports of machinery and chemicals. The group reported that in 2011 Chicago saw eighteen million more square feet of business space and $2.6 billion in new investment, leading *Site Selection* magazine to name it the top US metro area for business expansions.[27]

The mayor also prioritized high-tech "green" jobs: in November 2012 he announced that the company Smith Electric Vehicles would open a factory in Chicago producing zero-emissions electric trucks, which would create between fifty and two hundred jobs.[28]

Clearly, some things were going well with the Chicago economy, especially considering that the country was still struggling to emerge from the economic crisis. But skeptics wondered if the drumbeat of jobs announcements by the mayor's office was as good as it sounded, and who was benefiting from these positions.

BEHIND THE JOBS NUMBERS

Emanuel's office said that in his first year in City Hall, eight major companies committed to bringing their national or regional headquarters to Chicago and twenty-eight announced significant expansions, for a total of about twenty thousand new jobs.[29] (By January 2013 the estimate had risen to twenty-five thousand.)[30] JPMorgan Chase, GE Capital, SeatonCorp, Sara Lee, and Nokia were among the companies relocating headquarters or expanding their operations in Chicago.

Among the coups was United Airlines's August 2012 decision to expand and extend its lease through 2028 for office space in the Willis Tower, formerly the Sears Tower. The airline signed "one of the largest office leases ever in the history of Chicago," according to a press release from the mayor's office. "The fact that United has brought its company under one roof and extended their commitment to downtown is great news for all Chicagoans," Emanuel said. "This deal shows United's commitment to Chicago for a generation; it ensures our hometown airline will be here, and means that quality jobs and economic activity will remain in the area for years to come."[31]

At the time the airline made its move, companies nationwide were opting to locate in urban centers instead of in suburbs, in part because of the growing popularity—especially for young professionals—of living downtown. But when companies like United Airlines move huge operations, many longtime employees continue to live and pay taxes in their suburban homes. "There's all this focus on downtown, with the idea that it will trickle down to the neighborhoods—but in fact it's mostly making it harder for the neighborhoods," said Amisha Patel. "The mayor talks about bringing all these jobs downtown, but often they are jobs that already had workers, just moving downtown from the suburbs."[32]As the protesters at Fulton's on the River restaurant had pointed out, United Airlines received a

generous share of TIF dollars to relocate its headquarters to downtown Chicago
from the suburbs.[33] The agreement stipulated that by phase two of the project, the
headquarters must relocate at least 2,500 employees to the city and bring in another 2,500 new ones. So assuming the promises would be kept, many new jobs
were being created.[34] But in several prominent cases the shift of jobs from the suburbs to downtown Chicago actually resulted in net job cuts on a regional level. In
2011 Emanuel used between $5 and $6.5 million in TIF money to persuade Sara
Lee Corporation to bring the headquarters of its North American Meats company back to Chicago, where it had been located until a 2005 regional consolidation. But with the move back downtown the company cut almost half of the meat
division's staff—from about 1,000 at its suburban headquarters to between 500
and 650 at the new downtown location.[35]

In July 2012, Motorola Mobility announced it would move 3,000 employees to
Chicago from suburban Libertyville. A month later, the company reported it was
slashing its payroll by 20 percent, eliminating about 650 to 700 jobs that had been expected to move from Libertyville to Chicago.[36] Libertyville workers said they were
confused and stunned by the mixed messages, especially because Governor Quinn
had offered the company $100 million in tax incentives to stay in Libertyville just a
year earlier.[37]

The *Chicago Tribune* parsed Emanuel's job creation numbers:

> While about 60 percent of those job pledges are for new positions, the remainder likely
> will be transfers—good for the city but not providing direct opportunities for the 1 in
> 10 Chicagoans who are out of work and looking for jobs in a soggy economy. More-
> over, of the new jobs, more than 1,700 of the positions the mayor counts are construc-
> tion jobs, which aren't permanent. Of all the announced jobs, 2,200 are with
> companies that failed to provide a definitive date on when they would finish the hir-
> ing, and about 3,600 are on phased timetables that could stretch beyond 2015, raising
> the question of how firm those pledges could be.[38]

The *Tribune* noted a prime example of the squishiness of some of the job announcements: Lawson Products, which in late 2011 promised to relocate its headquarters from suburban Des Plaines to Chicago. Emanuel called it "a significant
commitment to the city," but the *Tribune* said "the move amounted to shifting the
company from one side of the Tri-State Tollway to the other, bringing the distribu-
tor of maintenance and repair supplies a bit closer to O'Hare International Airport.
The new location is less than four miles from the original spot."[39]

Lawson, which makes hose fittings, hydraulics, and other industrial supplies,
transferred about four hundred employees to the new Chicago headquarters in spring
2012. But a few months later, it laid off about one hundred employees, including
many at the Chicago headquarters. According to the *Tribune*, other cases where
Emanuel's announcements about hundreds of new jobs in Chicago had not panned

out months later included for-profit college Devry University and the German manufacturer ThyssenKrupp.[40]

In the view of Chicago Federation of Labor president Jorge Ramirez, Emanuel did create scores of jobs for Chicagoans of various skill levels. His plans to overhaul the city's aging water system created many union construction and pipefitting jobs, Ramirez noted. Building trades union members were generally supportive of the mayor, though they had clashed with him over contract issues, because they could see his ambitious plans for the city included significant job-creating infrastructure projects.

"He *is* creating manufacturing jobs," said Ramirez. "And we are working with him to train workers for high-skilled, high-road manufacturing jobs." Ramirez praised the mayor's efforts to focus curriculum at the City Colleges on specific in-demand sectors. "We're in jeopardy of losing out because we don't have a pipeline of skilled people" for modern blue-collar jobs like computerized machine operation, said Ramirez. "The mayor is attuned to that."[41]

Many critics countered that they would not be impressed by job creation numbers, even ones that materialized, as long as the mayor was simultaneously cutting and privatizing public sector jobs with solid union salaries and benefits—jobs of the type that sustain communities and employ people without the skills or education to work for a digital startup.

TRANSPARENCY

In the debate over job creation, as with other aspects of the city administration, both mayoral supporters and critics often brought up the concept of transparency. The mayor frequently touted his commitment to transparency, and his administration did indeed make public reams of documents and statistics that had not been accessible before, often by posting copious amounts of information online. In some ways Emanuel's office was a national model of transparency. So why was it often so hard for reporters and analysts, not to mention regular citizens, to actually figure out what was going on?

Emanuel told reporters that in his first hundred days in office he had improved accessibility, transparency, and public engagement with the mayor's office, including through "a groundbreaking Facebook town hall, answering questions during a telephone town hall, holding a live conversation during a virtual good government town hall and launching the city's first-ever interactive budget website, Chicagobudget.org." He also "published more than 200 data sets, allowing the people across Chicago to see city employee salaries, crime statistics, and contracts dating back to 1993."[42]

Reporters and media analysts described the Emanuel administration's version of "transparency" in terms that would be familiar to the increasingly frustrated press corps covering the Obama White House.[43] In both cases vast amounts of information was posted online, a boon for investigative reporters and statistics geeks. But dumping lots of data online didn't necessarily mean information was "accessible" for the average person, and reporters complained that Emanuel's office was often defensive and obstinate in responding to Freedom of Information Act requests and otherwise answering reporters' and citizens' specific questions.

The *Chicago Tribune* tested Emanuel's transparency promises by seeking emails, cellphone logs, and other records related to his decision-making on three topics: water rates, city vehicle stickers, and controversial new automated speed cameras to be placed around parks and schools.[44] The *Tribune's* mission was to shed light on how Emanuel governed—whom he consulted with and how he arrived at decisions—by examining these three issues.

The speed cameras were especially controversial because they could lead to numerous fines for regular Chicagoans picking up their kids or going about their business. Emanuel framed the cameras as a "safety zone" measure meant to protect children. Critical aldermen and residents saw them as a "cash grab" by the city, and the *Tribune* revealed that safety studies used by the Emanuel administration to back the plan were erroneous and misleading. The Traffic Safety Coalition, which promoted the plan, was funded by a camera company and run by Emanuel ally Greg Goldner—whose Resolute Consulting was tied to the scandal over payments to people to profess support for school closings.[45]

In a long February 2012 interview with *Tribune* reporter David Kidwell, Emanuel came across as defensive and patronizing. He essentially accused the *Tribune* of unfair coverage and told Kidwell, "You are going to write your little thing about what you've already concluded."[46] The *Tribune* countered the insinuations of bias by publishing the interview transcript in its entirety. Among other things, Kidwell probed why the mayor did not give the paper cellphone or email records. When pressed, Emanuel would not say whether he had a city-issued cellphone, and he claimed he didn't use email for his decision-making.

"I don't like to be lied to any more than you do," Kidwell told Emanuel during the interview. "And when we asked for a log of emails—of all emails—wait, I let you finish, let me finish—when I asked for a log of emails of all speed camera-related emails in the city, we got a list of 1,000, 1,200, 1,300 emails and not one email went to Rahm Emanuel or went to [schools CEO Jean-Claude] Brizard or went to the police chief. . . . We are just curious how it could possibly be that the mayor of this city hasn't received or sent or been copied on any emails regarding those three major issues."[47]

Emanuel's prickly interaction with Kidwell was generally indicative of his relationship with journalists. Almost all public officials are wary of the press for obvious reasons, but Emanuel was often known for taking a particularly guarded and even bullying approach when a journalist tried to drill down on a story—even as his office sent out numerous press releases about its achievements, no matter how small.

It soon became a running joke among reporters that Emanuel might as well issue a press release every day noting the sun rose in the east, so frequent were the press office missives trumpeting some action or other. Going back to his White House days it was known that Emanuel's strategy was to "capture" or "win" the news cycle each day, meaning to dominate the news with laudatory or at least lightweight stories that would continually keep him in the public eye and also obscure or distract from any negative coverage.[48]

Emanuel's press office got in hot water in November 2012 after *Tribune* reporters learned that his staff had recorded at least two phone interviews regarding the speed cameras and a 2011 interview with the police superintendent without asking the reporters' permission. This might not seem like a big deal, but recording someone without their knowledge is a felony in Illinois, and regular citizens had been prosecuted under the same eavesdropping law in recent years, specifically under a provision about recording police officers.[49] Emanuel's office said the recording happened "by mistake." The mayor himself invoked Shakespeare in calling the controversy "much ado about nothing."[50] It is not clear whether Emanuel knew about or condoned the recording, or whether it was common procedure in the press office.

The Better Government Association demanded that the mayor's office cooperate with an investigation by the city inspector general, and "come clean" about who else might have been recorded. The BGA sent Emanuel an open letter saying it worried his office had been recording conversations with its investigators, and demanding he reveal whether BGA staff had been recorded. In an editorial published in the *Sun-Times*, BGA president Andy Shaw said, "What's unfair is the mayor's characterization of this as small potatoes unworthy of further scrutiny. That attitude is also at odds with Emanuel's pledge to run an administration committed to transparency and accountability."[51]

THE INFRASTRUCTURE TRUST

Demands for true transparency were also central to the debate over one of Emanuel's most ambitious projects: the Chicago Infrastructure Trust. In March 2012, Emanuel announced "Building a New Chicago," a $7.3 billion plan to rebuild, repair, and retrofit Chicago's infrastructure, creating thirty thousand jobs in the process—even though the city was still facing a budget deficit of hundreds of millions of dollars.

"At a time when the nation is only beginning to pull itself painfully and delicately out of a deep recession, and when cities and states are cutting essential services and wondering how to keep the courthouses open and the lights on, an infrastructure proposal for a single city with an estimated cost in the billions—with a 'b'—is audacious," wrote John Schwartz in the *New York Times*.[52]

Experts pointed out that the plan did not break much new ground; rather, it involved cobbling together previously announced or nascent programs under one umbrella. The *Chicago Tribune* said Building a New Chicago "included very little that was new—except for its $7 billion price tag and its ambitious framing as a mission comparable to the city's rebuilding after the Great Chicago Fire."[53]

The most notable and novel part of Building a New Chicago was an initiative that had been announced a month earlier, called the Chicago Infrastructure Trust.[54] The trust would invite private financiers to invest in public projects, theoretically providing funding for propositions that might not be possible with traditional loans or bond sales.[55] The possibilities ranged from new airport runways to public transit overhauls to school improvements and arts programming, though city officials were cagey about specifics. The trust itself would be a nonprofit organization that would essentially be a conduit between investors and the city and its sister agencies, including the Chicago Public Schools and the Chicago Transit Authority. It would have an executive director and would be overseen by a board of experts appointed by the mayor.[56]

By spring 2012 a number of high-profile institutions had signed nonbinding agreements to work with the trust: Citibank NA, Citi Infrastructure Investors, Macquarie Infrastructure and Real Assets, and JPMorgan Asset Management Infrastructure Group.[57]

Macquarie's affiliate was part of the consortium that had leased Chicago's Skyway toll road for ninety-nine years under Mayor Daley. The company's website called it "the first privatization of an existing road in the United States."[58] The Skyway lease paved the way for more road privatizations, which raised concerns about steeply increased tolls and long-term maintenance and service. "The certainty of future toll hikes doesn't jibe with the uncertainty of service quality," noted *Bloomberg Businessweek* magazine. "Assets sold now could change hands many times over the next 50 years, with each new buyer feeling increasing pressure to make the deal work financially. It's hardly a stretch to imagine service suffering in such a scenario; already, the record in the U.S. has been spotty."[59]

Proponents stressed that the trust would not actually sell or lease public assets or services, like the Skyway or the parking meters. Rather, it would invite investment in public projects, offering investors potentially lucrative returns while allowing the city to retain some revenues and insulate itself from losses.

At least thirty-three states have infrastructure banks or similar revolving loan funds, according to a September 2012 Brookings Institution paper, but the great majority of that funding is used specifically for roads. The report identified the Chicago Infrastructure Trust, along with the New York Works Infrastructure Fund, a proposed state program, as "hybrid infrastructure funds" that are "innovative" in seeking private investment and offering a return to investors. It says the Chicago Infrastructure Trust is the first such fund developed at the city level.[60]

President Obama had even proposed a national infrastructure bank on a similar model. The bank Obama proposed would provide half of the funding for critical road, airport, bridge, and other projects, with the private sector putting up matching funds repaid by revenue generated by the projects.[61] The Chicago Infrastructure Trust, by contrast, would receive relatively minimal funding from city coffers and would rely primarily on the private sector—potentially including charitable foundations, union investment funds, and public pension funds along with corporations.

Emanuel unveiled the plan on March 1, 2012, at the Carpenters Union's Apprentice and Training Facility, underscoring the plan's appeal for building trade union members. He was joined by his former boss Bill Clinton, who was well known for backing public-private partnerships around the world, and Chicago chief financial officer Lois Scott.

While the three talked in broad strokes about the trust and what it would mean for Chicago, they offered specifics about only the first project—a plan called Retrofit Chicago, which would leverage private investment to improve the energy efficiency of more than a hundred municipal buildings.[62] With a $200 million investment to replace leaky windows, overhaul lighting systems, and otherwise reduce energy costs, the project would theoretically cut city energy bills by $20 million a year. This money would be used to pay back investors and award them a profit. And the retrofits were projected to create two thousand jobs to boot.[63]

The Retrofit plan was generally well received and praised by environmental groups. Who could be against fixing buildings and reducing their energy demand, helping to curb the need for dirty coal-fired power? But watchdog groups, community activists, and researchers were quick to point out serious concerns about the trust as a whole.

RISKS OF THE INFRASTRUCTURE TRUST

As a nonprofit organization, the trust would not be a government agency and would be exempt from state laws mandating freedom of information and open meetings, making it very hard for citizens and journalists to gain information about its inner workings. A board appointed by the mayor would be in charge of entering potentially lucrative agreements with private investors, a situation that could create strong potential for conflicts of interest.

And the trust would raise fundamental concerns about the privatization of public services and resources: whether the issue is schools or health care or water delivery, it is always risky and potentially very harmful to introduce a profit motive into an area where the government had previously provided a service for the public good. Private investors' entire reason for participating in the trust would be to make a profit on their investment. Hence, critics and community leaders worried, the people designing and managing these projects would naturally place a higher pri-

THE INFRASTRUCTURE TRUST COULD BE USED TO IMPROVE THE CITY'S ELEVATED TRAINS, BUT PRIVATE INVESTORS MIGHT TURN A PROFIT THROUGH DISTANCE-BASED FARES THAT FORCE SOUTH SIDE RESIDENTS TO PAY THE MOST. PHOTO BY KARI LYDERSEN.

ority on making money than on protecting public safety and well-being.

That could influence which projects were chosen to fund. New amenities or improvements in wealthier areas could be more likely to pay off, so the trust could be more likely to fund new parks, schools, and transit in better-off neighborhoods. And if revenue were raised through new or increased fees, it could disproportionately impact low-income people. That's because poorer people tend to be more dependent on public amenities, lacking access to private equivalents; and relatively small increases in fees eat up a larger portion of their household budget. Lois Scott stoked fears of such a regressive impact with her comment during the Infrastructure Trust launch that an extension of the city's red line L train could be funded through distance-based fares—people who travel further, primarily to and from low-income areas on the outskirts of the city, would pay more.[64]

The red line stretches from the North to the South Side of Chicago like a spine, connecting with other lines as it runs through downtown. The farthest north neighborhoods are moderate income and ethnically diverse, with populations getting wealthier and whiter as the train nears the Loop. As it heads south, the red line passes through neighborhoods that become increasingly low-income and populated largely by African Americans. Hence they would pay more if distance-based fares were instituted on the red line.

"It could continue the transit racism that already existed," noted Amisha Patel. "You already spend two hours on the train getting to your job; now you have to pay more. Our worry is that low-income people will pay more through taxes and fees and won't get the full benefit of the infrastructure."[65]

THE INFRASTRUCTURE TRUST AND THE CITY COUNCIL

The City Council finance committee voted on the ordinance creating the Infra-structure Trust on April 16, 2012, six weeks after the ambitious program was unveiled by the mayor's office. Before the vote, members of unions and community groups rallied at City Hall, urging the committee to vote no on the grounds that the trust could lead to union-busting and would short-change low-income communities.

The finance committee passed the ordinance by a vote of eleven to seven—a definite show of concern by a panel that often serves as a rubber stamp.[66] The full council vote was supposed to take place two days later, but aldermen demanded more time, more safeguards, and more information. They had probably learned from the criticism that rained down on them for passing Mayor Daley's parking meter privatization deal in a rush.

At least ten aldermen—including Brendan Reilly, Ricardo Muñoz, Leslie Hairston, John Arena, and Scott Waguespack—raised serious questions. Emanuel's proposal gave the City Council say only over deals involving city assets and city property, not the sister agencies such as the schools and the transit authority. Aldermen described this as undercutting their authority and transferring control of city services from elected representatives to nonelected appointees, namely Lois Scott and the Infrastructure Trust board. Aldermen also demanded that the trust be subject to freedom of information and open meetings laws. And they called for ethics provisions to prevent a "revolving door" wherein trust board members could accept jobs at companies with whom they'd made deals.

Emanuel eventually agreed to make some changes to the ordinance and delay the full council vote until a special meeting a week later. On April 24, the City Council passed the revised ordinance establishing the Infrastructure Trust by a vote of forty-one to seven.[67] It included some of the safeguards aldermen had demanded, like mandates that the trust would be subject to state freedom of information and open meetings laws.[68] But aldermen including Arena and Muñoz complained that major concerns remained unchanged.[69] Pundits described the vote as carrying larger symbolism: it showed that Emanuel was willing to compromise a bit but that he ultimately would get his way.[70] "He just said, 'I want to do this and I have the votes,'" remarked Muñoz, who opposed the very existence of the trust.[71]

Political scientist and former alderman Dick Simpson said the revised ordinance was better than the initial proposal, but still left many unanswered questions.

"For there to be a public-private partnership, the private side has to think they'll get their money," Simpson said. "If you're talking a major project of hundreds of mil lions or billions of dollars, that could be problematic. . . . The big danger is [Emanuel] will become too fixated on the bottom line and the private sector and what they can do, because they have the money."[72]

In June 2012, Emanuel named his handpicked five-member Infrastructure Trust board: retired Boeing executive James Bell; former Sara Lee executive Diana Ferguson; attorney David Hoffman, the city's former inspector general; Alderman John Pope, a longtime politico who represented the industrial Southeast Side; and Chicago Federation of Labor president Jorge Ramirez.[73]

Ramirez's participation underscored the fact that trust projects would likely cre-ate many union construction and tradesman jobs. One of the partners that signed on to the trust was the Union Labor Life Insurance Company (Ullico), a union-owned insurance and investment consortium founded in 1927 by labor leader Samuel Gompers to offer life insurance to union members who could not get it otherwise.[74] By 2012 Ullico was a large company with clients including individual unions, union-ized employers, and institutional investors.[75] Ramirez explained that the trust could offer Ullico a way to invest in projects that created jobs for American union mem-bers, as opposed to typical financial portfolios likely to include multinational compa-nies in foreign countries with bad labor records.[76]

"You could be investing in third-world countries, where labor leaders are get-ting killed and the governments are doing things we find abhorrent," said Ramirez. "The Infrastructure Trust is a way of putting people to work here, getting a good rate of return and relieving the burden [of financing infrastructure] on taxpayers."[77]

THE BEST DEAL?

In the wake of the Infrastructure Trust announcement, planning and finance ex-perts in Chicago and around the nation parsed the meaning of the plan. Many of these experts were not focused on equity and economic justice but whether this would be a good deal overall for the city. Especially given the lack of details emerg-ing from the administration, there was considerable skepticism. Among other things, finance experts questioned why the complicated trust structure would be preferable to plain-old municipal bonds of the type long used to finance public projects. Part of the justification for the trust was that it would allow the city to at-tract investment for riskier projects that might not be feasible with traditional fi-nancing. But as a *Chicago Tribune* editorial noted, "because these deals would put more risks on the investors than bond buyers typically accept, the investors likely would demand more lucrative paybacks."[78]

The finance industry newsletter *BondBuyer* noted that during the five-hour City Council hearing about the trust, Lois Scott acknowledged that "'absolutely' a portion of trust financing that relies on private investment would carry a higher borrowing cost than a traditional bond deal, and the overall package 'possibly' could be higher."[79] In other words, the projects undertaken by the Infrastructure Trust could ultimately be more expensive than they would have been if financed through regular bonds.

Jorge Ramirez predicted that the trust wouldn't displace bonds and other methods of financing for city projects but would simply add another option. "It's another arrow in the mayor's quiver," he said.[80]

TRUST IN CHICAGO'S CULTURE

Among his many other ambitious initiatives, during his second summer in office Emanuel set out to revamp the Chicago Cultural Plan, first formulated in 1986 under Mayor Harold Washington.[81] The new plan would be drafted with public input gathered through online comments and a series of community meetings. The goal was to "elevate the city as a global destination for creativity, innovation and excellence in the arts."[82] In bitingly humorous coverage for the *Chicago Reader*, Deanna Isaacs described how all the hype and process ultimately resulted in "92 pages of bureaucratese and unprioritized suggestions, all padded out with familiar-looking photographs of the city." The final plan was inauspiciously unveiled at a little-publicized event at an elementary school, albeit with a few national cultural stars on hand, including musician Yo-Yo Ma and former ballet dancer Damian Woetzel.[83]

The central component of the cultural plan would be increased arts education in schools, which gave Emanuel another opportunity to tout the longer school day. Teachers union president Karen Lewis praised the idea of more arts in the schools—this had been a request of the union throughout contract negotiations—but she noted that it was not clear where meaningful funding would come from. The city's 2013 proposed budget included $1 million for the cultural plan, $500,000 of which would go to arts in schools. But the city had spent $230,000 of mostly private money hiring a Canadian consulting company to host the public meetings and formulate the verbose, vague cultural plan.[84]

The plan listed many long-range, open-ended goals. Others were dubbed feasible in the next eighteen months, including establishment of the Infrastructure Trust as a way to fund cultural projects. Isaacs skeptically predicted the trust would "provide the appearance of a grassroots mandate for a mechanism that'll allow the private sector to profit from—and perhaps control—the brick-and-mortar assets that anchor our cultural heritage."[85]

Such fears might turn out to be unfounded. The trust could be a great success for all concerned, creating jobs and enabling important projects and renovations. Or it might end up being more spin than substance, frequently invoked in various contexts—energy efficiency overhauls, cultural programming—lending a sense of importance and action to projects that would materialize only if and when private investors decided the projects were worth their while.

In late November 2012, Emanuel published an opinion piece in the *Washington Post* trumpeting the Infrastructure Trust and the umbrella Building a New Chicago program:

> While infrastructure improvements have been neglected on a federal level for decades, Chicago is making one of the nation's largest coordinated investments, putting 30,000 residents to work over the next three years improving our roads, rails and runways; repairing our aged water system; and increasing access to gigabit-speed broadband. We are paying for these critical improvements through a combination of reforms, efficiencies and direct user fees, as well as creating the nation's first city-level public-private infrastructure bank. Democrats should champion these kinds of innovative financing tools at a national level.[86]

The piece certainly sounded inspiring. But it gave the impression that the Infrastructure Trust and the jobs and improvements it promised to create were already well under way. In reality, few details beyond the energy efficiency program had even been revealed, much less realized. Many readers thought the true message in the *Washington Post* op-ed was about Emanuel's future intentions. "Do you ever wonder why, when Mayor Rahm Emanuel has something important to say, he says it to *The Atlantic*, or *The New Republic*, or *The New York Times?*" asked NBC blogger Edward McClelland. "I don't. Emanuel owns all the votes he'll ever need in Chicago. But he's going to need a lot of votes outside Chicago to fulfill his goal of becoming, pound for pound, the most powerful world figure since Napoleon Bonaparte was Emperor of France."[87]

JEANETTE HANSEN SPOKE UP AT AN ALTERNATIVE BUDGET HEARING—
BECAUSE THE MAYOR CANCELED THE LONG-STANDING OFFICIAL COMMUNITY
HEARINGS. PHOTO BY KARI LYDERSEN.

12
ANOTHER BUDGET, ANOTHER BATTLE

AN ANNUAL RITUAL

The Chicago budget may be a complicated and voluminous document, but Chicagoans know it has real effects on their daily lives. It determines whether the pot holes on their streets will be fixed, whether their garbage will pile up in smelly mounds on top of overfilled dumpsters in the summer heat, whether police officers will respond quickly if they call 911, and sometimes whether they will even have a job come the new year.

People want to understand the budget and to have a say in it, and in 1984 Mayor Harold Washington started a process that would give them a chance. He pledged to release a draft budget well before the City Council voted on it, and to hold a series of evening meetings in various communities where the mayor and his staff would give residents a chance to voice their questions and concerns. "It was remarkable to witness: any resident could ask anything and get a concrete, substantive answer from the city's top decision-makers," wrote *Community Media Workshop* blogger Curtis Black.[1]

The budget hearings became a city institution, and one that outlived Washington. Mayor Daley continued the tradition, typically releasing draft budgets and then holding evening community hearings weeks before the City Council vote on the final document. Daley was not exactly rapt with attention or brimming with curiosity and sympathy during these sessions. He and his aides were known to look bored or distracted, and sometimes even left the room while constituents were talking in hearings that often dragged on late into the night. *Chicago Reader* reporter Ben Joravsky described the typical scene: "Mayor Daley would sit in the center of a long table with his cabinet members on either side. The people would line up at a microphone. And in that way the peasants could question the king. The press aides would give away all sorts of nifty little trinkets, like notepads, key chains, and pens."[2]

Daley's budgets didn't necessarily reflect changes based on the community hearings, and participants rarely got direct answers from the mayor. Nevertheless, Daley showed up and let people harangue, plead with, or even praise him, year after year.

Emanuel had tried to continue the tradition with two evening community budget hearings held at city colleges in August 2011. The mayor could not have been happy about how those turned out: people booed and heckled him as union members, Mental Health Movement activists, and other disgruntled residents questioned and denounced his policies. The political climate was even more fraught by the time the proposed 2013 budget was being finalized. Emanuel's battle with the teachers union was in full swing, and he was also facing contentious negotiations with the powerful police and firefighter unions. So there would be no community hearings.

"Thin-skinned dude that he is, he probably decided there and then—no more of this bullshit with these fuckers," wrote Joravsky. "As only Mayor Rahm could put it."[3]

THE 2013 BUDGET

By early October 2012, Emanuel had still not released a draft 2013 budget or details about what it might contain, so a coalition of unions and community groups sent him a letter demanding that the draft be immediately released and public hearings scheduled. The letter noted the "growing concern among Chicagoans about recent changes to the City Budget process that, taken together, represent a complete break with past precedent and serve to virtually eliminate public participation in the process." "Budgets are moral documents," the letter continued. "They lay out a city's values and priorities. Our members have credible solutions to offer—progressive revenue solutions that need to be heard. It is negligent to leave those who are most impacted by spending cuts—our neighborhoods and communities—out of the budget process."[4]

Grassroots Collaborative executive director Amisha Patel said that the mayor's office never responded to the letter.[5] Then on October 10 the mayor made his budget address to City Council and posted budget documents on the city website. The budget address had a stern yet hopeful tone. The mayor described an expected deficit of just under $300 million, the lowest since the economic crisis began. He struck a somber note describing fourteen thousand applicants for just seventy-five slots in a water infrastructure apprenticeship program, and noted the high number of foreclosures still plaguing the city. But these challenges were overshadowed by positive developments including thousands of new slots for youth summer jobs; early education programs and after-school activities; free eye exams and glasses for thirty thousand public school students; and the fact that Chicago home prices had climbed at more than double the national rate. He ticked off some of the companies moving their headquarters to Chicago, saying, "When it comes to creating jobs, the Second City is second to none. Chicago led the nation's large cities in job growth in the past year and experienced the largest drop in unemployment."[6]

Emanuel emphasized the role of labor unions in helping him save costs, citing deals he'd recently made with SEIU Local 73 and the IBEW Local 21 regarding 2,530 "non-sworn" public safety workers like traffic control aides, animal care and control workers, emergency dispatchers, and aviation inspectors.[7] The city's budget overview noted that the city and unions "have reached 11 agreements that are expected to save the City more than $42 million over the next six years, including an agreement with Laborers Local 1001 that will help save taxpayers more than $30 million in that period."[8]

The overview also noted the success of the recycling pickup managed competition and the victory of city workers in a similar competition for tree trimming. The city workers did such a good job that the city would save $1.3 million on tree trimming for 2013, the budget overview noted, promising, "these savings will be reinvested in maintaining and protecting the city's trees."[9]

Once the 2013 budget was finally released, community and union leaders set to work analyzing it. It did not sound alarm bells like the 2012 budget had. The total number of layoffs indicated was fairly low. And the city promised to hire almost five hundred more police officers and a handful of workers in other sectors, while funneling millions in TIF funds back to city coffers.[10] But union and community leaders feared there were less obvious impacts embedded in the budget document. Most important, they worried about privatization and increased efficiency measures that weren't reflected as layoffs but could lead to job cuts or service reductions down the road.

The City Council committee hearings on the proposed budget were relatively uneventful. But there was a flare-up around the decision to hire a subsidiary of a Japanese technology company to take over a water billing call center. The thirty-four call center city workers, 80 percent of whom were African American, would lose their jobs.[11] "You left them with no recourse. I'm a little ticked," said Budget Committee chair Carrie Austin, who represented a Far South Side neighborhood. "Every time there's elimination of employees, and you hire an outside firm to replace those employees, how are we strengthening the middle class?"[12]

PROGRESSIVE ALDERMEN STEP IN

In the absence of official evening budget hearings, a handful of aldermen from the City Council's progressive caucus decided to host their own community meetings. If the proposed 2013 budget looked relatively innocuous on paper, you wouldn't know it from the tenor of these gatherings. Many Chicagoans were still hurting because of

SPEAKERS—AND HOMEMADE POSTERS—AT
THE ALTERNATIVE BUDGET HEARINGS
DECRIED THE MAYOR'S LACK OF
TRANSPARENCY. PHOTO BY KARI LYDERSEN.

the cuts in the previous year's budget and larger economic forces. Though they probably hadn't waded through the massive budget overview for 2013, they feared more of the same was in store.

City workers—well organized, galvanized by the teachers strike, and fearing for their jobs—attended by the hundreds. At the second meeting, which took place at a high school on the city's Near West Side, one speaker after another—many wearing union stickers or T-shirts—stepped up to the microphone to voice concerns about privatization, discrimination, job cuts, and the city's priorities as a whole.

In one sad and awkward interlude, a meticulously dressed older African American woman spoke for much more than her allotted three minutes, reciting her résumé, qualifications, and personal attributes in a blatant plea for a job—she had been laid off from her position in the city office of emergency management. "I worked here for sixteen years and now a contractor is doing my job," she said, noting her bachelor's and master's degrees in computer science from the Illinois Institute of Technology. "I am dedicated, dependable.... I am job-ready. I was born and raised in this city, I love this city, and I love the people."

Lula White, a member of AFSCME Local 505 and an employee of the city's health department, scolded the aldermen for voting for the previous year's budget, which closed and privatized primary care clinics (not to be confused with the mental health clinics). She challenged the aldermen to go to the privatized primary care clinics and see if they could find the patients who were supposed to have been transferred from the city-run clinics. "The patients are not there," she cried. "The patients are not there. ... Where are they?"

AFSCME had been trying to study how clients of the primary care clinics were faring after privatization, but it was extremely difficult. That was partly because the Freedom of Information Act typically doesn't cover private contractors running public services like health clinics and outreach to the homeless. Jo Patton, a special projects director for AFSCME Council 31, figured that Emanuel wanted to privatize services like health care and homeless outreach not just to save money but also to ditch the political burden of serving such chronic and complicated needs. "You can't get pushed out of office for problems with services that you don't provide," she said.[13] "The more you can cut away at what the government does, the less [elected officials like the mayor] are vulnerable."

AFSCME member and librarian Caroline Broeren made the case that privatization does not necessarily pan out so well as a cost-cutting strategy in real life. She was one of several speakers who noted that unlike city workers, employees of contractors on city jobs do not need to live within the city limits. "Nonresidents are taking our jobs," she said. "We want to be able to continue providing services to the people who live in our communities, but we're having that taken away from us by privatization. And the low initial bids of contractors end up costing a lot more later—not just financially. As an employee of the city I care about what happens in the city. I don't know that private contractors will."

THE MENTAL HEALTH MOVEMENT MOBILIZES

On October 30, Jeanette Hansen and Margaret Sullivan met at Panera Bread in Beverly, the Southwest Side Irish neighborhood where they both lived, before the third and final community budget hearing hosted by the progressive aldermen.

"You look like a 1960s pimp!" Sullivan said playfully as Hansen walked up dressed strikingly in a velvety dark green tunic, leather hat, sparkly silver socks, and rose-colored glasses. She walked with a cane, her long graying hair straight and thick down her back.

Sullivan gave Hansen a peanut butter cookie she had saved for her—the free "birthday cookie" that the cafe gives regular customers once a year. Sullivan knew her friend had a sweet tooth. A typical conversation between the two ensued. Sullivan talked a mile a minute, making hilarious and biting remarks with wit worthy of a stand-up comedian, belying her struggle with manic depression and the serious health and financial problems she was facing. Hansen played the wry straight woman, offering small asides as they discussed their beloved therapist Eric Lindquist, their fellow mental health clinic consumers, and their mutual friend Helen Morley.

After drinking tea—Hansen stowed the cookie in her purse—they headed to the community budget hearing, where the Mental Health Movement planned to turn out in force. The event was being held at Hansen's alma mater, South Shore High School, though the building she attended had been torn down and replaced with spacious modern construction.

That day Lake Michigan was roiling with white caps and towering waves thanks to winds from Hurricane Sandy, which was at that moment pummeling New York City, destroying low-income beachfront housing projects, and leaving millions without power. Lake Michigan's waves were slamming against metal and concrete breakwaters, sending plumes of dirty spray forty feet in the air. There was a flood advisory in effect for the South Shore neighborhood, and Hansen worried the budget hearing would be canceled. But it went on as planned. While Sandy was laying bare deep inequities and desperation in New York City, Chicagoans lined up at the microphone in the high school auditorium to describe the poverty, anxiety, joblessness, homelessness, violence, and lack of health care that plagued their own communities on a daily basis.

Speakers praised the aldermen for holding the alternative hearings, and challenged them to stand up to the mayor, promising political support in return. They directed this message particularly at Alderman Robert Fioretti, whose ward had basically disappeared in recent redistricting—it had been disassembled and re-created as a squiggly shape that did not include Fioretti's own home.[14] Some speakers at the hearing described the gerrymandering as retaliation for Fioretti speaking out against Emanuel's 2012 budget, which he nonetheless voted for. More likely, it had been driven by unrelated political dynamics; but the fact that citizens would see it as retribution was revealing. Aldermen and regular Chicagoans alike had the sense that you took a risk by speaking out against the mayor.[15] "Some aldermen have concluded it's not possible to make up for getting off Emanuel's good side," said political scientist Dick Simpson. "With Daley it wasn't personal—it was about policy. With Emanuel, everything is personal."[16]

The hearing was moderated by Cliff Kelley, a popular radio host on historic African American radio station WVON and a former Chicago alderman himself. Kelley brought up the mental health clinics early in the evening, before members of the movement had even spoken. "You know what group has asked me to try to keep those mental health clinics open?" Kelley said. "The police." Mental Health Movement members handed attendees a hot-off-the-presses report they'd produced in conjunction with AFSCME indicating that at least 484 and as many as 2,200 patients had "disappeared" from the city mental health system.[17]

When Chuy Campuzano got his chance to address the aldermen, he waved the report and demanded they read it "line by line." He wore a T-shirt with Helen Morley's image, and he reminded the aldermen that "she passed away right after she told the mayor, 'If you close my clinic, I will die.'"

Sullivan and Hansen also addressed the aldermen. Sullivan sounded sarcastic and irascible—never a fan of authority, she explained later that "whenever I see aldermen I see red."

THE "OFFICIAL" HEARING

The day after the final community budget hearing, the full City Council convened for its monthly meeting. It would be followed by the city's official public hearing on the city budget—one such hearing was required by law. This hearing was completely different from the three unofficial community hearings hosted by the progressive aldermen.

Emanuel presided over the city council meeting, standing below the city seal between the Illinois and American flags and looking lithe and impeccable in a dark suit and purple tie. He joked cheerfully and smiled impishly as aldermen rambled on about the rivalry between the White Sox and the Cubs. He nodded reverently as the council passed a resolution honoring a police officer who had done CPR to save a toddler's life.

After the meeting, the chambers cleared out as the Spanish and sign language interpreters made their way to the front and the public budget hearing was called to order. City clerk Susana Mendoza pertly recited the official notice of the public budget meeting that had been published in the *Chicago Sun-Times* twelve days earlier, noting that "the budget document is in pamphlet form and has been conveniently made available for inspection at the city clerk's office and in the Harold Washington Library."

If someone had not happened to read the *Sun-Times* that day, it would have been hard to figure out that the budget hearing was going on. There was no obvious notice on the City Council calendar or the city's budget website. As the public hearing unfolded, only half the aldermen remained in their seats and Emanuel left the room, as did the press corps.

Chicagoland Chamber of Commerce vice president of public policy Mike Mini thanked the absent mayor for eliminating the "head tax" that made it more expensive to hire employees. He said, "It's more important than ever we enact policies to position ourselves as the most business-friendly city in America." Chicago Hilton general manager John Wells praised Emanuel on the same grounds and noted that hotel business was picking up and should be offering more jobs soon. The head of the state retail trade association also praised the budget, as did the business manager of the local plumbers union, James F. Coyne.

Emanuel had increased water rates to fund badly needed water infrastructure overhauls, which would create significant jobs for plumbers and other union tradesmen. "Since Mayor Emanuel is such a strong supporter of organized labor, the jobs made possible are also well-paying jobs," said Coyne. "We the plumbers at [Local] 130 wholeheartedly support Mayor Emanuel's budget and urge you, the City Council, to approve it." Coyne also invited veteran alderman Ed Burke, whose grandfather cofounded the union, to sing a ditty about plumbers "protecting the health of the nation." Burke recited the words: "So when your water is clear and bright, then you know your pipes are tight, and you know a union plumber put them there."

AFSCME Council 31 policy and legislative specialist Adrienne Alexander was the first critical voice, presenting the union's recent report on the impacts of closing the six city mental health clinics. She noted the hundreds of patients who had "disappeared" from the mental health system, and emphasized that African American and Latino staff had been disproportionately laid off at the clinics.[18] "Aldermen, at a point you're not doing more with less, you're just doing less," she said. "We ask you, don't support this budget that continues the privatization and diminishment of public services."

Then came Jorge Castellanos, wearing a purple SEIU T-shirt.[19] In slow, heavily accented English, he read from a statement:

> This summer I lost my job as a janitor at the water department when the city replaced my employer with an irresponsible contractor. When a new company took over, they fired me and my five coworkers, even though we had years of experience. The mayor's office changed to a non-union contractor.... Now we are struggling. It has been four months, and I still have not found a job. I'm worried about paying my bills and tuition for my son in college. The workers that replaced us are paid low wages and don't have insurance. I don't think that helps working families, to eliminate good middle-class jobs.... I tell Mayor Emanuel, Please don't cut good jobs for the peoples. Thank you so much and God bless you.

Responding to the previous speakers, the aldermen had gamely asked questions and made gushingly supportive comments. In contrast, Castellanos's remarks were met with complete silence.

Castellanos was followed by SEIU institutional services director Lonnell Saffold. "Taxpayers deserve transparency and community participation in the budget process," he said. "We need a budget that puts the needs of hardworking Chicagoans above corporate profits." By hiring a cheaper contractor who laid off Castellanos and his coworkers, Saffold continued, the city was just transferring costs to taxpayers in other ways. Deprived of their wages and health insurance, the laid-off workers would be relying on the county system for health care and collecting federal unemployment benefits.

"You don't take people making $14 an hour and take their jobs, their health care to balance the budget," he said. "You can do the right thing by asking Rahm—err, Mr. Emanuel and your colleagues—to look at these individuals right here. They did nothing wrong—they paid their taxes, they want to send their kids to school and have a good opportunity for the American Dream. But their dreams have been shattered because someone decided it was a good idea to give their jobs to nonunion contractors."

SEIU members in purple T-shirts stood in the chamber and clapped. Saffold invited the aldermen to ask questions about his testimony or about the proposed Responsible Bidders Ordinance, which would protect collective bargaining rights and workers' well-being in city jobs being done by private contractors. Among other things, the ordinance would require the city to consider past labor law violations in deciding whether to accept a bid. The proposed law had been on the docket for some months and sparked several protests at City Hall.[20] One alderman said he supported the ordinance, and Saffold stepped down.

By the time George Blakemore walked proudly to the front of the room, the number of aldermen in the room had dwindled even lower. For years Blakemore had been a constant fixture at public meetings of every sort, offering his long-winded opinions, often demanding more jobs and resources for the African American community and denouncing illegal immigration. Blakemore respectfully thanked the council for holding a public budget meeting and noted that "most of your comrades do not feel the need to be present at this public process."

Dressed sharply in a brown suit and patterned tie, he noted that he used to wear his old ratty clothes to the "dog and pony shows" around the annual budget. This year he'd decided to start dressing up to lend a little more dignity to the process. "But it's still the same thing—the Black community receives peanuts."

The next speaker, who had "endured indignities" making his way downtown from a poor West Side African American neighborhood, likewise pointed ruefully to the "empty chairs" and the chatting aldermen, who "don't even want to hear what I have to say because they're holding another meeting over there."

Then West Side resident Paul McKinley denounced "a Caligula-style mayor who refused to face the public, who refused to face society," before getting into a shouting match with his alderman over his allegations that she allowed a convenience store to openly sell bullets. The aldermen were still muttering over McKinley's outburst as the final speaker, Jeanette Hansen, made her case.

Earlier Hansen had removed her velvety rose-colored hat to carefully comb her hair, and composed her remarks in a small notebook in extremely neat handwriting. She extolled the skills and compassion of her therapist, Eric Lindquist, and reminded the few aldermen who were paying attention that Helen Morley had died after the clinic they attended was closed. "She was mentally ill and she knew it, but she knew she had rights and she worked for them," said Hansen.

Hansen said she herself had been employed by the city for fifteen years in a job writing parking tickets. Now she relied on food stamps but hoped to become self-sufficient by making artistic trinkets to sell with a peddler's license. "There's a stigma attached to mental illness, we know this," she said. "But it's an illness like any other, it's a chemical imbalance in the brain and it's not our fault." She noted that access to stable therapy and medication can help mentally ill people work and support themselves. Her conclusion about the budget: "All I can say is, penny-wise and pound-foolish. Thank you."

As soon as she finished speaking, the moderator called on Ed Burke to officially adjourn. But everyone had to wait for him to get off his cellphone.

THE VOTE

There was absolutely no doubt the budget would pass when the City Council considered it on November 15. Emanuel's inaugural budget had passed unanimously, and it included more controversial cuts to jobs and services—including the closing of the mental health clinics. But still there were stirrings of discontent, and the scoop was that up to five aldermen might actually vote against the 2013 budget. Five no votes would hardly be a rebellion, but it would be an annoying show of resistance for Emanuel.

The council meeting started in its usual way, with drawn-out resolutions praising law enforcement officers and local high achievers—a high school chess team, a firefighter, and a paramedic who had saved a ninety-four-year-old woman from a burning building. Alderman James Balcer, a Vietnam veteran, made his usual plug for the military—this time regarding the upcoming Toys for Tots parade.

When the resolution to pass the budget was introduced, aldermen proceeded to offer their thoughts. The first thirteen comments were overwhelmingly positive, with aldermen heaping accolades on the mayor and his budget team. There were frequent mentions of the elimination of the head tax to reduce costs on employers, the streamlining of small business licensing, and the increase in funding for school eye exams. Numerous aldermen also praised the plan to spend an additional $3 million on tree trimming, funds freed up in part by the city workers' bid to do the job more cheaply than private contractors. Alderman Leslie Hairston noted that overgrown trees block streetlights and create "a breeding ground for people to have their purses stolen" while walking around the University of Chicago.

"This budget is pro-business, pro-family, pro-cost-cutting, pro-economic development, and pro-safety," said Alderman George Cardenas, who represented Southwest Side Latino immigrant neighborhoods. "That's a lot to say in a sentence, but that's the reality."

Alderman Will Burns, whose ward included largely poor African American neighborhoods sandwiched between ritzy downtown and the University of Chicago, noted that "I represent a very skeptical corner of the city," people attuned to being marginalized and discriminated against. But without giving specifics, he praised Emanuel for "investing in programs that represent ladders of opportunity for poor people" and for using "city government to balance out the many inequalities that exist in our society." (AFSCME special projects director Jo Patton let out a disgusted murmur at that comment; she had been researching how the cuts in the city's 2012 budget disproportionately impacted low-income African American workers and communities.)

Danny Solis, the Pilsen alderman who likely owed his 2011 reelection to Emanuel, went beyond the budget to praise the mayor's leadership as a whole. "My colleagues have mentioned 90 to 95 percent of the reasons this is such a great budget. I want to focus on some of your good ideas that will benefit this city for many years to come."

Robert Fioretti was the first alderman from the progressive caucus to speak. Sitting in the front row near Emanuel and wearing a red satiny tie, he set the stage by saying, "The annual budget is more than a statement of our projected revenues and expenses . . . the budget tells us who we are as a city, it's a statement of our priorities, what we now agree to." Then he launched into the questions and criticisms. In a city where four people had recently been shot in front of the same liquor store on two consecutive nights, would enough police be on the streets? What about the thirty-four people laid off from the water call center when the operations were privatized? "Once we start outsourcing to entities in other cities, the future is being sold," Fioretti said. "A budget may be fiscally sound, but our priorities may be wrong."

Fioretti charged that the budget gap was being closed at the expense of middle-class jobs. He also questioned the financial wisdom of the mayor's proposed long-term leases for electronic digital billboards. Then he concluded saying he was confident the city could tackle its budget gap—but the "lack of transparency and lack of public input gives me great pause."

Alderman Pat Dowell, who represented the South Side neighborhood of Bronzeville—once a famous bastion of jazz and blues and the economic heart of the African American community—was sitting beside Fioretti, and she seemed to be directly responding to him when she said, "There's very little controversy associated with this budget, and I rise in support of it."

The next few speakers seemed similarly intent on reassuring Emanuel of their support in the face of Fioretti's blasphemy. Howard Brookins cited the plight of the laid-off water call center workers but thanked the mayor for trying to find them jobs elsewhere in city government. Anthony Beale, who represented a desperately poor Far South Side neighborhood, defended the mayor against citizen complaints about the lack of transparency. Patrick O'Connor appeared genuinely alarmed or angered by Fioretti's speech; he said he was glad the "luxury of dissent has crept back into the body" of the council after the previous year's unanimous vote, even as he tried to discourage such dissent.

Two years earlier Ed Burke had reportedly fought to keep Emanuel from running for mayor; he was widely identified as one of the masterminds behind the challenge to Emanuel's residency. But at the budget vote, Burke made clear his loyalty. He digressed about the heroism of local firefighters and seemed to imply that aldermen who opposed the budget were betraying those firefighters—though the firefighters union itself was battling Emanuel over proposed staffing cuts. Like O'Connor, Burke called for a return to the previous year's unanimous vote: "I would like to see today that unanimity ring through this chamber again to demonstrate that the mayor and members of City Council are acting together as one."

As part of the progressive caucus holding the community hearings, Toni Foulkes had listened to hours of testimony from residents about job losses, privatization, and the closing of mental health clinics. But that day in the council chambers she offered only praise for the budget, along with a rambling rumination on the idea that mental health is a serious problem and that people cannot necessarily recognize the "face of mental illness" among them. Nowhere in this tangent did she mention the closed mental health clinic patients.

None of the other progressive caucus members made a comment, and eventually the vote on the budget was called. Emanuel had stood through the entire meeting with his athletic posture, occasionally smiling at individual alderman and once eating an energy bar. As the "ayes" cascaded in one after another, he beamed at the reporters in the press box. The final tally: forty-six ayes, three nays, and one absence—Sandi Jackson, wife of Congressman Jesse Jackson Jr., who was battling mental illness and criminal corruption charges. The no votes on the budget were Fioretti and progressive caucus members John Arena and Scott Waguespack.

Emanuel gave a brief speech, describing a "budget that builds on the tough decisions we made in the first budget, to right a shift that went wrong, to deal with structural problems in a structural way." Though the aldermen had nearly all avoided mentioning the schools or education, Emanuel brought up the longer school day and his commitment to investing in children, including increased funds for summer jobs and after-school programs. He invoked one of his trademark images: "All of us have seen these kids with that distant look in their eye."

Most of the aldermen clapped enthusiastically after the speech, but not Fioretti, who rocked in his seat and maintained a blank expression. Nearly all spectators and reporters left the chambers after the budget vote, before another ordinance was introduced that could potentially be significant for Chicago public employees and taxpayers. And the action on this ordinance indicated that City Council members were actually more concerned about privatization and job cuts than they had let on while the cameras were rolling.

Thirty-two out of the council's fifty aldermen cosponsored the Privatization Accountability and Transparency Ordinance, which would mandate that the city must study the cost-effectiveness of privatizing any service before implementing the plan.[21] This might seem an obvious idea, but at that point the city could and often did wait to do any studies until after awarding a contract for public services to a private firm. The ordinance stipulated that the city also must prove that the economic benefits of privatization outweighed other public benefits that flowed from city employment. The ordinance also mandated that city officials work with potentially impacted employees and union leaders to find ways to address quality issues in-house before turning to a private contractor. This was an important provision to many union leaders because it was widely believed that city governments allowed public services to deteriorate intentionally or through understaffing and then used the poor service as a reason to turn it over to the private sector. With the new law, at least one public City Council committee hearing would have to be held on any privatization plan.

The ordinance was introduced by South Side alderman Roderick T. Sawyer. "I don't believe there are no good privatization deals," he said in a statement. "I just think we should be clear about which deals are in the best interest of the city and which are not. I have a concern about touting monetary savings if we haven't thought about the people that will lose a job, the families that could lose a home, and the local businesses that could lose a loyal customer."

AFSCME Council 31 and the Chicago Federation of Labor supported Sawyer's ordinance. "Privatizing as a long-term proposition doesn't seem to pan out so well," said labor federation president Ramirez at his office a few months later. "You're lowering wage rates and stripping benefits, all to save money. But it comes at a high cost. Contractors don't have residency requirements, so you're displacing people and communities and replacing them with people from out of town. If you displace someone in this economy, you are going to make them work for less or no money. You're blighting communities. A lot of folks have been burned by privatization in my world."[22]

MANAGED COMPETITION AND A QUESTIONABLE PLAYING FIELD

The concept of "managed competition" that had taken center stage in the 2011 face-off between public and private recycling pickup crews—and in 2012 between tree trimmers—was central to the city's privatization initiatives.

By comparing the costs and performance of public and private players, the city was giving unions and city workers a chance to protect their domain and use their own judgment in increasing efficiencies or cutting costs to match the private sector. But the playing field was not necessarily level. A number of union members complained during the alternative budget hearings that private, often nonunion contractors offered cheaper services than public union teams largely thanks to lower wages and benefits. Hence the city's bottom line might look better with a cheaper contractor in place, but that figure wouldn't take into account the economic ripple effects that follow when residents lose their jobs and hence reduce the amount of money flowing into the neighborhood economy. As people also pointed out often during the alternative budget hearings, city workers must live within Chicago but private contractors face no such restrictions; money paid for privatized jobs can go to people outside the city or even outside the state or country. In an analysis drafted around the 2013 budget proposal, AFSCME Council 31 experts noted that "the city's privatization initiatives have resulted in substituting lower-wage private sector jobs—as much as 40 percent lower—for city jobs that pay a decent, family-supporting wage."

Both AFSCME and SEIU leaders charged that they didn't trust the city to fairly carry out managed competition because, they said, Emanuel's administration had previously rejected or ignored union bids that were lower than those of the private contractors who got the jobs. As a briefing paper on privatization prepared by AFSCME stated:

> While the city claims that it is pursuing a policy of "managed competition" in which current employees can "bid" on the work along with outside firms, AFSCME has found this process to be little more than a sham, invoked to allow the administration to blame the victims of layoffs while proceeding with a systematic approach to contracting out city services. Proposals submitted by the union for ways in which city employees can perform work more efficiently have been rejected out of hand, with no explanation given.[23]

AFSCME gave several examples of cases in which the union had offered to do the job more cheaply than the private company awarded the deal. The city had laid off workers in the water call center, for example, and replaced them with the business services firm Keane, a US subsidiary of Tokyo-based NTT Data.[24] "Although the City has failed to provide full data to evaluate the NTT/Keane proposal, what it did provide indicates that NTT budgeted $800,000 more in personnel costs than the city personnel costs," said the AFSCME document.

The union said Emanuel treated employees of the Department of Family and Support Services' Mobile Emergency Outreach program the same way, outsourcing their work to the private organization Catholic Charities even though the city workers had already secured federal funding for their positions and felt confident they could do the job more efficiently.[25] "The Catholic Charities' proposal significantly cut staffing from forty-two frontline employees to the equivalent of thirty, which seriously jeopardizes services," said Jo Patton. "At the same time, employees in the privatized program will be paid on average 40 percent less than the city employees who had successfully provided these services for many years."[26] In his budget address Emanuel had touted the deal with Catholic Charities, saying the partnership would allow the city to serve 1,400 more homeless youth and 220 more adults.[27]

AFSCME was naturally fighting for its workers, and hence was generally motivated to win "managed competitions" and hold privatization at bay. But private contractors carrying out city services can be unionized, and in fact many of them are—the recycling competition pitted private-sector Teamsters against public-sector Teamsters. Union employees of private companies are often paid less or are working under less desirable terms than unionized public workers in similar jobs, but that doesn't necessarily have to be the case. So unions as a whole are not necessarily opposed to privatization or public private partnerships.

SEIU Local 1 represents janitors, security guards, and other employees working in Chicago public buildings through private contractors. Such workers were once hired directly by the city, but different sectors were bid out to private contractors be-

ANOTHER BUDGET, ANOTHER BATTLE 227

ginning in the 1990s, with much privatization happening in waves under Mayor Daley. Tom Balanoff, president of SEIU Local 1 and a longtime fighter for union rights in Chicago, said he had no beef with privatization per se. He thought some contracts, like security, might be best carried out by firms with specialized expertise. The most important thing, he stressed, was not whether people were hired directly by the city or by a contractor but whether protections were in place to make sure they had the right to unionize, to earn a decent living wage, and other basic provisions.[28]

A PRIVATE AIRPORT?

As people were debating the impacts of privatizing city services like call centers and garbage pickup, the mayor was in the midst of negotiating what could be one of the biggest privatization deals in the country.

Years earlier, Mayor Daley had tried to privatize Midway Airport, the city's smaller airport on the Southwest Side, which would have been the first such deal in the country. He laid the groundwork to lease the airport to private investors for $2.5 billion for ninety-nine years, but in 2009 the plan collapsed because financing could not be raised amid the economic crisis.[29] Many civic leaders called for the plan to be axed for good, and during his mayoral campaign Emanuel distanced himself from the idea.[30] But once in office he twice asked the Federal Aviation Administration to extend the deadline on a waiver allowing the possibility of privatization. In May 2012 the mayor and CFO Lois Scott also asked aldermen to approve refinancing of $1.15 billion in Midway-related debt.[31]

These moves—made while the Infrastructure Trust was being hashed out—kept the door to privatization open through at least the end of 2012.[32] Federal law allowed only one of the nation's largest twenty-nine hub airports to be privatized, so if Midway's waiver lapsed, another city could potentially jump in and lay claim to the country's first major privately run airport.[33] During 2012 San Juan, Puerto Rico, was negotiating a deal to lease its airport for up to fifty years for as much as $1 billion, but as that airport was not one of the country's twenty-nine largest, it was not subject to the federal rule.[34]

Months later, with the Federal Aviation Administration's December 31 deadline approaching, Emanuel announced that a Midway privatization deal was being explored. But, he promised, it would be a much shorter lease than the ninety-nine-year one proposed by Daley, and it would maintain a level of city ownership and include a traveler bill of rights to protect fliers from price increases and fees that could otherwise be instituted by private operators.[35] The city would get a share of ongoing revenues from Midway rather than signing away all profits during the lease term, as Daley had done in the disastrous parking meter deal. And aldermen would have thirty days to review any proposal.[36]

In late January 2013, Emanuel's office appointed an advisory council to study Midway privatization. A *Chicago Tribune* editorial urged caution, noting, "Though

MAYOR EMANUEL IS PUSHING TO PRIVATIZE MIDWAY AIRPORT, A CONTROVERSIAL
MOVE THAT FORMER MAYOR RICHARD M. DALEY FAILED TO PULL OFF. PHOTO BY
PAT LYDERSEN.

many airports outside the U.S. are privately owned and operated, this is largely un-
charted territory in the U.S." The *Tribune* said that the firm hired to evaluate a Midway proposal should have no self-interest in the deal getting made—for example, an
expectation of future contracts related to the airport. And nearby residents should
have a say in the whole process. The editorial board concluded, "A public-private
partnership will make sense if the city demonstrates a clear, long-term financial benefit. Parking meters aside, there are plenty of successful examples of such partnerships around the country and in Chicago. So mayor, aldermen, be deliberate and be
transparent. And be open to the very real possibility when the numbers come in that
the best option for Chicago is to say no."[37]

Emanuel was surely prepared for the scrutiny and skepticism around Midway
privatization. But he probably did not expect a bigger public relations headache related to Chicago airports that erupted around the same time: the uprising of O'Hare
International Airport janitors outraged at losing their jobs when the city awarded
their contract to a lower bidder . . . one who turned out to have unsavory connections.

SEIU LOCAL 1 JANITORS SAW UNION-BUSTING BEHIND THE CITY SIGNING CONTRACTS WITH CHEAPER CLEANING FIRMS. PHOTO BY KARI LYDERSEN.

13
"THE JOB KILLER" AND THE JANITORS

Outside the River North Westin hotel on a chilly morning in early November 2012, about twenty men and women stood quietly facing the entrance, holding flyers saying, "Mayor Rahm Emanuel, Stop Eliminating GOOD JOBS." Several hotel employees nodded and smiled as they took the flyers, which implored people to call the mayor on behalf of more than three hundred O'Hare airport janitors and window washers who would be out of work before Christmas if the city went through with its plan to hire a new contractor for their positions.

Inside the hotel, Mayor Emanuel was presiding over the fifth annual Airports Going Green conference, where airport and airline leaders from around the world were discussing the latest in sustainable airport management, including aviation biofuel development, electric vehicles, recycled asphalt, and LED flight information screens. Emanuel told the crowd that investing in energy efficiency and sustainability at airports like O'Hare and Midway is worth it because it creates jobs. "If you make that investment you find all the oars are pulling in the same direction," he said.

While Emanuel touted the value of extra spending on environmental and energy-efficient innovations, union leaders and workers were arguing he hadn't demonstrated such a commitment to investing in the loyal workers who kept the airports running smoothly day in and day out. The janitors, members of SEIU Local 1, feared losing their jobs because the city had recently signed a contract with a company offering to do the work more cheaply.[1]

Scrub Inc.—which, incidentally, had donated $20,000 to the mayoral campaign of Emanuel's rival Gery Chico[2]—had employed janitors at O'Hare since the jobs were privatized in 2005.[3] By fall 2012, most of them were making $15.45 an hour with decent benefits including health insurance.[4] But after Scrub's contract expired, the city awarded the job to United Maintenance Company, a subsidiary of a Chicago-based national cleaning firm hired for contracts at airports, trade shows, theaters, and other large institutions, including the Hyatt hotel chain.[5] United Maintenance's bid of $99.4 million for five years undercut Scrub's by about 10 percent, or $11 million. When United Maintenance took over on December 15, 2012, Scrub workers would lose their jobs and be replaced by United Maintenance hires with a starting wage of $11.90 an hour.[6] The former Scrub workers could apply for the jobs, but there was no guarantee they would be hired. And if they were, they would be bumped back to the starting wage like everyone else.

Another group of janitors (also represented by SEIU Local 1) who cleaned city police stations, health clinics, senior centers, and administrative satellite offices had recently suffered a similar fate. In summer 2012, their employer, Nationwide Maintenance, was replaced by Dayspring Janitorial Services, which had submitted a cheaper bid.

Pam Broughton had worked for eight years as a janitor at a police station on the city's Far South Side. As of spring 2012 she was making $15.45 an hour with benefits working for Nationwide. The new company, Dayspring, told workers that if they wanted to keep their jobs they would have to agree to $12 an hour, no benefits, and more part-time work, Broughton said. She and other janitors had agreed to the lower wage, she said, "because we needed jobs."[7]

Even so, Broughton was among fifty janitors laid off on June 29, 2012. Others were rehired by Dayspring but saw their pay drop from between $24,100 and $31,000 a year to a maximum of $23,800 per year. Many of those laid off had been in their jobs for decades. By fall 2012, Broughton was surviving on $167 a month in disability payments—or barely surviving, since she had diabetes and no health insurance.[8]

Things were even worse for one of Broughton's former coworkers, Catalina Bojorquez. She had been a police station janitor for three years but lost her job when Dayspring took over. That meant she had no health insurance when doctors discovered an ovarian tumor that might need surgery.[9]

SEIU Local 1 president Tom Balanoff said that while Broughton and her coworkers generally had full-time positions with health care benefits, Dayspring employed a largely part-time workforce without benefits. "We took workers who were making a real living wage with full health-care benefits, and turned them into part-time jobs," he said. "Now they are eligible for food stamps and all kinds of public aid. Maybe we helped fix the problems of the city budget, but we just transferred the costs. Without insurance, where will these workers go for health care? To the emergency room, which is the most expensive form of care."[10]

Balanoff is part of a Chicago family that's legendary in political and union circles, with relatives including elected officials, attorneys, and union leaders. He describes his family as an example of the American Dream that unions in their heyday

PAM BROUGHTON (RIGHT) AND OTHER UNION JANITORS FEARED SPIRALING
INTO POVERTY AFTER LOSING THEIR JOBS CLEANING CITY BUILDINGS.
PHOTO BY KARI LYDERSEN.

helped so many achieve. His father was able to send four kids to college and provide
a comfortable middle-class existence on a steelworker's union wages (he also became president of the steel union's largest local). And his parents were activists; they
took him to his first civil rights demonstration when he was nine years old.[11]

Balanoff had endorsed Rahm Emanuel in the 2002 Congressional race against
Nancy Kaszak. A decade later, he was describing Emanuel as a symbol of everything that was wrong with the way the Democratic Party treated working people.
"Chicago mayor is a big job nationally anyway, but Rahm Emanuel represents
something much bigger," he said in his downtown office as janitors were preparing
to make the latest in a series of visits to City Hall. "He represents the neoliberal
wing of the Democratic Party. Rahm Emanuel and [New York] Governor [An-
drew] Cuomo are the rising stars. This is a party that has to represent us, but they
haven't. . . . Workers are fighting over crumbs, over pieces of crumbs. If we unite, we
can forget the crumbs and say we want a piece of the pie."[12]

As he was overseeing the battles of the O'Hare and police station janitors, Balanoff was also gearing up for another standoff with the mayor. In spring 2013 contracts for the janitors who cleaned public schools would be expiring—these were

the same janitors who had been prepared to call their own walkout in solidarity during the teachers strike.[13]

REFORMS IN A "DARK HOLE"

For more than a year, SEIU Local 1 had been pushing City Council to adopt the Responsible Bidders Ordinance, which members had talked about during the one official hearing on the 2013 budget. The ordinance would apply to all contracts over $50,000 for window-washing, security, and janitorial services. It would require companies contracting with the city to comply with labor law, and it would disqualify companies charged with violating labor laws repeatedly in the past. Perhaps most important, it would mandate that when a new company took over a contract, it could not replace existing employees with new employees for at least a forty-five-day trial period. If people were laid off during this period, it would have to be done on the basis of seniority—so the new employer couldn't cherry-pick which workers it wanted to keep, and it couldn't selectively lay off union activists or rabble-rousers.[14]

As of fall 2012 the ordinance had the support of thirty-one aldermen, a majority. But it had to be called for a hearing in front of a City Council committee before going to a full council vote, where it would presumably pass. A year and a half into Emanuel's tenure, that still had not happened. The ordinance was stuck in the Workforce and Audit Committee, chaired by mayoral loyalist Alderman Pat O'Connor.[15] It is common knowledge that proposed ordinances don't progress through City Council without the mayor's support; even proposals popular with the aldermen will never see the light of day if the mayor doesn't give the green light.

The union UNITE HERE was pushing a similar ordinance meant to protect the concessions workers who staffed restaurants and gift shops at O'Hare. Like the janitors, they were afraid of losing their jobs if a new company was hired to take over their contract. The Stable Jobs, Stable Airports ordinance would mandate concessions workers be hired at least for a trial period when a new contractor was brought in, and it would force new contractors to remain neutral if workers tried to unionize. But like the Responsible Bidders Ordinance, it was languishing in a committee.[16]

On December 11, 2012, four aldermen supporting the Responsible Bidders Ordinance held a press conference in a small room at City Hall. Alderman Nick Sposato noted that without mayoral support the ordinance could easily remain stuck in a "dark hole." Along with Sposato, Aldermen Ricardo Muñoz, Scott Waguespack, and Roderick Sawyer described the SEIU janitors' situation as part of a larger trend: they said Emanuel was slashing middle-class union jobs and replacing them with low-paid and part-time positions.[17] "I believe what we are doing at O'Hare is socially irresponsible," Muñoz said. He lamented that the city might "save a nickel here and a nickel there" but would "put these families out on the street."

"These are people who are making $40,000 or $50,000 a year, paying taxes, many of them the only breadwinner in their family," added Waguespack. "And you're telling them to find another job, to go fish. . . . They're not going to be able to go to Boeing and get one of these jobs the mayor is bringing in."

Janitors Jermaine Samples and Mildred Rueda joined the aldermen at the press conference. They told reporters that they both turned in applications for jobs with United Maintenance at O'Hare, despite the severe pay cut and lack of benefits. But they never heard back. United Maintenance spokesman Steve Patterson later said the company did not have applications on file from Samples and Rueda, and that United Maintenance was hiring about one hundred former Scrub employees.[18] SEIU Local 1 spokesperson Izabela Miltko figured that the company conveniently lost the applications, given their activism with the union.[19]

Twenty-five-year-old Samples told reporters, "We had to stand in line like the general public to apply for our jobs—people were lining up at 5 a.m."

"They're taking my job away from me and giving it to someone else. It's not fair," added thirty-five-year-old Rueda. "People tell us we do a wonderful job, but we're living check to check and barely making it." When asked what she would do for the upcoming holidays, she said, "I'm grateful to have my family, but in terms of celebrating, there will not be any."

QUESTIONABLE CONNECTIONS

United Maintenance was headed by Richard Simon, a colorful, politically connected figure widely reported to have connections to organized crime.[20] A report by the Better Government Association described him as "a former cop and longtime neighbor of former mayor Richard M. Daley whose ties extend not only to politicians, but to union and reputed organized crime figures." The *Chicago Sun-Times* reported that from 1998 through 2011, Simon jointly managed another company with "alleged mob figure William Daddano Jr." The company was based in the same building as United Maintenance's offices, the *Sun-Times* reported.[21]

The questionable connections and behavior also involved unions. Federal investigators had probed allegations that Simon colluded with Teamsters union officials to illegally pay workers at Las Vegas trade shows lower than contract wages.[22] Another United Maintenance executive, Paul Fosco, had spent ten years in prison for racketeering related to mob corruption in the Laborers Union.[23]

The *Sun-Times* detailed how Simon had spent years working for former United Maintenance owner Ben Stein, known as a high-living "king of janitors." According to the *Sun-Times*, in 1980 Simon met with a woman the married Stein had been dating. On Stein's behalf, Simon offered her a luxury apartment and $10,000 to remove herself from Stein's life, the *Sun-Times* said. The woman, Karen Koppel, reportedly refused the offer. She was never seen again.[24]

As the media reported on Simon's associates and history, the *Sun-Times* quoted an Emanuel spokesman saying, "The city has no reason to believe that there is any wrongdoing with United Maintenance or its owner." The company gave the *Sun-Times* a statement saying that United Maintenance officials were not aware of allegations against its business partners, and that the since-terminated relationship with Daddano involved contracts to move heavy equipment at convention centers.[25]

Union leaders and watchdogs questioned whether the city government was playing favorites in selecting United Maintenance. The Better Government Association noted that another firm had offered to do the O'Hare job for significantly less than United Maintenance but was disqualified because city officials decided its financial predictions weren't realistic. The BGA quoted John W. Tyler, CEO of Kaleidoscope Cleaning, the Maryland firm that submitted the lowest bid for the O'Hare job, calling the situation "dirty dealing." The city "predetermined whom they wanted to give the contract to," he argued.[26]

Balanoff figured that the Emanuel administration was not only interested in cutting costs but also in dislodging the union at O'Hare. "This is a way to bust the union, and it's the wrong direction to be moving in," he said. He thought the mayor wanted to "privatize more and give what's already privatized to nonunion employees. We think he's manipulating bids to do this."[27]

A document filed as part of United Maintenance's bid mentioned paying up to $5 million (or 5 percent of the contract) to subcontract work out to the United Neighborhood Organization, the group run by top Emanuel adviser and vocal charter schools proponent Juan Rangel. In 2008 UNO had formed a janitorial operation employing about sixty people who mainly cleaned its charter schools.[28] After reporters picked up on the UNO angle, Rangel said that UNO would not actually be a subcontractor on the O'Hare deal. Rather, the organization would help recruit people for the United Maintenance jobs, and in fact it had already held two job fairs. Rangel told the Better Government Association that he expected UNO to be paid for its efforts. But in a statement United Maintenance said that UNO would not be paid, and that initial plans to hire fifteen janitors directly through UNO had been scrapped.[29]

The very idea that United Maintenance would need to recruit candidates for the janitorial jobs was strange, given that most of the union janitors employed by Scrub wanted to keep their jobs—not to mention the fact that hundreds of people had waited in line for six hours earlier that month to get into a city-sponsored job fair.[30]

BIRTHDAY WISHES

On November 29, 2012, Rahm Emanuel turned fifty-three. That afternoon, a procession of people marched to his house to wish him a happy birthday. The group included Latinos, African Americans, and many older Polish women, their hair neatly permed or tucked under head scarves. They were janitors at O'Hare, and they held tapered white candles and sang "Happy Birthday" in Polish, Spanish, and English as they walked toward Emanuel's house. Some had stickers affixed to their jackets with a photo of the mayor, the words "Rahm Emanuel, Job Killer," and the Twitter hashtags #millionairesmayor and #rahmjobkiller. Several said that they had voted for the mayor, and they called out, "Make our votes count!"

For a few weeks the janitors had been publicly asking Emanuel to "walk a day in our shoes"—to spend time with them at the airport and see how clean they kept the bathrooms and hallways despite the many thousands of harried travelers passing through each day. They had gotten no response.

Emanuel's house—mint green, spacious but not ostentatious, with a wide porch—was quiet. Two bright orange pumpkins perched on the steps. The janitors clustered around and made brief statements for the TV cameras that had seemingly materialized out of nowhere.

"These workers are working check to check already. This is going to create poverty jobs at the airport," said Laura Garza, secretary-treasurer of SEIU Local 1. "[Emanuel] claims to be creating jobs, but he's eliminating middle-class jobs. . . . They are mostly people of color, immigrants who came to make a better life for their families."

A hand pulled aside the edge of a curtain in the Emanuel house, and the small glow of a camera or smartphone could be seen apparently filming or snapping a photo of the gathering. Geneva Daniels, a middle-aged African American woman, held a cake with thick pink and blue frosting, the words "Happy Birthday Mayor Emanuel" in curvy script. Daniels had worked on the grueling night shift at O'Hare for nine years. Two of her brothers had recently died, so she was worried about being able to help provide for their kids. She wanted to be able to save enough money to take them on a little vacation. But on Emanuel's birthday, she was worried about just paying her own bills. "We don't want to be rich, we just want to get by," she said. "I have an apartment, the landlord wants rent—he doesn't want to wait for an unemployment check."[31]

The group soon crossed the street to mollify the police officers who were standing warily nearby; and then more workers addressed the reporters. Andy Cwanek spoke in Polish. "We don't want to be a burden to anyone, we want to support ourselves. We don't want to go to the unemployment office. Let us work."

Two weeks later, the janitors still had gotten no response from the mayor's office regarding their invitation to "walk a day in our shoes." So they held another festive protest, this one Christmas-themed. They gathered at City Hall, which was across the street from the big annual Christkindlmarket—a quaint faux-German village with beer gardens under heat lamps, a Santa's Workshop, and a towering Christmas tree.

A STATEMENT IN CHRISTMAS LIGHTS CAUGHT THE ATTENTION OF HOLIDAY
SHOPPERS. PHOTO BY KARI LYDERSEN.

The janitors and supporters from various faith-based, labor, and community groups marched out the City Hall doors, below giant holiday wreaths, toward the Christkindlmarket. They chanted, "Ho, ho, ho! Rahm Emanuel has got to go!" and "They took our jobs and they took our pay, right before the hol-i-day!" The group gathered below the Christmas tree and made speeches in the frosty air. Then everyone's attention turned across the street, where a twinkling spectacle was causing shoppers and revelers to pause and snap photos with their smartphones. Fourteen people each held a placard with a letter in blue Christmas lights. Together, they spelled "RAHM = JOB KILLER."

TIRED WORKERS AND DIRTY TOILETS

On her last Tuesday with a job at O'Hare, Geneva Daniels was despondent. She had only gotten an hour of sleep in the past twenty-four hours, having headed downtown after her night shift at the airport to visit the unemployment office and look for other work. She had previously gone to United Maintenance's office hoping to apply for a job at O'Hare, but she was told there were no more applications and that she should mail in her résumé. She had done that, but never heard back.[32] The next day Daniels was planning to fill out an application for a position through a different contractor in another airport terminal, but she wasn't hopeful.

"It's scary, it's sad. It's just really, really sad," she said. "They are destroying people, they just don't care. It's just a mess, it's the biggest mess I've ever seen in my life." Daniels was due back at O'Hare for one of her final shifts in a matter of hours, and she badly needed sleep. But she couldn't stop her mind from running. "You just have to go out there and keep looking for something," she said. "But I'm so tired, I just want to lay down."

On January 15, 2013, the *Sun-Times* reported that United Maintenance president Richard Simon had potentially violated city bidding requirements by failing to disclose that he had sold half of United Maintenance to an investment company called Invision Capital in December 2011. The paper noted tangential links between Emanuel and the new owners: Invision's managing partner, Robert Castillo, "formed the company after co-founding Valor Equity Partners, where he worked for seven years. Valor is headed by Antonio Gracias, who is on Emanuel's World Business Chicago board and was among seven co-chairs of the mayor's inaugural festivities in 2011."[33]

After the revelation, SEIU Local 1 held a press conference calling on the city to rebid the contract. And *Crain's Chicago Business* columnist Greg Hinz called on the city inspector general to look into the matter.[34] "This one just doesn't pass my sniff test," he wrote. "Not without a lot more questions being answered. A company involved in an extremely controversial city bid deal sells half of itself in the middle of the bid process and doesn't tell anyone until after? And the city says that's OK? I understand Mr. Emanuel's desire not to be seen giving in to SEIU. But this deal cries out for further investigation."

Many Chicagoans likely tuned out the news of complicated bidding issues and ownership deals. But soon the *Sun-Times* had another scoop about United Maintenance that attracted people's attention in a very personal way. Since taking over the contract United Maintenance had replaced the toilet seats at O'Hare, buying new "Sani Seats" with plastic wrap that rotates, theoretically to provide a clean surface for each new user. But suddenly it appeared the Sani Seats were not necessarily clean. *Sun-Times* reporter Dan Mihalopoulos, who had been on the Richard Simon beat, headed to the airport for a novel kind of investigative reporting. He poured orange juice on the rim of toilet bowls and then watched as the seats rotated. Apparently spray from the bowl was being trapped in the toilet mechanism and then brought out on the new stretch of plastic.[35] Mihalopoulos noted that the new seats also apparently violated two requirements of the contract: that a digital display let users know when a fresh seat was ready, and that the plastic not rotate when the seats were lifted.

SEIU Local 1 issued a press release warning of an "urgent health risk" at O'Hare, and calling on the health department to investigate. Workers handed out flyers with "urgent health warnings" at airport-bound L train stations.[36]

Meanwhile, in early 2013 SEIU Local 1 surveyed the former Scrub workers to see how everyone was faring. After talking with 178 of the 320 workers who had been laid off, the union found that thirty-five had been rehired by United Maintenance and five were on a wait-list. Ninety-seven people said they were still without work, and eighty of them reported relying on at least one form of public assistance (including food stamps, Temporary Assistance for Needy Families, and unemployment benefits).[37] Workers said they were relying on the county health system and worried they could not afford necessary health care. They feared losing their homes or being unable to pay rent, and some had taken to visiting soup kitchens and homeless shelters. One couple who had both worked as janitors at O'Hare were facing imminent bankruptcy. Contrary to expectations, the workers who were re-hired by United Maintenance said they did have health insurance. But as expected, their pay had fallen to $11.90 an hour from $15.45 under Scrub.[38]

For Jermaine Samples, losing his job right before Christmas created a sense of déjà vu. Two years earlier, Samples's mother had been laid off right before the holidays from her job at a hotel in downtown Chicago, where she had worked for a decade stocking minibars and other tasks. "They gave her a $1,000 check, a packet about unemployment, and an invitation to the Christmas party," Samples remembered drily.[39]

In 2012 Samples's mother's unemployment benefits ran out. Samples had split up with the mother of his son, so he moved in with his own mother in a West Side apartment. "My father isn't real reliable, so of course I was the breadwinner of the house," he said. When he found out just before Thanksgiving that he would soon be out of work, "I was stressed, destroyed, just trying to see how I could work things out. We tried not to turn to other means of making money. But when you get to that last option, everything gets thought about. People don't understand if they aren't put in this position—you can't judge." Nonetheless, he added, "I always have faith, I'm always optimistic."

On Christmas morning, while waiting to pick up his son, Samples ran into an acquaintance with whom he would often exchange greetings. The man had heard Samples was out of work, and told him that his own employer was hiring. He asked if Samples had a criminal record and if he had a valid driver's license. No and yes, Samples said. "So on the twenty-sixth I woke up at six thirty, went over there with the guy, with an application and résumé in a folder, looking presentable." He was hired on the spot to stock vending machines at hospitals and other institutions for $12.50 an hour, with no benefits or insurance.

"It's nothing like what I was making before, but you have to be grateful for what you have," he said. He didn't miss his overnight shifts at O'Hare. "I'm not going to lie, I never liked the job. I liked the pay and I liked the people. They become part of you. You develop a bond—like family. It's crazy just to know all these people are laid off. People I know and care about."[40]

MAYOR EMANUEL'S PLANS TO CLOSE SCORES OF PUBLIC SCHOOLS
WERE SEEN AS AN ATTACK ON LATINO AND BLACK NEIGHBORHOODS.
PHOTO BY KARI LYDERSEN.

CONCLUSION

As the second anniversary of his election approached, things were not going so well for Emanuel. Chicago had become a national, even international poster child for gun violence and homicides. The December 14, 2012, massacre of twenty students at Sandy Hook Elementary School in Connecticut had focused the country's attention on gun violence, and pundits were soon pointing out that a shooting death toll equivalent to Sandy Hook happened every few weeks in Chicago.

There were more than five hundred murders in Chicago in 2012, almost one hundred more than New York City despite the difference in population. And with forty-three murders in January 2013, Chicago was off to the bloodiest start since 2002.[1] The city had long been known for gang violence, and Emanuel could not be blamed directly for the uptick in murders. But critics were quick to point out that certain moves—cutting city jobs, closing mental health clinics, and closing schools—were likely to exacerbate the root causes of violence.

On February 21, 2013, a *Crain's*/Ipsos Illinois poll was released showing Emanuel's approval ratings had plummeted. Almost half of Illinois residents surveyed were on the disapproval side, while only 2 percent strongly approved of his performance and only 19 percent approved at all. This was significantly down from September 2012, when about a third of people had approved and a third had disapproved.[2]

The growing public disapproval was not mirrored in City Council. In April 2013 political scientist and former alderman Dick Simpson released an updated version of his "rubber stamp" report showing that aldermen were voting in line with Emanuel's wishes at even higher rates than under both Daleys and Ed Kelly, a Democratic Machine legend who served as mayor from 1933 to 1947.[3] On average aldermen voted with Emanuel 93 percent of the time in divided roll call votes, topping the 83–88 percent averages enjoyed by both Daleys and Kelly, as measured during key segments of their reigns. New aldermen were even more likely to vote with Emanuel than longstanding aldermen—at rates of 91 percent versus 90 percent.[4]

Simpson noted that independent opposition under Emanuel had been splintered in part by the split of so-called independent aldermen into two separate factions: the Progressive Reform Coalition, which voted with Emanuel 73 percent of the time, and the Paul Douglas Alliance, which voted with the mayor 92.5 percent of the time.

243

Simpson said that the increasing alliance with the mayor was partly the result of Emanuel's willingness to compromise more than Daley when facing solid opposition—for example, over the details of the NATO protest ordinances and the library closing plans.[5]

But many critics saw the cleaved progressive bloc as further evidence of Emanuel's bullying and manipulative style. They figured that even though the longstanding progressive bloc was hardly a fierce force of opposition, the Paul Douglas aldermen were even more afraid of offending Emanuel, and sought to keep their "progressive" label while essentially doing the mayor's bidding.

Emanuel's relationships with both City Council and the general public provided an important window into not only the political climate and future prospects of Chicago, but larger dynamics relevant to other American cities and on a national level. Chicago had long been a laboratory for the hottest new trends in urban planning, housing, finance, and education. This was eminently true during Emanuel's tenure. In his first two years he was at the forefront of pushing for charter schools, privatization, modern urban renewal, clean energy, and generally using a corporate, competition-based approach to examine and evaluate public services and structures. Other national and metropolitan leaders looked to Emanuel's Chicago for inspiration, and of course he wasted no chance to cultivate his national image, surely with higher ambitions in mind. He remained the consummate image of the New Democrat, a model for politicians and strategists nationwide.

How would Emanuel's tenure as mayor be judged through the lens of history? Would he be seen as popular and effective? Or autocratic and brutal? Or both? Would he be remembered for remaking Chicago in his own image: a fast-moving, efficient city driven by high finance and cutting-edge technology; the brawny working man's big shoulders of yore replaced by a triathlete's sleek pinstriped ones? And what would happen to the people who didn't find a place in the new Chicago?

That question was not a rhetorical one for the scores of parents and students who attended the more than a hundred meetings in the winter and spring of 2013 about plans to close up to a hundred or more public schools. In countless interviews with reporters, comments at public meetings, and chats with friends, the idea was often repeated: school closings were a clear sign that certain residents were no longer welcome in Chicago, that they weren't part of the future plan. Emanuel and his supporters continued repeating their talking points about creating schools where all students would have equal opportunity, about allowing low-income minority youth to fulfill their dreams. But increasingly many Chicagoans—particularly African American ones—were not buying it.

At the school closing hearings parents, teachers, and students begged the mayor and education board—often tearfully—to save their schools. In promoting charter schools Emanuel and other backers frequently invoked the image of "parent choice." With scores of public schools on the chopping block, hundreds of parents made their choice quite clear: they and their kids wanted their schools to stay open.

By March schools officials had, they said, analyzed the input from the community hearings. On March 21, the big news came: the list of schools to be closed. There were fifty-four: one small high school and fifty-three elementary schools. Additionally some schools would be combined with other schools, shoehorned into the same buildings. Parents across the city spread word and listened to public radio as education reporter Linda Lutton read the list in alphabetical order in a dirge-like monotone. The closings were mostly in low-income African American neighborhoods on the South and West Sides. It made national headlines as the largest ever mass school closing plan.

The reaction was immediate.

There were sighs of relief and cheers of celebration, as people learned their schools had survived. And there were cries of dismay and outrage, as parents and students saw their daily lives thrown unto uncertainty and chaos. Traveling an extra several miles to a new school might not seem like a significant change or ordeal. But as with the mental health clinic closures, various social and personal factors could turn a geographical mile into a de facto chasm for many vulnerable, frightened people.

Families saw the closing of their local school as the unmooring of one of their few anchors. Walking an extra mile—even an extra half mile—would mean significantly increased danger of violence. Parents and community activists demonstrated this point to reporters and some sympathetic aldermen by taking them on the new paths their kids would have to take, past loitering gang members, boarded up buildings, and busy intersections. The teachers union hosted a school closings bus tour, where union staffer and teacher Jackson Potter compared the plan to the demolition of public housing that displaced many and created new problems across large swaths of the city. "We were told that in order to improve housing we had to destroy it," Potter told bus tour participants including Alderman Robert Fioretti and African American congressmen Danny K. Davis and Bobby Rush.[6]

Parents' own schedules and even their jobs would be seriously affected by the need to escort children to new sites. And students lamented the impending separation from teachers they'd grown to know and love. Meanwhile teachers, custodians, and other staff at the schools—in many cases, residents of these same low-income minority neighborhoods—cringed in fear of losing their jobs.

Mayor Emanuel had not attended any of the community meetings leading up to the school closings. When the list of closures was announced, he was likewise not present to face outraged and terrified parents, students, and teachers. He was on the slopes in Utah, on the Emanuel family's annual ski vacation. The trip was timed with spring break at his children's school, his spokespeople explained. As critics frequently pointed out, that would be the University of Chicago Laboratory Schools, a

MASSIVE SCHOOL CLOSINGS COULD MEAN DANGER AND UPHEAVAL FOR LOW-
INCOME FAMILIES, AS MARCHERS MADE CLEAR. PHOTO BY KARI LYDERSEN.

pricey private institution not subject to the tumult facing the public schools.

Union president Karen Lewis called Emanuel's absence "cowardly." Musician and lawyer Matt Farmer tweeted, "Asked, while skiing in Utah, about closing 50 CPS schools, Mayor Emanuel said he is offering thousands of kids the chance to head downhill."[7]

Throughout the yearlong debate over closing schools, the administration had frequently changed its story about why the schools had to be closed and how the targets would be chosen. Sometimes they emphasized that "underutilized" schools with low student populations would be shuttered; critics noted that the Emanuel kids' private school would seemingly qualify as "underutilized" based on the same student-teacher and student-space ratios at play in the public schools. Other times the emphasis was on school performance. But in neither case did the actual list of schools targeted for closure consistently follow these criteria. Parents and teachers further revealed that the amount of money the administration said it would save by closing the schools seemed grossly inflated, by a factor of three or four in some cases.[8]

There would be another round of hearings on the school closings—almost two hundred more community meetings, at least three focused on each of the closing schools—before the board would vote in May 2013 to finalize the plan. The hearings were legally required to collect community input on the plan. But as Emanuel said in late March after returning wind-burned from his ski trip, it was a done deal.

"If nobody is going to be heard at the hearings, what's the use of having the hearings?" West Side pastor Marshall Hatch told the *Chicago Tribune*, as African

American ministers delivered a letter to Emanuel demanding a moratorium on school closings. "If it's a done deal, then stop wasting everybody's time."[9]

Around this time Emanuel stated publicly that he intended to run for re-election in 2015, and that if he won he would serve his entire term.[10] Experts and regular citizens across the political spectrum weren't convinced for a second that Emanuel did not harbor larger ambitions. And there were already stirrings from potential mayoral challengers. Cook County board president Toni Preckwinkle, a former alderman and relatively popular and connected African American leader, criticized the school closings and the public hearings, asking, "Was it all a charade?"[11] Like other critics, she demanded that Emanuel take to heart the recommendations of a panel of retired judges who had studied the issue and recommended sparing thirteen of the fifty-four schools on the list.[12]

Alderman Scott Waguespack, a member of the progressive caucus who was also floated as a possible mayoral candidate, publicly decried an administration "that has lost touch with the people and the citizens."[13] A *Chicago Tribune*/WGN poll showed that Emanuel's approval ratings had dropped considerably among whites and Latinos and had "reversed" among African Americans, from 44 percent approving of his performance a year earlier to 48 percent disapproving in spring 2013.[14]

Just before Mother's Day, school janitors represented by SEIU Local 1—the same union representing the airport janitors—held a press conference to announce that school closings would soon leave many of them without jobs, struggling to provide for their families.[15]

A week before the school board vote, students and activists staged a "die-in" on the South Side, near an elementary school slated for closure. They lay down in the street in white T-shirts adorned with fake blood; five were arrested.[16] Among them was Chuy Campuzano. The die-in was organized by Fearless Leading by Youth, the group of teenagers from the largely African American, low-income neighborhoods on the South Side. FLY had long been a close ally of the Mental Health Movement. "So when they asked me to help them, I'm like, 'Sure, anything for you guys,'" said Campuzano. The protest got him "eleven hours in lockup," as he recounted a week later, on charges of disorderly conduct. "Some people didn't believe I was up to that arrest, but I did it and I'm willing to do it again."

The weekend before the board vote, Karen Lewis was reelected president of the Chicago Teachers Union with 80 percent support.[17] Over the next three days, hundreds of parents, students, and teachers marched on various routes throughout the city visiting schools to be closed and protesting the plan.[18] They rallied at City Hall, and twenty-three were arrested for blocking elevators.[19] Students walked out of classes to join the demonstration—more than a hundred by organizers' count.

Not surprisingly, Campuzano was there all three days. It was a grueling week, but at times like that he would think of Helen Morley. He remembered her struggling with various physical ailments but refusing to go home, even when other activists would try to persuade her to. "I wonder what she would be doing if she was still around," mused Campuzano. "She was the one who taught me to stand up for what I believe in. She taught me not to let myself get bullied. The big bully in this town is the mayor. And if Helen were still here, he'd be having to deal with her every day."

The night before the vote, Campuzano sat in a brightly decorated Mexican taquería in Rogers Park, the North Side neighborhood where he'd been staying with friends since falling out with his parents. The air was humid and electric with the feel of a gathering storm; thunderheads amassed over downtown like a harbinger of the next day's impending drama. Campuzano chatted with the restaurant staff and sipped a chocolate shake as he flipped through photos from the past week on his cellphone. There was one of him being pushed roughly into a squad car at the die-in, a grimace on his face. There was a photo of him with Asean Johnson, a nine-year-old student at Marcus Garvey Elementary School known for his chant, "Education is a right, that's why we have to fight!" Johnson's great-grandfather was a union steelworker who joined the 1963 March on Washington and his great-grandmother was a union teacher. His grandfather was a union carpenter and his mother Shoneice Reynolds is a Chicago public schools clerk. "That union blood just runs through us—we're from a long line of union workers as well as fighters," said Reynolds.[20] People said Johnson should run for mayor, or even president. Johnson was a born organizer, starting in preschool when he successfully lobbied the principal to allow students to wear mohawks and other creative hairstyles.[21]

When he picked his fight with the teachers, Rahm Emanuel surely didn't realize that he was helping create a whole new class of Chicago leaders like Johnson. "When those children become adults, there will be a brighter future for the city," Campuzano concluded. "Thanks to the mayor, there will be a better Chicago."[22]

NOTES

INTRODUCTION
1. Interview with Shannon Bennett of KOCO, June 28, 2013. See also KOCO press release, January 6, 2012.

1. A GOLDEN BOY
1. Encyclopedia Britannica online, "Irgun Zvai Leumi," at www.britannica.com/EBchecked/topic/293947/Irgun-Zvai-Leumi. See also Noam Chomsky, *The Fateful Triangle* (Boston: South End Press, 1983), 94–96.
2. Cate Plys, "In Your Face," *Northwestern*, Spring 2012.
3. Naftali Bendavid, *The Thumpin': How Rahm Emanuel and the Democrats Learned to Be Ruthless and Ended the Republican Revolution* (New York: Doubleday, 2007), 33.
4. Jonathan Alter, *The Promise: President Obama, Year One* (New York: Simon & Schuster, 2010), 162.
5. Plys, "In Your Face."
6. Ibid.
7. Board of Jewish Education of Metropolitan Chicago website, 2011 Annual Tribute Event, at https://journals.eventjournal.com/view_custom.php?journal_id=331&id=24576. See also Elisabeth Bumiller, "The Brothers Emanuel," *New York Times*, June 15, 1997.
8. Though it has been widely reported, neither Emanuel nor the producers of *The West Wing* officially acknowledged that Emanuel was the inspiration for the character Josh Lyman.
9. Bumiller, "The Brothers Emanuel."
10. Plys, "In Your Face."
11. Ezekiel Emanuel, "Growing Up Emanuel," *Vanity Fair*, March 2013.
12. Ibid.
13. Ibid.
14. Rahm Emanuel's height is often reported as five-foot-six or five-foot-seven, and he has been quoted saying he is five-foot-eight.
15. US Census, State and County QuickFacts website, 2010. http://quickfacts.census.gov/qfd/states/17000.html.
16. Lynn Sweet, "Growing Up Emanuel: The Inside Story," *Chicago Sun-Times*, November 28, 2011.
17. Edward McClelland, "Does It Matter If Rahm Went to New Trier?," NBC Chicago, *Ward Room*, February 17, 2011.
18. Plys, "In Your Face."

19. Bumiller, "The Brothers Emanuel."
20. Alan Goldsher, "Rahm and Ari Emanuel Beat Me Up: Do Childhood Bullies Make Powerful Adult Leaders?" *Jewish Daily Forward*, November 3, 2012.
21. Ibid.
22. Emanuel, "Growing Up Emanuel."
23. Bumiller, "The Brothers Emanuel."
24. Plys, "In Your Face."
25. Emanuel, "Growing Up Emanuel."
26. Josh Duboff, "Rahm Emanuel Graphically Describes Finger Slicing for Katie Couric," *New York Magazine*, March 21, 2010.
27. Peter Baker, "The Limits of Rahmism," *New York Times Magazine*, March 8, 2010.
28. Caryn Rousseau, "Emanuel Wants Chicago to Be 'Heartbeat of Dance'," *ABC News*, August 26, 2011.
29. Bumiller, "The Brothers Emanuel."
30. Bernard Schoenburg, "Emanuel Learned the Ropes Here Way Back When," *State Journal-Register*, November 9, 2008.
31. Mark Jannot, "A Rahm for the Money," *Chicago Magazine*, August 1992.
32. Plys, "In Your Face."
33. David Wilhelm biography, Adena Ventures website. www.adenaventures.com/leadership/wilhelm.aspx.
34. The council was founded by Schakowsky's husband, veteran Democratic strategist Robert Creamer, who would later go to prison for a check fraud scheme. "Jan Schakowsky, Robert Creamer, and the Illinois Public Action Council," *Capitol Fax*, April 5, 2006.
35. William Neikirk, "Mr. Fixit," *Chicago Tribune*, November 23, 1997.
36. Robert Schlesinger, "Rahm Emanuel's Vision: Democrats Aim for a House Majority in 2006," *Campaigns & Elections*, June 1, 2005.
37. Neikirk, "Mr. Fixit."
38. Mark Jannot, "A Rahm for the Money," *Chicago Magazine*, August 1992.
39. Cate Plys, "Rahm's Grad School Days at Northwestern," *Northwestern*, Spring 2012. See also Bendavid, *The Thumpin'*, 36.
40. Cate Plys, "Rahm's Rhetoric: The Power of Persuasion," *Northwestern*, Spring 2012.
41. Ira Glass, "84: Harold," *This American Life*, Chicago Public Media, November 21, 1997.
42. Dirk Johnson, "Chicago's Mayor Washington Dies After a Heart Attack in His Office," *New York Times*, November 26, 1987.
43. Ben Joravsky, "Does Rahm Emanuel's Pick Mean the Chicago Machine Is Coming to Washington?" *American Prospect*, November 7, 2008.
44. Bendavid, *The Thumpin'*, 38.

2. THE ENFORCER—THE CLINTON YEARS

1. Chris Bury, "Interview: Rahm Emanuel," part of the PBS *Frontline* project "The Clinton Years," 2000.
2. Ibid.
3. Richard Blow, "Tough Guy Muzzled," *Mother Jones*, November/December 1993.
4. Jim VandeHei and Chris Cillizza, "In a Pivotal Year, GOP Plans to Get Personal," *Washington Post*, September 10, 2006.
5. Blow, "Tough Guy Muzzled."
6. William Neikirk, "Mr. Fixit," *Chicago Tribune*, November 23, 1997.
7. Fran Spielman, "Bill Clinton: I Knew Rahm Emanuel Was Big Time Decades Ago," *Chicago Sun-Times*, March 1, 2012.
8. Ibid.
9. Neikirk, "Mr. Fixit."

10. Mark Jannot, "A Rahm for the Money," *Chicago Magazine*, August 1992.

11. Bury, "Interview: Rahm Emanuel."

12. Robert Kurson, "Rahm Emanuel: Man of the Month," *Esquire*, July 1, 2004.

13. Robin Tower, "Tsongas Abandons Campaign, Leaving Clinton a Clear Path Toward Show-down with Bush," *New York Times*, March 20, 1992.

14. Neikirk, "Mr. Fixit."

15. Ron Suskind, *Confidence Men: Wall Street, Washington and the Education of a President* (New York: HarperCollins, 2011), 135.

16. Jodi Kantor, *The Obamas* (New York: Back Bay Books, 2012), 142.

17. Naftali Bendavid, *The Thumpin': How Rahm Emanuel and the Democrats Learned to Be Ruthless and Ended the Republican Revolution* (New York: Doubleday, 2007), 41.

18. "The A Team that Saved NAFTA's Bacon," *Businessweek*, December 5, 1993.

19. Andrea Ford, "A Brief History of NAFTA," *Time*, December 30, 2008.

20. Carol Felsenthal, "Is It Fair to Call Bill Daley a Lobbyist? Well, Actually, Yes It Is," *Huffington Post*, September 23, 2008.

21. Robert Novak, "GOP Turns Screws on NAFTA," *Chicago Sun-Times*, November 14, 1993.

22. Dan Balz and Kenneth Cooper, "Union Chief Jabs Clinton on NAFTA; AFL-CIO's Kirkland: President 'Abdicating' Role of Party Leader," *Washington Post*, November 16, 1993.

23. Ibid.

24. Bill summary and status for HR 3450 (North American Free Trade Agreement Implementation Act), at http://thomas.loc.gov/cgi-bin/bdquery/z?d103:HR3450.

25. Ibid. See also James Gerstenzang and Michael Ross, "House Passes NAFTA, 234–200: Clinton Hails Vote as Decision 'Not to Retreat,'" *LA Times*, November 18, 1993.

26. Neikirk, "Mr. Fixit."

27. David S. Broder, "Labor's NAFTA Math: 1 Trade Pact = 3-Month Cut in Funds for Democrats," *Washington Post*, December 7, 1993.

28. Robert L. Borosage and Katrina vanden Heuvel, "Progressives: Get Ready to Fight," *Nation*, November 29, 2004.

29. NAFTA had various devastating ripple effects on Mexico. The Zapatista movement was launched in the southern Mexican state of Chiapas on January 1, 1994, the day NAFTA took effect—a symbolic statement by indigenous campesino leaders about the impacts of neoliberalism and globalization. The rapid growth of maquiladoras provided jobs but also devastating social impacts in Mexico, drawing workers—largely young women prized for their small hands and supposedly docile personalities—from rural areas farther south. Arriving alone in border towns growing far more quickly than their infrastructure and social fabric could handle, women were often victimized, most horrifically in hundreds of unsolved murders in Juárez. The boom of maquiladora jobs at the border also coincided with another effect of NAFTA: as the market was flooded with cheap corn from the United States, Mexico's small-scale agricultural economies collapsed. In the lopsided implementation of NAFTA, US corn and other agricultural products remained subsidized, so corn grown in the Midwest could be sold at cut-rate prices in Mexico, making it impossible for local farmers to compete. Mexican family farmers were driven into poverty and displaced.

30. Sandra Polaski, "Mexican Employment, Productivity and Income a Decade After NAFTA," brief submitted to the Canadian Standing Senate Committee on Foreign Affairs by the Carnegie Endowment for International Peace, February 25, 2004.

31. Ibid.

32. Robert E. Scott, "Heading South: U.S.-Mexico Trade and Job Displacement After NAFTA," Economic Policy Institute, Briefing Paper No. 308, May 31, 2011.

33. Thomas Friedman, "Rabin and Arafat Seal Their Accord as Clinton Applauds 'Brave Gamble,'" *New York Times*, September 13, 1993.

34. "Struggle for Peace," CNN Special Section on the Oslo Accords, at www.cnn.com/WORLD/

struggle_for_peace/oslo.agreement.html.
35. "Camp David Accords," Encyclopedia Britannica online, at www.britannica.com/EBchecked/media/74951/Egyptian-President-Anwar-el-Sadat-US-President-Jimmy-Carter-and.
36. Bury, "Interview: Rahm Emanuel."
37. Tony G. Poveda, "The Congressional Crime Debate of 1993–1994," *Social Justice*, September 22, 1994.
38. US Department of Justice, "Violent Crime Control and Law Enforcement Act of 1994 Fact Sheet," October 24, 1994, at www.ncjrs.gov/txtfiles/billfs.txt.
39. Noam Scheiber, *The Escape Artists: How Obama's Team Fumbled the Recovery* (New York: Simon & Schuster, 2011), 143.
40. Bill Summary and Status for HR 3355 (Violent Crime Control and Law Enforcement Act of 1994), at http://thomas.loc.gov/cgi-bin/bdquery/z?d103:H.R.3355:.
41. "Too Little, Too Late: President Clinton's Prison Legacy," Justice Policy Institute, February 2001.
42. US Department of Justice, "Violent Crime Control and Law Enforcement Act of 1994 Fact Sheet," October 24, 1994, at www.ncjrs.gov/txtfiles/billfs.txt.
43. Carl T. Rowan, "Clinton Crime Initiative Is Flawed," *Chicago Sun-Times*, August 15, 1993.
44. Bill Summary and Status for HR 3355.
45. David J. Krajicek, "Boot Camps Lose Early Swagger: Correctional Boot Camps: A Brief History," *Youth Today*, November 1, 1999.
46. Patrick J. Lyons, "Acquittal Fits the Pattern in Boot Camp Deaths," *New York Times*, October 12, 2007.
47. Anna Crayton and Suzanne Rebecca Neusteter, "The Current State of Correctional Education," Paper to be presented at the Reentry Roundtable on Education, Prisoner Reentry Institute, John Jay College of Criminal Justice,18. See also Jon Marc Taylor (Missouri inmate), "Pell Grants for Prisoners: Why Should We Care?" *Straight Low Magazine* (Louisiana prison magazine) 9, no. 2, 2008.
48. Fox Butterfield, "First Federal 3-Strikes Conviction Ends a Criminal's 25-Year Career," *New York Times*, September 11, 1995.
49. Poveda, "Congressional Crime Debate."
50. Interview with Marc Mauer by Curtis Black, February 2013.
51. Lyle Denniston, "New Law Puts Heat on Crack Dealers: Clinton Signs Measure to Fight Cocaine Use," *Baltimore Sun*, October 31, 1995. See also Jeralyn Elise Merritt, "The Crack-Powder Cocaine Disparity: A Chronology," *TalkLeft*, December 12, 2007.
52. Ann Devro, "Clinton Retains Tough Law on Crack Cocaine; Panel's Call to End Disparity in Drug Sentencing Is Rejected," *Washington Post*, October 31, 1995.
53. Nina Easton, "Rahm Emanuel: Pitbull Politician," *Fortune*, September 25, 2006.
54. "The Killing of Troy Davis," *Nation*, September 21, 2011.
55. American Civil Liberties Union, "Analysis of Immigration Detention Policies," August 18, 1999, at www.aclu.org/immigrants-rights/analysis-immigration-detention-policies.
56. Geoff Rips, "The Way of RFK," *American Prospect*, November 7, 2001. See also Peter B. Edelman, *Searching for America's Heart: RFK and the Renewal of Hope* (New York: Houghton Mifflin, 2001).
57. "Welfare Reform, 10 Years Later," interview with Brookings Institution senior fellow Ron Haskins, Brookings Institution website, August 24, 2006.
58. David Ellwood, "Welfare Reform as I Knew It: When Bad Things Happen to Good Policies," *American Prospect*, November 19, 2001.
59. Rips, "The Way of RFK."
60. Richard Wolf, "How Welfare Reform Changed America," *USA Today*, July 18, 2006.
61. Easton, "Pitbull Politician."
62. "Clinton Signs Welfare Reform Bill, Angers Liberals," CNN, August 22, 1996.

63. Committee on Ways and Means, US House of Representatives, "Summary of Welfare Reforms Made by Public Law 104–193 The Personal Responsibility and Work Opportunity Reconciliation Act and Associated Legislation," November 6, 1996.

64. US Department of Health and Human Services, "Temporary Assistance for Needy Families Overview," at www.hhs.gov/recovery/programs/tanf/.

65. Barbara Vobejda and Judith Havemann, "2 HHS Officials Quit Over Welfare Changes," *Washington Post*, September 12, 1996.

66. Rips, "The Way of RFK."

67. Rahm Emanuel, "Recognizing the 10th Anniversary of Welfare Reform," remarks in Congress, July 25, 2006. Text published by Project VoteSmart, at https://votesmart.org/public-statement/202238/recognizing-the-10th-anniversary-of-welfare-reform#.USJUdGcw8TA.

68. Rahm Emanuel and Bruce Reed, *The Plan* (New York: PublicAffairs, 2006), 176.

69. Center on Budget and Policy Priorities, "Chart Book: TANF at 16," August 22, 2012.

70. "The Clinton Presidency: A Historic Era of Progress and Prosperity," The National Archives website, at clinton5.nara.gov.

3. CASHING IN

1. Nina Easton, "Rahm Emanuel: Pitbull Politician," *Fortune*, September 25, 2006.

2. Abdon Pallasch, "Rahm Emanuel's $18.5 Million Paychecks: How Did He Do It?" *Chicago Sun-Times*, February 7, 2011.

3. Michael Luo, "In Banking, Emanuel Made Money and Connections," *New York Times*, December 3, 2008.

4. Ibid.

5. Pallasch, "Rahm Emanuel's $18.5 Million Paychecks."

6. Luo, "In Banking, Emanuel Made Money and Connections."

7. Pallasch, "Rahm Emanuel's $18.5 Million Paychecks."

8. Lynn Sweet, "Rahm Emanuel: How He Made His Fortune," *Chicago Sun-Times*, February 7, 2011. See also Luo, "In Banking, Emanuel Made Money and Connections."

9. Ron Suskind, *Confidence Men: Wall Street, Washington and the Education of a President* (New York: HarperCollins, 2011), 135.

10. "CME Appoints Rahm Emanuel to Board," *Mondo Visione: Worldwide Exchange Intelligence*, July 5, 1999, at www.mondovisione.com/news/cme-appoints-rahm-emanuel-to-board.

11. Melissa Harris, "Chicago Confidential: With Tax Breaks on the Line, CME Group Hoping to Wield Clout at State Level," *Chicago Tribune*, November 9, 2011.

12. Sweet, "Rahm Emanuel: How He Got His Fortune."

13. Melita Marie Garza, "Daley Looks to Experience for New CHA Board," *Chicago Tribune*, June 23, 1999.

14. Chicago Housing Authority website, "The Plan for Transformation," at www.thecha.org/pages/the_plan_for_transformation/22.php.

15. Michaeljit Sandhu, "Unwelcomed," *Chicago Weekly*, May 2, 2012.

16. Gretchen Morgenson, "Housing Policy's Third Rail," *New York Times*, August 7, 2010.

17. Freddie Mac was officially known as the Federal Home Loan Mortgage Corporation; Fannie Mae was the Federal National Mortgage Association.

18. Dale Arthur Oesterle, "The Collapse of Fannie Mae and Freddie Mac: Victims or Villains?" *Ohio State Entrepreneurial Business Law Journal* 5, no. 2 (2010).

19. Bob Secter and Andrew Zajac, "Rahm Emanuel's Profitable Stint at Mortgage Giant," *Chicago Tribune*, March 26, 2009.

20. Ibid.

21. Jeanne Sahadi, "Mortgage Meltdown," *CNN Special Report*, July 30, 2008.

22. Oesterle, "Victims or Villains?"

23. "Freddie Mac, Four Former Executives Settle SEC Action Relating to Multi-Billion Dollar

Accounting Fraud," SEC press release, September 27, 2007.

24. Secter and Zajac, "Rahm Emanuel's Profitable Stint."
25. "Executive Summary of the Report of the Special Examination of Freddie Mac," Office of Federal Housing Enterprise Oversight, December 2003.
26. Ibid.
27. "Federal Home Loan Mortgage Corporation ("Freddie Mac") Pays Largest Fine in FEC History," Federal Election Commission press release, April 18, 2006.
28. Joe Brown, "Reporting on FEC Settlement, *NY Times, AP* Failed to Note That Most of Freddie Mac's Illegal Fundraising Events Benefited Republicans," *Media Matters*, April 21, 2006.
29. Secter and Zajac, "Rahm Emanuel's Profitable Stint."
30. Zeke Miller, "Book: Rahm Emanuel Dumped Tons of Freddie Mac Stock Days Before It Collapsed," *Business Insider*, November 14, 2011.
31. Secter and Zajac, "Rahm Emanuel's Profitable Stint."
32. Lynn Sweet, "Emanuel's Cash Clash," *Chicago Sun-Times*, August 14, 2003.
33. Miller, "Emanuel Dumped Tons of Freddie Mac Stock."
34. Stephanie Condon, "Obama Signs STOCK Act to Ban 'Congressional Insider Trading,'" CBS News, April 4, 2012.
35. Miller, "Emanuel Dumped Tons of Freddie Mac Stock."
36. Sahadi, "Mortgage Meltdown."
37. "HR 3221 (110th Congress) Housing and Economic Recovery Act of 2008," at www.govtrack.us/congress/bills/110/hr3221.
38. Binyamin Appelbaum, "U.S. Doubles Fannie, Freddie Backing to $400 Billion," *Washington Post*, February 19, 2009.
39. Zachary A. Goldfarb, "U.S. Promises Unlimited Financial Assistance to Fannie Mae, Freddie Mac," *Washington Post*, December 25, 2009.
40. Jane Hamsher, "Letter to U.S. Attorney General Eric Holder," *Firedoglake*, December 23, 2009.

4. RAHM GOES TO CONGRESS

1. US Census, Facts for Congress, for 106th Congress, Illinois Fifth Congressional District. www.census.gov/fastfacts.
2. Ibid.
3. Rob Paral, "The Polish Community in Metro Chicago," report published by the Polish American Association, June 2004.
4. David Bernstein, "Chicago Straight," *Chicago Magazine*, June 2009.
5. Pat Hickey, "There Will Be Blood: Quigley and Mikva and Rahm," *Chicago Daily Observer*, September 24, 2010.
6. Ellen Warren, "A Clash of Styles," *Chicago Tribune*, February 7, 2002. See also Nancy Kaszak Facebook page, "About Me."
7. Edward McClelland, "How Not to Get Rahmed," NBC Chicago, February 3, 2011.
8. Chris Hayes, "Polishing Up Her Image," *Chicago Reader*, February 15, 2002.
9. Warren, "A Clash of Styles."
10. Steve Neal, "Former House Allies Prepare for Battle," *Chicago Sun-Times*, February 28, 1993. See also Charles Nicodemus, "Blagojevich Takes Fifth: Political Pull Yanks Win from Kaszak," *Chicago Sun-Times*, March 20, 1993.
11. Mitchell Locin and Robert Becker, "Blagojevich Tops Flanagan," *Chicago Tribune*, November 6, 1996.
12. Hayes, "Polishing Up Her Image."
13. Ibid.
14. Steve Neal, "Byrne Gives Kaszak Thumbs Up in 5th," *Chicago Sun-Times*, March 16, 2002.
15. McClelland, "How Not to Get Rahmed."

16. John Conroy, "Rahm's Rough Road Ahead," *Daily Beast*, September 9, 2010.
17. Ben Joravsky, "Give 'Em What They Want," *Chicago Reader*, February 14, 2002.
18. Lynn Sweet, "Too Much Money a Bad Thing?" *Chicago Sun-Times*, January 3, 2002.
19. David Mendell and Gary Washburn, "Emanuel Wins in Big Costly Battle," *Chicago Tribune*, March 20, 2002.
20. Opensecrets.org, 2002 election for Illinois Fifth District Congress.
21. Chris Fusco, "Emanuel Digs Deeper into Pockets for Funds in 5th District, His Rival Kaszak Has Half as Much," *Chicago Sun-Times*, March 9, 2002.
22. Neil Steinberg, "Emanuel Turns on Charm for L Riders: Personable Candidate Isn't Like His Fire-Breathing Image," *Chicago Sun-Times*, November 22, 2010. See also Joravsky, "Give 'Em What They Want."
23. Joravsky, "Give 'Em What They Want."
24. John Nichols, "Trade Fights," *Nation*, April 1, 2002.
25. Thomas B. Edsall, "Emily's List Makes a Name for Itself; Pro-Choice Democratic Women's Lobby Is Proving a Powerful Opponent," *Washington Post*, April 21, 2002.
26. Lynn Sweet, "Emily's List Boosts Kaszak: Women's Group Buying Ads in Close 5th District Contest," *Chicago Sun-Times*, March 3, 2002.
27. Mendell and Washburn, "Emanuel Wins."
28. David Mendell, "Emanuel Hits, Kaszak Defends House Record," *Chicago Tribune*, January 31, 2002.
29. Interview with political researcher Don Wiener, September 2012.
30. Kaszak fundraising figure from Opensecrets.org, 2002 election for Illinois Fifth District. Emanuel primary campaign fundraising figure from Fusco, "Emanuel Digs Deeper into Pockets."
31. Lynn Sweet, "Bill Clinton to Campaign for Rahm Emanuel," *Chicago Sun-Times*, December 25, 2010.
32. Steve Neal, "Kaszak Emerges as the Favorite: Issues, Ethnic Background Give Her Edge in 5th District," *Chicago Sun-Times*, February 15, 2002.
33. David Mendell, "Emanuel, Kaszak Battling to Gain Edge with Voters," *Chicago Tribune*, March 10, 2002.
34. Endorsements, "U.S. Congress," *Chicago Sun-Times*, March 10, 2002.
35. Lynn Sweet, "Emanuel Hit with Anti-Semitic Remarks," *Chicago Sun-Times*, March 5, 2002.
36. "NJDC Denounces Anti-Semitic Comments Made Against Rahm Emanuel," National Jewish Democratic Council press release, March 7, 2002.
37. Sweet, "Emanuel Hit with Anti-Semitic Remarks."
38. Ibid. See also Mendell, "Emanuel, Kaszak Battling to Gain Edge."
39. "NJDC Denounces."
40. Lynn Sweet, "Bypassing the High Road Emanuel's Staff Could Have Put Unity Above Politics by Not Stalling on Allowing Kaszak to Speak," *Chicago Sun-Times*, March 7, 2002.
41. Ibid.
42. Chicago Board of Elections website.
43. Steve Neal, "Emanuel's Win One for the Books: Ex-Clinton Aide Took Opponent to School on Coalition-Building," *Chicago Sun-Times*, May 1, 2002.
44. Mendell and Washburn, "Emanuel Wins."
45. OurCampaigns.com candidate profile. See also Chicago Board of Elections website.
46. Tom Vanden Brook, "Indictments and Allegations Cloud Windy City," *USA Today*, October 4, 2005.
47. John Kass, "May the Farce Be with You, Obama and Daley," *Chicago Tribune*, September 17, 2009.
48. John Kass, "California Lawmaker Picking Rahmsian Beef," *Chicago Tribune*, August 6, 2009.
49. David Kidwell, "Emanuel Skirts Issue of How Insider Ties Helped Propel Him into Con-

gress," *Chicago Tribune*, February 5, 2011.

50. Dan Mihalopoulos and Rudolph Bush, "Court Told Jobs Built Patronage Battalion," *Chicago Tribune*, June 1, 2006.

51. Kidwell, "Emanuel Skirts Issue."

52. Mihalopoulos and Bush, "Court Told Jobs Built."

53. John F. Harris, "DLC on Brink of a Major Shakeup," *Politico*, March 6, 2009.

54. "The New Democrat Credo," Democratic Leadership Council website, January 1, 2001, at www.dlc.org/ndol_ciae29.html?kaid=86&subid=194&contentid=3775.

55. Harris, "DLC on Brink." See also Keith A. Halpern and Eliza R. Culbertson, "Blueprint for Change: Charter Schools, a Handbook for Action," Democratic Leadership Council, at www.dlc.org/documents/charter_schools.pdf.

56. Ben Smith, "Democratic Leadership Council Will Fold," *Politico*, February, 7, 2011.

57. Ari Berman, "Going Nowhere," *Nation*, March 21, 2005. Berman wrote, "The New Democratic movement of pro-free market moderates, which helped catapult Bill Clinton into the White House in 1992, has splintered, transformed by a reinvigoration of grassroots energy."

58. Harris, "DLC on Brink."

59. List and summary of bills sponsored by Emanuel in Congress (including the 108th,109th, and 110th Congresses), at Govtrack.us.

60. Analysis for Emanuel at Govtrack.us.

61. Highlights of Emanuel's voting record in Congress, OnTheIssues, at www.ontheissues.org/IL/Rahm_Emanuel.htm.

62. Ibid.

63. "H.R. 4437 (109th): Border Protection, Antiterrorism, and Illegal Immigration Control Act of . . . (On Passage of the Bill)," Govtrack.us.

64. Xochitl Bada et al., "Context Matters: Latino Civic Engagement in Nine U.S. Cities," report by the Woodrow Wilson International Center for Scholars, April 2010 (7–10).

65. Karen Jordan, "100,000 People Rally Over Controversial Immigration Bill," ABC Local, March 10, 2006.

66. Nick Moroni, "Once Foes, Rahm and Rep. Gutierrez Get Chummy Over Immigration Reform," *Chicago Reporter*, July 10, 2012. Video of Luis Gutierrez speech at www.chicagonow.com/chicago-muckrakers/2012/07/once-foes-rahm-and-rep-gutierrez-get-chumming-over-immigration-reform.

67. Eric Zorn, "Braun's 128 Beefs with Emanuel's Voting Record in Congress," *Chicago Tribune*, February 18, 2011.

68. Document provided by the Carol Moseley Braun campaign, February 2011, downloadable with story by Zorn, "Braun's 128 Beefs."

69. Ibid.

70. Ibid.

71. On the Issues website, at www.ontheissues.org/IL/Rahm_Emanuel.htm.

72. *Meet the Press*, NBC, transcript for January 16, 2005, at www.nbcnews.com/id/6832586/ns/meet_the_press/t/transcript-jan/#.URglLmcw8TA.

73. Ibid.

74. Democratic Congressional Campaign Committee website, at http://dccc.org/pages/about.

75. Shira Toeplitz, "An Inside Look at the DCCC Research Department," *Roll Call*, April 23, 2012; Jim VandeHei and Chris Cillizza, "In a Pivotal Year, GOP Plans to Get Personal," *Washington Post*, September 10, 2006.

76. Andrew Glass, "Congress Runs into 'Republican Revolution' November 8, 1994," *Politico*, November 8, 2007.

77. Holly Chmela, "A Vulnerable Republican," *New York Times*, April 9, 2006.

78. "Al From, Who Built the DLC and Changed American Politics, Announces Retirement," Democratic Leadership Council press release, March 5, 2009, at www.dlc.org/ndol_cid768

.html?kaid=85&subid=108&contentid=254926.

79. Emanuel and Reed, *The Plan*, xx–xxi.
80. Bendavid, *The Thumpin'*, 104.
81. Jacob S.Hacker and Paul Pierson,*Winner-Take-All Politics* (Simon & Schuster, Inc., Kindle Edition, 2009), 251–52.
82. US Census data from American FactFinder website, at www.factfinder2.census.gov, for Illinois 6th Congressional district, 109th Congress.
83. "IL-06: The Battle for Henry Hyde's Seat," *Time Magazine/CNNReal Clear Politics* blog, September 15, 2006.
84. "Where Are They Now? The Clinton Impeachment," *Time*, January 9, 2009.
85. Ourcampaigns.com website, IL-06, 2004 general election.
86. Bendavid, *The Thumpin'*, 93-100.
87. Ibid.,93.
88. Ibid., 96–104.
89. "Christine Cegelis," Ourcampaigns.com website, at www.ourcampaigns.com/CandidateDetail.html?CandidateID=33866, last visited February 10, 2013.
90. Rob Kall, "With Duckworth 43% Win, Democracy Not Served in Illinois; Make IRV National Dem Primary Policy," *Daily Kos*, March 22, 2006.
91. Bendavid, *The Thumpin'*, 106.
92. Illinois State Board of Elections website, General Elections, 6th District Congress, 2006.
93. Opensecrets.org website, 2006 Illinois House race.
94. Nina Easton, "Rahm Emanuel: Pitbull Politician," *Fortune*, September 25, 2006.
95. Kathrine Schmidt," DCCC Backing Craig in 1st District Primary," *Roll Call*, June 7, 2006.
96. Federal Election Commission, Official Election Results for United States House of Representatives, 2006 US House Campaigns, at www.fec.gov/pubrec/fe2006/2006house.pdf.
97. Paul Hogarth, "Three Democrats Worth Fighting For," *BeyondChron*, June 18, 2007.
98. Federal Election Commission, Official Election Results, 2006 US House Campaigns.
99. "Democrats Win House, Promise New Direction," CNN, November 8, 2006.
100. Edward McClelland, "The Legend of Rahm," *Salon*, May 8, 2007.
101. Opensecrets.org, Rahm Emanuel.
102. "Dresdner Buys Wasserstein Perella," ABC News, September 18, 2001.
103. Opensecrets.org, Rahm Emanuel, career donations to campaign committees.
104. *Politico*, "The Arena" profile of Rahm Emanuel, at www.politico.com/arena/bio/rahm_emanuel.html. See also House Financial Services Committee website, statement from Rahm Emanuel, "Hearing on FY2004 HUD Budget," March 5, 2003, at http://financialservices.house.gov/media/pdf/030503re.pdf.
105. Howard Fineman, "Obama Means to Control Washington. His Chief of Staff Will Be at the Wheel," *Newsweek*, December 19, 2008. See also James Pethokoukis, "Rahm Emanuel Leaves the White House," Reuters, October 1, 2010.
106. David M. Herszenhorn, "Bailout Plan Wins Approval; Democrats Vow Tighter Rules," *New York Times*, October 3, 2008.
107. "House Reverses Course, Approves Bailout Bill," *The Hill*, October 3, 2008. See also Final Vote Results for Roll Call 681 (on HR 1424), House Clerk's website, October 3, 2008.
108. Adam Nagourney, "Bracing for a Backlash Over Wall Street Bailouts," *New York Times*, March 15, 2009.
109. Tea Party website, "Congress Keeps Bailing Out Banks," at www.teapartypatriots.org/2013/01/congress-keeps-bailing-out-banks/.
110. Josh Brown, "Dear Wall Street, This Is Why the People Are Angry," *Marketplace Money*, American Public Media, October 14, 2011.

5. THE OBAMA WHITE HOUSE

1. Ben Smith, "Statements on Rahm," *Politico*, November 6, 2008.
2. Bob Woodward, *Obama's Wars* (New York: Simon & Schuster, 2010), 14.
3. Smith, "Statements on Rahm."
4. "Rahm Emanuel: Obama's Chief of Staff," AP/*Huffington Post*, updated November 6, 2008.
5. Peter Baker, "The Limits of Rahmism," *New York Times Magazine*, March 8, 2010.
6. Sarah Wheaton, "Emanuel Apologizes for Father's 'Arab' Comments," *New York Times, Caucus* (blog), November 13, 2008.
7. Lynn Sweet, "Rahm Emanuel Accepts Job as Obama Chief of Staff," *Chicago Sun-Times*, November 6, 2008. See also Scheiber, *The Escape Artists*, 143.
8. Woodward, *Obama's Wars*, 14.
9. Suskind, *Confidence Men*, 134.
10. "Daschle Withdraws as HHS Nominee," CNN, February 3, 2009.
11. Suskind, *Confidence Men*, 135.
12. Baker, "The Limits of Rahmism."
13. Laura Clawson, "Four years after the Lilly Ledbetter Act, we still need the Paycheck Fairness Act," *Daily Kos*, January 29, 2013.
14. Noam N. Levey, "Obama signs expansion of children's health insurance," *LA Times*, February 5, 2009.
15. "Recovery Act," Recovery.gov, at www.recovery.gov/About/Pages/The_Act.aspx.
16. Brad Plumer, "The Stimulus Bill, Three Years Later," *Washington Post*, February 17, 2012.
17. Ryan Lizza, "The Obama Memos: The Making of a Post-Partisan Presidency," *New Yorker*, January 30, 2012.
18. Kathryn A. Wolfe and Jessica Meyers, "Auto Bailout May Have Saved Obama," *Politico*, November 7, 2012.
19. Marcus Baram, "Rahm Emanuel's 'F—k the UAW': White House Pushes Back on Account in Rattner Book, UAW Prez Responds," *Huffington Post*, May 25, 2011.
20. "An American Made Recovery," CNBC, September 3, 2010.
21. Suskind, *Confidence Men*, 218–20.
22. Eric Pooley, "Rahm Emanuel Persuaded Obama to Play It Cool on Climate Bill. Post-Spill, Will the Game Plan Change?" *Grist*, June 14, 2010. See also Eric Pooley, *The Climate War: True Believers, Power Brokers, and the Fight to Save Planet Earth* (New York: Hyperion), 2010.
23. "Kyoto Protocol," United Nations Framework Convention on Climate Change, at http://un-fccc.int/kyoto_protocol/items/2830.php.
24. The Carbon Dioxide Information Analysis Center ranks countries on 2009 carbon emissions from fossil fuel burning, cement production, and gas flaring. China emitted 2.1 billion metric tons, the United States 1.4, India 0.5, the Russian Federation 0.4, and all other countries emitted significantly less. Rankings at http://cdiac.ornl.gov/trends/emis/top2009.tot. The US EPA website Global Greenhouse Gas Emissions Data notes that in 2008, the United States accounted for 19 percent of global carbon emissions from fossil-fuel burning and industrial processes, while China accounted for 23 percent, the European Union "EU-27" countries 13 percent, India 6 percent, Japan 4 percent, and Canada 2 percent. At www.epa.gov/climatechange/ghgemissions/global.html#four.
25. Emanuel and Reed, *The Plan*, 149, 165.
26. Kate Sheppard, "Everything You Always Wanted to Know about the Waxman-Markey Energy/Climate Bill—in Bullet Points," *Grist*, June 3, 2009. See also "H.R. 2454 (111th): American Clean Energy and Security Act of 2009," Govtrack.us.
27. Darren Samuelsohn, "Cap and Trade Dead, So Key Players Move On," *Politico*, July 22, 2011. See also "H.R. 2454 (111th): American Clean Energy and Security Act of 2009," Govtrack.us.
28. See, for example: Bo Cutter, "4 Reasons Why Obama Should Push for a Carbon Tax," *Salon*, May 3, 2013; Alan S. Blinder, "The Carbon Tax Miracle Cure," *Wall Street Journal*, January

31, 2011; and Hendrik Hertzberg, "Tax Vobiscum," *New Yorker*, December 3, 2012.

29. Pooley, "Rahm Emanuel Persuaded Obama."

30. Ibid.

31. "Emanuel Changes Tack on Solyndra Questions," *Chicago Tribune*, August 3, 2012. See also Carol Felsenthal, "Rahm 'Super Hot for This'—the Mayor's Role in Solyndra," *Chicago Magazine*, August 3, 2012.

32. Alter, *The Promise*, 244–45. See also Brian Montopoli, "Rahm Emanuel 'Begged' Obama Not to Push Health Care," CBS News, May 2010.

33. Alter, *The Promise*, 396.

34. Overview of Affordable Care Act, White House "Health Reform in Action" website, at www.whitehouse.gov/healthreform/healthcare-overview#healthcare-menu.

35. Suskind, *Confidence Men*, 307.

36. Kantor, *The Obamas*, 138.

37. Alter, *The Promise*, 395.

38. Suskind, *Confidence Men*, 271.

39. Alexander Bolton, "Lieberman Expresses Regret to Colleagues over Healthcare Tension," *The Hill*, December 15, 2009.

40. Glenn Greenwald, "White House as Helpless Victim on Health Care," *Salon*, December 16, 2009.

41. Jason Millman, "Health Secretary Sebelius: 'There Is No Taxpayer Funding for Abortion,'" *The Hill*, January 21, 2011.

42. John Harwood, "Health Care Reform Passed, but Just the Beginning," CNBC, March 22, 2010.

43. Overview of Affordable Care Act, White House "Health Reform in Action" website.

44. Politifact.com, The Obameter (analysis of campaign promises), "Introduce a Comprehensive Immigration Bill in the First Year." Source cited by Politifact: May 28, 2008, Jorge Ramos interview with then-candidate Barack Obama, aired on *This Week* (ABC), July 4, 2010.

45. Suzy Khimm, "Obama Is Deporting Immigrants Faster Than Bush. Republicans Don't Think That's Enough," *Washington Post*, Wonkblog, August 27, 2012.

46. Antonio Olivo, "'Secure Communities' Program Deportations Spur Frustration with Obama," *Chicago Tribune*, August 17, 2011.

47. Peter Nicholas, "Democrats Point the Finger at Obama's Chief of Staff for Immigration Reform's Poor Progress," *Los Angeles Times*, May 21, 2011.

48. Garance Franke-Ruta, "Obama's Game Changer on Young Illegal Immigrants," *Atlantic*, June 15, 2012.

49. Abdon M. Pallasch and Fran Spielman, "Rivals Jab Emanuel over Immigrants," *Chicago Sun-Times*, February 18, 2011.

50. Nicholas, "Democrats Point the Finger."

51. Ibid.

52. Ashley Parker and Jonathan Martin, "Senate, 68 to 32, Passes Overhaul for Immigration," *New York Times*, June 27, 2013.

53. Julie Percha, "Rahm Apologizes for Privately Calling Liberal Activists Retarded," ABC News, February 2, 2010.

54. Alter, *The Promise*, 407.

55. Peter Wallsten, "Chief of Staff Draws Fire from Left as Obama Falters," *Wall Street Journal*, January 26, 2010.

56. Cenk Uygur, "Why Rahm Was 100% Wrong," *Firedoglake*, September 10, 2010.

57. On page 316 of *Confidence Men*, Suskind writes, "The ongoing push and shove atop the administration, without leadership from either the president or the chief of staff, was leaving lines of authority blurred, roles ill defined, and deepening questions of who—at any given moment—was in charge."

58. See, for example, Suskind's *Confidence Men* and Kantor's *The Obamas.*
59. Scheiber, *The Escape Artists,* 171.
60. Edward Luce, "America: A Fearsome Foursome," *Financial Times,* February 3, 2010.
61. Suskind, *Confidence Men,* 316.
62. Alter, *The Promise,* 161.
63. Suskind, *Confidence Men,* 353.
64. Ibid., 364.
65. Dana Milbank, "Why Obama Needs Rahm at the Top," *Washington Post,* February 21, 2010.
66. Suskind, *Confidence Men,* 380–81.
67. Ibid., 12.

6. THE RACE FOR CITY HALL

1. Encyclopedia of Chicago, "Chicago Mayors 1837–2007," at www.encyclopedia.chicagohistory.org/pages/1443.html.
2. Rick Kogan, "Maggie Daley 1943–2011: Chicago's Longtime First Lady," *Chicago Tribune,* November 25, 2011.
3. "Chicago Mayor Daley Opts Against Re-election, Opens Door for Rahm," FoxNews.com, September 7, 2010.
4. Ted Klein, "Is Bobby Rush in Trouble? Two Formidable Opponents in the Race for His Congressional Seat Are Banking on It," *Chicago Reader,* March 17, 2000.
5. "Mayor Daley Back to Work after Announcement," ABC Local, September 9, 2010.
6. Azam Ahmed and Ofelia Casillas, "Sheriff: I Will Stop Enforcing Evictions," *Chicago Tribune,* October 9, 2008.
7. "Carol Moseley Braun," Biographical Directory of the United States Congress.
8. "Gery Chico," Chico & Nunes P.C. law firm website, at www.chiconunes.com/gery-chico.
9. "Biography," Congressman Danny K. Davis website, at http://davis.house.gov/index.php?option=com_content&task=view&id=13&Itemid=39.
10. Will Guzzardi, "Miguel Del Valle, Chicago Mayor Candidate: 'We Cannot Have a Polarized City,'" *Huffington Post,* January 13, 2011.
11. "Luis V. Gutierrez," Election 2012 Guide, *Wall Street Journal.*
12. "James Meeks Angers Gay Community While Discussing Possible Mayoral Run," *Huffington Post,* September 13, 2010.
13. "Mayor Daley Back to Work After Announcement," ABC Local, September 9, 2010.
14. Roland S. Martin, "Rahm Emanuel Faces Uphill Battle to Be Chicago Mayor," CNN, October 1, 2010.
15. Lynn Sweet, "Rahm Emanuel Chicago Mayor Polling Details; Carol Moseley Braun to Announce on Monday," *Chicago Sun-Times,* September 13, 2010.
16. "Dart Not Running for Mayor," CBS Local, October 27, 2010.
17. Samantha Abernathy, "Rahm Emanuel Announces Run for Mayor at Cooney Elementary," *Center Square Journal,* November 15, 2010. See also Chicago Public Schools, John C. Coonley School website, at www.cps.edu/Schools/Pages/school.aspx?id=609866.
18. "Rahm Emanuel Announces Run for Chicago Mayor," Associated Press, November 13, 2010.
19. Lynn Sweet, "Tenant in Rahm Emanuel Chicago Home Rebuffs Emanuel Plea to Leave," *Chicago Sun-Times,* September 28, 2010.
20. Kristen Mack and John Chase, "Emanuel Gets a Chicago Condo," *Chicago Tribune,* October 5, 2010.
21. Sweet, "Tenant in Rahm Emanuel Chicago Home."
22. Ben Joravsky, "Who Deserves to Be Disqualified?" *Chicago Reader,* December 31, 2009.
23. Abdon M. Pallasch, "Rahm Emanuel's Tenant Drops Out of Mayor's Race," *Chicago Sun-Times,* December 6, 2010.

24. "Ballot Shenanigans," *Chicago Tribune* editorial, November 30, 2010.
25. Edward McClelland, "Why Ed Burke Is at the Center of Rahm Conspiracies," NBC Chicago, *Ward Room*, January 27, 2011.
26. Emily Chow, Christopher Groskopf, Joe Germuska, Hal Dardick, and Brian Boyer, "Reshaping Chicago's Political Map: Race, Ward-by-Ward," *Chicago Tribune*, July 14, 2011. See also Fran Spielman, "Emanuel Praises Philly Police Chief," *Chicago Sun-Times*, March 14, 2011.
27. Scott Turow, "The One-Man Political Machine," *New York Times Magazine*, February 17, 2011. See also Charles Thomas, "Emanuel Takes Stand in Residency Hearing," ABC Local, December 14, 2011.
28. Dan Mihalopoulos, " Emanuel Testifies in Residency Challenge," *Chicago News Cooperative*, December 14, 2011.
29. David Heinzmann and Kristen Mack, "Chicago's Election Board Takes Center Stage in Emanuel's Residency Fight," *Chicago Tribune*, December 18, 2010. See also Mark Konkol and Abdon Pallasch, "Election board: Emanuel will remain on ballot," *Chicago Sun-Times,* December 23, 2010.
30. David Kidwell, "Emanuel Case Highlights Politics of Picking Judges," *Chicago Tribune*, January 24, 2011.
31. Jeff Coen, "Supreme Court Agrees to Hear Emanuel Residency Case," *Chicago Tribune*, January 25, 2011.
32. "Walter P. Maksym et al., appellees, v. The Board of Election Commissioners of the City of Chicago et al., appellants," Opinion by the Supreme Court of the State of Illinois, January 27, 2011.
33. Liam Ford, Jeff Coen, and David Heinzmann, "Supreme Court: Emanuel on Chicago Mayor Ballot," *Chicago Tribune*, January 27, 2012.
34. Amanda Paulson, "Yes, Rahm Emanuel Will Probably Run for Chicago Mayor. But Can He Win?" *Christian Science Monitor*, September 28, 2010.
35. Don Babwin, "Carol Moseley Braun Emerges as Main Black Candidate in Chicago Mayor's Race," *Huffington Post*, January 1, 2011.
36. Hal Dardick, "Emanuel Pulling Away from Rivals," *Chicago Sun-Times*, January 21, 2011.
37. Chris Fusco, Tim Novak, and Abdon Pallasch, "The $11.7 Million Man," *Chicago Sun-Times*, January 21, 2011.
38. Turow, "One-Man Political Machine."
39. Dardick, "Emanuel Pulling Away from Rivals."
40. Fusco, Novak, and Pallasch, "$11.7 Million Man." See also Tim Novak, "Chico Campaign Returns Donations from Partners of Taxicab Mogul," *Chicago Sun-Times*, January 27, 2011.
41. Achy Obejas, "Why Gery Chico Is the White Candidate for Mayor," WBEZ, February 18, 2011.
42. Chicago Mayor Rahm Emanuel's victory speech, February 23, 2011, video at www.YouTube.com/watch?v=sAm26OHElQU.
43. David Roeder, "Resetting Rahmbo," *Chicago Sun-Times*, February 6, 2011.
44. Turow, "One-Man Political Machine."
45. Nina Burleigh, "Rahm Emanuel 2.0: Less Screaming, More Smiling," *DuJour Magazine*, December 2012.
46. Mary Mitchell, "How Rahm Emanuel Won Black Voters," *Chicago Sun-Times*, February 26, 2011.
47. "Statement by Mayor Rahm Emanuel on the End of the Chicago Teachers Union Strike," City of Chicago Office of the Mayor, September 18, 2012.
48. Dan Sinker, *The F***ing Epic Twitter Quest of @MayorEmanuel* (New York: Simon & Schuster, 2011), 205.
49. Ibid., 85.
50. Ibid., 52.

51. Ibid. See also Alexis C. Madrigal, "Revealing the Man Behind @MayorEmanuel," *Atlantic*, February 28, 2011; and "Rahm Emanuel, Dan Sinker Meet: Young Chicago Authors Get $12,000 Donation," *Huffington Post*, March 2, 2011.

52. "Egg Thrown at Rahm Emanuel," *Fox Nation*, November 10, 2010.

53. Mark Brown, "New Rahm Ad Is Riling the Unions," *Chicago Sun-Times*, February 8, 2011.

54. Ibid.

55. Ibid.

56. Dan Mihalopoulus, "As the Election Looms, Candidates Skirt City's Financial Crisis," *New York Times* (Chicago edition), February 20, 2011.

57. Website of City Clerk Susana Mendoza, "Susana Mendoza Praises Rahm Emanuel for Backing Her City Sticker Idea," January 4, 2011.

58. Fran Spielman and Abdon M. Pallasch, "Teaming Up on Emanuel," *Chicago Sun-Times*, January 15, 2011.

59. Ibid.

60. Ibid.

61. Dardick, "Emanuel Pulling Away from Rivals."

62. Gery Chico campaign mailer, "The Rahm Tax."

63. John Kass, "Rahm Emanuel, Why'd You Have to Go and Mention Taxes?" *Chicago Tribune*, January 19, 2011. See also Abdon M. Pallasch, "Cut Sales Tax, but Tax More Services," *Chicago Sun-Times*, January 19, 2011.

64. Dardick, "Emanuel Pulling Away from Rivals."

65. Mitch Smith, "At Obama's Old Church, Pastor Declares 2008 Controversy Closed," *Chicago Tribune*, November 4, 2012.

66. Patrica Van Pelt-Watkins 2012 Illinois State Senate campaign website, at www.patriciaforchicago.com.

67. "Carol Moseley Braun Says Opponent Was 'On Crack' While She Was Starting a Business," *Huffington Post*, January 31, 2011.

68. Achy Obejas, "Watkins: I've Never Used Crack in My Life, I've Never Even Seen Crack," WBEZ, February 1, 2011.

69. "Sen. Patricia Van-Pelt—5th District," Illinois Senate Democrats website.

70. Election Results database, February 2011 Municipal General Election, Mayor, Chicago Board of Elections website.

71. Mitchell, "How Rahm Emanuel Won Black Voters."

72. Laura Washington, "Stories Behind Their Stories Tell the Tale of Braun vs. Watkins," *Chicago Sun-Times*, January 24, 2011.

73. Art Golab and Abdon M. Pallasch, "Rahm Nearly Swept Black Neighborhoods," *Chicago Sun-Times*, March 21, 2011.

74. Interview with an elected official who did not want to be named.

75. "Voter Turnout Just 41 Percent," *Chicago Sun-Times*, February 22, 2011.

76. David Kidwell, "Voter Turnout Proves Underwhelming," *Chicago Tribune*, February 22, 2011.

77. Abdon M. Pallasch, "Rahm Set to Launch PAC Attack," *Chicago Sun-Times*, March 6, 2011.

78. Carol Felsenthal, "Danny Solis: The Establishment Candidate, but Campaigning Like a Rookie," *Chicago Magazine*, March 29, 2011.

79. Kari Lydersen, "Chicago Election Twist Raises Hopes for Closing Coal Plants," *Midwest Energy News*, March 9, 2011.

80. Steve Daniels, "Midwest Generation Files for Chapter 11," *Crain's Chicago Business*, December 17, 2012.

81. Whet Moser, "What Does the For a Better Chicago PAC Want from Rahm Emanuel, Aldermen, and Us?" *Chicago Magazine*, March 3, 2011.

82. "For a Better Chicago, Pro-Business PAC, Can Keep Donor List Secret, Elections Board Rules," *Huffington Post*, March 11, 2011.

83. For details on the school closings controversy, see chapter 10.

7. GETTING DOWN TO BUSINESS

1. "Rahm Emanuel Inauguration: Chicago's New Mayor Sworn In," *Huffington Post*, May 16, 2011.
2. "Rahm Emanuel Inauguration Speech" transcript, *Chicago Sun-Times*, May 16, 2011.
3. Ibid.
4. Ibid.
5. Lisa Donovan, "The city has a new clerk, and she's not a 'go-along, get-along' politician," *Illinois Issues*, February 2012. As noted in chapter 5, Emanuel reportedly told a tongue-tied male staffer in the Obama White House to "take your fucking tampon out and tell me what you have to say."
6. Governor Pat Quinn signed the Illinois DREAM Act on August 1, 2011, several months into Emanuel's tenure as mayor. For more information, see "Illinois DREAM Act," Illinois Student Assistance Commission website, February 4, 2012.
7. "Rahm Emanuel Inauguration: Mayor Daley Leaves Office, Emanuel Sworn In," *Huffington Post*/Associated Press, May 16, 2011. See also Peter Kendall, "The Shooting of Anton Cermak," *Chicago Tribune*, February 15, 1933 (retroactively dated).
8. Kendall, "The Shooting of Anton Cermak."
9. Audio from wiretapped Blagojevich calls discussing Senate seat available on YouTube. See, for example, "Rod Blagojevich: 'F*ck Harry Reid'—Raw Unedited Wiretap Audio—NSFW," uploaded July 14, 2010, at www.YouTube.com/watch?v=3pXhoC9nLFA.
10. Jeff Coen and Bob Secter, "Emanuel Described as Shakedown Target," *Chicago Tribune*, May 12, 2011.
11. Alter, *The Promise*, 80.
12. Elizabeth Brackett, "Blagojevich Blog: Breakdown of the Alleged Shakedowns," WTTW, June 20, 2011.
13. Coen and Secter, "Emanuel Described as Shakedown Target."
14. John Chase and Kristen Mack, "Mayor Takes the Stand," *Chicago Tribune*, May 26, 2011. "Blagojevich Defense Team Seeks Tape with Emanuel," CBS, February 8, 2011.
15. Fran Spielman, "Mayor Rahm Emanuel Shifts 500 Police Officers, but Union Isn't Impressed," *Chicago Sun-Times*, May 24, 2011.
16. Cate Plys, "In Your Face," *Northwestern*, Spring 2012.
17. "The First 30 Days of the Emanuel Administration," City of Chicago Office of the Mayor press release, June 16, 2011.
18. Ibid. See also Eddie Arruza, "Mayor Emanuel's First 30 Days," *Chicago Tonight*, WTTW, June 16, 2011.
19. Ibid.
20. Ibid.
21. For more on SB 7, see chapter 10. See also "Legislation," Illinois General Assembly website, 97th Assembly and "Summary of Illinois Senate Bill 7," Chicago Teachers Union website (ctunet.com).
22. Jessen O'Brien, "Mayor Emanuel's First 100 Days: Debrief with Eddie Arruza," *Chicago Tonight*, WTTW, August 22, 2011.
23. Ibid.
24. Yasmin Rammohan, "Mayor Emanuel Debrief: Program Launched to Combat Foreclosure Crisis," *Chicago Tonight*, WTTW, August 17, 2011.
25. Emanuel and Reed, *The Plan*, xxii.
26. City of Chicago 2013 Budget Overview, Office of Management and Budget website, at www.cityofchicago.org/city/en/depts/obm/provdrs/city_budg/svcs/budget_documents

_documents.html.

27. City of Chicago 2012 Budget Overview, Office of Management and Budget website, at www.cityof chicago.org/content/dam/city/depts/obm/supp_info/2012%20Budget/2012BudgetOverview.pdf.

28. "School Board Votes to Cancel Teachers' Raise," CBS Local, June 15, 2011.

29. John Byrne and Hal Dardick, "Emanuel Challenges Unions to Help Cut Costs," *Chicago Tribune*, July 2, 2011.

30. Ibid.

31. Rich Miller, "AFSCME Says Emanuel Never Tried to Discuss Changes—Emanuel Essentially Gives Unions Another Month to Come to the Table," *Capitol Fax*, July 15, 2011.

32. Dan Mihalopoulos, "Rahm Emanuel and Unions Square Off Over Work Rules," *New York Times* (Chicago edition), July 9, 2011.

33. John Byrne, Hal Dardick, and Kristen Mack, "Mayor Rahm Emanuel to Unions: Contract Changes or Layoffs," *Chicago Tribune*, June 29, 2011.

34. Ibid.

35. Ibid.

36. Miller, "AFSCME Says Emanuel Never Tried to Discuss Changes."

37. Hal Dardick and Kristen Mack, "Emanuel to Send Out Layoff Notices Today," *Chicago Tribune*, July 15, 2011.

38. Chicago Federation of Labor spokesman Nick Kaleba said COUPE officially represents 6,400 city workers, while about 10,000 workers total are directly affected by COUPE negotiations.

39. Miller, "AFSCME Says Emanuel Never Tried to Discuss Changes."

40. "Unions Present $242 Million in Savings to Mayor," Chicago Federation of Labor press release, July 26, 2011. See also "City of Chicago 2012 Budget Efficiency Report," submitted by Coalition of Unionized Public Employees (COUPE), July 26, 2011. Report compiled by Public Works LLC.

41. "Unions Present $242 Million in Savings."

42. "Making Managed Competition Fair Competition," Chicago Federation of Labor brief, 2011. For more details, see CFL website, at www.chicagolabor.org/faircomp.

43. "Unions Present $242 Million in Savings."

44. Interview with Laborers 1001 business manager Lou Phillips, February 7, 2013.

45. "Labor Deal at McCormick Place Revives Work Rule Changes," CBS Chicago, October 21, 2011.

46. Interview with Chicago Federation of Labor president Jorge Ramirez, January 30, 2013.

47. City of Chicago 2013 Budget Overview.

48. Kristen Mack, "Emanuel's 'Managed Competition' Push Goes into Full Swing on Recycling Pickups," *Chicago Tribune*, September 30, 2011.

49. Fran Spielman, "65k More Households to Switch to Grid Garbage Collection System," *Chicago Sun-Times*, August 29, 2012.

50. John Byrne and Hal Dardick, "Daley Aide, Aldermen Clash Over Delay of Blue-Cart Recycling Program," *Chicago Tribune*, October 29, 2009.

51. Mick Dumke, "Why Can't Chicago Recycle?" *Chicago Reader*, July 22, 2010.

52. Interview with Lou Phillips, February 7, 2013.

53. Ibid.

54. Kristen Mack and Hal Dardick, "Emanuel Hires Private Firms for City Recycling," *Chicago Tribune*, July 18, 2011.

55. Mack, "Emanuel's 'Managed Competition' Push."

56. Mack and Dardick, "Emanuel Hires Private."

57. Mack, "Emanuel's 'Managed Competition' Push."

58. Ibid.

59. Interview with Lou Phillips, February 7, 2013.

60. Ibid.

61. Ibid.
62. Greg Basich, "Chicago Dept. of Sanitation Improves Recycling Fleet Efficiency in Managed Competition," *Government Fleet*, January 20, 2012. See also Fran Spielman, "Taxpayers the Winners in Recycling Competition, Emanuel Says," *Chicago Sun-Times*, January 3, 2012.
63. Interview with Lou Phillips, February 7, 2013.
64. Spielman, "Taxpayers the Winners."
65. Interview with Jorge Ramirez, January 30, 2013; interview with Lou Phillips, February 7, 2013.
66. "City of Chicago 2012 Budget Efficiency Report," submitted by COUPE, July 26, 2011.
67. Ben Joravsky and Mick Dumke, "The Mayor's Millionaire Club," *Chicago Reader*, October 27 2011.
68. Mayor Emanuel's "In-House" Schedules for June 2011, *Chicago Reader* online, October 27, 2011.
69. Interview with Robert Bruno, professor in the School of Labor and Employment Relations at the University of Illinois, December 2012.
70. Joravsky and Dumke, "The Mayor's Millionaire Club."
71. Interview with an elected official who declined to use his name for fear of political consequences, October 2012.
72. "Brief Biography of Dick Simpson," University of Illinois at Chicago website.
73. Interview with political scientist Dick Simpson, December 2012.
74. Ibid.
75. "Mayor Rahm Emanuel Outlines 2012 Budget Proposal to Secure Chicago's Future," City of Chicago Office of the Mayor press release, October 12, 2011.
76. The City of Chicago's website includes a page titled "Just the Facts: Answers to Frequent City Pension Questions," which lists the projected unfunded city pension liability through the end of FY2012 as $26.8 billion. The unfunded liability refers to pension payments, which public employees have already earned through their service. The city pension liability includes six separate pension funds: firefighters, police, Laborers, municipal employees, park district employees, and teachers. The breakdown of the projected liabilities through FY2012 was as follows: Municipal Employees' Annuity and Benefit Fund of Chicago (MEABF): $8.2 billion; Laborers' and Retirement Board Employees' Annuity and Benefit Fund (LABF): $0.9 billion; Policemen's Annuity and Benefit Fund (PABF): $7.0 billion; Firemen's Annuity and Benefit Fund (FABF): $3.1 billion; Chicago Teachers Pension Fund (CTPF): $7.1 billion; Park Employees Annuity and Benefit Fund (PEABF): $0.4 billion. For additional pension liability information, see the Civic Federation report "City of Chicago Pensions See Continued Decline," November 7, 2012.
77. "Mayor Rahm Emanuel Outlines 2012 Budget Proposal."
78. Ibid.
79. Fran Spielman, "Who Will Be Hit by Emanuel's 517 Layoffs?" *Chicago Sun-Times*, October 15, 2011. See also City of Chicago 2012 Budget Overview.
80. "Mayor Rahm Emanuel Outlines 2012 Budget Proposal."
81. Kristen Mack and Hal Dardick, "City Budget with Higher Fines, Fees Expected to Be Approved Today," *Chicago Tribune*, November 16, 2011.
82. "Mayor Emanuel's 2012 Budget Address," prepared remarks published by Eric Zorn, *Chicago Tribune*, October 12, 2011.
83. Ibid.
84. Mary Mitchell, "How Rahm Emanuel Won Black Voters," *Chicago Sun-Times*, February 26, 2011.
85. Dan Mihalopuolos, Lisa Donovan, and Dave McKinney, "Rahm Emanuel's Cabinet Comes Up Short in Diversity," *Chicago Sun-Times*, July 8, 2012.
86. Fran Spielman, "Emanuel Touts His Administration's Diversity—in Experience, Race and Results," *Chicago Sun-Times*, July 9, 2012.
87. Dick Johnson, "Rahm Town Hall Gets Testy," NBC Chicago, August 30, 2011.
88. Jessica D'Onofrio and Ben Bradley, "Chicago Budget Town Hall Draws Opinions," ABC,

August 30, 2011.

89. Interview with activist Matt Ginsberg-Jaeckle, January 2013.

90. D'Onofrio and Bradley, "Chicago Budget Town Hall Draws Opinions."

91. Ibid.

92. Johnson, "Rahm Town Hall Gets Testy."

93. "Rahm Emanuel Budget Town Hall Gets Heated (VIDEO)," *Huffington Post*, August 30, 2011.

94. Ibid.

95. Ibid.

96. "Chicago Traffic Control Layoffs: City Axes Aides to Save City an Estimated $2.3 Million," *Huffington Post*, August 2, 2011.

97 Jeff Goldblatt, "Emanuel Demands 'Ideas, Not Insults' at Second Budget Town Hall," NBC Chicago, January 3, 2012.

98. Jim Vail, "CTU Mobilizing and Energized Following Mayor's Demagogic Attacks on Public School Teachers. . . . Rahm Emanuel His Own Worst Enemy?" *Substance News*, September 26, 2011.

99. Goldblatt, "Emanuel Demands 'Ideas, Not Insults.'"

100. Interview with Dick Simpson, December 2012.

101. Ibid. The report "The Last of the Daley Years, Chicago City Council Voting Report #5, May 21, 2007–January 13, 2011," by Simpson and colleagues,describes the "rubber stamp" council under Mayor Daley. Between 2007 and 2011, aldermen voted with Daley 82 percent of the time, and only seven out of fifty aldermen voted with him less than 70 percent of the time.

102. "Aldermen Wringing Hands over Budget," NBC Chicago, *Ward Room*, November 16, 2011.

103. "Emanuel Budget Changes: Will Ease Library Cuts, Raise City Sticker Fees for All Drivers," *Huffington Post*, November 4, 2011.

104. Hal Dardick and John Byrne, "Emanuel's Budget Unanimously Approved," *Chicago Tribune*, November 16, 2011.

105. Ibid.

106. Fran Spielman, "Why Chicago Commissioner Had to Go," *Chicago Sun-Times*, January 25, 2011.

107. Interview with library page Sara Doe, January 2012.

108. Ibid.

109. Interview with AFSCME Council 31 spokesman Anders Lindall, January 2012.

110. Interview with Chicago blogger and mother Natasha Nicholes, January 2012.

111. Interview with Anders Lindall, January 2012.

112. Ibid.

113. John Byrne, "Branch Libraries to Reopen Monday Afternoons," *Chicago Tribune*, January 22, 2012.

114. Interview with Chicago alderman who did not want his name used.

115. Interview with Mental Health Movement member Margaret Sullivan, October 2012.

116. Interview with Dick Simpson, December 2012.

8. THE MENTAL HEALTH MOVEMENT

1. Steve Bogira, "Starvation Diet: Coping with Shrinking Budgets in Publicly Funded Mental Health Services," *Health Affairs Journal*, May/June 2009.

2. Ibid.

3. Ibid.

4. Map of mental health clinics, Chicago Department of Public Health, at www.cityofchicago.org/city/en/depts/cdph/dataset/mental_health_clinics.html.As of February 2013, the website showed only the remaining six clinics.

5. Megan Cottrell, "City to Close Five Mental Health Centers," *Chi-Town Daily News*, January 13, 2009.

6. Hal Dardick, "Chicago Mental Health Centers Closing: After Sit-in at Mayor Richard Daley's Office, Supporters Meet with Top Aide," *Chicago Tribune*, April 7, 2009.

7. Kari Lydersen, "A Chicago Youth Group Continues Its Slain Leader's Fight for Safety, Housing and Health Care," *Chicago Reporter*, February 8, 2012.

8. STOP website, at www.stopchicago.org.

9. Alex Parker, "Exclusive: Billing Glitch Led to Mental Health Closures," *Chi-Town Daily News*, April 7, 2009.

10. Hal Dardick and Dan Mihalopoulos, "City Hall to Use Stimulus Money to Keep Four Mental Health Clinics Open," *Chicago Tribune*, April 9, 2009. Hal Dardick and Dan Mihalopoulos, "City Hall: 4 Mental Clinics to Reopen Soon," *Chicago Tribune*, April 10, 2009.

11. Hal Dardick, "Chicago Targets Mental Health Clinics for Cuts," *Chicago Tribune*, August 26, 2009.

12. Steve Rhodes, "A Mental Health Moment," NBC Chicago, August 28, 2009.

13. Ibid.

14. Chika S. Oduah, "Community Groups Demand Adequate Staffing for City Mental Health Centers," Medill News Service, October 6, 2009.

15. "2012 Mental Health Services: Overview," City of Chicago Department of Public Health website, at www.cityofchicago.org/city/en/depts/cdph/provdrs/clinic/svcs/2012_mental _healthservices.html.

16. Ibid.

17. Bridget O'Shea, "County Jail a Large Mental Ward: Dart," Chicago News Cooperative, February 20, 2012.

18. "Dumping Responsibility: The Case Against Closing CDPH Mental Health Clinics," prepared by the Mental Health Movement and AFSCME Council 31, January 2012.

19. Interview with Mental Health Movement member Margaret Sullivan, October 2012.

20. Don Terry, "A Sit-In Fails to Save Clinics, But the Fight Continues," *New York Times* (Chicago edition), November 19, 2011.

21. Samuel Richardson's 1740 novel *Pamela, Or Virtue Rewarded* told the tale of a teenage maid whose employer attempts to seduce and rape her.

22. Interview with Mental Health Movement member Jeanette Hansen, October 2012.

23. Interview with Jesus "Chuy" Campuzano, October 2012.

24. StopChicago, "Mayor Emanuel: The Grinch Who Stole Clinics," December 17, 2011, at www.YouTube.com/watch?v=_zS4ijeT-p0.

25. StopChicago, "Helen Morley Speaking Truth to Power," June 6, 2012, at www.youtube .com/watch?v=Fwxq4FiMCtA.

26. Interview with Allen McNair, January 2013.

27. Interview with Jeanette Hansen and Margaret Sullivan, October 2012.

28. Lauren Fliegelman, "Access Living Celebrates the Life and Contributions of Helen Morley," Access Living website, June 27, 2012.

29. Interview with Mental Health Movement member Matt Ginsberg-Jaeckle, January 2013.

30. StopChicago, "Mayor Emanuel: The Grinch who Stole Clinics."

31. Interviews with Margaret Sullivan, Jeanette Hansen, Matt Ginsberg-Jaeckle, and other Mental Health Movement members.

32. YouTube video posted by "schoolofdissent," April 12, 2012. One comment says of N'Dana Carter, "That woman should be the mayor!"

33. Interviews with Margaret Sullivan, Jeanette Hansen, Matt Ginsberg-Jaeckle, and other Mental Health Movement members.

34. Rachel Allshiny, "Woodlawn Mental Health Clinic Occupation," *Occupied Stories* website, updated April 17, 2012.

35. Interview with Matt Ginsberg-Jaeckle, February 2013.

36. Interview with Jesus "Chuy" Campuzano, October 2012.

37. Statement from Debbie Delgado at a meeting of the Mental Health Movement, January 2013.
38. Ibid.
39. City of Chicago 2012 Budget Overview, Office of Management and Budget website, at www.cityofchicago.org/content/dam/city/depts/obm/supp_info/2012%20Budget/2012Budget Overview.pdf.
40. "Dumping Responsibility."
41. Ibid., 8.
42. Ibid.
43. "Abandoning the Most Vulnerable: The Real Consequences of Closing City of Chicago Mental Health Clinics," produced by AFSCME Council 31 and the Mental Health Movement, October 2012.
44. "Mental Health Services Transition Report," Chicago Department of Public Health, July 24, 2012.
45. "Report on Chicago Health Reforms," Chicago Department of Public Health, August 2012, at www.cityofchicago.org/content/dam/city/depts/cdph/clinical_care_and_more/RevisedHealthReport.August.pdf.
46. "Abandoning the Most Vulnerable."
47. Ibid.
48. "Dumping Responsibility."
49. Jo Patton, testimony at alternative community budget hearing hosted by aldermen with the Progressive Caucus of City Council, October 30, 2012.
50. "Mental Health Services Transition Report."
51. Interview with AFSCME special projects director Jo Patton, February 2013. Patton said that specific layoffs were in part governed by seniority provisions in the union contract, but the union maintained the city should have laid off fewer therapists.
52. Interview with Mental Health Movement activist N'Dana Carter, August 2012.

9. NATO AND THE GLOBAL CITY

1. Nina Burleigh, "Rahm Emanuel 2.0: Less Screaming, More Smiling," *DuJour Magazine*, December 2012.
2. "NATO Summit Meetings," North Atlantic Treaty Organization website, at www.nato.int/cps/en/natolive/topics_50115.htm.
3. "About the G8," US Department of State website, at www.state.gov/e/eb/ecosum/2012g8/about/index.htm.
4. "G8 Summit Locations and Dates," Government of Canada website, at www.canadainternational.gc.ca/g8/summit-sommet/past-passe.aspx?view=d.
5. Fran Spielman and Lynn Sweet, "Obama Bringing World Leaders to Chicago for NATO, G-8 Meetings," *Chicago Sun-Times*, June 22, 2011.
6. Ibid.
7. Robert Morgenthau, "Chicago Mayor Rahm Emanuel Is Latest to Reject 'Secure Communities' Immigration Law," *Daily Beast*, July 13, 2012. Daley, like other county and city officials nationwide, refused to participate in the federal Secure Communities program, meant to funnel undocumented immigrants picked up by police into immigration and possibly deportation proceedings.
8. "Boisterous Protesters March at G-20 Summit," Associated Press, September 25, 2009.
9. "Parades, Public Assemblies and Athletic Events," Proposed Ordinance Briefing from Mayor Rahm Emanuel's office and the Chicago Department of Cultural Affairs and Special Events, January 2012.
10. Frank Main, "Garry McCarthy to NATO, G-8 Protesters: Police Will Be Ready," *Chicago Sun-Times*, July 15, 2011.
11. Andy Grimm and Cynthia Dizikes, "FBI Raids Anti-war Activists' Homes," *Chicago Tribune*, September 24, 2010.

12. Ibid. See also "SEIU Local 73 Resolution Supporting Joe Iosbaker & Condemning FBI Raids," November 26, 2011, published on the Committee to Stop FBI Repression website, at www .stopfbi.net/2010/11/26/seiu-local-73-resolution-supporting-joe-iosbaker-condemning-fbi-raids.
13. Interview with activist Joe Iosbaker, December 31, 2012.
14. Main, "Garry McCarthy to NATO, G-8 protesters."
15. Interview with Joe Iosbaker, December 31, 2012.
16. "About,"CANG8 website, at http://cang8.wordpress.com/about.
17. Kim Janssen, "G-8 Protest Organizer Agent of 'Change' or 'Pain in the Butt'?" *Chicago Sun-Times*, January 16, 2012.
18. Erin Meyer, "Gay rights prosteters don't accept cardinal's apology for KKK statement," *Chicago Tribune*, January 9, 2012.
19. Mark Cassello, "Occupy Chicago Petitions Rahm Emanuel," *Huffington Post*, October 22, 2011.
20. Kristen Mack, Dahleen Glanton, and Becky Schlikerman, "Occupy Chicago Arrests Are Seen as a Trial Run for International Summits to Come Next Year," *Chicago Tribune*, October 16, 2012.
21. "Jailed Occupy Chicago Protesters Describe Harsh Treatment by Police, Plan to Picket Rahm Emanuel's Office," *Huffington Post*, October 24, 2011.
22. Charles Pierce, "Rahm Emanuel Gets the Spanking He Deserves," *Esquire Magazine* blog, September 28, 2012.
23. Mack, Glanton, and Schlikerman, "Occupy Chicago Arrests."
24. Interview with Joe Iosbaker, December 31, 2012.
25. Edward McClelland, "Mayor One Percent Catches On," NBC, *Ward Room*, January 18, 2012.
26. "Brief History of Chicago's 1968 Democratic Convention," CNN, 1996, at www.cnn .com/ALLPOLITICS/1996/conventions/chicago/facts/chicago68/index.shtml.
27. "Amendment of Various Provisions of Municipal Code Regarding Parades, Athletic Events and Public Assemblies," ordinance introduced to Chicago City Council Committee on Special Events, Cultural Affairs, and Recreation, December 14, 2011.
28. Ibid.
29. Ibid.
30. "Call for Hearing(s) on Use of Sound Devices," resolution introduced in Chicago City Council, December 14, 2011.
31. "Amendment of Various Provisions of Municipal Code."
32. "No Games Chicago: Chicago Citizens Against the 2016 Olympic Bid," at http:// nogames.wordpress.com.
33. Interview with Joe Iosbaker, December 31, 2012.
34. "Parades, Public Assemblies and Athletic Events," Proposed Ordinance Briefing from Mayor Rahm Emanuel's office and the Chicago Department of Cultural Affairs and Special Events, January 2012.
35. Don Babwin, "Chicago Backs Off Tough Measures for World Summits," Associated Press, January 17, 2012.
36. "Amendment of Various Provisions of Municipal Code."
37. "Emanuel's 'Improvements' to Permit Ordinances Leave Intact Grave Violations to Civil Liberties," CANG8 press release, January 13, 2012.
38. Though their most serious concerns about the proposed changes to the parade ordinance had been addressed, CANG8 organizers still opposed both the amendments to the existing parade/public assembly ordinance and the ordinance specifically related to the summits.
39. Interview with SEIU Local 73 division director Wayne Lindwall, January 18, 2012.
40. Joe Macare, *Gapers Block*, February 2012.
41. Joe Moreno, "My Vote on the NATO/G-8 Ordinance," *Huffington Post*, January 18, 2012.
42. "Emanuel's 'Improvements,'" CANG8 press release.
43. People's Summit website, at www.peoplessummitchicago.org.
44. National Nurses United website, at www.nationalnursesunited.org.

45. Ina Jaffe, "The Political Clout of California's Nurses," NPR, August 8, 2006.

46. "Financial Transaction Tax,"National Nurses United website.see also Ashok Selvan, "Nurses union urges Wall Street tax at NATO meeting," Modernhealthcare.com, May 18, 2012 (reprinted on National Nurses United website).The actual tax on each individual transaction as proposed by the nurses union would be minimal—50 cents on every $100 worth of transactions, which backers say would add as much as $350 billion a year for health care and other services.

47. Blair Kamin, "Cook County May Rescue Old Beaux Arts Hospital," *Chicago Tribune*, March 1, 2010.

48. BJ Lutz and Phil Rogers, "Obama Moves G8 Summit to Camp David," *Chicago Sun-Times*, March 6, 2012.

49. Laura MacInnis, "Obama Opens Up Camp David for Rustic VIP Sleepover," Reuters, May 19, 2012.

50. Interview with CANG8 organizer Andy Thayer, August 2012.

51. Dan Hyman, "Tom Gets Fired Up at Chicago Nurses Rally," *Rolling Stone*, May 18, 2012.

52. "Nurses, Veterans Furious with City's Changes to NATO Protests," CBS Local, May 9, 2012.

53. "City of Chicago Pulls Permit for Nurses Rally After Event Adds Tom Morello Performance," *Rolling Stone*, May 8, 2012.

54. Jeremy Gorner, Becky Schlikerman, and Rosemary R. Sobol, "Mystery over Bridgeport Arrests: Molotov Cocktails or Brewing Equipment?" *Chicago Tribune*, May 19, 2012.

55. Ken Armstrong, "The 1919 Race Riots," *Chicago Tribune*, July 27, 1919 (postdated).

56. Don Terry, "Chicago Neighborhood Reveals an Ugly Side," *New York Times*, March 27, 1997.

57. Gorner, Schlikerman, and Sobol, "Mystery over Bridgeport Arrests."

58. David Heinzmann and Jeff Coen, "Lawyers for NATO Protesters Allege Improper Arrests," *Chicago Tribune*, May 17, 2012.

59. Alex Perez and Andy Fies, "NATO Summit: 3 Protesters Arrested, Charged with Conspiracy to Commit Terrorism," ABC News, May 19, 2012.

60. "NATO 3 to Appear in Court Tuesday,"WLSAM.com, June 11, 2012.

61. Perez and Fies, "NATO Summit: 3 Protesters Arrested, Charged." See also NewsPowerTV, "Police Intimidating NATO/Occupy Protestors in Chicago On," audio of encounter posted on YouTube, May 10, 2012, at www.YouTube.com/watch?v=TudIyxxAboA.

62. Ibid.

63. Michael Tarm, "NATO Summit Chicago: 2 More Activists Arrested, Charged with Terrorism-Related Activities," *Huffington Post*, May 20, 2012.

64. "2 More Arrested on Terror, Explosives Charges in Chicago During NATO Protests," Associated Press, May 20, 2012.

65. "Occupy Chicago Releases Additional Photos of Both Suspected Police Informants Involved in NATO Terrorism-Related Cases," Occupy Chicago press release, May 22, 2012.

66. Ibid.

67. "NATO 3 to Appear in Court Tuesday."

68. Matt Stroud and Steve Horn, "Revealed: The Story Behind the 'NATO 3' Domestic Terrorism Arrests," *TruthOut*, June 21, 2013. See also People of the State of Illinois v. Brian Church, Jared Chase, Brent Betterly, Circuit Court of Cook County, County Department-Criminal Division, "People's Response to Defendants' Motion to Compel Discovery," filed April 16, 2013.

69. Jason Lewis, "Federal Court Rules NYPD's Mass Arrests During 2004 Republican National Convention Unlawful," *Village Voice*, October 2, 2012.

70. Diana Novak, "Garry McCarthy Named Chicago Police Superintendent," *Chicago Tonight*, WTTW, May 2, 2011.

71. Deborah Jacobs, "Newark Police Department Investigated as Director Garry McCarthy Heads to Chicago," AP/*Huffington Post*, May 9, 2011.

72. As noted in Jacobs, "Newark Police Department Investigated." A statement from the ACLU of New Jersey said, "Director McCarthy came to Newark promising to reform Internal Affairs,

and it simply hasn't happened."

73. Gary Younge, "Rahm Emanuel, King of Chicago, Goes into Battle as NATO Comes to Town," *Guardian*, May 20, 2012.
74. Michelle Manchir, "Boy, 14, Killed in Brighton Park," *Chicago Tribune*, May 20, 2012.
75. Interview with Amisha Patel, September 2012.
76. Perez and Fies, "NATO Summit: 3 Protesters Arrested, Charged."
77. Fran Spielman, "Police Union Gets Personal with Emanuel in NATO Pay Dispute," *Chicago Sun-Times*, May 30, 2012.
78. Perez and Fies, "NATO Summit: 3 Protesters Arrested, Charged."
79. Ryan Ori, "What Not to Wear During the NATO Summit," *Crain's Chicago Business*, May 8, 2012.
80. Perez and Fies, "NATO Summit: 3 Protesters Arrested, Charged."
81. Press release issued on *PRWeb*, February 27, 2012, at www.prweb.com/releases/2012/2/prweb9228221.htm.
82. Hyman, "Tom Morello Gets Fired Up."
83. "NATO Blog Day 2: Some Protesters Detained as Evening March Snakes Through Loop," *Chicago Tribune*, May 20, 2012.
84. "Chicago, Mental Health Movement Stage Sit-In at Mayor's House, Demand Health Care Not Warfare!" Occupy Wall Street website, May 19, 2012, at http://occupywallst.org/article/today-chicago-health-care-not-warfare-watch-live.
85. Rick Pearson, Bob Secter, and Kristen Mack, "NATO Blog Day 3: Anti-War March and Rally End with Confrontations," *Chicago Tribune*, May 21, 2012.
86. Interview with Jesus "Chuy" Campuzano, October 2012.
87. Kathleen Hennessey, "NATO Blog Day 3."
88. Photo by Brian Cassella, "NATO Blog Day 3."
89. Matt Walberg, "NATO Blog Day 3."
90. "NATO Blog Day 4: After One Last March Through Loop, Most Protesters Heading Home," *Chicago Tribune*, May 22, 2012.
91. Ibid.
92. Helene Cooper and Matthew Rosenberg, "NATO Agrees on Afghan Security Transition in 2013," *New York Times*, May 21, 2012. See also Margaret Talev and Hans Nichols, "Obama Seeks Afghan Commitments as NATO Summit Closes," *Bloomberg News*, May 21, 2012.
93. "NATO Summit: Obama, Karzai Affirm Plan to Withdraw Troops from Afghanistan," CBS Local, May 20, 2012.
94. "Chicago Summit Declaration on Afghanistan," North Atlantic Treaty Organization website, May 21, 2012, at www.nato.int/cps/en/natolive/official_texts_87595.htm.
95. Mike Flannery, "Emanuel Calls the NATO Summit a Huge Success for Chicago," *Fox 32*, May 21, 2012.
96. Rick Pearson, "NATO Blog Day 4."
97. Ibid.
98. John Byrne, "Mayor Makes a Play for the Super Bowl," *Chicago Tribune*, June 1, 2012.
99. Greg Hinz, "Olympics Door Opens Again for Chicago," *Crain's Chicago Business*, May 24, 2012.
100. "NATO Blog Day 4."
101. Interview with CANG8 organizer Andy Thayer, August 2012.
102. Phil Vettel, "NATO Blog Day 2."
103. Jeff Coen, "Emanuel Has $4 Million After NATO Tab Settled," *Chicago Tribune*, November 20, 2012.
104. "Mayor Emanuel Announces $1 million Investment in Learning Gardens Located at CPS Schools Through NATO Legacy Funds," City of Chicago Office of the Mayor press release, December 16, 2012. See also "Mayor Emanuel Announces $2 million in Neighborhood Park

Investments with NATO Legacy Funds," City of Chicago Office of the Mayor press release, January 6, 2013.

10. RAHM GETS SCHOOLED

1. Casey Banas and Devonda Byers, "Education Chief: City Schools Worst," *Chicago Tribune*, November 8, 1987.
2. Andrew Sum, "High School Dropouts in Chicago and Illinois: The Growing Labor Market, Income, Civic, Social and Fiscal Costs of Dropping Out of High School," Center for Labor Market Studies, Northeastern University, November 2011. (For Chicago youth age 19–24, 27 percent of Hispanic males and 30 percent of Black males have no high school diploma, while the number is only 4 percent for white males.)
3. "Stats and Facts," Chicago Public Schools website, at www.cps.edu/about_cps/at-a-glance/pages/stats_and_facts.aspx.
4. Interview with Chicago Teachers Union vice president Jesse Sharkey, February 4, 2013.
5. Sevil Omer, "Chicago Pushes Longer School Days as Key to Achievement," NBC News, June 14, 2012.
6. "Emanuel Scales Back Longer School Day," Chicago CBS, April 10, 2012.
7. Rosalind Rossi, "1,000 CPS Teachers Protest Canceled Raises While Execs Get Higher Salaries," *Chicago Sun-Times*, June 22, 2011.
8. Brian Montopoli, "Chris Christie in Hostile Interaction on Jersey Shore," CBS News, July 6, 2012.
9. Jason Song, "Schwarzenegger Backs Bill That Would Change Teachers' Dismissal Standards," *Los Angeles Times*, April 20, 2010.
10. "About Us," Chicago Teachers Union website, at www.ctunet.com/about.
11. "Renaissance 2010," Chicago Public Schools website, at www.cps.edu/PROGRAMS/DISTRICTINITIATIVES/Pages/Renaissance2010.aspx.
12. "Contract" and "Charter," Chicago Public Schools website, at www.cps.edu/Schools/Elementary_schools/Pages/Contract.aspx and www.cps.edu/Schools/Elementary_schools/Pages/Charter.aspx.
13. "Renaissance 2010."
14. Joanne Barkan, "Hired Guns on Astroturf: How to Buy and Sell School Reform," *Dissent*, Spring 2012.
15. Motoko Rich, "Push to Add Charter Schools Hangs Over Strike," *New York Times*, September 12, 2012.
16. Rick Pearson, "Emanuel Adviser Bruce Rauner Blasts Chicago Teachers Union Leadership," *Chicago Tribune*, September 19, 2012.
17. Stephanie Simon, "Privatizing Public Schools: Big Firms Eyeing Profits from U.S. K-12 Market," Reuters, August 2, 2012.
18. Interview with Kenwood Oakland Community Organization education organizer Jitu Brown, December 2012.
19. "Englewood Basketball Player Killed Helping His Sister," *Chicago Tribune*, December 17, 2002.
20. Interview with Chicago Public Schools teacher and Chicago Teachers Union staff coordinator Jackson Potter, March 3, 2013.
21. A. L. Loy, "Who Failed Englewood High?" *Third Coast Press*.
22. Ann Heppermann and Kara Oehler, "RE-Forming Englewood," WBEZ, *Chicago Matters* series, October 5, 2006.
23. "A Cauldron of Opposition in Duncan's Hometown—Rank-and-File Teachers Score Huge Victory: An Interview with Jackson Potter and Karen Lewis," *Rethinking Schools*, Fall 2010.
24. Ben Goldberger, "Karen Lewis, Street Fighter," *Chicago Magazine*, November 2012.
25. "Teaching Ambassador Fellowship: Xian (Sean) Barrett, Alumni Classroom Fellow," U.S. Department of Education, Office of Communications and Outreach website, 2009.
26. Potter saw British Columbia Teachers' Federation leader Jinny Sims speak at a conference and

was inspired. "She reengaged members to fight—she provided a template for us in CORE," he said. Sims later served as a member of Canada's House of Commons with the New Democratic Party (NDP). See "Jinny Sim," New Democratic Party website, at www.parl.gc.ca/Members OfParliament/ProfileMP.aspx?Key=170673&Language=E.

27. Interview with teacher Xian Barrett, August 2012.

28. Rebecca Harris, "Union Election Heads to Runoff; Stewart to Face Challenger from CORE," *Catalyst*, May 22, 2010. See also "Teachers Union Has New Leadership Team," NBC Chicago website, June 12, 2010.

29. Chris Cillizza, "Chicago Mayor Richard M. Daley to Retire, Speculation Swirls Around Rahm Emanuel Candidacy," *Washington Post*, September 7, 2010.

30. Rebecca Vevea, "Teachers Union Confronts Some Crucial Decisions," *New York Times* (Chicago edition), June 16, 2011.

31. Kristen McQueary, "CTU Calls Bill Language 'Atomic Bomb,'" WBEZ, May 5, 2011.

32. James Warren, "In Springfield, a Week of Change in Education," *New York Times* (Chicago Edition), April 16, 2011.

33. Lee Sustar, "A Crisis for Teachers Union Reformers?" *Socialistworker.org*, April 21, 2011.

34. "Amendment to Senate Bill 7," filed by Senator Kimberly Lightford, Illinois General Assembly, April 13, 2011.

35. Illinois General Assembly website, 97th Congress, SB0007.

36. Karen Lewis, "Senate Bill 7—Letter from President Lewis," published on Chicago Teachers Union website, April 14, 2011.

37. "Delegates to Union: Put the Brakes on Senate Bill 7," *Catalyst Chicago*, May 5, 2011. See also Jim Vail, "Delegates Reject CTU's Support of Illinois Senate Bill 7, Demand Major Changes," *Substance News*, May 7, 2011.

38. Illinois General Assembly website, 97th Congress, SB0007.

39. Will Guzzardi and Joy Resmovits, "Illinois Education Reform: Gov. Pat Quinn Signs Bill into Law," *Huffington Post*, June 13, 2011.

40. Jonah Edelman, "Stand for Children Co-Founder Describes Illinois Take Down of Teachers and Their Unions," video from 2011 Aspen Ideas Festival, at www.aspenideas.org/session/if-it-can -happen-there-it-can-happen-anywhere-transformational-education-legislation.

41. Joel Hood, "Teachers at 3 Small Schools Act Early to Approve Longer School Day," *Chicago Tribune*, September 2, 2011.

42. Matthew Blake, "Battle Lines Being Drawn in Push for Longer School Day," *Progress Illinois*, September 12, 2011.

43. Interview with Jesse Sharkey, February 4, 2013.

44. Rosalind Rossi, "Teachers Union President Says Mayor Emanuel 'Exploded' at Her," *Chicago Sun-Times*, September 9, 2011.

45. Becky Schlikerman, "CPS Chief Defends Move Closing, Reorganizing Schools," *Chicago Tribune*, February 26, 2012.

46. Joel Hood and Noreen S. Ahmed-Ullah, "Jean-Claude Brizard, Chicago's New Schools Chief, Doesn't Back Down from a Challenge," *Chicago Tribune*, May 8, 2011.

47. CPS Biography of Jean-Claude Brizard, May 26, 2011, at www.cps.edu/About_CPS/ The_Board_of_Education/BoardBios/Pages/Jean-ClaudeBrizard.aspx.

48. Mark Gruba, "Brizard Given No Confidence Vote," Rochesterhomepage.net, February 11, 2011.

49. Carol Felsenthal, "A Chat with Jean-Claude Brizard: The Personal and the Professional," *Chicago Magazine*, September 21, 2011.

50. Ibid.

51. Goldberger, "Karen Lewis, Street Fighter."

52. "Stats and Facts," Chicago Public Schools website, at www.cps.edu/about_cps/at-a -glance/pages/stats_and_facts.aspx.

53. United Neighborhood Organization website, at www.uno-online.org. See also Dan Mihalopoulos, "A Lifetime of Close Ties and Growing Influence," *New York Times* (Chicago edition), January 14, 2012.
54. Mihalopoulos, "A Lifetime of Close Ties."
55. Chicago Teachers Union political director Stacey Gates Davis, "Legislative Update," sent by email, January 7, 2013.
56. Joel Hood, "St. Scholastica Academy Leased for Charter School," *Chicago Tribune*, August 2, 2012.
57. Dan Mihalopoulos, "For Insiders, Community Group's Charter Schools Pay," *Chicago Sun-Times*, February 4, 2013.
58. Monique Garcia, Hal Dardick, and Antonio Olivo, "State Turns Off UNO Money Spigot after Charter School Scandal," *Chicago Tribune*, April 26, 2013.
59. Dan Mihalopoulos, "Work Is Stopped on UNO High School after State Halts Funding," *Chicago Sun-Times*, April 30, 2013.
60. Linda Lutton, "Embattled UNO Charter School Leader Steps Aside, Stops Short of Resigning," WBEZ, May 28, 2013.
61. Noble Network website, at www.noblenetwork.org.
62. Kyle Olson and Juan Williams, *A Tale of Two Missions*, abridged version of film available on Education Action Group website, at http://eagnews.org/short-films/two-missions/.
63. Education Action Group website, at http://eagnews.org/.
64. Two young self-proclaimed "reporters" working with Breitbart posed as a prostitute and pimp asking suspicious ACORN staff for advice on illegal activity. Details recounted by Joe Conason, "ACORN Video: Lies from Coast to Coast," *Salon*, April 7, 2010. Right-wing pundits including Bill O'Reilly later acknowledged that a Breitbart video appearing to show discrimination on the part of African American US Agriculture Department official Shirley Sherrod was blatantly misconstrued. Details recounted by Matea Gold, "Bill O'Reilly Apologizes to Shirley Sherrod for 'Not Doing My Homework,'" *Los Angeles Times*, July 21, 2010.
65. Rahm Emanuel Facebook Town Hall (live), January 30, 2012.
66. Kristen Mack, "Judge Orders Chicago Public Schools to Discuss Transfers with Fenger Students," *Chicago Tribune*, November 17, 2009.
67. Noreen S. Ahmed-Ullah, "CPS to Add 12 Charters Despite Weak Scores," *Chicago Tribune*, December 13, 2011.
68. Interview with Chicago Public Schools teacher and Chicago Teachers Union staff coordinator Jackson Potter, March 3, 2013.
69. Linda Lutton, "Paid Protesters a New Force in School Closings Debate," WBEZ, January 24, 2012.
70. Ibid.
71. Noreen S. Ahmed-Ullah, Kristen Mack and Jeff Coen, "Church Groups with City Contracts Back Emanuel's School Agenda," *Chicago Tribune*, January 27, 2012.
72. Jennifer Brandel, "CPS Inspector General to Investigate Paid Protesters," WBEZ, January 26, 2012.
73. Noreen S. Ahmed-Ullah and Kristen Mack, "Consulting Firm with Ties to Mayor Rahm Emanuel Bolsters Education Agenda by Backing Community Groups with Money, Expertise," *Chicago Tribune*, February 13, 2012.
74. Rhoda Rae Gutierrez and Pauline Lipman, University of Illinois at Chicago, Collaborative for Equity and Justice in Education, "Dyett High School and the Three D's of Chicago School Reform: Destabilization, Disinvestment, Disenfranchisement," flyer prepared for the Kenwood Oakland Community Organization.
75. Ibid.
76. Walter H. Dyett High School website, at http://schools.cuip.net/dyett/.
77. Noreen S. Ahmed-Ullah, "CPS: Poorer-Performing Schools Less Likely to Get Funds,"

Chicago Tribune, December 15, 2011.
78. "Chicago Parents, Students Occupy Piccolo Elementary, School Targeted for 'Turnaround,'" *Huffington Post*, February 18, 2012.
79. "Piccolo School Occupation," posted on YouTube, February 17, 2012, at www.youtube.com/watch?v=jXrhgC0CYoo.
80. John Byrne, "Activists End Sit-In at Piccolo School," *Chicago Tribune*, February 18, 2012.
81. John Byrne, "Emanuel Says School Protest Outside His House a Response to Change," *Chicago Tribune*, February 21, 2012.
82. Linda Lutton, "Chicago School Protest Turns Up in an Unusual Location: Winnetka," WBEZ, February 20, 2012.
83. Stacey Baca, "Board Approves School Closings, Turnarounds," ABC Local, February 22, 2012.
84. Bob Roberts, "Chicago School Board Approves School Closings, Turnarounds," CBS Local, February 22, 2012.
85. Tisha Lewis, Fox Chicago News, February 26, 2012.
86. Joel Hood and Noreen Ahmed-Ullah, "Parents Plead with CPS to Put Off Vote on School Closings," *Chicago Tribune*, February 22, 2012.
87. Hyde Park Johnny, "Massive Chicago Teachers Union Rally Takes Over Downtown," *Daily Kos*, May 24, 2012.
88. Edelman, video from 2011 Aspen Ideas Festival.
89. "Chicago Teachers Vote to Authorize Strike," CBS Local, June 11, 2012.
90. Rosalind Rossi, "Arbitrator: Give Chicago Teachers 35.7% Raise Over Four Years," *Chicago Sun-Times*, July 16, 2012.
91. Ibid.
92. "Teachers Reach Accord in 4-week Strike," Associated Press, October 4, 1987.
93. Sources including Joel Wendland, Political Affairs, February 26, 2008, and Coalition of Black Trade Unionists website.
94. Don Babwin and Carla Johnson, "Chicago Teachers Union, CPS Reach Interim Agreement on Longer School Day," *Huffington Post*, July 24, 2012. See also Joel Hood and Noreen S. Ahmed-Ullah, "Like Richard, Like Rahm," *Chicago Tribune*, July 31, 2012.
95. Memo published on *Mike Klonsky's Small Talk Blog*, August 20, 2012, at http://michaelklonsky.blogspot.com/2012/08/in-mailbox_20.html.
96. Nick Carey, "Thousands of Chicago Teachers Rally on First Day of Strike," Reuters, September 10, 2012.
97. Chicago City Club video, Juan Rangel, CEO of United Neighborhood Organization, August 29, 2012, at http://cityclubvideo.wordpress.com/2012/08/29/juan-rangel-ceo-united-neighborhood-organization-2.
98. Fran Spielman, "Rahm Emanuel to Cut Short Democratic Convention Trip," *Chicago Sun-Times*, September 3, 2012.
99. "Chicago Teachers Strike: At Labor Day Rally, Union President Calls Rahm 'a Liar and a Bully,'" *Huffington Post* Chicago, September 4, 2012.
100. Rahm Emanuel speech at 2012 Democratic National Convention, September 4, 2012, video and text posted by *Politico*.
101. Bill Clinton's speech at the 2012 Democratic National Convention, September 5, 2012, video posted by CBS News. For more on Emanuel's Infrastructure Trust, see chapter 11.
102. BJ Lutz and Carol Marin, "Chicago Mayor Emanuel Exits Obama 2012 Campaign, Joins Super PAC," *Chicago Sun-Times*, September 6, 2012.
103. Shushannah Walshe, "Paul Ryan on Chicago Teachers' Strike: 'We Stand with Mayor Rahm Emanuel,'" ABC News, September 10, 2012.
104. Ibid.
105. "House of Delegates to Review New Contract Language This Sunday at 3 p.m.," Chicago Teachers Union press release, September 15, 2012, including summary of contract provisions.

106. Ibid.
107. Ibid.
108. Ibid.
109. Ibid.
110. Ibid.
111. Noreen S. Ahmed-Ullah and Ellen Jean Hirst, "Teachers Union Challengers Say Karen Lewis Failed to Deliver During Strike," *Chicago Tribune*, February 20, 2013.
112. Rosalind Rossi, "CPS Teachers Overwhelmingly Approve New Contract," *Chicago Sun-Times*, October 3, 2012.
113. See, for example, Jena McGregor, "How Rahm Emanuel Handled the Chicago Teachers Strike," *Washington Post*, September 19, 2012, and James Warren, "Mayor Rahm Emanuel Reaches Flawed Deal to End Chicago Teachers Strike," *Daily Beast*, September 19, 2012.
114. TV ad available on YouTube, uploaded by *Capitol Fax*. Story by *Huffington Post Chicago*, September 20, 2012.
115. Bruce Rauner, "It's Time We Say 'Enough,'" *Chicago Tribune*, September 12, 2012.
116. Carol Marin, *Chicago Tonight*, WTTW, September 18, 2012.
117. Carol Marin, "Is It Ever OK for a Politician to Deceive the Public?" *Chicago Sun-Times*, October 12, 2012.
118. "Lewis: Brizard Was Set Up to Fail as CPS Chief Executive," CBS Local, October 12, 2012.
119. Marin, "Is It Ever OK?"
120. Dahleen Glanton, Antonio Olivo, and Cynthia Dizikes, "Mostly High Marks for New CPS Chief," *Chicago Tribune*, October 14, 2012.
121. Cassandra West, "In the News: Byrd-Bennett's Honeymoon Begins," *Catalyst Chicago*, October 15, 2012. See also "Lewis: Brizard Was Set Up." Interview with Robert Bruno, professor in the School of Labor and Employment Relations at the University of Illinois, December 2012.
122. Pauline Lipman and Eric "Rico" Gutstein, "Should Chicago Have an Elected Representative School Board? A Look at the Evidence," University of Illinois at Chicago, Collaborative for Equity and Justice in Education, February 2011.
123. Ibid.
124. Joel Hood, "Teachers Union, Community Groups Want Elected School Board," *Chicago Tribune*, February 26, 2012.
125. Ben Joravsky, "Moore and Emanuel Block Elected School Board," *Chicago Reader*, August 1, 2012.
126. Fran Spielman, "Ald. Moore Nixes Elected School Board Referendum," *Chicago Sun-Times*, July 23, 2012.
127. Joravsky, "Moore and Emanuel Block."
128. Curtis Black, "On the Ballot: Elected School Board," *Community Media Workshop Newstips*, October 22, 2012. There are 2,034 precincts in the city's fifty wards; the referendum about an elected school board appeared on the ballot in 327 precincts in thirty-five different wards.
129. Spreadsheet published by the Raise Your Hand coalition for public education in Illinois, at www.ilraiseyourhand.org. See also Becky Vevea, "Elected School Board Referendum Results Give Supporters a Boost," WBEZ, November 7, 2012.
130. Jason Grotto and Alex Richards, "CPS Finances Tell a Grim Tale," *Chicago Tribune*, September 16, 2012.
131. "Editorial: CPS Must Come Clean on School Closings," *Chicago Sun-Times*, September 19, 2012.
132. Rosalind Rossi, "Byrd-Bennett Proposes 5-Year Ban on CPS Closures after This Year," *Chicago Sun-Times*, November 26, 2012.
133. "Editorial: CPS Must Come Clean."
134. "Statement from Mayor Emanuel on CPS Launching a Comprehensive Community Engagement Process Around School Actions," City of Chicago Office of the Mayor press release,

November 2, 2012.
135. "Editorial: CPS Must Come Clean."
136. In *Community Media Workshop Newstips* on November 28, 2012, Curtis Black explained, "One-quarter of a school's classrooms are allowed to be 'ancillary'—going for 'non-homeroom uses' like art, science or computer labs, recreation rooms if there's no gym, and other purposes. All the rest are expected to have 30 students. If it's a kindergarten class with 21 students, those are nine 'empty seats'.... It doesn't matter if the room actually has 18 pre-K students or if it's a self-contained special ed room with five autistic students—those rooms have 12 and 25 'empty seats' respectively. There's no accounting for whether the school has a gym or lunchroom or playground, or whether a classroom converted to a science lab can fit the same number of bodies as a classroom full of desks."
137. Sarah Karp, "Minimal Cost Savings for Closing Schools: Analysis," *Catalyst Chicago*, October 2012.
138. "Editorial: CPS Must Come Clean."
139. Rosalind Rossi, "School Upheavals Blasted as 'Insane,'" *Chicago Sun-Times*, June 22, 2012.
140. Hal Dardick and Kristen Mack, "Talks Drag On, with School Closings in Spotlight," *Chicago Tribune*, September 12, 2012.
141. Grotto and Richards, "CPS Finances Tell a Grim Tale."
142. Lauren Fitzpatrick, "New CPS Chief Bennett Seeks Delay in School Closing List Release," *Chicago Sun-Times*, November 2, 2012.
143. "CTU President Lewis Responds to CPS Request to Skip Mandated December 1 School Closing Deadline," statement from Chicago Teachers Union, November 2, 2012.
144. Fitzpatrick, "New CPS chief Bennett seeks delay."
145. Julie Woestehoff, "Mayor Wants to Stop the School Closing Beatings—After This Year," blog post for the grassroots parents group PURE, at www.pureparents.org/?p=20056, November 26, 2012.
146. Noreen S. Ahmed-Ullah and John Chase, "Document Shows Emanuel Administration Had Detailed School Closing Plans," *Chicago Tribune*, December 19, 2012.
147. Ibid.
148. Lauren Fitzpatrick, "Leave All City High Schools Open, CPS School-Closing Panel Says," *Chicago Sun-Times*, January 10, 2013.
149. "CPS Chief Agrees High Schools Should Not Be Closed," WGN, January 14, 2013.
150. Sarah Karp, "For the Record: Walton Foundation Funds Community Engagement," *Catalyst*, January 30, 20013.
151. Ibid.

11. TIFS, JOBS, AND THE INFRASTRUCTURE TRUST

1. River Point website, at www.chicagoriverpoint.com.
2. Merchandise Mart website, at www.merchandisemart.com.
3. Up to $29.5 million in TIF funds are promised under the city development agreement with L&M Riverbend Venture, submitted by the City Council Finance Committee on September 10, 2008. Agreement available on the city's LaSalle/Central TIF website, at www.city-ofchicago.org/city/en/depts/dcd/supp_info/tif/lasalle_central_tif.html. As noted in "Eight TIF Districts Would Be Eliminated Under Mayoral Plan," an October 31, 2012, press release from the mayor's office, L&M Riverbend Ventures became part of River Point LLC.
4. Up to $24.39 million would be available to United Airlines under a redevelopment agreement with the city. "LaSalle Central Redevelopment Project Area United Airlines Redevelopment Agreement," filed with Cook County Recorder of Deeds, November 19, 2011. See the city's LaSalle/Central TIF website.
5. Under its redevelopment agreement with the city, MillerCoors could access up to $5.78 million

in TIF funds. "Execution of redevelopment agreement with MillerCoors 11 C and provision of tax increment allocation financing for rehabilitation of corporate headquarters at 250 S. Wacker Dr.," submitted by the City Council Committee on Finance, September 9, 2009. See the city's LaSalle/Central TIF website.

6. The City of Chicago Department of Housing and Economic Development website includes a page on the LaSalle/Central TIF, which defines the specific TIF's mission in part: "The LaSalle/Central TIF is characterized by older commercial buildings and mixed-use structures, many possessing excess vacancies due to ongoing economic and geographic shifts involving central business district office properties. The TIF was designated to provide resources for their rehabilitation for current and new uses, especially projects that involve the district's numerous historic structures." See also www.cityofchicago.org/city/en/depts/dcd/supp_info/tif/lasalle_central_tif.html.

7. TIF money could also be used specifically for projects involving schools, libraries, parks, or other public services and buildings. In an August 29, 2011, story in the *Chicago Sun-Times*, Fran Spielman noted, "In the ten-year period ending in 2010, the city spent $3 billion in TIF funds. Projects undertaken by private developers got $637.6 million. The Chicago Public Schools got $548 million while $98.7 million bankrolled CTA station and track improvements and $72.7 million went to the Chicago Park District." But critics say the money going to private developers should also be going to public services, and that TIF funds spent on public services are subject to political favoritism in a way general budget funds are not.

8. Matthew Blake, "TIF Piggybank Running Low," *Progress Illinois*, July 18, 2012.

9. Description of TIFs available at Cook County Clerk's Office website, "TIFs 101: A Taxpayer's Primer for Understanding TIFs," at www.cookcountyclerk.com/tsd/tifs/pages/tifs101.aspx. Annual reports about Cook County and Chicago TIFs also available on county clerk's website, at www.cookcountyclerk.com/tsd/tifs/Pages/TIFReports.aspx.

10. Colin Briskman and Hailey Witt, "Jobs and TIF: An Analysis of Job Creation and Tax Increment Financing," report by Illinois PIRG, August 2012.

11. Fran Spielman, "Rahm Emanuel Embraces Reform of Special TIF Taxing Districts," *Chicago Sun-Times*, August 29, 2011.

12. Briskman and Witt, "Jobs and TIF."

13. Yvette Shields, "Chicago's Emanuel Offers a Scary Prognosis About City's Fiscal Woes," *Bond Buyer*, August 2, 2011.

14. Briskman and Witt, "Jobs and TIF." See also www.cookcountyclerk.com/newsroom/newsfromclerk/Pages/2010TIFReportReleased.aspx.

15. "Rahm Proposes Shutting Down Eight TIF Districts—But Don't Call It TIF Reform," *Chicagoist*, November 1, 2012. See also "United Airlines to Return Economic Development Incentives for 77 W. Wacker to City," City of Chicago Office of the Mayor press release, November 12, 2012.

16. "Eight TIF Districts Would Be Eliminated Under Mayoral Plan," City of Chicago Office of the Mayor press release, October 31, 2012.

17. Curtis Black, "Penny Pritzker's TIF," *Community Media Workshop Newstips*, August 8, 2012. See also Ben Joravsky, "The Shrinking Slush Fund: As the TIF Stream Slows, Mayor Emanuel Dips in Anyway," *Chicago Reader*, July 18, 2012. See also "Eight TIF Districts Would Be Eliminated" press release.

18. Alejandra Cancino and Kathy Bergen, "CME Group Has Tax Breaks from '08 It Has Yet to Use," *Chicago Tribune*, November 10, 2011.

19. Melissa Harris, "Chicago Confidential: With Tax Breaks on the Line, CME Group Hoping to Wield Clout at State Level," *Chicago Tribune*, November 9, 2011. See also Cancino and Bergen, "CME Group Has Tax Breaks."

20. Interview with Grassroots Collaborative executive director Amisha Patel, September 2012.

21. Kari Lydersen, "The Golden Toilet Marches on, Inspires Call for Development Reform," *In*

These Times, February 7, 2012.
22. "Local, Activists Bring Golden Toilet to City Hall, Protest Grant to CME," CBS, February 8, 2012.
23. Donald Wilson, "Why Chicago Business Needs Protected Bike Lanes," *Crain's Business Chicago*, December 11, 2012.
24. "Chicago Forward: Conversations About the Future," event hosted by the Chicago Tribune Foundation at the Field Museum, January 16, 2013.
25. World Business Chicago, "Chicago's Business Growth Profile: New and Expanded Companies," year-end report, 2011.
26. "Chicago Forward: Conversations About the Future."
27. World Business Chicago, "Chicago's Business Growth Profile."
28. Kari Lydersen, "With New Battery Hub, Chicago Seeks to Lead Nation on Electric Vehicles," *Midwest Energy News*, January 25, 2013.
29. Kathy Bergen, Kristen Mack, and Wailin Wong, "Emanuel's Job Pipeline Somewhat Leaky," *Chicago Tribune*, August 19, 2012.
30. "About the Mayor," City of Chicago website, at www.cityofchicago.org/city/en/depts/mayor/supp_info/about_the_mayor.html.
31. "Mayor Emanuel, United Airlines and U.S. Equities Announce United Will Move HQ to Willis Tower," City of Chicago Office of the Mayor press release, August 13, 2012.
32. Interview with Amisha Patel, September 2012.
33. "LaSalle Central Redevelopment Project Area United Airlines Redevelopment Agreement," filed with Cook County Recorder of Deeds, November 19, 2011.
34. Ibid. Along with the job creation requirements, as a condition of the TIF money the company promised that 50 percent of construction workers hired for the move would be city residents, that a quarter of contractors would be minority-owned businesses, and that 4 percent would be women-owned.
35. Alejandra Cancino and Emily Bryson York, "Slimmer Sara Lee Moving to Chicago," *Chicago Tribune*, December 8, 2011.
36. Bergen, Mack, and Wong, "Emanuel's Job Pipeline."
37. John Roszkowski, "Layoffs Are 'One More Broken Promise,'" *Libertyville Review*, August 20, 2012.
38. Bergen, Mack, and Wong, "Emanuel's Job Pipeline."
39. Ibid.
40. Ibid.
41. Interview with Chicago Federation of Labor president Jorge Ramirez, January 30, 2013.
42. Jessen O'Brien, "Mayor Emanuel's First 100 Days: Debrief with Eddie Arruza," *Chicago Tonight*, WTTW, August 22, 2011.
43. Regarding the Emanuel administration and transparency, coverage and commentary including: Mick Dumke, "The Most Transparent Government Chicago Has Ever Seen, Part 1," *Chicago Reader*, December 1, 2012; Steve Rhodes, "Rahm's Fake Transparency," *Beachwood Reporter*, November 4, 2012; and Ben Bradley, "Rahm's April Fools' resolution," ABC Local, April 2, 2012. Regarding the Obama White House, see coverage and commentary including: Ned Potter, "Just How 'Transparent' Is the Obama White House? Scientists Try to Help," ABC News, November 16, 2010; and Josh Gerstein, "President Obama's Muddy Transparency Record," *Politico*, March 5, 2012.
44. Kristen Mack, Hal Dardick, and John Byrne, "Emanuel Speed Camera Ticket Measure Approved," *Chicago Tribune*, April 18, 2012.
45. David Kidwell, Jeff Coen, and Bob Secter, "Mayor's Speed Cameras Would Help Political Ally," *Chicago Tribune*, March 13, 2012.
46. David Kidwell, "Transcript: Tribune Interview with Mayor Rahm Emanuel," *Chicago Tribune*, February 12, 2012.

47. Ibid.
48. James Warren, "The City That Works (Even Better!): Emanuel's Strategy for Chicago Growth," *Atlantic*, March 1, 2012. Warren called Emanuel "Chicago's hyperkinetic mayor and an obsessive when it comes to winning the next news cycle."
49. Ryan Haggerty and Jason Meisner, "Constitutionality of Illinois Eavesdropping Law Challenged in Court," *Chicago Tribune*, February 14, 2012.
50. Robert Channick, "Emanuel: Taping of Reporters 'Much Ado About Nothing,'" *Chicago Tribune*, November 12, 2012.
51. Andy Shaw, "Emanuel's Recording Explanation—Much Ado About Something," *Chicago Sun-Times*, November 16, 2012.
52. John Schwartz, "$7 Billion Public-Private Plan in Chicago Aims to Fix Transit, Schools and Parks," *New York Times*, March 29, 2012.
53. John Byrne and Jon Hilkevitch, "Emanuel Puts $7 Billion Price Tag on Infrastructure Plans," *Chicago Tribune*, March 29, 2012.
54. "A Question of Trust: Chicago Pioneers a New Way of Paying for Infrastructure," *Economist*, May 12, 2012.
55. "Mayor Emanuel Announces Chicago Infrastructure Trust to Invest in Transformative Projects," City of Chicago Office of the Mayor press release, March 1, 2012.
56. Yvette Shields, "Chicago Eyes Mayor's Plan for an Infrastructure Trust," *Bond Buyer*, April 17, 2012.
57. "Mayor Emanuel Announces Chicago Infrastructure Trust" press release. See also "More Mega Projects Turning to Private Investors," Associated Press, July 5, 2012.
58. Macquarie MQA website, "Chicago Skyway" section under "Asset Portfolio," at www.macquarie.com/mgl/com/mqa/asset-portfolio/chicago-skyway.
59. Emily Thornton, "Roads to Riches," *Bloomberg Businessweek*, May 7, 2006.
60. Robert Puentes and Jennifer Thompson, "Banking on Infrastructure: Enhancing State Revolving Funds for Transportation," Brookings Institution, September 2012, at www.brookings.edu/~/media/research/files/papers/2012/9/12%20state%20infrastructure%20investmen%20puentes/12%20state%20infrastructure%20investment%20puentes.pdf.
61. Matt Compton, "Five Facts About a National Infrastructure Bank," *White House Blog*, November 3, 2011.
62. Fran Spielman, "Emanuel, Clinton Announce $1.7 Billion Trust for Chicago Projects," *Chicago Sun-Times*, March 1, 2012.
63. "Mayor Emanuel Announces Chicago Infrastructure Trust" press release.
64. Spielman, "Emanuel, Clinton Announce $1.7 Billion Trust."
65. Interview with Amisha Patel, September 2012.
66. Hal Dardick and Kristen Mack, "Some Aldermen Raising Concerns as Hearing Set on Mayor's Trust Plan," *Chicago Tribune*, April 17, 2012.
67. "City Council Passes Chicago Infrastructure Trust," City of Chicago Office of the Mayor press release, April 24, 2012.
68. "Substitute Ordinance Establishing the Chicago Infrastructure Trust and Providing for Certain Related Matters," Section 5, submitted to City Council March 14, 2012.
69. Hal Dardick, Kristen Mack, and John Byrne, "Emanuel's Trust Win Shows He's Firmly in Control," *Chicago Tribune*, April 24, 2012.
70. Ibid.
71. Interview with Alderman Ricardo Muñoz, December 2012.
72. Interview with political scientist Dick Simpson, December 2012.
73. The Infrastructure Trust also included a nonvoting advisory board.
74. Ullico website, "About Ullico" section, at www.ullico.com/about-ullico. Ullico's enthusiasm over the Retrofit Chicago component of the Infrastructure Trust is described at the Ullico website, at www.ullico.com/news-item/mayor-rahm-emanuel-announces-chicago.

75. Ibid.
76. Interview with Jorge Ramirez, December 2012.
77. Interview with Jorge Ramirez, January 30, 2013.
78. Editorial, "'Oops, Here We Go Again'—Did the Aldermen Learn Nothing from Their Parking Meter Debacle?" *Chicago Tribune*, April 17, 2012.
79. Shields, "Chicago Eyes Mayor's Plan."
80. Interview with Jorge Ramirez, January 30, 2013.
81. "About the Chicago Cultural Plan,"City of Chicago website, at www.cityofchicago.org/city/en/depts/dca/supp_info/cultural_plan0.html.
82. "Chicago Cultural Plan," City of Chicago website, at www.cityofchicago.org/city/en/depts/dca/supp_info/cultural_plan.html.
83. Mark Caro and Heather Gillers, "Cultural Plan Emphasizes Arts in Schools," *Chicago Tribune*, October 15, 2012.
84. Ibid.
85. Deanna Isaacs, "The Final Version of the Chicago Cultural Plan 2012 Arrives as a Photo Op," *Chicago Reader*, October 24, 2012.
86. Rahm Emanuel, "How to Rebuild America," *Washington Post*, November 23, 2012.
87. Edward McClelland, "Opinion: Rahm Writes WaPo OpEd on Why He Should Be President," NBC Chicago, *Ward Room,* November 26, 2012.

12. ANOTHER BUDGET, ANOTHER BATTLE

1. Curtis Black, "Public Left Out of Emanuel's Budget," *Community Media Workshop Newstips*, October 4, 2012.
2. Ben Joravsky, "Mayor Rahm Meets the People No More," *Chicago Reader*, October 10, 2012.
3. Ibid.
4. "An Open Letter to Mayor Emanuel Calling for Transparency and Community Participation in the City Budget Process," signed by Action Now, Albany Park Neighborhood Council, and numerous other unions and groups, October 3, 2012.
5. Interview with Grassroots Collaborative executive director Amisha Patel, September 2012.
6. "Mayor Rahm Emanuel Remarks as Prepared for Delivery on City of Chicago 2013 Budget," City of Chicago website, October 10, 2012, at www.cityofchicago.org/city/en/depts/mayor/press_room/press_releases/2012/october_2012/mayor_emanuel_presents2013budgettocitycouncil.html. See also Office of Management and Budget, City of Chicago 2013 Budget Overview, at www.cityofchicago.org/city/en/depts/obm/provdrs/city_budg/svcs/budget_documents.html.
7. "Mayor Rahm Emanuel Remarks," October 10, 2012. The nonsworn safety employees' four-year contracts limited raises to 6 percent and substituted one-time modest signing bonuses for retroactive pay that otherwise would have been due. See also Fran Spielman, "Chicago Reaches Labor Deal with Non-Sworn Public Safety Workers," *Chicago Sun-Times*, October 1, 2012.
8. City of Chicago 2013 Budget Overview.
9. Ibid.
10. Ibid. See also Fran Spielman, "Emanuel Budget Hearing: 'Calm Before the Storm,'" *Chicago Sun-Times*, October 16, 2012.
11. Ibid.
12. Ibid.
13. Interview with AFSCME Council 31 special projects director Jo Patton, October 2012.
14. Ben Meyerson, "Ward Remap Passes: 2nd Ward Blown Up, 3rd and 4th Wards Split South Loop," *Chicago Journal*, January 19, 2012.
15. Jennifer Brandel and Alex Keefe, "Majority of Aldermen Call for Budget Changes,"WBEZ, November 2, 2011.
16. Interview with political scientist Dick Simpson, December 2012.

17. The report "Abandoning the Most Vulnerable: The Real Consequences of Closing City of Chicago Mental Health Clinics," produced by AFSCME Council 31 and the Mental Health Movement, was discussed in chapter 8.
18. Alexander was referring to "Abandoning the Most Vulnerable."
19. Kari Lydersen, "City Janitors Are Latest to Feel the Sting of Emanuel's Cuts," *In These Times, Working*, August 31, 2012.
20. SEIU Local 1 fact sheet, "Responsible Bidders Ordinance."
21. "Amendment of Chapter 2-92 of Municipal Code to Establish Privatization Transparency and Accountability Ordinance." The ordinance was introduced to the Committee on Committees, Rules and Ethics, in Chicago City Council, November 15, 2012. Text available on City of Chicago Clerk's Legistar website, at http://chicago.legistar.com/Legislation.aspx.
22. Interview with Chicago Federation of Labor president Jorge Ramirez, January 30, 2013.
23. "City of Chicago Privatization ('Managed Competition') Initiatives—Problems and Pitfalls," AFSCME Council 31, November 2012.
24. Tokyo-based NTT Data bought Boston-based Keane in 2010. "NTT Data to Buy Keane for $1.2 Billion in U.S. Push: Report," Reuters, October 21, 2010.
25. "City of Chicago Privatization," AFSCME Council 31, November 2012.
26. Interview with AFSCME Council 31 special projects director Jo Patton, October 2012.
27. "Mayor Rahm Emanuel Remarks as Prepared for Delivery on City of Chicago 2013 Budget," City of Chicago, October 10, 2012.
28. Interview with SEIU Local 1 president Tom Balanoff, November 20, 2012.
29. "The Daybook: Midway Airport Deal Dead, 4/20 Confusion," WBEZ, April 20, 2009.
30. Paul Merrion, "Has Midway Airport Missed Its Takeoff?" *Crain's Chicago Business*, December 12, 2012.
31. Fran Spielman, "Emanuel Close to Reviving Midway Privatization—with Key Changes," *Chicago Sun-Times*, December 1, 2012.
32. Fran Spielman, "Is Midway Airport Privatization Deal Back in the Works?" *Chicago Sun-Times*, April 3, 2012.
33. Merrion, "Has Midway Airport Missed Its Takeoff?"
34. "Puerto Rico Picks Two Finalists for Airport Privatization," Reuters, May 2, 2012.
35. Spielman, "Emanuel Close to Reviving Midway Privatization."
36. "The New Battle of Midway," *Chicago Tribune* editorial, January 20, 2013.
37. Ibid.

13. "THE JOB KILLER" AND THE JANITORS

1. For details on the contract, see United Maintenance Company, "Comprehensive Custodial/Window Cleaning and Related Hygiene and Disposal Services for Chicago O'Hare Int'l Airport," Contract PO number 26971, filed with Department of Aviation, available on the City of Chicago website.
2. Chris Fusco, Tim Novak, and Abdon M. Pallasch, "Business, Hollywood Big Shots Help Stock Emanuel's War Chest," *Chicago Sun-Times*, January 20, 2011.
3. Fran Spielman, "Contract for New Janitor Service at O'Hare Criticized by Powerful Union Boss," *Chicago Sun-Times*, November 2, 2012.
4. Interview with SEIU Local 1 president Tom Balanoff, November 20, 2012.
5. United Service Companies (parent company of United Maintenance Company) website, at www.unitedhq.com/maintenance.html.
6. Spielman, "Contract for New Janitor Service."
7. Interview with SEIU Local 1 janitor Pam Broughton, August 30, 2012.
8. Ibid.
9. "Janitors and Faith Community Hold Prayer Vigil at City Hall ... On the Day the Supreme Court Upholds Health Care Reform, Chicago Janitors Lose Their Health Insurance and In-

come," SEIU Local 1 press release, June 28, 2012.

10. Interview with Tom Balanoff, November 20, 2012.
11. "Tom Balanoff: SEIU Local 1 President," SEIU Local 1 website, posted July 8, 2011. Interview with Tom Balanoff, November 20, 2012.
12. Interview with SEIU Local 1 president Tom Balanoff, November 20, 2012.
13. Ibid.
14. "Responsible Bidders Ordinance," SEIU Local 1 fact sheet.
15. Ibid.
16. Kari Lydersen, "Airports Go Green and, Labor Leaders Fear, Bust Unions," *In These Times*, November 13, 2012.
17. Press conference at Chicago City Hall, December 11, 2012.
18. Email from United Maintenance spokesman Steve Patterson, in response to questions from this author, December 11, 2012.
19. Interview with SEIU Local 1 spokesperson Izabela Miltko, January 2013.
20. Dan Mihalopoulos, "Richard Simon: Chicago's 'King of the Janitors," *Chicago Sun-Times*, December 11, 2012.
21. Dan Mihalopoulos and Mitch Dudek, "Owner of Firm with O'Hare Deal Has Links to Reputed Mob Figure," *Chicago Sun-Times*, November 29, 2012.
22. Jeff Coen, "Union Fights to Keep O'Hare Janitor Jobs," *Chicago Tribune*, July 4, 2012.
23. Dan Mihalopoulos, "More Mob Ties to Contractor in O'Hare Cleaning Deal," *Chicago Sun-Times*, January 7, 2013.
24. Mihalopoulus, "Richard Simon."
25. Mihalopoulos and Dudek, "Owner of Firm with O'Hare Deal Has Links."
26. Andrew Schroedter, "Cleaning Up? Curious Questions Arise about O'Hare Airport Janitorial Contract and the Mayoral Ally Who Stands to Benefit," Better Government Association, December 3, 2012.
27. Interview with Tom Balanoff, November 20, 2012.
28. Schroedter, "Cleaning Up?"
29. Ibid. United Maintenance spokesman Steve Patterson responded to this author's questions about the contract in a December 11, 2012, email saying, "United has no subcontract with UNO. UNO is a community supporter and United makes the group aware when job opportunities are available, but otherwise has no relationship with UNO."
30. Maudlyne Ihejirika, "Long Lines, Frustration at First City Government-Wide Job Fair," *Chicago Sun-Times*, November 9, 2012.
31. Interview with janitor Geneva Daniels, November 29, 2012.
32. Interview with Geneva Daniels, December 11, 2012.
33. Dan Mihalopoulus, "Hidden Investors in Controversial City Janitorial Contract," *Chicago Sun-Times*, January 15, 2013.
34. Greg Hinz, "City Inspector Needs to Probe O'Hare Deal," *Crain's Chicago Business*, January 16, 2013.
35. Dan Mihalopoulos, "New 'Hygienic' Toilet Seats at O'Hare Aren't All That Clean," *Chicago Sun-Times*, January 28, 2013.
36. "Laid Off Workers Call on City's Public Health Department to Investigate Urgent Health Risk at O'Hare," SEIU Local 1 press release, January 29, 2013.
37. Preliminary results of SEIU Local 1 survey of former Scrub Inc. janitors and window washers at O'Hare, provided by Izabela Miltko, January 31, 2013. The study elaborated on the use of public assistance by laid-off workers: "Seventy percent (68/97) of these workers indicated they are on unemployment and 37 percent (36/97) of them indicated they are using SNAP. 31 percent (30/97) of these workers participated in two or more public assistance program; two workers indicated they were on three or more different public assistance programs."
38. Ibid.

39. Interview with janitor Jermaine Samples, January 2013.
40. Ibid.

CONCLUSION

1. "Homicide Tracker," *RedEye*, at http://homicides.redeyechicago.com.
2. Greg Hinz, "Emanuel's Poll Rating Turns Negative," *Crain's Chicago Business*, February 21, 2013.
3. Melissa Mouritsen Zmuda and Dick Simpson, "Continuing the Rubber Stamp City Council: Chicago City Council Report #6, June 8, 2011 to February 13, 2013," University of Illinois at Chicago, Department of Political Science, April 13, 2013.
4. Ibid.
5. Interview with political scientist Dick Simpson, April 30, 2013.
6. Linda Lutton, "Bus Tour Shows 'Collateral Damage' from School Closings," WBEZ, April 5, 2013.
7. Ted Cox, Mark Konkol, and Lizzie Schiffman, "Rahm on Vacation as School Closings List Leaks," DNAInfo.com, March 21, 2013.
8. Linda Lutton, "'Zero Trust' after CPS Admits It Overstated Savings from Closing Schools," WBEZ, May 6, 2013.
9. John Byrne and Hal Dardick, "Emanuel: Time to Move Forward with School Closings Plan," *Chicago Tribune*, March 27, 2013.
10. "Rahm Emanuel to Seek Second Term as Chicago Mayor," Associated Press, May 12, 2013.
11. Carol Marin, "Cloudy Days Roll In for Emanuel," *Chicago Sun-Times*, May 17, 2013.
12. Fran Spielman and Lauren Fitzpatrick, "Handful of CPS Schools Slated to Close May Be Spared," *Chicago Sun-Times*, May 17, 2013.
13. Mark Brown, "Two Take On Weakened Mayor," *Chicago Sun-Times*, May 19, 2013.
14. Editorial, "Mayor Difficult: Has Emanuel Alienated Chicagoans?" *Chicago Tribune*, May 19, 2013.
15. "Moms Call On CPS CEO Barbara Byrd-Bennett to Celebrate Mother's Day by Halting School Closings," SEIU Local 1press release, May 9, 2013.
16. Darryl Holliday, "Students Stage Die-In at School Closing Protest," DNAInfo.com, May 15, 2013.
17. Lauren Fitzpatrick and Art Golab, "Karen Lewis Easily Wins Second Term Leading Chicago Teachers Union," *Chicago Sun-Times*, May 17, 2013.
18. Kim Geiger, "School Closings Protesters: Route to New School a 'Danger Zone,'" *Chicago Tribune*, May 19, 2013.
19. Ibid.
20. Colleen Mastony, "Littlest Orator Moves People on Both Sides of CPS Debate," *Chicago Tribune*, May 25, 2013.
21. Asean Johnson video available on YouTube, at www.youtube.com/watch?v=pkZRbfN2z5A.
22. On May 22, 2013, the Board of Education voted to close fifty schools, sparing four that had been on the list, including Garvey. Noreen S. Ahmed-Ullah, John Chase, and Bob Secter, "CPS Approves Largest School Closing in Chicago History," *Chicago Tribune*, May 23, 2013.

INDEX

ABOUT THE AUTHOR

Kari Lydersen has worked since 1997 as a Chicago-based journalist, including in the Midwest bureau of the *Washington Post* and for the Chicago News Cooperative, specializing in environment, energy, labor, and immigration. She is a regular contributor to *Midwest Energy News* and to *In These Times* magazine, and she has written for numerous local and national outlets including the *Chicago Reporter*, the *Chicago Reader*, *People Magazine*, *Alternet*, and the *Progressive*. She is the author of three previous books, including *Revolt on Goose Island: The Chicago Factory Takeover and What It Says About the Economic Crisis*. She teaches journalism at Chicago colleges and universities and with youth in marginalized communities. She graduated from the Medill School of Journalism at Northwestern University in 1997.